*Robert Burns*

# INTRODUCTION

*'That I for poor auld Scotland's sake
Some useful plan or book could make,
Or sing a sang at least.'*

EVERYONE, or at least every Scotsman (Burns's work has not traditionally been a female taste), has his own image of Burns, whether it be the untutored ploughboy-poet, the hard-drinking womaniser and satirist of Calvinist hypocrisy, the socialite in the Edinburgh awash with the ideas of Hume and Smith, or simply as an icon of the Scottish democratic spirit to be celebrated with copious amounts of whisky once a year on 25 January by misty-eyed Scots from Hong Kong to Alberta wearing a distinctly inappropriate conventionalised form of Highland Dress. In a way, Burns may, to a degree, be some of these things, but these images taken singly are at best only partial and at worst grossly misleading.

Although born (on 25 January 1759) into miserable poverty, Burns had by the age of eighteen acquired a good knowledge of English literature and a grounding in Latin, Greek, French and trigonometry (he was to retain a lifelong interest in mathematics). This was achieved through the determination of his father who was described by Thomas Carlyle as 'a man of thoughtful intense character, as the best of our [ie Scotland's] peasants are, valuing knowledge, possessing some and open minded for more . . .'. Although his mother was largely uneducated, Burns nevertheless imbibed from her a great love for the rich tradition of Scottish balladry.

Despite the desperate hardship of the farm – where by the age of thirteen Burns threshed the corn with his own hands – he would always have a small volume in his pocket, usually a collection of the Scottish ballads ready to read in any spare moment 'gathering round him the memories and tradition of his country till they became a mantle and a crown'. It is also during this period that Burns's intense feeling for the day-to-day minutiae of the lowland fields developed. The detail of observation in much of Burns's nature poetry makes that of, for example the English Romantics, often seem generalised and effete, with a diction sometimes chosen more for its mellifluousness than its content.

In 1781 Burns went to Irvine to train as a flax dresser – linen was one of the staples of the eighteenth-century Scottish economy. It was a disastrous venture compounded by an unsuccessful love affair and Burns began to take solace in public houses and wild company. (There had been signs of this propensity much earlier when he was suffering one of the many bouts of deep melancholy which were probably brought about by the sheer physical harshness of his life at that time.)

In 1784 Burns moved to Mossgiel and again tried to make a living as a farmer. During this period he met his future wife, Jean Armour, but because of the objections of her father the marriage was not yet to be and Burns resolved to emigrate to the West Indies. Luckily for literature his fortunes changed with his first collection, *Poems Chiefly in the Scottish Dialect*, which was published in Kilmarnock in June 1786 and Burns decided to stay. This volume contains some of his most popular early songs as well as 'To a Mouse', 'To a Mountain Daisy', 'The Cotter's Saturday Night' and 'The Epistle to Davie'. Although Burns never received more than £20 for it, the book was a huge popular success, being admired by everyone from ploughboys to the *literati* of Edinburgh, some of whom now began to lionise him while others were merely content to patronise him as a rustic prodigy.

Eighteenth-century Edinburgh was culturally a highly schizophrenic capital, unsure whether to look southwards or inwards, forwards or back, and it may have been politically convenient to pigeon-hole Burns – the admirer of Locke, reader of Hume and Adam Smith, and sympathiser with the ideals of the French Revolution – as the untutored 'natural'. There is also some evidence of traces of an artificial gentility and imitative Augustan tone creeping into some of Burns's writings of this period. However, he successfully rode out this period of cultural confusion and after the second edition of the poems was published in 1787 – which brought Burns sufficient financial security to allow him to return to Ayrshire in 1788 – he was to write two of his best-loved works, 'Auld Lang Syne' (probably adapted from traditional sources) and 'Tam o' Shanter' – his last major work and many would say his masterpiece. By this time he was married to Jean Armour and having lost his money felt compelled to take up a position as an Excise Officer – anathema to any right-thinking Scottish drinker.

For the next few years Burns's major literary commitment was his work on James Johnson's *Scots Musical Museum* (published between 1787 and 1803) and George Thomson's *Select Collection of Original Scottish Airs* (published between 1793 and 1818). Working without payment, Burns effectively became the editor of the former, collecting and collating old songs as well as writing over two hundred of his own to old airs in order that the tunes could be kept alive. From this work come some of Burns's most familiar and popular songs, including 'Mary Morison', 'My Love is like a Red Red Rose', 'Highland Mary', 'Scots Wha Hae' and 'Coming Through the Rye'. Although these songs became instantly popular and are still to be heard in informal gathering of songsters throughout Scotland (to the extent that one suspects that the participants think of the songs as traditional and have no idea of their actual provenance), the critical reaction was for a long time, most unfairly, dismissive. Stevenson's comment is typical, '. . . that a man who first attacked literature with a hand that seemed capable of moving mountains, should have spent his later years in whittling cherry stones'. Indeed it is only recently that the songs have come to be properly appreciated.

By 1790 Burns's health was beginning to suffer, partly as a result of the rheumatic heart disorder probably first contracted in his youth and partly because of the strain of constantly travelling on behalf of the Excise, for whom he was now working more-or-less full time. However, in that year 'Tam o' Shanter' was published and he continued to produce a steady flow of work for the *Scots Musical Museum*. In the winters of 1794 and 1795 he was ill with rheumatic fever although he still managed his work for the Excise. However, the illness continued through the winter and spring of 1796 and he died on 21 July of that year.

How then, is the modern reader to approach Burns's work? Unfortunately, the answer has, to a certain extent, to be 'With some difficulty'. His reputation has never fully recovered from his being cast as the ploughboy-poet of the Romantics. It has not been helped by more recent overlays of sentimentalism either. Partly because of different literary traditions and partly because of his language, he has tended to be marginalised (outside Scotland) from the mainstream of literature in English so that there is no real continuing tradition of Burns criticism or scholarship. Even to a Scot it is hard to dispose of the partial myths alluded to already and to look at the poetry for what it is in itself.

Firstly, because of the myths and the paucity of serious study,

Burns's technical virtuosity has been badly overlooked. The first poem in the 1786 Kilmarnock edition, 'The Twa Dogs', is written in perfect, formal, octosyllabic couplets. Yet even at this early age he was also fully conversant with some of the fiendishly difficult traditional Scottish verse forms although the tone of the poetry is always natural and conversational with the diction moving quickly and smoothly between English and Scots as required.

Secondly, to consider Burns as a moralist it is important to remember not only his own background but also that Scotland was a poor country. His hatred of injustice is not born of a fashionable eighteenth-century intellectual radicalism but is firmly rooted in personal experience. It is sometimes hard to see a consistency between the author of 'Holy Willie's Prayer' and the masonic Whig which Burns was to become in his later years; between the writer of the patriotic 'Does Haughty Gaul' and the collector of Jacobite airs. There is, however, a deep moral and political core to Burns's work which is best characterised as a faith in fundamental human decency, a loathing of hypocrisy and a deep mistrust of the pomposity of rank and the dangers of wealth and power. In this respect Burns is profoundly at one with the history of Scotland and in tune with a sentiment which dates back as far as that early and most robust limitation on the powers of a monarchy, the 1320 Declaration of Arbroath (by comparison Magna Carta seems positively limp-wristed), which has it that, 'It is not for glory, riches or honours that we fight: it is for liberty alone, the liberty that no good man relinquishes but with his life.' The sentiment of 'For a' that and a' that' could scarcely be more similar.

> *The rank is but the guinea stamp;*
> *The man's the gowd for a' that.*

Exactly.

*Donald McFarlan, Oxfordshire, 1994*

## FURTHER READING

*Biography and Criticism*

Bentman, Raymond, *Robert Burns*, 1987.
Ferguson, J. DeLancey, (revised by G. Ross Roy), *The Letters of Robert Burns* (2 volumes), 1985.
Lindsay, Maurice, *The Burns Encyclopedia*, 3rd edition, 1980.
Low, Donald, ed., *Robert Burns: The Critical Heritage*, 1974.
Mackay, James, *A Biography of Robert Burns, 1992.*

*General Background*

Daiches, David, The Paradox of Scottish Culture: The Eighteenth Century Experience, 1964.

# CONTENTS

———◆◆———

## POEMS, EPISTLES, &c.

## SONGS AND BALLADS.

# ADDENDA.

# I.

# POEMS, EPISTLES, ETC.

## TAM O' SHANTER.

When chapman billies leave the street,
And drouthy neibors neibors meet,
As market-days are wearing late,
An' folk begin to tak the gate;
While we sit bousing at the nappy,
An' getting fou and unco happy,
We think na on the lang Scots miles,
The mosses, waters, slaps, and styles,
That lie between us and our hame,
Where sits our sulky sullen dame,                    10
Gathering her brows like gathering storm,
Nursing her wrath to keep it warm.
    This truth fand honest Tam o' Shanter,
As he frae Ayr ae night did canter—
(Auld Ayr, wham ne'er a town surpasses
For honest men and bonnie lasses .
    O Tam! hadst thou but been sae wise
As ta'en thy ain wife Kate's advice!
She tauld thee weel thou was a skellum,
A bletherin', blusterin', drunken blellum;           20
That frae November till October,
Ae market-day thou was na sober;
That ilka melder wi' the miller
Thou sat as lang as thou had siller;
That every naig was ca'd a shoe on,
The smith and thee gat roarin' fou on;

That at the Lord's house, even on Sunday,
Thou drank wi' Kirkton Jean till Monday.
She prophesied that, late or soon,
Thou would be found deep drown'd in Doon;          30
Or catch'd wi' warlocks in the mirk
By Alloway's auld ha·nted kirk.

  Ah, gentle dames! it gars me greet
To think how mony counsels sweet,
How mony lengthen'd sage advices,
The husband frae the wife despises!

  But to our tale: Ae market night,
Tam had got planted unco right,
Fast by an ingle, bleezing finely,
Wi' reaming swats, that drank divinely;          40
And at his elbow, Souter Johnny,
His ancient, trusty, drouthy crony;
Tam lo'ed him like a very brither;
They had been fou for weeks thegither.
The night drave on wi' sangs and clatter.
And aye the ale was growing better:
The landlady and Tam grew gracious,
Wi' favours secret, sweet, and precious;
The souter tauld his queerest stories;
The landlord's laugh was ready chorus:          50
The storm without might rair and rustle,
Tam did na mind the storm a whistle.

  Care, mad to see a man sae happy,
E'en drown'd himsel amang the nappy.
As bees flee hame wi' lades o' treasure,
The minutes wing'd their way wi' pleasure;
Kings may be blest, but Tam was glorious,
O'er a' the ills o' life victorious!

  But pleasures are like poppies spread—
You seize the flow'r, its bloom is shed;          60
Or like the snow falls in the river—
A moment white, then melts for ever;
Or like the borealis race,
That flit ere you can point their place;
Or like the rainbow's lovely form
Evanishing amid the storm.
Nae man can tether time nor tide;
The hour approaches Tam maun ride;

That hour, o' night's black arch the key-stane,
That dreary hour, he mounts his beast in;　　　70
And sic a night he taks the road in,
As ne'er poor sinner was abroad in.
　The wind blew as 'twad blawn its last ;
The rattling show'rs rose on the blast ;
The speedy gleams the darkness swallow'd ;
Loud, deep, and lang, the thunder bellow'd :
That night, a child might understand,
The Deil had business on his hand.
　Weel mounted on his gray mare, Meg,
A better never lifted leg,　　　80
Tam skelpit on thro' dub and mire,
Despising wind, and rain, and fire ;
Whiles holding fast his gude blue bonnet ;
Whiles crooning o'er some auld Scots sonnet ;
Whiles glow'ring round wi' prudent cares,
Lest bogles catch him unawares.
Kirk-Alloway was drawing nigh,
Whare ghaists and houlets nightly cry.
　By this time he was cross the ford,
Where in the snaw the chapman smoor'd ;　　　90
And past the birks and meikle stane,
Where drunken Charlie brak 's neck-bane ;
And thro' the whins, and by the cairn,
Where hunters fand the murder'd bairn ;
And near the thorn, aboon the well,
Where Mungo's mither hang'd hersel.
Before him Doon pours all his floods ;
The doubling storm roars thro' the woods ;
The lightnings flash from pole to pole ;
Near and more near the thunders roll :　　　100
When, glimmering thro' the groaning trees,
Kirk-Alloway seem'd in a bleeze ;
Thro' ilka bore the beams were glancing ;
And loud resounded mirth and dancing.
　Inspiring bold John Barleycorn !
What dangers thou canst make us scorn !
Wi' tippenny, we fear nae evil ;
Wi' usquebae, we'll face the devil !
The swats sae ream'd in Tammie's noddle,
Fair play, he car'd na deils a boddle !　　　110

But Maggie stood right sair astonish'd,
Till, by the heel and hand admonish'd,
She ventur'd forward on the light;
And, vow! Tam saw an unco sight!
Warlocks and witches in a dance!
Nae cotillon brent new frae France,
But hornpipes, jigs, strathspeys, and reels,
Put life and mettle in their heels.
A winnock-bunker in the east,
There sat auld Nick, in shape o' beast—        120
A touzie tyke, black, grim, and large!
To gie them music was his charge:
He screw'd the pipes and gart them skirl.
Till roof and rafters a' did dirl.
Coffins stood round like open presses,
That shaw'd the dead in their last dresses:
And by some devilish cantraip sleight
Each in its cauld hand held a light,
By which heroic Tam was able
To note upon the haly table                     130
A murderer's banes in gibbet-airns;
Twa span-lang, wee, unchristen'd bairns;
A thief new-cutted frae the rape—
Wi' his last gasp his gab did gape;
Five tomahawks, wi' blude red rusted;
Five scymitars, wi' murder crusted;
A garter, which a babe had strangled;
A knife, a father's throat had mangled,
Whom his ain son o' life bereft—
The gray hairs yet stack to the heft;           140
Wi' mair of horrible and awfu',
Which even to name wad be unlawfu'.
    As Tammie glowr'd, amaz'd, and curious,
The mirth and fun grew fast and furious:
The piper loud and louder blew;
The dancers quick and quicker flew;
They reel'd, they set, they cross'd, they cleekit,
Till ilka carlin swat and reekit,
And coost her duddies to the wark,
And linkit at it in her sark!                    150
    Now Tam, O Tam! had thae been queans,
A' plump and strapping in their teens;

Their sarks, instead o' creeshie flannen,
Been snaw-white seventeen hunder linen!
Thir breeks o' mine, my only pair,
That ance were plush, o' gude blue hair,
I wad hae gi'en them off my hurdies,
For ae blink o' the bonnie burdies!
But wither'd beldams, auld and droll,
Rigwoodie hags wad spean a foal,                    160
Louping and flinging on a crummock,
I wonder didna turn thy stomach.
But Tam kent what was what fu' brawlie
There was ae winsome wench and walie
That night enlisted in the core,
Lang after kent on Carrick shore!
(For mony a beast to dead she shot,
And perish'd mony a bonnie boat,
And shook baith meikle corn and bear,
And kept the country-side in fear.)                 170
Her cutty sark, o' Paisley harn,
That while a lassie she had worn,
In longitude tho' sorely scanty,
It was her best, and she was vauntie.
Ah! little kent thy reverend grannie
That sark she coft for her wee Nannie
Wi' twa pund Scots ('twas a' her riches)
Wad ever grac'd a dance of witches!
But here my muse her wing maun cour:
Sic flights are far beyond her pow'r—               180
To sing how Nannie lap and flang,
(A souple jade she was, and strang);
And how Tam stood, like ane bewitch'd,
And thought his very een enrich'd;
Even Satan glowr'd, and fidg'd fu' fain,
And hotch'd and blew wi' might and main:
Till first ae caper, syne anither,
Tam tint his reason a' thegither,
And roars out 'Weel done, Cutty-sark!'
And in an instant all was dark!                     190
And scarcely had he Maggie rallied,
When out the hellish legion sallied.
As bees bizz out wi' angry fyke
When plundering herds assail their byke,

As open pussie's mortal foes
When pop! she starts before their nose,
As eager runs the market-crowd,
When 'Catch the thief!' resounds aloud.
So Maggie runs; the witches follow,
Wi' mony an eldritch skriech and hollow.        200
    Ah, Tam! ah, Tam! thou'll get thy fairin'!
In hell they'll roast thee like a herrin'!
In vain thy Kate awaits thy comin'!
Kate soon will be a woefu' woman!
Now do thy speedy utmost, Meg,
And win the key-stane o' the brig:
There at them thou thy tail may toss,
A running stream they darena cross.
But ere the key-stane she could make,
The fient a tail she had to shake!        210
For Nannie, far before the rest,
Hard upon noble Maggie prest,
And flew at Tam wi' furious ettle;
But little wist she Maggie's mettle!
Ae spring brought off her master hale,
But left behind her ain gray tail:
The carlin claught her by the rump,
And left poor Maggie scarce a stump.
    Now, wha this tale o' truth shall read,
Each man and mother's son, take heed;        220
Whene'er to drink you are inclin'd,
Or cutty-sarks rin in your mind,
Think! ye may buy the joys o'er dear;
Remember Tam o' Shanter's mare.

## THE JOLLY BEGGARS.

WHEN lyart leaves bestrow the yird,
Or, wavering like the baukie bird,
   Bedim cauld Boreas' blast;
When hailstanes drive wi' bitter skyte,
And infant frosts begin to bite,
   In hoary cranreuch drest;
Ae night at e'en a merry core
  O' randie gangrel bodies
In Poosie Nansie's held the splore,
  To drink their orra duddies.               10
     Wi' quaffing and laughing,
      They ranted and they sang;
     Wi' jumping and thumping
      The very girdle rang.

First, niest the fire, in auld red rags,
Ane sat, weel brac'd wi' mealy bags,
   And knapsack a' in order;
His doxy lay within his arm;
Wi' usquebae and blankets warm,
  She blinket on her sodger;               20
An' aye he gies the tosy drab
  The tither skelpin' kiss,
While she held up her greedy gab,
  Just like an aumous dish:
     Ilk smack still did crack still
      Just like a cadger's whip;
     Then staggering, and swaggering,
      He roar'd this ditty up—

I am a son of Mars, who have been in many wars,
  And show my cuts and scars wherever I come;     30
This here was for a wench, and that other in a trench,
  When welcoming the French at the sound of the drum.
          Lal de daudle, &c.

My 'prenticeship I pass'd where my leader breath'd his
    last,
When the bloody die was cast on the heights of Abrám ;
And I servèd out my trade when the gallant game was
    play'd,
And the Moro low was laid at the sound of the drum.


I lastly was with Curtis, among the floating batt'ries,
    And there I left for witness an arm and a limb :
Yet let my country need me, with Elliot to head me,  40
    I'd clatter on my stumps at the sound of a drum.


And now tho' I must beg, with a wooden arm and leg,
    And many a tatter'd rag hanging over my bum,
I'm as happy with my wallet, my bottle, and my callet,
    As when I used in scarlet to follow a drum.


What tho' with hoary locks I must stand the winter
    shocks,
Beneath the woods and rocks oftentimes for a home ?
When the t'other bag I sell, and the t'other bottle tell,
    I could meet a troop of hell at the sound of the drum.


      He ended ; and the kebars sheuk      50
        Aboon the chorus roar ;
      While frighted rattons backward leuk,
        And seek the benmost bore.
      A fairy fiddler frae the neuk,
        He skirled out *Encore!*
      But up arose the martial chuck,
        And laid the loud uproar.


I once was a maid, tho' I cannot tell when,
And still my delight is in proper young men ;
Some one of a troop of dragoons was my daddie,  60
No wonder I'm fond of a sodger laddie.
                Sing, Lal de dal, &c.

The first of my loves was a swaggering blade,
To rattle the thundering drum was his trade;
His leg was so tight, and his cheek was so ruddy,
Transported I was with my sodger laddie.

But the godly old chaplain left him in the lurch;
The sword I forsook for the sake of the church;
He ventur'd the soul, and I riskèd the body,—
'Twas then I prov'd false to my sodger laddie.          70

Full soon I grew sick of my sanctified sot,
The regiment at large for a husband I got;
From the gilded spontoon to the fife I was ready,
I askèd no more but a sodger laddie.

But the peace it reduced me to beg in despair,
Till I met my old boy at a Cunningham fair;
His rags regimental they flutter'd so gaudy,
My heart it rejoiced at a sodger laddie.

And now I have liv'd—I know not how long,
And still I can join in a cup or a song;               80
But whilst with both hands I can hold the glass steady,
Here's to thee, my hero, my sodger laddie!


Poor Merry Andrew in the neuk
    Sat guzzling wi' a tinkler hizzie;
They mind't na wha the chorus teuk,
    Between themselves they were sae busy.
    At length, wi' drink and courting dizzy,
He stoitered up an' made a face;
    Then turn'd, an' laid a smack on Grizzy,
Syne tun'd his pipes wi' grave grimace.               90


Sir Wisdom's a fool when he's fou,
    Sir Knave is a fool in a session;
He's there but a 'prentice I trow,
    But I am a fool by profession.

My grannie she bought me a beuk,
   And I held awa to the school;
I fear I my talent misteuk,
   But what will ye hae of a fool?

For drink I would venture my neck;
   A hizzie's the half o' my craft;      100
But what could ye other expect,
   Of ane that's avowedly daft?

I ance was tied up like a stirk,
   For civilly swearing and quaffing;
I ance was abused i' the kirk,
   For touzling a lass i' my daffin.

Poor Andrew that tumbles for sport,
   Let naebody name wi' a jeer;
There's even, I'm tauld, i' the Court,
   A tumbler ca'd the Premier.      110

Observ'd ye yon reverend lad
   Maks faces to tickle the mob?
He rails at our mountebank squad—
   It's rivalship just i' the job.

And now my conclusion I'll tell,
   For, faith! I'm confoundedly dry;
The chiel that's a fool for himsel',
   Gude Lord! he's far dafter than I.

Then niest outspak a raucle carlin,
Wha kent fu' weel to cleek the sterling,    120
For mony a pursie she had hookit,
And had in mony a well been dookit;
Her love had been a Highland laddie,
But weary fa' the waefu' woodie!
Wi' sighs and sobs, she thus began
To wail her braw John Highlandman:—

A Highland lad my love was born,
The Lawlan' laws he held in scorn;
But he still was faithfu' to his clan,
My gallant braw John Highlandman.                    130

CHORUS.

Sing hey, my braw John Highlandman!
Sing ho, my braw John Highlandman!
There's no a lad in a' the lan'
Was match for my John Highlandman.

With his philibeg an' tartan plaid,
And gude claymore down by his side,
The ladies' hearts he did trepan,
My gallant braw John Highlandman.

We rangèd a' from Tweed to Spey,
And lived like lords and ladies gay;                    140
For a Lawlan' face he fearèd nane,
My gallant braw John Highlandman.

They banish'd him beyond the sea;
But ere the bud was on the tree,
Adown my cheeks the pearls ran,
Embracing my John Highlandman.

But oh! they catch'd him at the last,
And bound him in a dungeon fast;
My curse upon them every one!
They've hang'd my braw John Highlandman.  150

And now a widow I must mourn
The pleasures that will ne er return;
No comfort but a hearty can,
When I think on John Highlandman.

A pigmy scraper wi' his fiddle,
Wha used at trysts and fairs to driddle,
Her strappin' limb and gaucy middle
            (He reach'd nae higher)
Had holed his heartie like a riddle,
            And blawn't on fire.                    160

Wi' hand on haunch, and upward ee,
He croon'd his gamut, one, two, three,
Then, in an arioso key,
            The wee Apollo
Set aff, wi' allegretto glee,
            His giga solo.

Let me ryke up to dight that tear,
And go wi' me and be my dear,
And then your every care and fear
    May whistle owre the lave o't.                  170

### CHORUS.

I am a fiddler to my trade,
And a' the tunes that e'er I play'd,
The sweetest still to wife or maid,
    Was whistle owre the lave o't.

At kirns and weddings we'se be there,
And oh! sae nicely 's we will fare;
We'll bouse about, till Daddie Care
    Sings whistle owre the lave o't.

Sae merrily 's the banes we'll pyke,
And sun oursels about the dyke,                     180
And at our leisure, when ye like,
    We'll whistle owre the lave o't.

But bless me wi' your heav'n o' charms,
And while I kittle hair on thairms,
Hunger and cauld, and a' sic harms,
    May whistle owre the lave o't.

Her charms had struck a sturdy caird,
   As well as poor gut-scraper ;
He taks the fiddler by the beard,
   And draws a roosty rapier—       190

He swoor, by a' was swearing worth,
   To spit him like a pliver,
Unless he would from that time forth
   Relinquish her for ever.

Wi' ghastly ee, poor tweedle-dee
   Upon his hunkers bended,
And pray'd for grace wi' ruefu' face,
   And sae the quarrel ended.

But tho' his little heart did grieve
   When round the tinkler prest her,      200
He feign'd to snirtle in his sleeve,
   When thus the caird address'd her :—

My bonnie lass, I work in brass,
   A tinkler is my station ;
I've travell'd round all Christian ground
   In this my occupation ;
I've ta'en the gold, I've been enroll'd
   In many a noble squadron ;
But vain they search'd, when off I march'd
   To go and clout the cauldron.      210

Despise that shrimp, that wither'd imp,
   Wi' a' his noise and caperin' ;
And tak a share wi' those that bear
   The budget and the apron ;
And, by that stoup, my faith and houp !
   And by that dear Kilbaigie,
If e'er ye want, or meet wi' scant,
   May I ne'er weet my craigie.

The caird prevail'd—th' unblushing fair
  In his embraces sunk,                                    220
Partly wi' love o'ercome sae sair,
  And partly she was drunk.
Sir Violino, with an air
  That show'd a man o' spunk,
Wish'd unison between the pair,
  And made the bottle clunk
          To their health that night.

But urchin Cupid shot a shaft
  That play'd a dame a shavie ;
The fiddler rak'd her fore and aft,                       230
  Behint the chicken cavie.
Her lord, a wight of Homer's craft,
  Tho' limpin' wi' the spavie,
He hirpled up, and lap like daft,
  And shor'd them *Dainty Davie*
          O' boot that night.

He was a care-defying blade
  As ever Bacchus listed ;
Tho' Fortune sair upon him laid,
  His heart she ever miss'd it.                            240
He had nae wish, but to be glad,
  Nor want but when he thirsted ;
He hated nought but to be sad,
  And thus the Muse suggested
          His sang that night.

I am a bard of no regard
  Wi' gentlefolks, and a' that ;
But Homer-like, the glowrin' byke,
  Frae town to town I draw that.

CHORUS.

For a' that, and a' that,
  And twice as meikle 's a' that ;                         250
I've lost but ane, I've twa behin',
  I've wife eneugh for a' that.

I never drank the Muses' stank,
  Castalia's burn, and a' that;
But there it streams, and richly reams!
  My Helicon I ca' that.

Great love I bear to a' the fair,
  Their humble slave, and a' that;
But lordly will, I hold it still              260
  A mortal sin to thraw that.

In raptures sweet this hour we meet
  Wi' mutual love, and a' that;
But for how lang the flee may stang,
  Let inclination law that.

Their tricks and craft hae put me daft,
  They've ta'en me in, and a' that;
But clear your decks, and *Here's the sex!*
  I like the jads for a' that.

    For a' that, and a' that,              270
      And twice as meikle 's a' that,
    My dearest bluid, to do them guid,
      They're welcome till't, for a' that.


So sung the bard—and Nansie's wa's
Shook with a thunder of applause,
  Re-echo'd from each mouth;
They toom'd their pocks, an' pawn'd their duds.
They scarcely left to co'er their fuds,
  To quench their lowin' drouth.
Then owre again the jovial thrang          280
  The poet did request
To lowse his pack, an' wale a sang,
  A ballad o' the best;
    He rising, rejoicing,
      Between his twa Deborahs,
    Looks round him. an' found them
      Impatient for the chorus.

See the smoking bowl before us,
　Mark our jovial ragged ring;
Round and round take up the chorus,　　　290
　And in raptures let us sing—


CHORUS.

A fig for those by law protected!
　Liberty's a glorious feast!
Courts for cowards were erected,
　Churches built to please the priest.


What is title? what is treasure?
　What is reputation's care?
If we lead a life of pleasure,
　'Tis no matter how or where!


With the ready trick and fable,　　　300
　Round we wander all the day;
And at night, in barn or stable,
　Hug our doxies on the hay.


Does the train-attended carriage
　Thro' the country lighter rove?
Does the sober bed of marriage
　Witness brighter scenes of love?


Life is all a variorum,
　We regard not how it goes;
Let them cant about decorum　　　310
　Who have characters to lose.


Here's to budgets, bags, and wallets!
　Here's to all the wandering train!
Here's our ragged brats and callets!
　One and all cry out *Amen!*

[The Sailor's Song.]

Tho' women's minds, like winter winds,
  May shift, an' turn, and a' that,
The noblest breast adores them maist—
  A consequence I draw that.

CHORUS.

For a' that, and a' that,
  An' twice as meikle's a' that;
The bonnie lass that I lo'e best,
  She'll be my ain for a' that!

Great love I bear to a' the fair,
  Their humble slave and a' that;
But lordly will, I hold it still
  A mortal sin to thraw that.

But there is ane aboon the lave
  Has wit, an' sense, and a' that;
A bonnie lass, I like her best,
  An' wha a crime dare ca' that?

In rapture sweet this hour we meet
  Wi' mutual love, and a' that;
But for how lang the flee may stang,—
  Let inclination law that.

Their tricks an' craft hae put me daft;
  They've ta'en me in, and a' that;
But clear your decks, an' *Here's the sex!*
  I like the jads for a' that!

[THE CAIRD'S SECOND SONG.]

O merry hae I been teethin' a heckle,                    340
  An' merry hae I been shapin' a spoon;
O merry hae I been cloutin' a kettle,
  An' kissin' my Katie when a' was done.
O a' the lang day I ca' at my hammer,
  An' a' the lang day I whistle and sing,
A' the lang night 1 cuddle my kimmer,
  An' a' the lang night am as happy 's a King.


Bitter in dool I lickit my winnins,
  O' marrying Bess, to gie her a slave:
Bless'd be the hour she cool'd in her linens,           350
  And blythe be the bird that sings on her grave.
Come to my arms, my Katie, my Katie.
  O come to my arms, an' kiss me again!
Drucken or sober, here 's to thee, Katie!
  And bless'd be the day I did it again.


———◆———


## HALLOWEEN.

Upon that night, when fairies light
  On Cassilis Downans dance,
Or owre the lays, in splendid blaze,
  On sprightly coursers prance;
Or for Colean the rout is ta'en,
  Beneath the moon's pale beams;
There, up the Cove, to stray an' rove
  Amang the rocks and streams
        To sport that night;

Amang the bonnie winding banks 10
  Where Doon rins wimplin' clear,
Where Bruce ance ruled the martial ranks
  An' shook his Carrick spear,
Some merry friendly country-folks
  Together did convene
To burn their nits, an' pou their stocks,
  An' haud their Halloween
        Fu' blythe that night:


The lasses feat, an cleanly neat,
  Mair braw than when they're fine; 20
Their faces blythe fu' sweetly kythe
  Hearts leal, an' warm, an' kin':
The lads sae trig, wi' wooer-babs
  Weel knotted on their garten,
Some unco blate, an' some wi' gabs
  Gar lasses' hearts gang startin'
        Whyles fast at night.


Then, first an foremost, thro' the kail,
  Their stocks maun a' be sought ance:
They steek their een, an' grape an' wale 30
  For muckle anes an' straught anes.
Poor hav'rel Will fell aff the drift,
  An' wander'd thro' the bow-kail,
An' pou'd, for want o' better shift,
  A runt was like a sow-tail,
        Sae bow'd, that night.


Then, straught or crooked, yird or nane,
  They roar an' cry a' throu'ther;
The very wee things toddlin' rin—
  Wi' stocks out-owre their shouther; 40
An' gif the custock's sweet or sour,
  Wi' joctelegs they taste them;
Syne coziely, aboon the door,
  Wi' cannie care they've plac'd them
        To lie that night.

The lasses staw frae 'mang them a'
  To pou their stalks o' corn ;
But Rab slips out, an' jinks about,
  Behint the muckle thorn :
He grippit Nelly hard an' fast ;        50
  Loud skirled a' the lasses ;
But her tap-pickle maist was lost,
    When kiutlin' i' the fause-house
        Wi' him that night.


The auld guidwife's well-hoordit nits
  Are round an' round divided,
An' mony lads' an' lasses' fates
  Are there that night decided :
Some kindle, couthie, side by side,
  An' burn thegither trimly ;        60
Some start awa, wi' saucy pride,
  An' jump out-owre the chimlie
        Fu' high that night.


Jean slips in twa, wi' tentie e'e ;
  Wha 'twas, she wadna tell ;
But this is Jock, an' this is me,
  She says in to hersel :
He bleez'd owre her, an' she owre him,
  As they wad never mair part ;
Till fuff! he started up the lum,        70
  An' Jean had e'en a sair heart
        To see't that night.


Poor Willie, wi' his bow-kail runt,
  Was brunt wi' primsie Mallie,
An' Mary, nae doubt, took the drunt,
  To be compar'd to Willie :
Mall's nit lap out, wi' pridefu' fling,
  An' her ain fit it brunt it ;
While Willie lap, an' swoor by jing,
  'Twas just the way he wanted        80
        To be that night.

Nell had the fause-house in her min',
  She pits hersel an' Rob in;
In loving bleeze they sweetly join,
  Till white in ase they're sobbin:
Nell's heart was dancin' at the view:
  She whisper'd Rob to leuk for't:
Rob, stownlins, prie'd her bonnie mou',
  Fu' cozie in the neuk for't,
        Unseen that night. 90


But Merran sat behint their backs,
  Her thoughts on Andrew Bell;
She lea'es them gashin' at their cracks,
  An' slips out by hersel:
She thro' the yard the nearest taks,
  An' to the kiln she goes then,
An' darklins grapit for the bauks,
  And in the blue-clue throws then,
        Right fear'd that night.


An' aye she win't, an' aye she swat, 100
  I wat she made nae jaukin';
Till something held within the pat,
  Guid Lord! but she was quaukin'!
But whether 'twas the Deil himsel,
  Or whether 'twas a bauk-en',
Or whether it was Andrew Bell,
  She did na wait on talkin
        To spier that night.


Wee Jenny to her grannie says,
  'Will ye go wi' me, grannie? 110
I'll eat the apple at the glass,
  I gat frae uncle Johnie:'
She fuff't her pipe wi' sic a lunt,
  In wrath she was sae vap'rin,
She noticed na an aizle brunt
  Her braw new worset apron
        Out-thro' that night.

'Ye little skelpie-limmer's face!
  I daur you try sic sportin',
As seek the foul Thief ony place,          120
  For him to spae your fortune!
Nae doubt but ye may get a sight!
  Great cause ye hae to fear it;
For mony a ane has gotten a fright,
  An' lived an' died deleerit,
          On sic a night.


'Ae hairst afore the Sherra-moor,—
  I mind't as weel 's yestreen,
I was a gilpey then, I'm sure
  I was na past fyfteen:          130
The simmer had been cauld an' wat,
  An' stuff was unco green;
An' aye a rantin' kirn we gat,
  An' just on Halloween
          It fell that night.


Our stibble-rig was Rab M'Graen,
  A clever, sturdy fallow;
His sin gat Eppie Sim wi' wean,
  That liv'd in Achmacalla;
He gat hemp-seed, I mind it weel,          140
  An' he made unco light o't;
But mony a day was by himsel,
  He was sae sairly frighted
          That vera night.'


Then up gat fechtin' Jamie Fleck,
  An' he swoor by his conscience
That he could saw hemp-seed a peck;
  For it was a' but nonsense:
The auld guidman raught down the pock,
  An' out a handfu' gied him;          150
Syne bad him slip frae 'mang the folk,
  Sometime when nae ane see'd him,
          An' try't that night.

He marches thro' amang the stacks,
  Tho' he was something sturtin';
The graip he for a harrow taks,
  An' haurls at his curpin:
An' ev'ry now an' then, he says,
  'Hemp-seed! I saw thee,
An' her that is to be my lass      160
  Come after me an' draw thee
      As fast this night.'


He whistled up Lord Lennox' march,
  To keep his courage cheery;
Altho' his hair began to arch,
  He was sae fley'd an' eerie:
Till presently he hears a squeak,
  An' then a grane an' gruntle;
He by his shouther gae a keek,
  An' tumbl'd wi' a wintle      170
      Out-owre that night.


He roar'd a horrid murder-shout,
  In dreadfu' desperation!
An' young an' auld come rinnin' out,
  An' hear the sad narration:
He swoor 'twas hilchin Jean M'Craw,
  Or crouchie Merran Humphie,
Till stop! she trotted thro' them a';
  An' wha was it but grumphie
      Asteer that night!      180


Meg fain wad to the barn gane
  To winn three wechts o' naething;
But for to meet the Deil her lane,
  She pat but little faith in:
She gies the herd a pickle nits,
  And twa red-cheekit apples,
To watch, while for the barn she sets,
  In hopes to see Tam Kipples
      That very night.

She turns the key wi' cannie thraw,                    190
   An' owre the threshold ventures ;
But first on Sawnie gies a ca',
   Syne bauldly in she enters ;
A ratton rattl'd up the wa',
   An' she cried 'Lord preserve her !'
An' ran thro' midden-hole an' a',
   An' pray'd wi' zeal an' fervour
               Fu' fast that night.


They hoy't out Will, wi' sair advice ;
   They hecht him some fine braw ane ;    200
It chanced the stack he faddom'd thrice
   Was timmer-propt for thrawin' :
He taks a swirlie auld moss-oak
   For some black gruesome Carlin ;
An' loot a winze, an' drew a stroke,
   Till skin in blypes cam haurlin'
               Aff's nieves that night.


A wanton widow Leezie was,
   As cantie as a kittlin ;
But och ! that night, amang the shaws,    210
   She gat a fearfu' settlin' !
She thro' the whins, an' by the cairn,
   An' owre the hill gaed scrievin' ;
Where three laird's lands met at a burn,
   To dip her left sark-sleeve in,
               Was bent that night.


Whyles owre a linn the burnie plays,
   As thro' the glen it wimpled ;
Whyles round a rocky scaur it strays ;
   Whyles in a wiel it dimpled ;          220
Whyles glitter'd to the nightly rays,
   Wi' bickering, dancing dazzle ;
Whyles cookit underneath the braes,
   Below the spreading hazel,
               Unseen that night.

Amang the brackens on the brae,
  Between her an' the moon,
The Deil, or else an outler quey,
  Gat up an' gae a croon:
Poor Leezie's heart maist lap the hool;                    230
  Near lav'rock height she jumpit,
But miss'd a fit, an' in the pool
  Out-owre the lugs she plumpit,
            Wi' a plunge that night.


In order, on the clean hearth-stane,
  The luggies three are ranged;
And every time great care is ta'en,
  To see them duly changed:
Auld uncle John, wha wedlock's joys
  Sin' Mar's year did desire,                              240
Because he gat the toom dish thrice,
  He heav'd them on the fire
            In wrath that night.


Wi' merry sangs, an' friendly cracks,
  I wat they did na weary;
And unco tales, an' funny jokes,—
  Their sports were cheap and cheery;
Till butter'd sow'ns, wi' fragrant lunt,
  Set a' their gabs a-steerin';
Syne, wi' a social glass o' strunt,                        250
  They parted aff careerin'
            Fu' blythe that night.

## THE COTTER'S SATURDAY NIGHT.

My lov'd, my honour'd, much respected friend!
 No mercenary bard his homage pays:
With honest pride I scorn each selfish end,
 My dearest meed a friend's esteem and praise:
To you I sing, in simple Scottish lays,
The lowly train in life's sequester'd scene;
 The native feelings strong, the guileless ways;
What Aiken in a cottage would have been—
Ah! tho' his worth unknown, far happier there, I ween.


November chill blaws loud wi' angry sough;       10
 The short'ning winter-day is near a close;
The miry beasts retreating frae the pleugh;
 The black'ning trains o' craws to their repose:
The toil-worn Cotter frae his labour goes,
This night his weekly moil is at an end,
 Collects his spades, his mattocks, and his hoes,
Hoping the morn in ease and rest to spend,
And weary, o'er the moor, his course does hameward bend.


At length his lonely cot appears in view,
 Beneath the shelter of an agèd tree;       20
Th' expectant wee things, toddlin', stacher through
 To meet their Dad, wi' flichterin' noise an' glee.
His wee bit ingle, blinkin bonnilie,
His clean hearth-stane, his thrifty wifie's smile,
 The lisping infant prattling on his knee,
Does a' his weary kiaugh and care beguile,
An' makes him quite forget his labour an' his toil.


Belyve, the elder bairns come drapping in,
 At service out, amang the farmers roun';
Some ca' the pleugh, some herd, some tentie rin       30
 A cannie errand to a neibor town:

Their eldest hope, their Jenny, woman-grown,
In youthfu' bloom, love sparkling in her e'e,
Comes hame, perhaps to shew a braw new gown,
Or deposite her sair-won penny-fee,
To help her parents dear, if they in hardship be.


With joy unfeign'd brothers and sisters meet,
An' each for other's weelfare kindly spiers:
The social hours, swift-wing'd, unnoticed fleet;
Each tells the uncos that he sees or hears;          40
The parents, partial, eye their hopeful years;
Anticipation forward points the view.
The mother, wi' her needle an' her sheers,
Gars auld claes look amaist as weel 's the new;
The father mixes a' wi' admonition due.


Their master's an' their mistress's command,
The younkers a' are warnèd to obey;
An' mind their labours wi' an eydent hand,
An' ne'er, tho' out o' sight, to jauk or play:
'And O ! be sure to fear the Lord alway,          50
An' mind your duty, duly, morn an' night !
Lest in temptation's path ye gang astray,
Implore His counsel and assisting might:
They never sought in vain that sought the Lord aright !'


But hark ! a rap comes gently to the door ;
Jenny, wha kens the meaning o' the same,
Tells how a neibor lad cam o'er the moor,
To do some errands, and convoy her hame.
The wily mother sees the conscious flame
Sparkle in Jenny's e'e, and flush her cheek ;          60
Wi' heart-struck anxious care, inquires his name,
While Jenny hafflins is afraid to speak ;
Weel pleased the mother hears it's nae wild worthless rake.


Wi' kindly welcome, Jenny brings him ben ;
A strappin' youth ; he takes the mother's eye ;
Blythe Jenny sees the visit 's no ill ta'en ;
The father cracks of horses, pleughs, and kye.

The youngster's artless heart o'erflows wi' joy,
But blate and laithfu', scarce can weel behave;
   The mother, wi' a woman's wiles, can spy    70
What makes the youth sae bashfu' an' sae grave;
Weel-pleased to think her bairn's respected like the lave.

O happy love! where love like this is found;
   O heart-felt raptures! bliss beyond compare!
I've pacèd much this weary mortal round,
   And sage experience bids me this declare—
' If Heaven a draught of heavenly pleasure spare,
One cordial in this melancholy vale,
   'Tis when a youthful, loving, modest pair
In other's arms breathe out the tender tale,    80
Beneath the milk-white thorn that scents the evening gale.'

Is there, in human form, that bears a heart—
   A wretch, a villain, lost to love and truth—
That can, with studied, sly, ensnaring art,
   Betray sweet Jenny's unsuspecting youth?
   Curse on his perjur'd arts, dissembling smooth!
Are honour, virtue, conscience, all exil'd?
   Is there no pity, no relenting ruth,
Points to the parents fondling o'er their child?
Then paints the ruin'd maid, and their distraction wild?   90

But now the supper crowns their simple board,
   The halesome parritch, chief of Scotia's food:
The sowpe their only hawkie does afford,
   That 'yont the hallan snugly chows her cood;
   The dame brings forth in complimental mood,
To grace the lad, her weel hain'd kebbuck, fell;
   And aft he's prest, and aft he ca's it good;
The frugal wifie, garrulous, will tell
How 'twas a towmond auld sin' lint was i' the bell.

The cheerfu' supper done, wi' serious face    100
   They round the ingle form a circle wide;
The sire turns o'er, wi' patriarchal grace,
   The big ha'-bible, ance his father's pride:

His bonnet rev'rently is laid aside,
His lyart haffets wearing thin an' bare;
 Those strains that once did sweet in Zion glide—
He wales a portion with judicious care,
And 'Let us worship God!' he says with solemn air.


They chant their artless notes in simple guise;
 They tune their hearts, by far the noblest aim:   110
Perhaps Dundee's wild warbling measures rise,
 Or plaintive Martyrs, worthy of the name;
 Or noble Elgin beets the heav'nward flame,
The sweetest far of Scotia's holy lays:
 Compared with these, Italian trills are tame;
The tickled ears no heartfelt raptures raise;
Nae unison hae they with our Creator's praise.


The priest-like father reads the sacred page,
 How Abram was the friend of God on high;
Or Moses bade eternal warfare wage          120
 With Amalek's ungracious progeny;
 Or how the royal bard did groaning lie
Beneath the stroke of Heaven's avenging ire;
 Or Job's pathetic plaint, and wailing cry;
 Or rapt Isaiah's wild seraphic fire;
Or other holy seers that tune the sacred lyre.


Perhaps the Christian volume is the theme,
 How guiltless blood for guilty man was shed;
How He who bore in Heaven the second name
 Had not on earth whereon to lay His head;   130
 How His first followers and servants sped;
The precepts sage they wrote to many a land:
 How he, was lone in Patmos banishèd,
Saw in the sun a mighty angel stand,
And heard great Bab'lon's doom pronounced by Heaven's
    command.


Then kneeling down to Heaven's Eternal King
 The saint, the father, and the husband prays:
Hope 'springs exulting on triumphant wing'
 That thus they all shall meet in future days:

There ever bask in uncreated rays,                    140
  No more to sigh, or shed the bitter tear,
  Together hymning their Creator's praise,
    In such society, yet still more dear ;
While circling Time moves round in an eternal sphere.


Compared with this, how poor Religion's pride,
  In all the pomp of method and of art,
When men display to congregations wide
    Devotion's every grace, except the heart !
  The Power, incensed, the pageant will desert,
The pompous strain, the sacerdotal stole ;          150
    But haply, in some cottage far apart,
May hear, well pleased, the language of the soul ;
And in His Book of Life the inmates poor enrol.


Then homeward all take off their several way ;
  The youngling cottagers retire to rest :
The parent-pair their secret homage pay,
    And proffer up to Heav'n the warm request,
  That He who stills the raven's clamorous nest,
And decks the lily fair in flowery pride,
    Would, in the way His wisdom sees the best,     160
For them and for their little ones provide ;
But chiefly in their hearts with grace divine preside.


From scenes like these old Scotia's grandeur springs,
  That makes her loved at home, revered abroad :
Princes and lords are but the breath of kings,
    ' An honest man 's the noblest work of God ;'
  And certes, in fair virtue's heavenly road,
The cottage leaves the palace far behind ;
    What is a lordling's pomp ? a cumbrous load,
Disguising oft the wretch of human kind,            170
Studied in arts of hell, in wickedness refin'd !


O Scotia ! my dear, my native soil !
  For whom my warmest wish to Heaven is sent !
Long may thy hardy sons of rustic toil
    Be blest with health, and peace, and sweet content !

And O may Heaven their simple lives prevent
From luxury's contagion, weak and vile;
 Then, howe'er crowns and coronets be rent,
A virtuous populace may rise the while,   179
And stand a wall of fire around their much-loved isle.


O Thou! who poured the patriotic tide
 That streamed thro' Wallace's undaunted heart,
Who dared to nobly stem tyrannic pride,
 Or nobly die—the second glorious part,
 (The patriot's God, peculiarly thou art,
His friend, inspirer, guardian, and reward!)
 O never, never, Scotia's realm desert;
But still the patriot, and the patriot-bard,
In bright succession raise, her ornament and guard!


---&#8224;---


## THE HOLY FAIR.

*A robe of seeming truth and trust*
 *Hid crafty observation;*
*And secret hung, with poison'd crust,*
 *The dirk of defamation:*
*A mask that like the gorget show'd,*
 *Dye-varying on the pigeon;*
*And for a mantle large and broad,*
 *He wrapt him in religion.*
    HYPOCRISY À LA MODE.


UPON a simmer Sunday morn,
 When Nature's face is fair,
I walkèd forth to view the corn,
 An' snuff the callor air.
The risin' sun, owre Galston muirs,
 Wi' glorious light was glintin';
The hares were hirplin' down the furrs,
 The lav'rocks they were chantin'
    Fu' sweet that day.

As lightsomely I glowr'd abroad,                    10
    To see a scene sae gay,
Three hizzies, early at the road,
    Cam skelpin' up the way.
Twa had manteeles o' dolefu' black,
    But ane wi' lyart lining;
The third, that gaed a wee a-back,
    Was in the fashion shining
                    Fu' gay that day.


The twa appear'd like sisters twin,
    In feature, form, an' claes;                    20
Their visage wither'd, lang an' thin,
    An' sour as ony slaes:
The third cam up, hap-stap-an'-lowp,
    As light as ony lambie,
An' wi' a curchie low did stoop,
    As soon as e'er she saw me,
                    Fu' kind that day.


Wi' bonnet aff, quoth I, 'Sweet lass,
    I think ye seem to ken me;
I'm sure I've seen that bonnie face,                 30
    But yet I canna name ye.'
Quo' she, an' laughin' as she spak,
    An' taks me by the hands,
'Ye, for my sake, hae gi'en the feck
    Of a' the ten commands
                    A screed some day.


'My name is Fun—your crony dear,
    The nearest friend ye hae;
An' this is Superstition here,
    An' that's Hypocrisy.                            40
I'm gaun to Mauchline Holy Fair,
    To spend an hour in daffin':
Gin ye'll go there, yon runkled pair,
    We will get famous laughin'
                    At them this day.'

Quoth I, 'Wi' a' my heart, I'll do't;
  I'll get my Sunday's sark on,
An' meet you on the holy spot;
  Faith, we'se hae fine remarkin'!'
Then I gaed hame at crowdie-time,            50
  An' soon I made me ready;
For roads were clad, frae side to side,
  Wi' mony a wearie bodie
                In droves that day.


Here farmers gash in ridin' graith
  Gaed hoddin' by their cotters;
There swankies young in braw braid-claith
  Are springin' owre the gutters.
The lasses, skelpin' barefit, thrang,
  In silks an' scarlets glitter,            60
Wi' sweet-milk cheese, in mony a whang,
  An' farls bak'd wi' butter,
                Fu' crump that day.


When by the plate we set our nose,
  Weel heapèd up wi' ha'pence,
A greedy glow'r Black Bonnet throws,
  An' we maun draw our tippence.
Then in we go to see the show:
  On ev'ry side they're gath'rin';
Some carryin' deals, some chairs an' stools,   70
  An' some are busy bleth'rin'
                Right loud that day.


Here stands a shed to fend the show'rs,
  An' screen our country gentry;
There racer Jess an' twa-three whores
  Are blinkin' at the entry.
Here sits a raw o' tittlin' jades,
  Wi' heavin' breasts an' bare neck,
An' there a batch o' wabster lads,
  Blackguardin' frae Kilmarnock            80
                For fun this day.

Here some are thinkin' on their sins,
  An' some upo' their claes ;
Ane curses feet that fyl'd his shins,
  Anither sighs an' prays :
On this hand sits a chosen swatch,
  Wi' screw'd up, grace-proud faces ;
On that a set o' chaps, at watch,
  Thrang winkin' on the lasses
             To chairs that day.    90


O happy is that man an' blest !
  Nae wonder that it pride him !
Wha's ain dear lass, that he likes best,
  Comes clinkin' down beside him !
Wi' arm repos'd on the chair-back
  He sweetly does compose him ;
Which, by degrees, slips round her neck,
  An 's loof upon her bosom,
             Unkenn'd that day.


Now a' the congregation o'er         100
  Is silent expectation ;
For Moodie speels the holy door,
  Wi' tidings o' damnation.
Should Hornie, as in ancient days,
  'Mang sons o' God present him,
The very sight o' Moodie's face
  To 's ain het hame had sent him
             Wi' fright that day.


Hear how he clears the points o' faith
  Wi' rattlin' an' wi' thumpin' !     110
Now meekly calm, now wild in wrath,
  He 's stampin' an' he 's jumpin' !
His lengthen'd chin, his turned-up snout,
  His eldritch squeal an' gestures,
O how they fire the heart devout,
  Like cantharidian plaisters,
             On sic a day !

But, hark ! the tent has chang'd its voice ;
   There 's peace an' rest nae langer ;
For a' the real judges rise,            120
   They canna sit for anger.
Smith opens out his cauld harangues,
   On practice and on morals ;
An' aff the godly pour in thrangs
   To gie the jars an' barrels
                A lift that day.


What signifies his barren shine
   Of moral pow'rs an' reason ?
His English style an' gesture fine
   Are a' clean out o' season.        130
Like Socrates or Antonine,
   Or some auld pagan Heathen,
The moral man he does define,
   But ne'er a word o' faith in
               That 's right that day.


In guid time comes an antidote
   Against sic poison'd nostrum ;
For Peebles, frae the water-fit,
   Ascends the holy rostrum :
See, up he 's got the word o' God,   140
   An' meek an' mim has view'd it,
While Common Sense has ta'en the road,
   An' aff, an' up the Cowgate
             Fast, fast, that day.


Wee Miller, neist, the Guard relieves,
   An' Orthodoxy raibles,
Tho' in his heart he weel believes,
   An' thinks it auld wives' fables :
But, faith ! the birkie wants a Manse,
   So cannilie he hums them ;      150
Altho' his carnal wit an' sense
   Like hafflins-wise o'ercomes him
             At times that day.

Now, butt an' ben, the Change-house fills,
　　Wi' yill-caup Commentators ;
Here 's crying out for bakes an' gills,
　　An' there the pint-stowp clatters ;
While thick an' thrang, an' loud an' lang,
　　Wi' logic, an' wi' Scripture,
They raise a din, that in the end                    160
　　Is like to breed a rupture
　　　　　　　　O' wrath that day.


Leeze me on drink ! it gi'es us mair
　　Than either school or college :
It kindles wit, it waukens lair,
　　It pangs us fou o' knowledge.
Be't whisky gill, or penny wheep,
　　Or ony stronger potion,
It never fails, on drinkin' deep,
　　To kittle up our notion                         170
　　　　　　　　By night or day.


The lads an' lasses, blythely bent
　　To mind baith saul an' body,
Sit round the table, weel content,
　　An' steer about the toddy.
On this ane's dress, an' that ane's leuk,
　　They're makin observations ;
While some are cosy i' the neuk,
　　An' formin' assignations
　　　　　　　　To meet some day.      180


But now the Lord's ain trumpet touts,
　　Till a' the hills are rairin',
An' echoes back return the shouts ;
　　Black Russel is na sparin' :
His piercing words, like Highlan' swords,
　　Divide the joints an' marrow ;
His talk o' Hell, where devils dwell,
　　Our very ' sauls does harrow '
　　　　　　　　Wi' fright that day !

A vast, unbottom'd, boundless pit,                    190
　Fill'd fou o' lowin' brunstane,
Wha's ragin' flame, an' scorchin' heat,
　Wad melt the hardest whun-stane!
The half-asleep start up wi' fear
　An' think they hear it roarin',
When presently it does appear
　'Twas but some neebor snorin'
　　　　　　　　　Asleep that day.


'Twad be owre lang a tale to tell
　How mony stories past,                    200
An' how they crowded to the yill,
　When they were a' dismist;
How drink gaed round, in cogs an' caups,
　Amang the furms and benches;
An' cheese an' bread, frae women's laps,
　Was dealt about in lunches,
　　　　　　　　　An' dawds that day.


In comes a gawsie, gash guidwife,
　An' sits down by the fire,
Syne draws her kebbuck an' her knife;                    210
　The lasses they are shyer.
The auld guidmen, about the grace,
　Frae side to side they bother,
Till some ane by his bonnet lays,
　An' gi'es them't like a tether,
　　　　　　　　　Fu' lang that day.


Waesucks! for him that gets nae lass,
　Or lasses that hae naething!
Sma' need has he to say a grace,
　Or melvie his braw claithing!                    220
O wives, be mindfu', ance yoursel
　How bonnie lads ye wanted,
An' dinna for a kebbuck-heel
　Let lasses be affronted
　　　　　　　　　On sic a day!

Now Clinkumbell, wi' rattlin' tow,
   Begins to jow an' croon ;
Some swagger hame the best they dow,
   Some wait the afternoon.
At slaps the billies halt a blink,                    230
   Till lasses strip their shoon :
Wi' faith an' hope, an' love an' drink,
   They're a' in famous tune
               For crack that day.


How mony hearts this day converts
   O' sinners and o' lasses !
Their hearts o' stane, gin night, are gane
   As saft as ony flesh is.
There's some are fou o' love divine,
   There's some are fou o' brandy ;                    240
An' mony jobs that day begin,
   May end in houghmagandie
              Some ither day.


—•—

## THE TWA DOGS.

'Twas in that place o' Scotland's Isle,
That bears the name o' auld King Coil,
Upon a bonnie day in June,
When wearin' through the afternoon,
Twa dogs, that werena thrang at hame,
Forgather'd ance upon a time.

   The first I'll name, they ca'd him Caesar,
Was keepit for his Honour's pleasure ;
His hair, his size, his mouth, his lugs,
Show'd he was nane o' Scotland's dogs,                    10
But whalpit some place far abroad,
Where sailors gang to fish for cod.
   His lockèd, letter'd, braw brass collar,
Shew'd him the gentleman and scholar ;

But though he was o' high degree,
The fient a pride, nae pride had he ;
But wad hae spent ane hour caressin'
E'en wi' a tinkler-gipsy's messan :
At kirk or market, mill or smiddie,
Nae tawted tyke, though e'er sae duddie,                    20
But he wad stand as glad to see him,
An' stroan'd on stanes an' hillocks wi' him.

The tither was a ploughman's collie,
A rhyming, ranting, raving billie ;
Wha for his friend and comrade had him,
And in his freaks had Luath ca'd him,
After some dog in Highland sang,
Was made lang syne—Lord knows how lang.

He was a gash an' faithfu' tyke,
As ever lap a sheugh or dyke ;                             30
His honest, sonsie, bawsent face
Aye gat him friends in ilka place.
His breast was white, his tousie back
Weel clad wi' coat o' glossy black ;
His gawsie tail, wi' upward curl,
Hung o'er his hurdies wi' a swirl.

Nae doubt but they were fain o' ither,
And unco pack and thick thegither ;
Wi' social nose whyles snuff'd and snowkit ;
Whyles mice and moudieworts they howkit ;                  40
Whyles scour'd awa in lang excursion,
And worried ither in diversion ;
Until wi' daffin' weary grown,
Upon a knowe they sat them down,
And there began a lang digression
About the lords of the creation.

### CAESAR.

I've aften wonder'd, honest Luath,
What sort o' life poor dogs like you have ;
An' when the gentry's life I saw,
What way poor bodies liv'd ava.                            50

Our Laird gets in his rackèd rents,
His coals, his kain, and a' his stents ;
He rises when he likes himsel' ;
His flunkies answer at the bell :
He ca's his coach ; he ca's his horse ;
He draws a bonny silken purse
As lang's my tail, where, through the steeks,
The yellow-letter'd Geordie keeks.
    Frae morn to e'en it's nought but toiling
At baking, roasting, frying, boiling ;          60
And though the gentry first are stechin',
Yet e'en the ha' folk fill their pechan
Wi' sauce, ragouts, and sic like trashtrie,
That's little short o' downright wastrie.
Our whipper-in, wee blastit wonner !
Poor worthless elf ! it eats a dinner
Better than ony tenant man
His Honour has in a' the lan' ;
An' what poor cot-folk pit their painch in,
I own it's past my comprehension.          70

### LUATH.

Trowth, Caesar, whyles they're fash'd eneugh ;
A cottar howkin' in a sheugh,
Wi' dirty stanes biggin' a dyke,
Baring a quarry, and sic like ;
Himsel', a wife, he thus sustains,
A smytrie o' wee duddy weans,
And nought but his han'-darg to keep
Them right and tight in thack and rape.
    And when they meet wi' sair disasters,
Like loss o' health, or want o' masters,          80
Ye maist wad think, a wee touch langer
And they maun starve o' cauld and hunger ;
But how it comes I never kent yet,
They're maistly wonderfu' contented ;
An' buirdly chiels and clever hizzies
Are bred in sic a way as this is.

### CAESAR.

But then, to see how ye're negleckit,
How huff'd, and cuff'd, and disrespeckit,

Lord, man! our gentry care sae little
For delvers, ditchers and sic cattle; 90
They gang as saucy by poor folk
As I wad by a stinking brock.
    I've noticed, on our Laird's court-day,
An' mony a time my heart's been wae,
Poor tenant bodies, scant o' cash,
How they maun thole a factor's snash;
He'll stamp and threaten, curse and swear,
He'll apprehend them, poind their gear:
While they maun stan', wi' aspect humble,
An' hear it a', an' fear an' tremble! 100
I see how folk live that hae riches;
But surely poor folk maun be wretches!

LUATH.

They're no' sae wretched's ane wad think,
Though constantly on poortith's brink:
They're sae accustom'd wi' the sight,
The view o't gi'es them little fright.
    Then chance and fortune are sae guided,
They're aye in less or mair provided;
An' though fatigued wi' close employment,
A blink o' rest's a sweet enjoyment. 110
    The dearest comfort o' their lives,
Their grushie weans an' faithfu' wives;
The prattling things are just their pride,
That sweetens a' their fireside.
    And whyles twalpenny-worth o' nappy
Can mak the bodies unco happy;
They lay aside their private cares
To mind the Kirk and State affairs:
They'll talk o' patronage and priests,
Wi' kindling fury in their breasts; 120
Or tell what new taxation's comin',
And ferlie at the folk in Lon'on.
    As bleak faced Hallowmas returns
They get the jovial rantin' kirns,
When rural life o' every station
Unite in common recreation;
Love blinks, Wit slaps, and social Mirth
Forgets there's Care upo' the earth.

That merry day the year begins
They bar the door on frosty win's;                    130
The nappy reeks wi' mantling ream,
And sheds a heart-inspiring steam;
The luntin' pipe and sneeshin'-mill
Are handed round wi' right gude-will;
The canty auld folk crackin' crouse,
The young anes ranting through the house—
My heart has been sae fain to see them
That I for joy hae barkit wi' them.

Still it's owre true that ye hae said,
Sic game is now owre aften play'd.                    140
There's mony a creditable stock
O' decent, honest, fawsont folk,
Are riven out baith root and branch
Some rascal's pridefu' greed to quench,
Wha thinks to knit himsel the faster
In favour wi' some gentle master,
Wha, aiblins, thrang a-parliamentin',
For Britain's gude his saul indentin—

CAESAR.

Haith, lad, ye little ken about it;
For Britain's gude!—guid faith! I doubt it!          150
Say rather, gaun as Premiers lead him,
And saying ay or no's they bid him!
At operas and plays parading,
Mortgaging, gambling, masquerading.
Or maybe, in a frolic daft,
To Hague or Calais taks a waft,
To make a tour, an' tak a whirl,
To learn *bon ton* an' see the worl'.
There, at Vienna, or Versailles,
He rives his father's auld entails;                   160
Or by Madrid he takes the rout,
To thrum guitars and fecht wi' nowt;
Or down Italian vista startles,
Whore-hunting amang groves o' myrtles;
Then bouses drumly German water,
To make himsel' look fair and fatter,
And clear the consequential sorrows,
Love-gifts of Carnival signoras.

For Britain's gude !—for her destruction !
Wi' dissipation, feud, and faction !                    170

### LUATH.

Hech man ! dear sirs ! is that the gate
They waste sae mony a braw estate ?
Are we sae foughten and harass'd
For gear to gang that gate at last ?
O would they stay aback frae courts,
An' please themselves wi' country sports,
It wad for every ane be better,
The laird, the tenant, an' the cotter !
For thae frank, rantin', ramblin' billies,
Fient haet o' them 's ill-hearted fellows :            180
Except for breakin' o' their timmer,
Or speaking lightly o' their limmer,
Or shootin' o' a hare or moor-cock,
The ne'er-a-bit they're ill to poor folk.
But will ye tell me, Master Caesar ?
Sure great folk's life 's a life o' pleasure ;
Nae cauld nor hunger e'er can steer them,
The very thought o't needna fear them.

### CAESAR.

Lord, man, were ye but whyles where I am,
The gentles ye wad ne'er envý 'em,                      190
It 's true, they needna starve or sweat,
Thro' winter's cauld or simmer's heat ;
They've nae sair wark to craze their banes,
An' fill auld age wi' grips an' granes :
But human bodies are sic fools,
For a' their colleges and schools,
That when nae real ills perplex them,
They make enow themselves to vex them,
An' aye the less they hae to sturt them,
In like proportion less will hurt them.                200
A country fellow at the pleugh,
His acres till'd, he 's right eneugh ;
A country lassie at her wheel,
Her dizzens done, she 's unco weel ;
But gentlemen, an' ladies warst,
Wi' ev'ndown want o' wark are curst.

They loiter, lounging, lank, and lazy;
Though de'il haet ails them, yet uneasy;
Their days insipid, dull and tasteless;
Their nights unquiet, lang, and restless.          210
And e'en their sports, their balls, and races,
Their galloping through public places;
There's sic parade, sic pomp and art,
The joy can scarcely reach the heart.
The men cast out in party matches,
Then sowther a' in deep debauches:
Ae night they're mad wi' drink and whoring,
Neist day their life is past enduring.
The ladies arm-in-arm, in clusters,
As great and gracious a' as sisters;          220
But hear their absent thoughts o' ither,
They're a' run de'ils and jades thegither.
Whyles, owre the wee bit cup and platie,
They sip the scandal-potion pretty;
Or lee-lang nights, wi' crabbit leuks,
Pore owre the devil's picture beuks;
Stake on a chance a farmer's stack-yard,
And cheat like ony unhang'd blackguard.
    There's some exception, man and woman;
But this is gentry's life in common.          230


    By this the sun was out o' sight,
And darker gloamin brought the night;
The bum-clock humm'd wi' lazy drone,
The kye stood rowtin' i' the loan;
When up they gat and shook their lugs,
Rejoiced they werena men but dogs;
And each took aff his several way,
Resolved to meet some ither day.

## THE BRIGS OF AYR.

THE simple Bard, rough at the rustic plough,
Learning his tuneful trade from every bough;
The chanting linnet, or the mellow thrush,
Hailing the setting sun, sweet, in the green thorn bush;
The soaring lark, the perching red-breast shrill,
Or deep-ton'd plovers gray, wild-whistling o'er the hill;
Shall he, nurst in the peasant's lowly shed,
To hardy independence bravely bred,
By early poverty to hardship steel'd,
And train'd to arms in stern Misfortune's field,—    10
Shall he be guilty of their hireling crimes,
The servile, mercenary Swiss of rhymes?
Or labour hard the panegyric close,
With all the venal soul of dedicating prose?
No! though his artless strains he rudely sings,
And throws his hand uncouthly o'er the strings,
He glows with all the spirit of the Bard,
Fame, honest fame, his great, his dear reward.
Still, if some patron's generous care he trace,
Skill'd in the secret to bestow with grace;    20
When Ballantyne befriends his humble name
And hands the rustic stranger up to fame,
With heartfelt throes his grateful bosom swells,
The godlike bliss, to give, alone excels.

'Twas when the stacks get on their winter-hap,
And thack and rape secure the toil-won crap;
Potatoe-bings are snuggèd up frae skaith
O' coming Winter's biting, frosty breath;
The bees, rejoicing o'er their summer toils,
Unnumber'd buds an' flowers' delicious spoils,    30
Seal'd up with frugal care in massive waxen piles,
Are doom'd by Man, that tyrant o'er the weak,
The death o' devils, smoor'd wi' brimstone reek:
The thund'ring guns are heard on ev'ry side,
The wounded coveys, reeling, scatter wide;

The feather'd field-mates, bound by Nature's tie,
Sires, mothers, children, in one carnage lie:
(What warm, poetic heart, but inly bleeds,
And execrates man's savage, ruthless deeds!)
Nae mair the flow'r in field or meadow springs;          40
Nae mair the grove with airy concert rings,
Except perhaps the Robin's whistling glee, .
Proud o' the height o' some bit half-lang tree:
The hoary morns precede the sunny days,
Mild, calm, serene, wide spreads the noontide blaze,
While thick the gossamour waves wanton in the rays.

'Twas in that season when a simple Bard,
Unknown and poor, simplicity's reward,
Ae night, within the ancient brugh of Ayr,
By whim inspir'd, or haply prest wi' care,          50
He left his bed and took his wayward route,
And down by Simpson's wheel'd the left about:
(Whether impell'd by all-directing Fate,
To witness what I after shall narrate;
Or whether, rapt in meditation high,
He wander'd out he knew not where nor why:)
The drowsy Dungeon clock had number'd two,
And Wallace Tower had sworn the fact was true:
The tide-swoln Firth, wi' sullen-sounding roar,
Through the still night dash'd hoarse along the shore: 60
All else was hush'd as Nature's closèd e'e;
The silent moon shone high o'er tow'r and tree:
The chilly frost, beneath the silver beam,
Crept, gently-crusting, owre the glittering stream—
   When, lo! on either hand the list'ning Bard,
The clanging sough of whistling wings is heard;
Two dusky forms dart thro' the midnight air,
Swift as the gos drives on the wheeling hare;
Ane on th' Auld Brig his airy shape uprears,
The ither flutters o'er the rising piers:          70
Our warlock Rhymer instantly descried
The Sprites that owre the Brigs of Ayr preside.
(That Bards are second-sighted is nae joke,
And ken the lingo of the sp'ritual folk;
Fays, Spunkies, Kelpies, a', they can explain them,
And ev'n the very deils they brawly ken them.)

Auld Brig appear'd o' ancient Pictish race,
The very wrinkles Gothic in his face ;
He seem'd as he wi Time had warstl'd lang,
Yet, teughly doure, he bade an unco bang. 80
New Brig was buskit, in a braw new coat,
That he, at Lon'on, frae ane Adams got ;
In 's hand five taper staves as smooth 's a bead,
Wi' virls an' whirlygigums at the head.
The Goth was stalking round with anxious search,
Spying the time-worn flaws in ev'ry arch ;
It chanc'd his new-come neebor took his e'e,
And e'en a vex'd and angry heart had he !
Wi' thieveless sneer to see his modish mien,
He, down the water, gies him this guid-een :— 90

AULD BRIG.

I doubtna, frien', ye'll think ye're nae sheep-shank.
Ance ye were streekit owre frae bank to bank !
But gin ye be a brig as auld as me—
Tho', faith ! that date, I doubt, ye'll never see—
There'll be, if that day come, I'll wad a boddle,
Some fewer whigmaleeries in your noddle.

NEW BRIG.

Auld Vandal ! ye but show your little mense,
Just much about it wi' your scanty sense ;
Will your poor narrow foot-path of a street,
Where twa wheel-barrows tremble when they meet, 100
Your ruin'd formless bulk o' stane and lime,
Compare wi' bonnie brigs o' modern time ?
There 's men of taste wou'd tak the Ducat stream,
Tho' they should cast the very sark and swim,
Ere they would grate their feelings wi' the view
O' sic an ugly Gothic hulk as you.

AULD BRIG.

Conceited gowk ! puff'd up wi' windy pride !
This mony a year I've stood the flood an' tide ;
And tho' wi' crazy eild I'm sair forfairn,
I'll be a brig, when ye're a shapeless cairn ! 110

As yet ye little ken about the matter,
But twa-three winters will inform ye better.
When heavy, dark, continued, a'-day rains,
Wi' deepening deluges o'erflow the plains;
When from the hills where springs the brawling Coil,
Or stately Lugar's mossy fountains boil,
Or where the Greenock winds his moorland course,
Or haunted Garpal draws his feeble source,
Arous'd by blust'ring winds an' spotting thowes,
In mony a torrent down the snaw-broo rowes;                    120
While crashing ice, borne on the roaring spate,
Sweeps dams, an' mills, an' brigs, a' to the gate;
And from Glenbuck, down to the Ratton-key,
Auld Ayr is just one lengthen'd, tumbling sea;
Then down ye'll hurl, deil nor ye never rise!
And dash the gumlie jaups up to the pouring skies!
A lesson sadly teaching, to your cost,
That architecture's noble art is lost!


### NEW BRIG.

Fine architecture, trowth, I needs must say't o't,
The Lord be thankit that we've tint the gate o't!            130
Gaunt, ghastly, ghaist-alluring edifices,
Hanging with threat'ning jut, like precipices;
O'er-arching, mouldy, gloom-inspiring coves,
Supporting roofs, fantastic, stony groves;
Windows and doors in nameless sculptures drest,
With order, symmetry, or taste unblest;
Forms like some bedlam Statuary's dream,
The craz'd creations of misguided whim;
Forms might be worshipp'd on the bended knee,
And still the second dread command be free,                  140
Their likeness is not found on earth, in air, or sea!
Mansions that would disgrace the building taste
Of any mason reptile, bird, or beast;
Fit only for a doited monkish race,
Or frosty maids forsworn the dear embrace,
Or cuifs of later times wha held the notion
That sullen gloom was sterling, true devotion;
Fancies that our guid Brugh denies protection,
And soon may they expire, unblest with resurrection!

### AULD BRIG.

O ye, my dear-remember'd, ancient yealings,   150
Were ye but here to share my wounded feelings!
Ye worthy Proveses, an' mony a Bailie,
Wha in the paths o' righteousness did toil aye;
Ye dainty Deacons, an' ye douce Conveeners,
To whom our moderns are but causey-cleaners!
Ye godly Councils wha hae blest this town;
Ye godly Brethren o' the sacred gown,
Wha meekly gie your hurdies to the smiters;
And (what would now be strange ye godly Writers:
A' ye douce folk I've borne aboon the broo,   160
Were ye but here, what would ye say or do!
How would your spirits groan in deep vexation,
To see each melancholy alteration;
And agonizing, curse the time and place
When ye begat the base degen'rate race!
Nae langer rev'rend men, their country's glory,
In plain braid Scots hold forth a plain braid story;
Nae langer thrifty citizens, an' douce,
Meet owre a pint, or in the Council-house;
But staumrel, corky-headed, graceless Gentry,   170
The herryment and ruin of the country;
Men, three-parts made by tailors and by barbers,
Wha waste your wool-hain'd gear on damn'd new brigs and
  harbours!

### NEW BRIG.

Now haud you there! for faith ye've said enough,
And muckle mair than ye can mak to through:
As for your Priesthood, I shall say but little,
Corbies and Clergy are a shot right kittle;
But, under favour o' your langer beard,
Abuse o' Magistrates might weel be spar'd;
To liken them to your auld-warld squad,   180
I must needs say, comparisons are odd.
In Ayr, wag-wits nae mair can have a handle
To mouth 'a Citizen,' a term o' scandal;
Nae mair the Council waddles down the street,
In all the pomp of ignorant conceit;

Men wha grew wise priggin' owre hops an' raisins,
Or gather'd liberal views in bonds and seisins.
If haply Knowledge, on a random tramp,
Had shor'd them wi' a glimmer of his lamp,
And would to Common-sense for once betray'd them,  190
Plain dull Stupidity stept kindly in to aid them.

WHAT farther clishmaclaver might been said,
What bloody wars, if Sprites had blood to shed,
No man can tell ; but all before their sight
A fairy train appear'd in order bright ;
Adown the glittering stream they featly danc'd ;
Bright to the moon their various dresses glanc'd :
They footed o'er the watery glass so neat,
The infant ice scarce bent beneath their feet ;
While arts of Minstrelsy among them rung,          200
And soul-ennobling Bards heroic ditties sung.
O had M'Lauchlan, thairm-inspiring sage,
Been there to hear this heavenly band engage,
When thro' his dear strathspeys they bore with Highland rage,
Or when they struck old Scotia's melting airs,
The lover's raptur'd joys or bleeding cares,
How would his Highland lug been nobler fired,
And ev'n his matchless hand with finer touch inspired !
No guess could tell what instrument appear'd,
But all the soul of Music's self was heard ;        210
Harmonious concert rung in every part,
While simple melody pour'd moving on the heart.
   The Genius of the Stream in front appears,
A venerable Chief, advanced in years ;
His hoary head with water-lilies crown'd,
His manly leg with garter-tangle bound.
Next came the loveliest pair in all the ring,
Sweet Female Beauty hand in hand with Spring ;
Then, crown'd with flow'ry hay, came Rural Joy,
And Summer, with his fervid-beaming eye ;          220
All-cheering Plenty, with her flowing horn,
Led yellow Autumn wreath'd with nodding corn ;
Then Winter's time-bleach'd locks did hoary show,
By Hospitality with cloudless brow ;
Next follow'd Courage with his martial stride,
From where the Feal wild-woody coverts hide ;

Benevolence, with mild benignant air,
A female form, came from the towers of Stair:
Learning and Worth in equal measures trode
From simple Catrine, their long-loved abode;            230
Last, white-robed Peace, crown'd with a hazel wreath,
To rustic Agriculture did bequeath
The broken iron instruments of death:
At sight of whom our Sprites forgat their kindling wrath.

---

## THE VISION.

### DUAN FIRST.

THE sun had closed the winter day,
The curlers quat their roarin' play,
An' hunger'd maukin taen her way
    To kail-yards green,
While faithless snaws ilk step betray
    Where she has been.

The thresher's weary flingin'-tree
The lee-lang day had tirèd me;
And when the day had clos'd his e'e,
    Far i' the west,            10
Ben i' the spence, right pensivelie,
    I gaed to rest.

There lanely by the ingle-cheek
I sat and eyed the spewing reek,
That fill'd, wi' hoast-provoking smeek,
    The auld clay biggin';
An' heard the restless rattons squeak
    About the riggin'.

All in this mottie misty clime,
I backward mused on wasted time,            20
How I had spent my youthfu' prime,
    An' done nae-thing,
But stringin' blethers up in rhyme.
    For fools to sing.

Had I to guid advice but harkit,
I might, by this, hae led a market,
Or strutted in a bank, and clarkit
    My cash-account:
While here, half-mad, half-fed, half-sarkit,
    Is a' th' amount.        30

I started, mutt'ring 'blockhead! coof!'
And heaved on high my waukit loof,
To swear by a' yon starry roof,
    Or some rash aith,
That I, henceforth, would be rhyme-proof
    Till my last breath—

When click! the string the snick did draw;
An' jee! the door gaed to the wa';
And by my ingle-lowe I saw,
    Now bleezin' bright,
A tight outlandish hizzie, braw,        40
    Come full in sight.

Ye need na doubt I held my whisht;
The infant aith, half-form'd, was crusht;
I glowr'd as eerie 's I'd been dusht
    In some wild glen;
When sweet, like modest worth, she blusht,
    An' steppèd ben.

Green, slender, leaf-clad holly-boughs
Were twisted, gracefu', round her brows;    50
I took her for some Scottish Muse
    By that same token;
And come to stop these reckless vows,
    Would soon been broken.

A hare-brain'd, sentimental trace,
Was strongly markèd in her face;
A wildly-witty rustic grace
    Shone full upon her;
Her eye, ev'n turn'd on empty space,
    Beam'd keen with honour.        60

Down flow'd her robe, a tartan sheen,
Till half a leg was scrimply seen ;
An' such a leg ! my bonnie Jean
      Could only peer it ;
Sae straught, sae taper, tight, and clean,
      Nane else came near it.

Her mantle large, of greenish hue,
My gazing wonder chiefly drew ;
Deep lights and shades, bold-mingling, threw
      A lustre grand ;      70
And seem'd to my astonish'd view
      A well-known land.

Here rivers in the sea were lost ;
There mountains to the skies were tost :
Here tumbling billows mark'd the coast
      With surging foam ;
There, distant shone Art's lofty boast,
      The lordly dome.

Here Doon pour'd down his far-fetch'd floods ;
There well-fed Irwine stately thuds ;      80
Auld hermit Ayr staw thro' his woods,
      On to the shore ;
And many a lesser torrent scuds,
      With seeming roar.

Low in a sandy valley spread,
An ancient borough rear'd her head ;
Still, as in Scottish story read,
      She boasts a race,
To ev'ry nobler virtue bred,
      And polish'd grace.      90

By stately tower or palace fair,
Or ruins pendent in the air,
Bold stems of heroes, here and there,
      I could discern ;
Some seem'd to muse, some seem'd to dare,
      With feature stern.

My heart did glowing transport feel,
To see a race heroic wheel,
And brandish round, the deep-dyed steel
          In sturdy blows ;                         100
While back-recoiling seem'd to reel
          Their Suthron foes.


His Country's Saviour, mark him well!
Bold Richardton's heroic swell ;
The Chief—on Sark who glorious fell,
          In high command ;
And he whom ruthless fates expel
          His native land.


There, where a sceptred Pictish shade
Stalk'd round his ashes lowly laid,            110
I mark'd a martial race, pourtray'd
          In colours strong ;
Bold, soldier-featur'd, undismay'd
          They strode along.


Thro' many a wild romantic grove,
Near many a hermit-fancied cove
(Fit haunts for Friendship or for Love
          In musing mood)
An agèd Judge, I saw him rove
          Dispensing good.                          120


With deep-struck reverential awe
The learned Sire and Son I saw ;
To Nature's God and Nature's law
          They gave their lore ;
This, all its source and end to draw,
          That, to adore.


Brydon's brave ward I well could spy,
Beneath old Scotia's smiling eye ;
Who call'd on Fame, low standing by,
          To hand him on,                           130
Where many a patriot name on high,
          And hero shone.

DUAN SECOND.

WITH musing-deep astonish'd stare,
I view'd the heavenly-seeming Fair;
A whisp'ring throb did witness bear
   Of kindred sweet,
When with an elder Sister's air
   She did me greet.

'All hail! my own inspired bard!
In me thy native Muse regard!     140
Nor longer mourn thy fate is hard,
   Thus poorly low;
I come to give thee such reward
   As we bestow.

'Know the great Genius of this land
Has many a light aërial band,
Who, all beneath his high command,
   Harmoniously,
As arts or arms they understand,
   Their labours ply.     150

'They Scotia's race among them share:
Some fire the soldier on to dare;
Some rouse the patriot up to bare
   Corruption's heart:
Some teach the bard, a darling care,
   The tuneful art.

''Mong swelling floods of reeking gore,
They, ardent, kindling spirits pour;
Or, 'mid the venal senate's roar,
   They, sightless, stand,   160
To mend the honest patriot lore,
   And grace the hand.

'And when the bard, or hoary sage,
Charm or instruct the future age,
They bind the wild poetic rage
   In energy,
Or point the inconclusive page
   Full on the eye.

'Hence Fullarton, the brave and young;
Hence Dempster's zeal-inspirèd tongue;          170
Hence sweet harmonious Beattie sung
          His Minstrel lays,
Or tore, with noble ardour stung,
          The sceptic's bays.


'To lower orders are assign'd
The humbler ranks of human-kind,
The rustic bard, the lab'ring hind,
          The artisan ;
All choose, as various they're inclin'd,
          The various man.          180


'When yellow waves the heavy grain,
The threat'ning storm some strongly rein ;
Some teach to meliorate the plain
          With tillage-skill ;
And some instruct the shepherd-train,
          Blythe o'er the hill.


'Some hint the lover's harmless wile ;
Some grace the maiden's artless smile ;
Some soothe the lab'rer's weary toil
          For humble gains,          190
And make his cottage-scenes beguile
          His cares and pains.


'Some, bounded to a district-space,
Explore at large man's infant race,
To mark the embryotic trace
          Of rustic bard ;
And careful note each op'ning grace,
          A guide and guard.


'Of these am I—Coila my name ;
And this district as mine I claim,          200
Where once the Campbells, chiefs of fame,
          Held ruling pow'r :
I mark'd thy embryo-tuneful flame,
          Thy natal hour.

'With future hope I oft would gaze,
Fond, on thy little early ways,
Thy rudely-caroll'd, chiming phrase,
          In uncouth rhymes,—
. Fired at the simple artless lays
          Of other times.                              210


'I saw thee seek the sounding shore,
Delighted with the dashing roar;
Or when the North his fleecy store
          Drove thro' the sky,
I saw grim Nature's visage hoar
          Struck thy young eye.


'Or when the deep green-mantled Earth
Warm-cherish'd ev'ry flow'ret's birth,
And joy and music pouring forth
          In ev'ry grove,                                220
I saw thee eye the gen'ral mirth
          With boundless love.


'When ripen'd fields and azure skies
Call'd forth the reapers' rustling noise,
I saw thee leave their ev'ning joys,
          And lonely stalk,
To vent thy bosom's swelling rise
          In pensive walk.


'When youthful love, warm-blushing strong,
Keen-shivering shot thy nerves along,                   230
Those accents, grateful to thy tongue,
          Th' adorèd Name,
I taught thee how to pour in song,
          To soothe thy flame.


'I saw thy pulse's maddening play
Wild send thee pleasure's devious way,
Misled by fancy's meteor ray,
          By passion driven;
But yet the light that led astray
          Was light from Heaven.                         240

'I taught thy manners-painting strains,
The loves, the ways of simple swains,
Till now, o'er all my wide domains
　　　　Thy fame extends ;
And some, the pride of Coila's plains,
　　　　Become thy friends.


'Thou canst not learn, nor can I show,
To paint with Thomson's landscape-glow ;
Or wake the bosom-melting throe
　　　　With Shenstone's art ;　　　　250
Or pour with Gray the moving flow
　　　　Warm on the heart.


'Yet all beneath th' unrivall'd rose
The lowly daisy sweetly blows ;
Tho' large the forest's monarch throws
　　　　His army shade,
Yet green the juicy hawthorn grows
　　　　Adown the glade.


'Then never murmur nor repine ;
Strive in thy humble sphere to shine ;　　　260
And trust me, not Potosi's mine,
　　　　Nor king's regard,
Can give a bliss o'ermatching thine,
　　　　A rustic Bard.


'To give my counsels all in one,
Thy tuneful flame still careful fan ;
Preserve the dignity of Man,
　　　　With Soul erect ;
And trust the Universal Plan
　　　　Will all protect.　　　　270


'And wear thou this' : She solemn said,
And bound the holly round my head :
The polish'd leaves and berries red
　　　　Did rustling play ;
And, like a passing thought, she fled
　　　　In light away.

# THE DEATH AND DYING WORDS OF POOR MAILIE, THE AUTHOR'S ONLY PET YOWE.

As Mailie, an' her lambs thegither,
Was ae day nibbling on the tether,
Upon her cloot she coost a hitch,
An' owre she warsled in the ditch ;
There, groaning, dying, she did lie,
When Hughoc he cam doytin by.
　Wi' glowrin' een, an' lifted han's,
Poor Hughoc like a statue stan's ;
He saw her days were near-hand ended,
But, wae's my heart ! he could na mend it !　　10
He gapèd wide, but naething spak ;
At length poor Mailie silence brak :—

　'O thou, whase lamentable face
Appears to mourn my woefu' case !
My dying words attentive hear,
An' bear them to my Master dear.
　'Tell him, if e'er again he keep
As muckle gear as buy a sheep,—
O bid him never tie them mair
Wi' wicked strings o' hemp or hair !　　20
But ca' them out to park or hill,
An' let them wander at their will ;
So may his flock increase, an' grow
To scores o' lambs, an' packs o' woo' !
　'Tell him he was a Master kin',
An' aye was guid to me an' mine ;
An' now my dying charge I gie him,
My helpless lambs, I trust them wi' him.
　'O bid him save their harmless lives
Frae dogs, an' tods, an' butchers' knives !　　30
But gie them guid cow-milk their fill,
Till they be fit to fend themsel :
An' tent them duly, e'en an' morn,
Wi' teats o' hay an' ripps o' corn.

'An' may they never learn the gates
Of ither vile wanrestfu' pets—
To slink thro' slaps, an' reave an' steal,
At stacks o' pease, or stocks o' kail.
So may they, like their great forbears,
For mony a year come thro' the shears ;          40
So wives will gie them bits o' bread,
  An' bairns greet for them when they're dead.
  'My poor tup-lamb, my son an' heir,
O bid him breed him up wi' care !
An', if he live to be a beast,
To pit some havins in his breast !
An' warn him, what I winna name,
To stay content wi' yowes at hame ;
An' no to rin an' wear his cloots,
Like ither menseless graceless brutes.          50
  'An' neist my yowie, silly thing,
Gude keep thee frae a tether string !
O may thou ne'er forgather up
Wi' ony blastit moorland tup ;
But ay keep mind to moop an' mell,
Wi' sheep o' credit like thysel !
  'And now, my bairns, wi' my last breath
I lea'e my blessin wi' you baith ;
An' when you think upo' your mither,
Mind to be kind to ane anither.          60
  'Now, honest Hughoc, dinna fail
To tell my master a' my tale ;
An' bid him burn this cursed tether ;
An', for thy pains, thou'se get my blether.'

This said, poor Mailie turn'd her head,
An' closed her een amang the dead !

## POOR MAILIE'S ELEGY.

LAMENT in rhyme, lament in prose,
Wi' saut tears tricklin' down your nose;
Our bardie's fate is at a close,
        Past a' remead;
The last sad cape-stane of his woes—
        Poor Mailie's dead!

It's no the loss o' warl's gear
That could sae bitter draw the tear,
Or mak our bardie, dowie, wear
        The mourning weed:    10
He's lost a friend and neibor dear
        In Mailie dead.

Thro' a' the toun she trotted by him;
A lang half-mile she could descry him;
Wi' kindly bleat. when she did spy him,
        She ran wi' speed:
A friend mair faithfu' ne'er cam nigh him
        Than Mailie dead.

I wat she was a sheep o' sense,
An' could behave hersel wi' mense;    20
I'll say't, she never brak a fence
        Thro' thievish greed.
Our bardie, lanely, keeps the spence
        Sin' Mailie's dead.

Or, if he wanders up the howe,
Her living image in her yowe
Comes bleating to him, owre the knowe,
        For bits o' bread,
An' down the briny pearls rowe
        For Mailie dead.    30

She was nae get o' moorland tups,
Wi' tawted ket, an' hairy hips;
For her forbears were brought in ships
        Frae yont the Tweed:
A bonnier fleesh ne'er cross'd the clips
        Than Mailie's, dead.

Wae worth the man wha first did shape
That vile wanchancie thing—a rape!
It maks guid fellows girn an' gape,
      Wi' chokin' dread;      40
An' Robin's bonnet wave wi' crape
      For Mailie dead.


O a' ye bards on bonnie Doon!
An' wha on Ayr your chanters tune!
Come, join the melancholious croon
      O' Robin's reed;
His heart will never get aboon
      His Mailie dead!


## DEATH AND DOCTOR HORNBOOK.

Some books are lies frae end to end,
And some great lies were never penn'd:
Ev'n ministers, they hae been kenn'd,
      In holy rapture,
A rousing whid at times to vend,
      And nail't wi' Scripture.


But this that I am gaun to tell,
Which lately on a night befell,
Is just as true 's the Deil 's in hell
      Or Dublin city:      10
That e'er he nearer comes oursel
      'S a muckle pity.


The Clachan yill had made me canty,
I wasna fou, but just had plenty;
I stacher'd whyles, but yet took tent aye
      To free the ditches;
An' hillocks, stanes, an' bushes kent aye
      Frae ghaists an' witches.

The rising moon began to glowre
The distant Cumnock hills out-owre :                    20
To count her horns, wi' a' my pow'r,
                    I set mysel ;
But whether she had three or four
                    I cou'd na tell.


I was come round about the hill,
And todlin' down on Willie's mill,
Setting my staff, wi' a' my skill,
                    To keep me sicker ;
Tho' leeward whyles, against my will,
                    I took a bicker.                    30


I there wi' Something did forgather,
That pat me in an eerie swither ;
An awfu' scythe, out-owre ae shouther,
                    Clear-dangling, hang ;
A three-tae'd leister on the ither
                    Lay large an' lang.


Its stature seem'd lang Scotch ells twa,
The queerest shape that e'er I saw,
For fient a wame it had ava ;
                    And then its shanks,                    40
They were as thin, as sharp an' sma'
                    As cheeks o' branks.


'Guid-een,' quo' I ; 'Friend ! hae ye been mawin,
When ither folk are busy sawin ?'
It seem'd to mak a kind o' stan',
                    But naething spak ;
At length says I, 'Friend, wh'are ye gaun ?
                    Will ye go back ?'


It spak right howe—'My name is Death,
But be na fley'd.'—Quoth I, 'Guid faith,                    50
Ye're maybe come to stap my breath ;
                    But tent me, billie :
I red ye weel, tak care o' skaith,
                    See, there's a gully !'

'Gudeman,' quo' he, 'put up your whittle,
I'm no design'd to try its mettle ;
But if I did—I wad be kittle
    To be mislear'd—
I wad na mind it, no that spittle
    Out-owre my beard.' 60


'Weel, weel !' says I, 'a bargain be't ;
Come, gies your hand, an' sae we're gree't ;
We'll ease our shanks an' tak a seat—
    Come, gies your news ;
This while ye hae been mony a gate,
    At mony a house.'


'Ay, ay !' quo' he, an' shook his head,
'It 's e'en a lang lang time indeed
Sin' I began to nick the thread,
    An' choke the breath : 70
Folk maun do something for their bread,
    An' sae maun Death.


'Sax thousand years are near-hand fled,
Sin' I was to the butching bred ;
An' mony a scheme in vain 's been laid
    To stap or scaur me ;
Till ane Hornbook 's ta'en up the trade,
    An' faith ! he'll waur me.


'Ye ken Jock Hornbook i' the clachan—
Deil mak his king's-hood in a spleuchan ! 80
He 's grown sae well acquaint wi' Buchan
    An' ither chaps,
The weans haud out their fingers laughin',
    And pouk my hips.


'See, here 's a scythe, and there 's a dart—
They hae pierc'd mony a gallant heart ;
But Doctor Hornbook, wi' his art
    And cursed skill,
Has made them baith no worth a fart !
    Damn'd haet they'll kill. 90

' 'Twas but yestreen, nae farther gane,
I threw a noble throw at ane—
Wi' less, I'm sure, I've hundreds slain—
        But deil may care !
It just play'd dirl on the bane,
        But did nae mair.

' Hornbook was by wi' ready art,
And had sae fortified the part
That, when I lookèd to my dart,
        It was sae blunt,     100
Fient haet o't wad hae pierc'd the heart
        O' a kail-runt.

' I drew my scythe in sic a fury
I near-hand cowpit wi' my hurry,
But yet the bauld Apothecary
        Withstood the shock ;
I might as weel hae tried a quarry
        O' hard whin rock.

' E'en them he canna get attended,
Altho' their face he ne'er had kenn'd it,     110
Just sh— in a kail-blade, and send it,
        As soon 's he smells 't,
Baith their disease, and what will mend it,
        At once he tells 't.

' And then a' doctor's saws and whittles,
Of a' dimensions, shapes, an' mettles,
A' kinds o' boxes, mugs, an' bottles,
        He 's sure to hae ;
Their Latin names as fast he rattles
        As A B C.     120

' Calces o' fossils, earths, and trees ;
True sal-marinum o' the seas ;
The farina of beans and pease,
        He has 't in plenty ;
Aqua-fortis, what you please,
        He can content ye.

'Forbye some new uncommon weapons,—
Urinus spiritus of capons ;
Or mite-horn shavings, filings, scrapings,
                    Distill'd per se ;          130
Sal-alkali o' midge-tail clippings,
                    And mony mae.'


'Wae 's me for Johnny Ged's Hole now,'
Quoth I, 'if that thae news be true !
His braw calf-ward where gowans grew
                    Sae white and bonnie,
Nae doubt they'll rive it wi' the plew ;
                    They'll ruin Johnie !'


The creature grain'd an eldritch laugh,
And says 'Ye needna yoke the pleugh,          140
Kirk-yards will soon be till'd eneugh,
                    Tak ye nae fear ;
They'll a' be trench'd wi' mony a sheugh
                    In twa-three year.


'Where I kill'd ane, a fair strae-death,
By loss o' blood or want o' breath,
This night I'm free to tak my aith
                    That Hornbook's skill
Has clad a score i' their last claith,
                    By drap and pill.          150


'An honest wabster to his trade,
Whase wife's twa nieves were scarce weel-bred,
Gat tippence-worth to mend her head
                    When it was sair ;
The wife slade cannie to her bed,
                    But ne'er spak mair.


'A country laird had ta'en the batts,
Or some curmurring in his guts,
His only son for Hornbook sets,
                    An' pays him well :          160
The lad, for twa guid gimmer-pets,
                    Was laird himsel.

'A bonnie lass, ye kenn'd her name,
Some ill-brewn drink had hov'd her wame ;
She trusts hersel, to hide the shame,
    In Hornbook's care ;
Horn sent her aff to her lang hame,
    To hide it there.

' That's just a swatch o' Hornbook's way ;
Thus goes he on from day to day,     170
Thus does he poison, kill, an' slay,
    An's weel pay'd for 't ;
Yet stops me o' my lawfu' prey
    Wi' his damn'd dirt.

' But, hark ! I'll tell you of a plot,
Tho' dinna ye be speaking o't ;
I'll nail the self-conceited sot
    As dead's a herrin' :
Niest time we meet, I'll wad a groat,
    He gets his fairin' ! '   180

But, just as he began to tell,
The auld kirk-hammer strak the bell
Some wee short hour ayont the twal,
    Which rais'd us baith :
I took the way that pleas'd mysel,
    And sae did Death.

———•◦•———

# A DREAM.

GUID-MORNIN' to your Majesty !
 May heaven augment your blisses
On ev'ry new birth-day ye see—
 A humble poet wishes !
My bardship here, at your levee,
 On sic a day as this is,
Is sure an uncouth sight to see
 Amang thae birth-day dresses
    Sae fine this day.

I see ye're complimented thrang,                    10
  By mony a lord an' lady ;
' God save the King ! ' 's a cuckoo sang
  That 's unco easy said aye ;
The poets, too, a venal gang,
  Wi' rhymes well-turn'd an' ready,
Wad gar you trow ye ne'er do wrang,
  But aye unerring steady,
            On sic a day.


For me, before a monarch's face—
  Ev'n there I winna flatter ;                      20
For neither pension, post, nor place,
  Am I your humble debtor :
So nae reflection on your Grace,
  Your kingship to bespatter ;
There 's mony waur been o' the race,
  And aiblins ane been better
            Than you this day.


'Tis very true, my sovereign King,
  My skill may weel be doubted ;
But Facts are chiels that winna ding,               30
  An' downa be disputed :
Your royal nest, beneath your wing,
  Is e'en right reft an' clouted,
An' now the third part of the string,
  An' less, will gang about it,
            Than did ae day.


Far be 't frae me that I aspire
  To blame your legislation,
Or say ye wisdom want, or fire,
  To rule this mighty nation ;                      40
But faith ! I muckle doubt, my Sire,
  Ye've trusted ministration
To chaps wha in a barn or byre
  Wad better fill'd their station
            Than courts yon day.

And now ye've gien auld Britain peace
   Her broken shins to plaister,
Your sair taxation does her fleece
   Till she has scarce a tester.
For me, thank God! my life's a lease,      50
   Nae bargain wearing faster,
Or faith! I fear that with the geese
   I shortly boost to pasture
               I' the craft some day.


I'm no mistrusting Willie Pitt
   When taxes he enlarges
(An' Will's a true guid fallow's get,
   A name not envy spairges)
That he intends to pay your debt,
   An' lessen a' your charges;      60
But God's sake! let nae saving fit
   Abridge your bonnie barges
               An' boats this day.


Adieu, my Liege! may freedom geck
   Beneath your high protection;
An' may ye rax Corruption's neck,
   And gie her for dissection!
But since I'm here, I'll no neglect,
   In loyal true affection,
To pay your Queen, with due respect,      70
   My fealty an' subjection
               This great Birth-day.


Hail, Majesty most Excellent!
   While nobles strive to please ye,
Will ye accept a compliment
   A simple poet gies ye?
Thae bonny bairntime Heav'n has lent,
   Still higher may they heeze ye
In bliss, till fate some day is sent
   For ever to release ye      80
               Frae care that day.

For you, young Potentate o' Wales,
   I tell your Highness fairly,
Down pleasure's stream wi' swelling sails
   I'm tauld ye're driving rarely ;
But some day ye may gnaw your nails,
   An' curse your folly sairly,
That ere ye brak Diana's pales,
    Or rattled dice wi' Charlie,
         By night or day.      90


Yet aft a ragged cowt's been known
   To mak a noble aiver ;
So ye may doucely fill a throne,
   For a' their clish-ma-claver ;
There, him at Agincourt wha shone,
   Few better were or braver ;
And yet, wi' funny queer Sir John,
   He was an unco shaver
         For mony a day.


For you, right rev'rend Osnaburg,      100
   Nane sets the lawn-sleeve sweeter,
Altho' a ribban' at your lug
   Wad been a dress completer :
As ye disown yon paughty dog
   That bears the keys of Peter,
Then swith ! an' get a wife to hug,
   Or trouth ! ye'll stain the mitre
         Some luckless day.


Young royal Tarry Breeks, I learn
   Ye've lately come athwart her—    110
A glorious galley, stem and stern,
   Weel rigg'd for Venus' barter ;
But first hang out, that she'll discern
   Your hymeneal charter ;
Then heave aboard your grapple airn,
   An' large upon her quarter
         Come full that day.

Ye, lastly, bonnie blossoms a',
  Ye royal lasses dainty,
Heav'n mak you guid as weel as braw,    120
  An' gie you lads a-plenty:
But sneer na British boys awa',
  For kings are unco scant aye;
An' German gentles are but sma',
  They're better just than want aye
          On ony day.


God bless you a'! Consider now
  Ye're unco muckle dautit;
But, e'er the course o' life be through,
  It may be bitter sautit:    130
An' I hae seen their coggie fou
  That yet hae tarrow't at it;
But or the day was done, I trow,
  The laggen they hae clautit
          Fu' clean that day.


# ADDRESS TO THE DEIL.

O THOU! whatever title suit thee,
Auld Hornie, Satan, Nick, or Clootie,
Wha in yon cavern grim an' sootie,
         Clos'd under hatches,
Spairges about the brunstane cootie,
         To scaud poor wretches!


Hear me, auld Hangie, for a wee,
An' let poor damnèd bodies be;
I'm sure sma' pleasure it can gie,
         Ev'n to a deil,    10
To skelp an' scaud poor dogs like me,
         An' hear us squeal!

Great is thy pow'r, an' great thy fame;
Far kenn'd an' noted is thy name;
An', tho' yon lowin heugh's thy hame,
          Thou travels far;
An' faith! thou's neither lag nor lame,
          Nor blate nor scaur.


Whyles rangin' like a roarin' lion
For prey, a' holes an' corners tryin';          20
Whyles on the strong-wing'd tempest flyin',
          Tirlin' the kirks;
Whyles, in the human bosom pryin',
          Unseen thou lurks.


I've heard my reverend grannie say,
In lanely glens ye like to stray;
Or, where auld ruin'd castles gray
          Nod to the moon,
Ye fright the nightly wand'rer's way,
          Wi' eldritch croon.          30


When twilight did my grannie summon
To say her pray'rs, douce, honest woman!
Aft yont the dyke she's heard you bummin',
          Wi' eerie drone;
Or, rustlin', thro' the boortrees comin',
          Wi' heavy groan.


Ae dreary windy winter night
The stars shot down wi' sklentin' light,
Wi' you mysel I gat a fright
          Ayont the lough;          40
Ye like a rash-buss stood in sight
          Wi' waving sough.


The cudgel in my nieve did shake,
Each bristled hair stood like a stake,
When wi' an eldritch stoor 'quaick, quaick,'
          Amang the springs,
Awa ye squatter'd like a drake
          On whistlin' wings.

Let warlocks grim an' wither'd hags
Tell how wi' you on ragweed nags                                    50
They skim the muirs, an' dizzy crags
          Wi' wicked speed ;
And in kirk-yards renew their leagues
          Owre howkit dead.


Thence country wives, wi' toil an' pain,
May plunge an' plunge the kirn in vain ;
For oh ! the yellow treasure 's taen
          By witchin' skill ;
An' dawtit twal-pint Hawkie's gane
          As yell 's the bill.                                      60


Thence mystic knots mak great abuse
On young guidmen, fond, keen, an' crouse ;
When the best wark-lume i' the house,
          By cantrip wit,
Is instant made no worth a louse,
          Just at the bit.


When thowes dissolve the snawy hoord,
An' float the jinglin' icy-boord,
Then water-kelpies haunt the foord,
          By your direction,                                        70
An' 'nighted trav'llers are allur'd
          To their destruction.


An' aft your moss-traversing spunkies
Decoy the wight that late an' drunk is :
The bleezin, curst, mischievous monkies
          Delude his eyes,
Till in some miry slough he sunk is,
          Ne'er mair to rise.


When masons' mystic word an' grip
In storms an' tempests raise you up,                                80
Some cock or cat your rage maun stop,
          Or, strange to tell !
The youngest brither ye wad whip
          Aff straught to hell.

Lang syne, in Eden's bonnie yard,
When youthfu' lovers first were pair'd,
And all the soul of love they shar'd,
          The raptur'd hour,
Sweet on the fragrant flow'ry swaird,
          In shady bow'r;                    90


Then you, ye auld snick-drawing dog!
Ye cam to Paradise incog.
An' play'd on man a cursed brogue,
          (Black be you fa!)
An' gied the infant warld a shog,
          'Maist ruin'd a'.


D'ye mind that day, when in a bizz,
Wi' reekit duds, an' reestit gizz,
Ye did present your smoutie phiz
          'Mang better folk,
An' sklented on the man of Uz           100
          Your spitefu' joke?


An' how ye gat him i' your thrall,
An' brak him out o' house an' hal',
While scabs an' blotches did him gall
          Wi' bitter claw,
An' lows'd his ill-tongu'd wicked scawl,
          Was warst ava?


But a' your doings to rehearse,
Your wily snares an' fechtin' fierce,   110
Sin' that day Michael did you pierce,
          Down to this time,
Wad ding a' Lallan tongue, or Erse,
          In prose or rhyme.


An' now, auld Cloots, I ken ye're thinkin',
A certain Bardie's rantin', drinkin',
Some luckless hour will send him linkin',
          To your black pit;
But faith! he'll turn a corner jinkin',
          An' cheat you yet.                  120

But fare you weel, auld Nickie-ben!
O wad ye tak a thought an' men'!
Ye aiblins might—I dinna ken—
   Still hae a stake:
I'm wae to think upo' yon den,
   Ev'n for your sake!

# THE ORDINATION.

KILMARNOCK wabsters, fidge and claw,
 An' pour your creeshie nations;
An' ye wha leather rax an' draw,
 Of a' denominations;
Swith to the Laigh Kirk, ane an' a',
 An' there tak up your stations;
Then aff to Begbie's in a raw,
 An' pour divine libations
   For joy this day.

Curst Common-sense, that imp o' hell,    10
 Cam in wi' Maggie Lauder;
But Oliphant aft made her yell,
 An' Russel sair misca'd her;
This day Mackinlay takes the flail,
 An' he's the boy will blaud her!
He'll clap a shangan on her tail,
 An' set the bairns to daud her
   Wi' dirt this day.

Mak haste an' turn king David owre,
 An' lilt wi' holy clangor;    20
O' double verse come gie us four,
 An' skirl up the Bangor:
This day the Kirk kicks up a stoure,
 Nae mair the knaves shall wrang her,
For Heresy is in her pow'r,
 And gloriously she'll whang her
   Wi' pith this day.

Come, let a proper text be read,
    An' touch it aff wi' vigour,
How graceless Ham leugh at his dad,                30
    Which made Canaan a nigger;
Or Phineas drove the murdering blade,
    Wi' whore-abhorring rigour;
Or Zipporah, the scauldin jad,
    Was like a bluidy tiger
                        I' th' inn that day.


There try his mettle on the creed,
    And bind him down, wi' caution
That stipend is a carnal weed
    He takes but for the fashion;                 40
An' gie him o'er the flock,—to feed,
    And punish each transgression;
Especial, rams that cross the breed—
    Gie them sufficient threshin',
                        Spare them nae day.


Now, auld Kilmarnock, cock thy tail,
    An' toss thy horns fu' canty;
Nae mair thou 'lt rowte out-owre the dale,
    Because thy pasture 's scanty;
For lapfu's large o' gospel kail                   50
    Shall fill thy crib in plenty,
An' runts o' grace the pick an' wale,
    No gi'en by way o' dainty,
                        But ilka day.


Nae mair by Babel streams we'll weep,
    To think upon our Zion;
And hing our fiddles up to sleep,
    Like baby-clouts a-dryin':
Come, screw the pegs wi' tunefu' cheep,
    And o'er the thairms be tryin';                60
O rare! to see our elbucks wheep,
    And a' like lamb-tails flyin'
                        Fu' fast this day!

Lang patronage, wi' rod o' airn,
　　Has shor'd the Kirk's undoin',
As lately Fenwick, sair forfairn,
　　Has proven to its ruin :
Our patron, honest man ! Glencairn,
　　He saw mischief was brewin' :
An' like a godly elect bairn,　　　　　　　　　70
　　He 's wal'd us out a true ane,
　　　　　　　　And sound this day.


Now Robertson, harangue nae mair,
　　But steek your gab for ever ;
Or try the wicked town of Ayr,
　　For there they'll think you clever ;
Or, nae reflection on your lear,
　　Ye may commence a shaver ;
Or to the Netherton repair,
　　And turn a carpet-weaver　　　　　　　　80
　　　　　　　　Aff-hand this day.


Mu'trie and you were just a match,
　　We never had sic twa drones ;
Auld Hornie did the Laigh Kirk watch,
　　Just like a winkin' baudrons ;
And aye he catch'd the tither wretch,
　　To fry them in his caudrons ;
But now his Honour maun detach,
　　Wi' a' his brimstone squadrons,
　　　　　　　　Fast, fast this day.　　　　　　　90


See, see auld Orthodoxy's faes
　　She 's swingein' thro' the city ;
Hark how the nine-tail'd cat she plays !
　　I vow it 's unco protty !
There Learning, with his Greekish face,
　　Grunts out some Latin ditty ;
And Common-sense is gaun, she says,
　　To mak to Jamie Beattie
　　　　　　　　Her plaint this day.

But there 's Morality himsel,                    100
   Embracing all opinions ;
Hear how he gies the tither yell,
   Between his twa companions ;
See how she peels the skin an' fell,
   As ane were peelin onions !
Now there, they're packèd aff to hell,
   And banish'd our dominions
         Henceforth this day.


O happy day ! rejoice, rejoice !
   Come bouse about the porter !          110
Morality's demure decoys
   Shall here nae mair find quarter :
Mackinlay, Russel, are the boys
   That heresy can torture ;
They'll gie her on a rape a hoyse,
   And cowe her measure shorter
         By th' head some day.


Come, bring the tither mutchkin in,
   And here 's, for a conclusion,
To every New Light mother's son          120
   From this time forth, Confusion !
If mair they deave us wi' their din,
   Or patronage intrusion,
We'll light a spunk, and, ev'ry skin,
   We'll rin them aff in fusion
         Like oil, some day.

# THE AUTHOR'S EARNEST CRY AND PRAYER

TO THE SCOTCH REPRESENTATIVES IN THE HOUSE OF COMMONS.

Ye Irish lords, ye knights an' squires,
Wha represent our brughs an' shires,
An' doucely manage our affairs
        In Parliament,
To you a simple poet's prayers
        Are humbly sent.

Alas! my roupit muse is hearse;
Your Honours' heart wi' grief 'twad pierce
To see her sitten on her arse
        Low i' the dust,      10
An' screechin' out prosaic verse,
        An' like to brust!

Tell them wha hae the chief direction,
Scotland an' me 's in great affliction,
E'er sin' they laid that curst restriction
        On aqua vitæ;
An' rouse them up to strong conviction,
        An' move their pity.

Stand forth, an' tell yon Premier youth
The honest, open, naked truth:      20
Tell him o' mine an' Scotland's drouth,
        His servants humble:
The muckle devil blaw ye south,
        If ye dissemble!

Does ony great man glunch an' gloom?
Speak out, an' never fash your thumb!
Let posts an' pensions sink or soom
        Wi' them wha grant them;
If honestly they canna come,
        Far better want them.      30

In gath'rin' votes you were na slack;
Now stand as tightly by your tack;
Ne'er claw your lug, an' fidge your back,
   An' hum an' haw;
But raise your arm, an' tell your crack
   Before them a'.

Paint Scotland greetin owre her thrissle;
Her mutchkin stoup as toom's a whissle:
An' damn'd Excisemen in a bussle,
   Seizin a stell,    40
Triumphant crushin't like a mussle
   Or limpet shell.

Then on the tither hand present her,
A blackguard smuggler, right behint her,
An' cheek-for-chow, a chuffie vintner,
   Colleaguing join,
Pickin' her pouch as bare as Winter
   Of a' kind coin.

Is there, that bears the name o' Scot,
But feels his heart's bluid rising hot,   50
To see his poor auld mither's pot
   Thus dung in staves,
An' plunder'd o' her hindmost groat
   By gallows knaves?

Alas! I'm but a nameless wight,
Trode i' the mire out o' sight!
But could I like Montgomeries fight,
   Or gab like Boswell,
There's some sark-necks I wad draw tight,
   An' tie some hose well.   60

God bless your Honours, can ye see't,
The kind, auld, cantie carlin greet,
An' no get warmly to your feet
   An' gar them hear it?
An' tell them wi' a patriot-heat,
   Ye winna bear it?

Some o' you nicely ken the laws
To round the period an' pause,
An' with rhetoric clause on clause
        To mak harangues ;          70
Then echo thro' Saint Stephen's wa's
        Auld Scotland's wrangs.


Dempster, a true blue Scot I'se warran' ;
Thee, aith-detesting, chaste Kilkerran ;
An' that glib-gabbèd Highland Baron,
        The Laird o' Graham ;
An' ane, a chap that 's damn'd auldfarran,
        Dundas his name ;


Erskine, a spunkie Norland billie ;
True Campbells, Frederik an' Ilay ;          80
An' Livingston, the bauld Sir Willie ;
        An' mony ithers,
Whom auld Demosthenes or Tully
        Might own for brithers.


Arouse, my boys! exert your mettle
To get auld Scotland back her kettle ;
Or faith ! I'll wad my new pleugh-pettle,
        Ye 'll see 't or lang,
She 'll teach you, wi' a reekin whittle,
        Anither sang.          90


This while she 's been in crankous mood ;
Her lost Militia fir'd her bluid
(Deil nor they never mair do guid
        Play'd her that pliskie !)
An' now she 's like to rin red-wud
        About her whisky.


An' Lord, if ance they pit her till 't,
Her tartan petticoat she 'll kilt,
An', durk an' pistol at her belt,
        She 'll tak the streets,          100
An' rin her whittle to the hilt
        I' th' first she meets !

For God sake, sirs! then speak her fair,
An' straik her cannie wi' the hair,
An' to the muckle house repair
    Wi' instant speed
An' strive, wi' a' your wit and lear,
    To get remead.


Yon ill-tongu'd tinkler, Charlie Fox,
May taunt you wi' his jeers an' mocks;   110
But gie him 't het, my hearty cocks!
    E'en cowe the cadie,
An' send him to his dicing-box
    An' sportin' lady.


Tell yon guid bluid o' auld Boconnock's
I'll be his debt twa mashlum bannocks,
An' drink his health in auld Nanse Tinnock's
    Nine times a-week,
If he some scheme, like tea an' winnocks,
    Wad kindly seek.   120


Could he some commutation broach,
I'll pledge my aith in guid braid Scotch,
He need na fear their foul reproach
    Nor erudition,
Yon mixtie-maxtie queer hotch-potch,
    The Coalition.


Auld Scotland has a raucle tongue;
She's just a devil wi' a rung;
An' if she promise auld or young
    To tak their part,   130
Tho' by the neck she should be strung,
    She'll no desert.


An' now, ye chosen Five-and-Forty,
May still your Mither's heart support ye;
Then, though a minister grow dorty,
    An' kick your place,
Ye'll snap your fingers, poor an' hearty,
    Before his face.

God bless your Honours a' your days
Wi' sowps o' kail an' brats o' claes,          140
In spite o' a' the thievish kaes
    That haunt St. Jamie's!
Your humble poet sings an' prays,
    While Rab his name is.


### Postscript.

Let half-starv'd slaves in warmer skies
See future wines rich-clust'ring rise;
Their lot auld Scotland ne'er envies,
    But, blythe an' frisky,
She eyes her free-born martial boys
    Tak aff their whisky.          150


What tho' their Phœbus kinder warms,
While fragrance blooms an' beauty charms,
When wretches range in famish'd swarms
    The scented groves,
Or, hounded forth, dishonour arms
    In hungry droves.


Their gun's a burden on their shouther;
They downa bide the stink o' powther;
Their bauldest thought's a hank'ring swither
    To stan' or rin,          160
Till skelp! a shot—they're aff, a' throu'ther,
    To save their skin.


But bring a Scotsman frae his hill,
Clap in his cheek a Highland gill,
Say 'Such is royal George's will,
    An' there's the foe!'
He has nae thought but how to kill
    Twa at a blow.


Nae cauld faint-hearted doubtings tease him;
Death comes, wi' fearless eye he sees him;          170
Wi' bluidy hand a welcome gies him;
    An', when he fa's,
His latest draught o' breathin' lea'es him
    In faint huzzas.

Sages their solemn een may steek,
An' raise a philosophic reek,
An' physically causes seek
         In clime an' season ;
But tell me whisky's name in Greek,
         I'll tell the reason.      180


Scotland, my auld respected Mither!
Tho' whyles ye moistify your leather,
Till where ye sit, on craps o' heather,
         Ye tine your dam—
Freedom and Whisky gang thegither!
         Tak aff your dram !

———◆◆———

# ADDRESS TO THE UNCO GUID, OR THE RIGIDLY RIGHTEOUS.

*My son, these maxims make a rule,*
   *And lump them aye thegither :*
*The rigid righteous is a fool,*
   *The rigid wise anither :*
*The cleanest corn that e'er was dight,*
   *May hae some pyles o' caff in ;*
*So ne'er a fellow-creature slight*
   *For random fits o' daffin.*
            SOLOMON (Eccles. vii. 16).


O ye wha are sae guid yoursel.
   Sae pious and sae holy,
Ye've nought to do but mark and tell
   Your neibour's fauts and folly!
Whase life is like a weel-gaun mill,
   Supplied wi' store o' water :
The heapèd happer's ebbing still,
   And still the clap plays clatter :

Hear me, ye venerable core,
    As counsel for poor mortals,                    10
That frequent pass douce Wisdom's door,
    For glaikit Folly's portals;
I, for their thoughtless careless sakes,
    Would here propone defences,—
Their donsie tricks, their black mistakes,
    Their failings and mischances.


Ye see your state wi' their's compar'd,
    And shudder at the niffer;
But cast a moment's fair regard—
    What maks the mighty differ?                    20
Discount what scant occasion gave,
    That purity ye pride in,
And (what's aft mair than a' the lave)
    Your better art o' hidin'.


Think, when your castigated pulse
    Gies now and then a wallop,
What ragings must his veins convulse,
    That still eternal gallop!
Wi' wind and tide fair i' your tail,
    Right on ye scud your sea-way;                  30
But in the teeth o' baith to sail,
    It maks an unco leeway.


See Social life and Glee sit down,
    All joyous and unthinking,
Till, quite transmogrified, they're grown
    Debauchery and Drinking:
O would they stay to calculate
    Th' eternal consequences;
Or your more dreaded hell to state,
    Damnation of expenses!                          40


Ye high, exalted, virtuous Dames,
    Tied up in godly laces,
Before ye gie poor Frailty names,
    Suppose a change o' cases;

A dear lov'd lad, convenience snug,
    A treacherous inclination—
But, let me whisper i' your lug,
    Ye're aiblins nae temptation.

Then gently scan your brother man,
    Still gentler sister woman;                    50
Tho' they may gang a kennin wrang,
    To step aside is human.
One point must still be greatly dark,
    The moving why they do it;
And just as lamely can ye mark
    How far perhaps they rue it.

Who made the heart, 'tis He alone
    Decidedly can try us;
He knows each chord, its various tone,
    Each spring, its various bias.                60
Then at the balance let's be mute,
    We never can adjust it;
What's done we partly may compute,
    But know not what's resisted.

------◆------

## HOLY WILLIE'S PRAYER.

O Thou, wha in the Heavens dost dwell,
Wha, as it pleases best thysel',
Sends ane to heaven and ten to hell,
            A' for thy glory,
And no for ony guid or ill
            They've done afore thee!

I bless and praise thy matchless might,
Whan thousands thou hast left in night,
That I am here afore thy sight,
            For gifts an' grace                   10
A burnin' an' a shinin' light,
            To a' this place.

What was I, or my generation,
That I should get sic exaltation?
I, wha deserve most just damnation,
   For broken laws,
Sax thousand years 'fore my creation,
   Thro' Adam's cause.

When frae my mither's womb I fell,
Thou might hae plungèd me in hell,
To gnash my gums, to weep and wail,
   In burnin' lakes,
Where damnèd devils roar and yell,
   Chain'd to their stakes;   20

Yet I am here a chosen sample,
To show thy grace is great and ample;
I'm here a pillar in thy temple,
   Strong as a rock,
A guide, a buckler, an example
   To a' thy flock.   30

O Lord, thou kens what zeal I bear,
When drinkers drink, and swearers swear,
And singin' there and dancin' here,
   Wi' great an' sma':
For I am keepit by thy fear
   Free frae them a'.

But yet, O Lord! confess I must
At times I'm fash'd wi' fleshy lust;
An' sometimes too, in warldly trust,
   Vile self gets in;
But thou remembers we are dust,
   Defil'd in sin.   40

O Lord! yestreen, thou kens, wi' Meg—·
Thy pardon I sincerely beg;
O! may't ne'er be a livin' plague
   To my dishonour,
An' I'll ne'er lift a lawless leg
   Again upon her.

Besides I farther maun allow,
Wi' Lizzie's lass, three times I trow—          50
But, Lord, that Friday I was fou,
          When I cam near her,
Or else thou kens thy servant true
          Wad never steer her.


May be thou lets this fleshly thorn
Beset thy servant e'en and morn
Lest he owre high and proud should turn,
          That he 's sae gifted ;
If sae, thy hand maun e'en be borne,
          Until thou lift it.          60


Lord, bless thy chosen in this place,
For here thou hast a chosen race ;
But God confound their stubborn face,
          And blast their name,
Wha bring thy elders to disgrace
          An' public shame.


Lord, mind Gawn Hamilton's deserts,
He drinks, an' swears, an' plays at cartes,
Yet has sae mony takin' arts
          Wi' grit an' sma',          70
Frae God's ain priest the people's hearts
          He steals awa'.


An' when we chasten'd him therefor,
Thou kens how he bred sic a splore
As set the warld in a roar
          O' laughin' at us ;
Curse thou his basket and his store,
          Kail and potatoes.


Lord, hear my earnest cry an' pray'r,
Against that presbyt'ry o' Ayr ;          80
Thy strong right hand, Lord, make it bare
          Upo' their heads ;
Lord, weigh it down, and dinna spare,
          For their misdeeds.

O Lord my God, that glib-tongu'd Aiken,
My very heart and soul are quakin',
To think how we stood sweatin', shakin',
      An' piss'd wi' dread,
While he, wi' hingin' lips and snakin',
      Held up his head.      90


Lord, in the day of vengeance try him;
Lord, visit them wha did employ him,
And pass not in thy mercy by them,
      Nor hear their pray'r:
But, for thy people's sake, destroy them,
      And dinna spare.


But, Lord, remember me and mine
Wi' mercies temp'ral and divine,
That I for gear and grace may shine
      Excell'd by nane,      100
And a' the glory shall be thine,
      Amen, Amen!


## EPISTLE TO A YOUNG FRIEND.

I LANG hae thought, my youthfu' friend,
    A something to have sent you,
Tho' it should serve nae ither end
    Than just a kind memento;
But how the subject theme may gang,
    Let time and chance determine;
Perhaps it may turn out a sang,
    Perhaps turn out a sermon.


Ye'll try the world soon, my lad,
    And, Andrew dear, believe me,      10
Ye'll find mankind an unco squad,
    And muckle they may grieve ye:

For care and trouble set your thought,
   Ev'n when your end 's attained ;
And a' your views may come to nought,
   Where ev'ry nerve is strained.


I'll no say men are villains a' ;
   The real harden'd wicked,
Wha hae nae check but human law,
   Are to a few restricked :            20
But och ! mankind are unco weak,
   An' little to be trusted ;
If self the wavering balance shake,
   It 's rarely right adjusted !


Yet they wha fa' in fortune's strife,
   Their fate we shouldna censure ;
For still th' important end of life
   They equally may answer.
A man may hae an honest heart,
   Tho' poortith hourly stare him ;       30
A man may tak a neibor's part,
   Yet hae nae cash to spare him.


Aye free, aff han', your story tell,
   When wi' a bosom crony ;
But still keep something to yoursel
   Ye scarcely tell to ony.
Conceal yoursel as weel 's ye can
   Frae critical dissection ;
But keek thro' ev'ry other man
   Wi' sharpen'd sly inspection.        40


The sacred lowe o' weel-plac'd love,
   Luxuriantly indulge it ;
But never tempt th' illicit rove,
   Tho' naething should divulge it :
I wave the quantum o' the sin,
   The hazard of concealing ;
But och ! it hardens a' within,
   And petrifies the feeling !

To catch dame Fortune's golden smile,
   Assiduous wait upon her;          50
And gather gear by ev'ry wile
   That's justified by honour;
Not for to hide it in a hedge,
   Nor for a train attendant;
But for the glorious privilege
   Of being independent.


The fear o' hell's a hangman's whip
   To haud the wretch in order;
But where ye feel your honour grip,
   Let that aye be your border:      60
Its slightest touches, instant pause—
   Debar a' side pretences;
And resolutely keep its laws,
   Uncaring consequences.


The great Creator to revere
   Must sure become the creature;
But still the preaching cant forbear,
   And ev'n the rigid feature:
Yet ne'er with wits profane to range
   Be complaisance extended;     70
An atheist laugh's a poor exchange
   For Deity offended.


When ranting round in pleasure's ring,
   Religion may be blinded;
Or, if she gie a random sting,
   It may be little minded;
But when on life we're tempest-driv'n,
   A conscience but a canker—
A correspondence fix'd wi' Heav'n
   Is sure a noble anchor.      80


Adieu, dear amiable youth!
   Your heart can ne'er be wanting!
May prudence, fortitude, and truth
   Erect your brow undaunting.

In ploughman phrase, God send you speed
Still daily to grow wiser;
And may ye better reck the rede
Than ever did th' adviser!

———•+•———

## TAM SAMSON'S ELEGY.

Has auld Kilmarnock seen the deil?
Or great Mackinlay thrawn his heel?
Or Robertson again grown weel,
        To preach an' read?
'Na, waur than a'!' cries ilka chiel,
        'Tam Samson's dead!'

Kilmarnock lang may grunt an' grane,
An' sigh, an' sab, an' greet her lane,
An' cleed her bairns, man, wife, an' wean,
        In mourning weed;          10
To death, she's dearly paid the kane,—
        Tam Samson's dead!

The Brethren o' the mystic level
May hing their head in woefu' bevel,
While by their nose the tears will revel,
        Like ony bead;
Death's gien the Lodge an unco devel,—
        Tam Samson's dead!

When Winter muffles up his cloak,
And binds the mire like a rock;          20
When to the loughs the curlers flock
        Wi' gleesome speed,
Wha will they station at the cock?
        Tam Samson's dead!

He was the king o' a' the core
To guard, or draw, or wick a bore,
Or up the rink like Jehu roar
      In time o' need ;
But now he lags on Death's hogscore,—
      Tam Samson 's dead !    30

Now safe the stately sawmont sail,
And trouts bedropp'd wi' crimson hail,
And eels weel kent for souple tail,
      And geds for greed,
Since dark in Death's fish-creel we wail
      Tam Samson dead !

Rejoice, ye birring paitricks a' ;
Ye cootie moorcocks, crousely craw ;
Ye maukins, cock your fud fu' braw,
      Withouten dread ;    40
Your mortal fae is now awa',—
      Tam Samson 's dead !

That woefu' morn be ever mourn'd
Saw him in shootin graith adorn'd,
While pointers round impatient burn'd,
      Frae couples freed ;
But oh ! he gaed and ne'er return'd !
      Tam Samson 's dead !

In vain auld age his body batters ;
In vain the gout his ancles fetters ;    50
In vain the burns cam down like waters,
      An acre braid !
Now ev'ry auld wife, greetin', clatters
      ' Tam Samson 's dead ! '

Owre mony a weary hag he limpit,
An' aye the tither shot he thumpit,
Till coward Death behind him jumpit
      Wi' deadly feide ;
Now he proclaims, wi' tout o' trumpet,
      ' Tam Samson 's dead ! '    60

When at his heart he felt the dagger,
He reel'd his wonted bottle-swagger,
But yet he drew the mortal trigger
        Wi' weel-aim'd heed ;
'Lord, five!' he cried, an' owre did stagger;
        Tam Samson's dead !


Ilk hoary hunter mourn'd a brither ;
Ilk sportsman youth bemoan'd a father ;
Yon auld grey stane, amang the heather,
        Marks out his head,      70
Where Burns has wrote, in rhyming blether,
        'Tam Samson's dead !'


There low he lies in lasting rest;
Perhaps upon his mould'ring breast
Some spitfu' muirfowl bigs her nest,
        To hatch and breed ;
Alas ! nae mair he'll them molest !
        Tam Samson's dead !


When August winds the heather wave,
And sportsmen wander by yon grave,      80
Three volleys let his memory crave
        O' pouther an' lead,
Till Echo answer frae her cave
        'Tam Samson's dead !'


Heav'n rest his saul, where'er he be !
Is th' wish o' mony mae than me :
He had twa faults, or maybe three,
        Yet what remead ?
Ae social honest man want we :
        Tam Samson's dead !      90


### THE EPITAPH.

Tam Samson's weel-worn clay here lies :
    Ye canting zealots, spare him !
If honest worth in heaven rise,
    Ye'll mend ere ye win near him.

*Per Contra.*

Go, Fame, an' canter like a filly
Thro' a' the streets an' neuks o' Killie,
Tell ev'ry social honest billie
    To cease his grievin',
For yet, unskaith'd by Death's gleg gullie,
    Tam Samson's livin' !    100

———◆———

# A WINTER NIGHT.

WHEN biting Boreas, fell and doure,
Sharp shivers thro' the leafless bow'r ;
When Phœbus gies a short-liv'd glow'r,
    Far south the lift,
Dim-dark'ning thro' the flaky show'r
    Or whirling drift ;

Ae night the storm the steeples rocked,
Poor Labour sweet in sleep was locked,
While burns, wi' snawy wreaths up-choked,
    Wild-eddying swirl,    10
Or, thro' the mining outlet bocked,
    Down headlong hurl ;

List'ning the doors an' winnocks rattle
I thought me on the ourie cattle,
Or silly sheep, wha bide this brattle
    O' winter war,
And thro' the drift, deep-lairing, sprattle
    Beneath a scar.

Ilk happing bird, wee, helpless thing !
That, in the merry months o' spring,    20
Delighted me to hear thee sing,
    What comes o' thee ?
Where wilt thou cow'r thy chittering wing,
    An' close thy e'e ?

Ev'n you, on murd'ring errands toil'd,
Lone from your savage homes exil'd,—
The blood-stained roost and sheep-cote spoil'd
    My heart forgets,
While pitiless the tempest wild
    Sore on you beats.       30

Now Phœbe, in her midnight reign,
Dark muffl'd, view'd the dreary plain ;
Still crowding thoughts, a pensive train,
    Rose in my soul,
When on my ear this plaintive strain,
    Slow, solemn, stole :—

'Blow, blow, ye winds, with heavier gust !
And freeze, thou bitter-biting frost !
Descend, ye chilly smothering snows !
Not all your rage, as now united, shows    40
  More hard unkindness unrelenting,
  Vengeful malice unrepenting,
Than heav'n-illumin'd man on brother man bestows !
See stern Oppression's iron grip,
  Or mad Ambition's gory hand,
Sending, like blood-hounds from the slip,
  Woe, want, and murder o'er a land !
Ev'n in the peaceful rural vale,
Truth, weeping, tells the mournful tale
How pamper'd Luxury, Flatt'ry by her side,    50
  The parasite empoisoning her ear,
  With all the servile wretches in the rear,
Looks o'er proud property, extended wide ;
  And eyes the simple rustic hind,
  Whose toil upholds the glitt'ring show,
A creature of another kind,
Some coarser substance, unrefin'd,
Plac'd for her lordly use thus far, thus vile, below.

Where, where is Love's fond, tender throe,
With lordly Honour's lofty brow,    60
  The pow'rs you proudly own ?
Is there, beneath Love's noble name,
Can harbour, dark, the selfish aim
  To bless himself alone ?

Mark maiden-innocence a prey
   To love-pretending snares ;
This boasted honour turns away,
Shunning soft pity's rising sway,
Regardless of the tears, and unavailing pray'rs !
   Perhaps this hour, in mis'ry's squalid nest,      70
   She strains your infant to her joyless breast,
And with a mother's fears shrinks at the rocking blast !


Oh ye ! who, sunk in beds of down,
Feel not a want but what yourselves create,
Think, for a moment, on his wretched fate,
   Whom friends and fortune quite disown !
Ill satisfied keen nature's clam'rous call,
   Stretch'd on his straw he lays himself to sleep,
While thro' the ragged roof and chinky wall,
Chill o'er his slumbers piles the drifty heap !      80
Think on the dungeon's grim confine,
Where guilt and poor misfortune pine !
Guilt, erring man, relenting view !
But shall thy legal rage pursue
   The wretch, already crushèd low,
   By cruel fortune's undeservèd blow ?
Affliction's sons are brothers in distress ;
A brother to relieve, how exquisite the bliss ! '


I heard nae mair ; for Chanticleer
   Shook off the pouthery snaw,      90
And hail'd the morning with a cheer,
   A cottage-rousing craw.


But deep this truth impress'd my mind—
   Thro' all His works abroad,
The heart benevolent and kind
   The most resembles God.

## SCOTCH DRINK.

*Gie him strong drink, until he wink,*
*That's sinking in despair;*
*An' liquor guid to fire his bluid,*
*That's prest wi' grief an' care;*
*There let him bouse, an' deep carouse,*
*Wi' bumpers flowing o'er,*
*Till he forgets his loves or debts,*
*An' minds his griefs no more.*
SOLOMON (Proverbs xxxi. 6, 7).

LET other Poets raise a fracas
'Bout vines, an' wines, an' drunken Bacchus,
An' crabbèd names an' stories wrack us,
          An' grate our lug;
I sing the juice Scotch bear can mak us,
          In glass or jug.


O thou, my Muse! guid auld Scotch Drink,
Whether thro' wimplin worms thou jink,
Or, richly brown, ream owre the brink,
          In glorious faem,                              10
Inspire me, till I lisp an' wink,
          To sing thy name!


Let husky wheat the haughs adorn,
An' aits set up their awnie horn,
An' pease an' beans at een or morn,
          Perfume the plain;
Leeze me on thee, John Barleycorn,
          Thou King o' grain!


On thee aft Scotland chows her cood,
In souple scones, the wale o' food!                       20
Or tumblin' in the boiling flood
          Wi' kail an' beef;
But when thou pours thy strong heart's blood,
          There thou shines chief.

Food fills the wame, an' keeps us livin';
Tho' life 's a gift no worth receivin',
When heavy-dragg'd wi' pine an' grievin';
   But, oil'd by thee,
The wheels o' life gae down-hill, scrievin'
    Wi' rattlin' glee.   30

Thou clears the head o' doited Lear:
Thou cheers the heart o' drooping Care;
Thou strings the nerves o' Labour sair,
   At 's weary toil:
Thou even brightens dark Despair
    Wi' gloomy smile.

Aft, clad in massy siller weed,
Wi' gentles thou erects thy head;
Yet humbly kind, in time o' need,
   The poor man's wine,  40
His wee drap parritch, or his bread,
    Thou kitchens fine.

Thou art the life o' public haunts;
But thee, what were our fairs and rants?
Ev'n godly meetings o' the saunts,
   By thee inspir'd,
When gaping they besiege the tents,
    Are doubly fir'd.

That merry night we get the corn in!
O sweetly then thou reams the horn in! 50
Or reekin' on a New-Year mornin'
   In cog or bicker,
An' just a wee drap sp'ritual burn in,
    An' gusty sucker!

When Vulcan gies his bellows breath,
An' ploughmen gather wi' their graith,
O rare to see thee fizz an' freath
   I' th' luggèd caup!
Then Burnewin comes on like death
    At ev'ry chaup.   60

Nae mercy, then, for airn or steel;
The brawnie, banie, ploughman chiel,
Brings hard owrehip, wi' sturdy wheel,
   The strong forehammer,
Till block an' studdie ring an' reel
   Wi' dinsome clamour.

When skirlin' weanies see the light,
Thou maks the gossips clatter bright
How fumblin' cuifs their dearies slight—
   Wae worth the name!  70
Nae Howdie gets a social night,
   Or plack frae them.

When neibors anger at a plea,
An' just as wud as wud can be,
How easy can the barley-bree
   Cement the quarrel!
It's aye the cheapest lawyer's fee
   To taste the barrel.

Alake! that e'er my Muse has reason
To wyte her countrymen wi' treason;  80
But mony daily weet their weasan'
   Wi' liquors nice,
An' hardly, in a winter's season,
   E'er spier her price.

Wae worth that brandy, burning trash!
Fell source o' mony a pain an' brash!
Twins mony a poor, doylt, drucken hash,
   O' half his days;
An' sends, beside, auld Scotland's cash
   To her warst faes.  90

Ye Scots, wha wish auld Scotland well,
Ye chief, to you my tale I tell,
Poor plackless devils like mysel'!
   It sets you ill,
Wi' bitter, dearthfu' wines to mell,
   Or foreign gill.

May gravels round his blather wrench,
An' gouts torment him, inch by inch,
Wha twists his gruntle wi' a glunch
    O' sour disdain,     100
Out owre a glass o' whisky punch
    Wi' honest men!

O Whisky! soul o' plays an' pranks!
Accept a bardie's gratefu' thanks!
When wanting thee, what tuneless cranks
    Are my poor verses!
Thou comes—they rattle i' their ranks
    At ither's arses!

Thee, Ferintosh! O sadly lost!
Scotland, lament frae coast to coast!     110
Now colic-grips an' barkin' hoast
    May kill us a';
For loyal Forbes' charter'd boast
    Is ta'en awa!

Thae curst horse-leeches o' th' Excise,
Wha mak the whisky stells their prize—
Haud up thy hand, deil! Ance—twice—thrice!
    There, seize the blinkers!
An' bake them up in brunstane pies
    For poor damn'd drinkers.   120

Fortune! if thou 'll but gie me still
Hale breeks, a bannock, and a gill,
An' rowth o' rhyme to rave at will,
    Tak' a' the rest,
An' deal'd about as thy blind skill
    Directs thee best.

# ELEGY ON CAPT. MATTHEW HENDERSON,

### A GENTLEMAN WHO HELD THE PATENT FOR HIS HONOURS
### IMMEDIATELY FROM ALMIGHTY GOD.

O DEATH! thou tyrant fell and bloody!
The meikle devil wi' a woodie
Haurl thee hame to his black smiddie
        O'er hurcheon hides,
And like stock-fish come o'er his studdie
        Wi' thy auld sides!

He's gane, he's gane! he's frae us torn,
The ae best fellow e'er was born!
Thee, Matthew, Nature's sel' shall mourn
        By wood and wild,      10
Where, haply, Pity strays forlorn,
        Frae man exil'd.

Ye hills, near neibors o' the starns,
That proudly cock your cresting cairns!
Ye cliffs, the haunts of sailing earns,
        Where echo slumbers!
Come join, ye Nature's sturdiest bairns,
        My wailing numbers!

Mourn, ilka grove the cushat kens!
Ye haz'lly shaws and briery dens!      20
Ye burnies, wimplin' down your glens,
        Wi' toddlin din,
Or foaming strang wi' hasty stens
        Frae lin to lin.

Mourn, little harebells o'er the lea;
Ye stately foxgloves fair to see;
Ye woodbines hanging bonnilie,
        In scented bow'rs;
Ye roses on your thorny tree,
        The first o' flow'rs.      30

At dawn when ev'ry grassy blade
Droops with a diamond at his head,
At ev'n when beans their fragrance shed
        I' th' rustling gale,
Ye maukins, whiddin' thro' the glade,
        Come join my wail.


Mourn, ye wee songsters o' the wood ;
Ye grouse that crap the heather bud ;
Ye curlews calling thro' a clud ;
        Ye whistling plover ;                      40
And mourn, ye whirring paitrick brood—
        He 's gane for ever !


Mourn, sooty coots, and speckled teals ;
Ye fisher herons, watching eels ;
Ye duck and drake, wi' airy wheels
        Circling the lake ;
Ye bitterns, till the quagmire reels,
        Rair for his sake.


Mourn, clamouring craiks at close o' day,
'Mang fields o' flowering clover gay ;               50
And, when ye wing your annual way
        Frae our cauld shore,
Tell thae far warlds wha lies in clay,
        Wham we deplore.


Ye houlets, frae your ivy bow'r
In some auld tree, or eldritch tow'r,
What time the moon wi' silent glowr
        Sets up her horn,
Wail thro' the dreary midnight hour
        Till waukrife morn !                        60


O rivers, forests, hills, and plains !
Oft have ye heard my canty strains ;
But now, what else for me remains
        But tales of woe ?
And frae my een the drapping rains
        Maun ever flow.

Mourn, Spring, thou darling of the year!
Ilk cowslip cup shall kep a tear:
Thou, Simmer, while each corny spear
  Shoots up its head,     70
Thy gay green flow'ry tresses shear
  For him that's dead!

Thou, Autumn, wi' thy yellow hair,
In grief thy sallow mantle tear!
Thou, Winter, hurling thro' the air
  The roaring blast,
Wide o'er the naked world declare
  The worth we've lost!

Mourn him, thou sun, great source of light!
Mourn, empress of the silent night!   80
And you, ye twinkling starnies bright,
  My Matthew mourn!
For through your orbs he's ta'en his flight,
  Ne'er to return.

O Henderson! the man! the brother!
And art thou gone, and gone for ever?
And hast thou crost that unknown river,
  Life's dreary bound?
Like thee, where shall I find another,
  The world around?     90

Go to your sculptur'd tombs, ye great,
In a' the tinsel trash o' state!
But by thy honest turf I'll wait,
  Thou man of worth!
And weep the ae best fellow's fate
  E'er lay in earth.

### THE EPITAPH.

Stop, passenger! my story's brief,
 And truth I shall relate, man;
I tell nae common tale o' grief,
 For Matthew was a great man.   100

If thou uncommon merit hast,
  Yet spurn'd at fortune's door, man;
A look of pity hither cast,
  For Matthew was a poor man.

If thou a noble sodger art,
  That passest by this grave, man,
There moulders here a gallant heart;
  For Matthew was a brave man.

If thou on men, their works and ways,
  Canst throw uncommon light, man;    110
Here lies wha weel had won thy praise,
  For Matthew was a bright man.

If thou at friendship's sacred ca'
  Wad life itself resign, man;
The sympathetic tear maun fa',
  For Matthew was a kind man.

If thou art staunch without a stain,
  Like the unchanging blue, man;
This was a kinsman o' thy ain,
  For Matthew was a true man.    120

If thou hast wit, and fun, and fire,
  And ne'er guid wine did fear, man;
This was thy billie, dam, and sire,
  For Matthew was a queer man.

If ony whiggish whingein' sot,
  To blame poor Matthew dare, man;
May dool and sorrow be his lot,
  For Matthew was a rare man.

But now his radiant course is run,
  For Matthew's was a bright one;    130
His soul was like the glorious sun,
  A matchless, Heav'nly Light, man.

# THE AULD FARMER'S NEW-YEAR MORNING SALUTATION TO HIS AULD MARE, MAGGIE,

### ON GIVING HER THE ACCUSTOMED RIPP OF CORN TO HANSEL IN THE NEW YEAR.

A GUID New-Year I wish thee, Maggie!
Hae, there's a ripp to thy auld baggie :
Tho' thou's howe-backit now, an' knaggie,
            I've seen the day,
Thou could hae gane like ony staggie
            Out-owre the lay.

Tho' now thou's dowie, stiff, an' crazy,
An' thy auld hide's as white's a daisie,
I've seen thee dappled, sleek an' glaizie,
            A bonnie gray :               10
He should been tight that daur't to raize thee,
            Ance in a day.

Thou ance was i' the foremost rank,
A filly buirdly, steeve, an' swank,
An' set weel down a shapely shank,
            As e'er tread yird ;
An' could hae flown out-owre a stank,
            Like ony bird.

It's now some nine-an'-twenty year,
Sin' thou was my guid-father's meere ;      20
He gied me thee, o' tocher clear,
            An' fifty mark ;
Tho' it was sma', 'twas weel-won gear,
            An' thou was stark.

When first I gaed to woo my Jenny,
Ye then was trottin' wi' your minnie :
Tho' ye was trickie, slee, an' funnie,
            Ye ne'er was donsie ;
But hamely, tawie, quiet, an' cannie,
            An' unco sonsie.               30

That day ye pranc'd wi' muckle pride
When ye bure hame my bonnie bride ;
An' sweet an' gracefu' she did ride,
   Wi' maiden air !
Kyle-Stewart I could braggèd wide
  For sic a pair.

Tho' now ye dow but hoyte and hobble,
An' wintle like a saumont-coble,
That day ye was a jinker noble
   For heels an' win' !    40
An' ran them till they a' did wobble
  Far, far behin'.

When thou an' I were young and skeigh,
An' stable-meals at fairs were driegh,
How thou wad prance, an' snore, an' skriegh
   An' tak the road !
Town's-bodies ran, and stood abeigh,
  An' ca't thee mad.

When thou was corn't, an' I was mellow,
We took the road aye like a swallow :   50
At brooses thou had ne'er a fellow
   For pith an' speed ;
But ev'ry tail thou pay't them hollow,
  Where'er thou gaed.

The sma', droop-rumpled, hunter cattle,
Might aiblins waur'd thee for a brattle ;
But sax Scotch miles, thou tried their mettle,
   An' gart them whaizle :
Nae whip nor spur, but just a wattle
   O' saugh or hazel.    60

Thou was a noble fittie-lan',
As e'er in tug or tow was drawn !
Aft thee an' I, in aucht hours' gaun,
   On guid March-weather,
Hae turn'd sax rood beside our han',
   For days thegither.

Thou never braindg't, an' fetch't, an' fliskit,
But thy auld tail thou wad hae whiskit,
An' spread abreed thy weel-fill'd brisket,
   Wi' pith an' pow'r,    70
Till spritty knowes wad rair't and riskit,
   An' slypet owre.


When frosts lay lang, an' snaws were deep,
An' threaten'd labour back to keep,
I gied thy cog a wee bit heap
   Aboon the timmer ;
I kenn'd my Maggie wad na sleep
   For that, or simmer.


In cart or car thou never reestit ;
The steyest brae thou wad hae faced it ;  80
Thou never lap, an' stenned, and breastit,
   Then stood to blaw ;
But, just thy step a wee thing hastit,
   Thou snoov't awa.


My pleugh is now thy bairn-time a',
Four gallant brutes as e'er did draw ;
Forbye sax mae I've sell't awa
   That thou hast nurst :
They drew me thretteen pund an' twa,
   The very warst.    90


Mony a sair darg we twa hae wrought,
An' wi' the weary warl' fought !
An' mony an anxious day I thought
   We wad be beat !
Yet here to crazy age we're brought,
   Wi' something yet.


And think na, my auld trusty servan',
That now perhaps thou 's less deservin',
An' thy auld days may end in starvin' ;
   For my last fou,    100
A heapit stimpart I'll reserve ane
   Laid by for you.

We've worn to crazy years thegither;
We'll toyte about wi' ane anither;
Wi' tentie care I'll flit thy tether
      To some hain'd rig,
Where ye may nobly rax your leather,
      Wi' sma' fatigue.

———••———

# TO A MOUSE, ON TURNING HER UP IN HER NEST WITH THE PLOUGH, NOVEMBER, 1785.

Wee, sleekit, cow'rin', tim'rous beastie,
O what a panic's in thy breastie!
Thou need na start awa sae hasty,
      Wi' bickering brattle!
I wad be laith to rin an' chase thee
      Wi' murd'ring pattle!

I'm truly sorry man's dominion
Has broken Nature's social union,
An' justifies that ill opinion
      Which makes thee startle     10
At me, thy poor earth-born companion,
      An' fellow-mortal!

I doubt na, whiles, but thou may thieve;
What then? poor beastie, thou maun live!
A daimen-icker in a thrave
      'S a sma' request:
I'll get a blessin' wi' the lave,
      And never miss't!

Thy wee bit housie, too, in ruin!
Its silly wa's the win's are strewin'!     20
An' naething, now, to big a new ane,
      O' foggage green!
An' bleak December's winds ensuin',
      Baith snell an' keen!

Thou saw the fields laid bare and waste,
An' weary winter comin' fast,
An' cozie here, beneath the blast,
        Thou thought to dwell,
Till crash! the cruel coulter past
        Out-thro' thy cell.      30

That wee bit heap o' leaves an' stibble
Has cost thee mony a weary nibble!
Now thou's turn'd out, for a' thy trouble,
        But house or hald,
To thole the winter's sleety dribble,
        An' cranreuch cauld!

But, Mousie, thou art no thy lane,
In proving foresight may be vain:
The best laid schemes o' mice an' men
        Gang aft a-gley,      40
An' lea'e us nought but grief an' pain
        For promis'd joy.

Still thou art blest compar'd wi' me!
The present only toucheth thee:
But oh! I backward cast my e'e
        On prospects drear!
An' forward tho' I canna see,
        I guess an' fear!

---

## MAN WAS MADE TO MOURN.

WHEN chill November's surly blast
  Made fields and forests bare,
One ev'ning as I wander'd forth
  Along the banks of Ayr,
I spied a man, whose agèd step
  Seem'd weary, worn with care;
His face was furrow'd o'er with years,
  And hoary was his hair.

'Young stranger, whither wand'rest thou?'
  Began the rev'rend sage;                          10
'Does thirst of wealth thy step constrain,
  Or youthful pleasure's rage?
Or, haply, prest with cares and woes,
  Too soon thou hast began
To wander forth with me to mourn
  The miseries of man.


'The sun that overhangs yon moors,
  Out-spreading far and wide,
Where hundreds labour to support
  A haughty lordling's pride—                       20
I've seen yon weary winter-sun
  Twice forty times return,
And ev'ry time has added proofs
  That man was made to mourn.


'O man! while in thy early years,
  How prodigal of time!
Mis-spending all thy precious hours,
  Thy glorious youthful prime!
Alternate follies take the sway;
  Licentious passions burn;                         30
Which tenfold force give nature's law,
  That man was made to mourn.


'Look not alone on youthful prime,
  Or manhood's active might;
Man then is useful to his kind,
  Supported is his right;
But see him on the edge of life,
  With cares and sorrows worn,
Then age and want, oh! ill-match'd pair!
  Show man was made to mourn.                       40


'A few seem favourites of fate,
  In pleasure's lap carest;
Yet think not all the rich and great
  Are likewise truly blest.

But oh! what crowds in ev'ry land
    All wretched and forlorn,
Thro' weary life this lesson learn—
    That man was made to mourn.


'Many and sharp the num'rous ills
    Inwoven with our frame!                         50
More pointed still we make ourselves
    Regret, remorse, and shame!
And man, whose heaven-erected face
    The smiles of love adorn—
Man's inhumanity to man
    Makes countless thousands mourn!


'See yonder poor o'erlabour'd wight,
    So abject, mean, and vile,
Who begs a brother of the earth
    To give him leave to toil;                      60
And see his lordly fellow-worm
    The poor petition spurn,
Unmindful tho' a weeping wife
    And helpless offspring mourn.


'If I'm design'd yon lordling's slave,—
    By nature's law design'd,—
Why was an independent wish
    E'er planted in my mind?
If not, why am I subject to
    His cruelty, or scorn?                          70
Or why has man the will and pow'r
    To make his fellow mourn?


'Yet let not this too much, my son,
    Disturb thy youthful breast;
This partial view of human-kind
    Is surely not the last!
The poor oppressèd honest man,
    Had never sure been born,
Had there not been some recompense
    To comfort those that mourn!                    80

'O Death, the poor man's dearest friend,
  The kindest and the best!
Welcome the hour my agèd limbs
  Are laid with thee at rest!
The great, the wealthy, fear thy blow.
  From pomp and pleasure torn;
But oh! a blest relief to those
  That weary-laden mourn.'

## TO A MOUNTAIN DAISY,

### ON TURNING ONE DOWN WITH THE PLOUGH, IN APRIL, 1786.

WEE modest crimson-tippèd flow'r,
Thou 's met me in an evil hour;
For I maun crush amang the stoure
     Thy slender stem:
To spare thee now is past my pow'r,
     Thou bonnie gem.

Alas! it 's no thy neibor sweet,
The bonnie lark, companion meet,
Bending thee 'mang the dewy weet
     Wi' spreckl'd breast,     10
When upward springing, blythe to greet
     The purpling east.

Cauld blew the bitter-biting north
Upon thy early humble birth;
Yet cheerfully thou glinted forth
     Amid the storm,
Scarce rear'd above the parent-earth
     Thy tender form.

The flaunting flow'rs our gardens yield
High shelt'ring woods and wa's maun shield,   20
But thou, beneath the random bield
     O' clod or stane,
Adorns the histie stibble-field,
     Unseen, alane.

There, in thy scanty mantle clad,
Thy snawy bosom sun-ward spread,
Thou lifts thy unassuming head
          In humble guise ;
But now the share uptears thy bed,
          And low thou lies !     30

Such is the fate of artless maid,
Sweet flow'ret of the rural shade,
By love's simplicity betray'd,
          And guileless trust,
Till she like thee, all soil'd, is laid
          Low i' the dust.

Such is the fate of simple bard,
On life's rough ocean luckless starr'd :
Unskilful he to note the card
          Of prudent lore,     40
Till billows rage, and gales blow hard,
          And whelm him o'er !

Such fate to suffering worth is giv'n,
Who long with wants and woes has striv'n,
By human pride or cunning driv'n
          To mis'ry's brink,
Till wrench'd of ev'ry stay but Heav'n,
          He, ruin'd, sink !

Ev'n thou who mourn'st the Daisy's fate,
That fate is thine—no distant date ;     50
Stern Ruin's ploughshare drives elate
          Full on thy bloom,
Till crush'd beneath the furrow's weight
          Shall be thy doom !

## TO RUIN.

ALL hail! inexorable lord,
At whose destruction-breathing word
  The mightiest empires fall!
Thy cruel woe-delighted train,
The ministers of grief and pain,
  A sullen welcome, all!
With stern-resolv'd despairing eye,
  I see each aimèd dart;
For one has cut my dearest tie,
  And quivers in my heart.                          10
    Then low'ring, and pouring,
      The storm no more I dread,
    Tho' thick'ning and black'ning
      Round my devoted head.


And, thou grim pow'r, by life abhorr'd,
While life a pleasure can afford,
  Oh! hear a wretch's pray'r!
No more I shrink appall'd, afraid;
I court, I beg thy friendly aid,
  To close this scene of care!                      20
When shall my soul, in silent peace,
  Resign life's joyless day?
My weary heart its throbbings cease,
  Cold-mould'ring in the clay?
    No fear more, no tear more,
      To stain my lifeless face,
    Enclaspèd, and graspèd
      Within thy cold embrace!

## ON A SCOTCH BARD, GONE TO THE
## WEST INDIES.

A' ye wha live by sowps o' drink,
A' ye wha live by crambo-clink,
A' ye wha live an' never think,
      Come mourn wi' me!
Our billie 's gi'en us a' a jink,
      An' owre the sea.

Lament him, a' ye rantin core,
Wha dearly like a random-splore ;
Nae mair he'll join the merry roar,
      In social key ;      10
For now he 's taen anither shore,
      An' owre the sea !

The bonnie lasses weel may wiss him,
And in their dear petitions place him ;
The widows, wives, an' a' may bless him,
      Wi' tearfu' e'e ;
For weel I wat they'll sairly miss him
      That 's owre the sea !

O Fortune, they hae room to grumble !
Hadst thou taen aff some drowsy bummle,      20
Wha can do nought but fyke an' fumble,
      'Twad been nae plea ;
But he was gleg as ony wumble,
      That 's owre the sea !

Auld cantie Kyle may weepers wear,
An' stain them wi' the saut saut tear :
'Twill mak her poor auld heart, I fear,
      In flinders flee ;
He was her Laureat mony a year,
      That 's owre the sea !      30

He saw misfortune's cauld nor-west
Lang mustering up a bitter blast;
A jillet brak his heart at last—
        Ill may she be!
So took a berth afore the mast,
        An' owre the sea.


To tremble under Fortune's cummock
On scarce a bellyfu' o' drummock,
Wi' his proud independent stomach,
        Could ill agree;        40
So row'd his hurdies in a hammock,
        An' owre the sea.


He ne'er was gi'en to great misguidin',
Yet coin his pouches wad na bide in;
Wi' him it ne'er was under hidin',
        He dealt it free:
The Muse was a' that he took pride in,
        That 's owre the sea.


Jamaica bodies, use him weel,
An' hap him in a cozie biel;        50
Ye'll find him aye a dainty chiel,
        And fu' o' glee;
He wad na wrang'd the vera deil,
        That 's owre the sea.


Fareweel, my rhyme-composing billie!
Your native soil was right ill-willie;
But may ye flourish like a lily,
        Now bonnilie!
I'll toast ye in my hindmost gillie,
        Tho' owre the sea!        60

## ADDRESS TO EDINBURGH.

EDINA ! Scotia's darling seat,
  All hail thy palaces and tow'rs,
Where once beneath a monarch's feet
  Sat Legislation's sov'reign pow'rs.
  From marking wildly-scatter'd flow'rs,
As on the banks of Ayr I stray'd,
  And singing lone the ling'ring hours,
I shelter in thy honour'd shade.


Here Wealth still swells the golden tide,
  As busy trade his labours plies ;        10
There Architecture's noble pride
  Bids elegance and splendour rise ;
  Here Justice, from her native skies,
High wields her balance and her rod ;
  There Learning, with his eagle eyes,
Seeks Science in her coy abode.


Thy sons, Edina, social, kind,
  With open arms the stranger hail ;
Their views enlarg'd, their lib'ral mind,
  Above the narrow rural vale ;        20
  Attentive still to sorrow's wail,
Or modest merit's silent claim :
  And never may their sources fail !
And never envy blot their name !


Thy daughters bright thy walks adorn,
  Gay as the gilded summer sky,
Sweet as the dewy milk-white thorn,
  Dear as the raptur'd thrill of joy.
  Fair Burnet strikes th' adoring eye,
Heaven's beauties on my fancy shine ;      30
  I see the Sire of Love on high,
And own his work indeed divine !

There watching high the least alarms,
   Thy rough rude fortress gleams afar ;
Like some bold veteran, gray in arms,
   And mark'd with many a seamy scar :
The pond'rous wall and massy bar,
Grim-rising o'er the rugged rock,
   Have oft withstood assailing war,
And oft repell'd th' invader's shock.         40


With awe-struck thought, and pitying tears,
   I view that noble stately dome,
Where Scotia's kings of other years,
   Fam'd heroes, had their royal home ;
Alas, how chang'd the times to come !
Their royal name low in the dust,
   Their hapless race wild-wand'ring roam ;
Tho' rigid law cries out 'twas just !


Wild beats my heart to trace your steps,
   Whose ancestors, in days of yore,         50
Thro' hostile ranks and ruin'd gaps
   Old Scotia's bloody lion bore.
Ev'n I who sing in rustic lore,
Haply my sires have left their shed,
   And faced grim danger's loudest roar,
Bold-following where your fathers led !


Edina ! Scotia's darling seat,
   All hail thy palaces and tow'rs,
Where once beneath a monarch's feet
   Sat Legislation's sov'reign pow'rs !        60
   From marking wildly-scatter'd flow'rs,
As on the banks of Ayr I stray'd,
   And singing lone the ling'ring hours,
I shelter in thy honour'd shade.

# LAMENT FOR JAMES, EARL OF GLENCAIRN.

THE wind blew hollow frae the hills ;
    By fits the sun's departing beam
Look'd on the fading yellow woods
    That waved o'er Lugar's winding stream.
Beneath a craigy steep, a bard,
    Laden with years and meikle pain,
In loud lament bewail'd his lord,
    Whom death had all untimely taen.


He lean'd him to an ancient aik,
    Whose trunk was mould'ring down with years ;  10
His locks were bleachèd white wi' time,
    His hoary cheek was wet wi' tears ;
And as he touch'd his trembling harp,
    And as he tun'd his doleful sang,
The winds, lamenting thro' their caves,
    To echo bore the notes alang.


'Ye scatter'd birds that faintly sing,
    The reliques of the vernal quire !
Ye woods that shed on a' the winds
    The honours of the agèd year !                20
A few short months, and glad and gay,
    Again ye'll charm the ear and e'e ;
But nocht in all revolving time
    Can gladness bring again to me.


'I am a bending agèd tree,
    That long has stood the wind and rain ,
But now has come a cruel blast,
    And my last hold of earth is gane :
Nae leaf o' mine shall greet the spring,
    Nae simmer sun exalt my bloom ;              30
But I maun lie before the storm,
    And others plant them in my room.

'I've seen so many changefu' years,
　On earth I am a stranger grown ;
I wander in the ways of men,
　Alike unknowing and unknown :
Unheard, unpitied, unreliev'd,
　I bear alane my lade o' care,
For silent, low, on beds of dust,
　Lie a' that would my sorrows share.　　40


'And last (the sum of a' my griefs !)
　My noble master lies in clay ;
The flow'r amang our barons bold,
　His country's pride, his country's stay :
In weary being now I pine
　For a' the life of life is dead,
And hope has left my agèd ken,
　On forward wing for ever fled.


'Awake thy last sad voice, my harp !
　The voice of woe and wild despair ;　　50
Awake, resound thy latest lay,
　Then sleep in silence evermair !
And thou, my last, best, only, friend,
　That fillest an untimely tomb,
Accept this tribute from the bard
　Thou brought from fortune's mirkest gloom.


'In poverty's low barren vale,
　Thick mists obscure involv'd me round ;
Though oft I turn'd the wistful eye,
　No ray of fame was to be found :　　60
Thou found'st me, like the morning sun
　That melts the fogs in limpid air ;
The friendless bard and rustic song
　Became alike thy fostering care.


'O why has worth so short a date
　While villains ripen grey with time ?
Must thou, the noble, gen'rous, great,
　Fall in bold manhood's hardy prime ?

Why did I live to see that day,
  A day to me so full of woe?
O had I met the mortal shaft
  Which laid my benefactor low!      70

'The bridegroom may forget the bride
  Was made his wedded wife yestreen;
The monarch may forget the crown
  That on his head an hour has been;
The mother may forget the child
  That smiles sae sweetly on her knee;
But I'll remember thee, Glencairn,
  And a' that thou hast done for me!'     80

———◆◆———

# LAMENT OF MARY QUEEN OF SCOTS, ON THE
## APPROACH OF SPRING.

Now Nature hangs her mantle green
  On every blooming tree,
And spreads her sheets o' daisies white
  Out-owre the grassy lea;
Now Phoebus cheers the crystal streams,
  And glads the azure skies;
But nought can glad the weary wight
  That fast in durance lies.

Now laverocks wake the merry morn,
  Aloft on dewy wing;     10
The merle, in his noontide bow'r,
  Makes woodland echoes ring;
The mavis mild wi' many a note,
  Sings drowsy day to rest:
In love and freedom they rejoice,
  Wi' care nor thrall opprest.

Now blooms the lily by the bank,
　　The primrose down the brae ;
The hawthorn's budding in the glen,
　　And milk-white is the slae :　　　　　　20
The meanest hind in fair Scotland
　　May rove their sweets amang ;
But I, the Queen of a' Scotland,
　　Maun lie in prison strang.


I was the Queen o' bonnie France,
　　Where happy I hae been ;
Fu' lightly rase I in the morn,
　　As blythe lay down at e'en :
And I'm the sov'reign of Scotland,
　　And mony a traitor there ;　　　　　　30
Yet here I lie in foreign bands,
　　And never-ending care.


But as for thee, thou false woman,
　　My sister and my fae,
Grim vengeance yet shall whet a sword
　　That thro' thy soul shall gae !
The weeping blood in woman's breast
　　Was never known to thee ;
Nor th' balm that draps on wounds of woe
　　Frae woman's pitying e'e.　　　　　　40


My son ! my son ! may kinder stars
　　Upon thy fortune shine ;
And may those pleasures gild thy reign,
　　That ne'er wad blink on mine.
God keep thee frae thy mother's faes,
　　Or turn their hearts to thee ;
And where thou meet'st thy mother's friend,
　　Remember him for me !


Oh ! soon to me may summer-suns
　　Nae mair light up the morn !　　　　　50
Nae mair to me the autumn winds
　　Wave o'er the yellow corn !

And, in the narrow house o' death,
   Let winter round me rave ;
And the next flow'rs that deck the spring
   Bloom on my peaceful grave !

———◆———

## THE TWA HERDS.

O a' ye pious godly flocks,
Weel fed on pastures orthodox,
Wha now will keep you frae the fox,
      Or worrying tykes ?
Or wha will tent the waifs and crocks,
      About the dykes ?

The twa best herds in a' the wast
That e'er gae gospel horn a blast
These five-and-twenty summers past,
      O dool to tell !         10
Hae had a bitter black out-cast
      Atween themsel.

O Moodie, man, and wordy Russel,
How could you raise so vile a bustle ?
Ye'll see how new-light herds will whistle
      And think it fine !
The Lord's cause ne'er gat sic a twistle,
      Sin' I hae min'.

O sirs, whae'er wad hae expeckit
Your duty ye wad sae negleckit        20
Ye wha were ne'er by lairds respeckit
      To wear the plaid,
But by the brutes themselves eleckit
      To be their guide.

What flock wi' Moodie's flock could rank,
Sae hale and hearty every shank?
Nae poison'd soor Arminian stank
        He let them taste;
Frae Calvin's well, aye clear, they drank—
        O' sic a feast!                    30

The thummart, wil'-cat, brock and tod,
Weel kenn'd his voice thro' a' the wood;
He smell'd their ilka hole and road
        Baith out and in,
And weel he lik'd to shed their bluid
        And sell their skin.

What herd like Russel tell'd his tale?
His voice was heard thro' muir and dale;
He kenn'd the Lord's sheep, ilka tail,
        O'er a' the height,
And saw gin they were sick or hale      40
        At the first sight.

He fine a mangy sheep could scrub,
Or nobly fling the gospel club,
And new-light herds could nicely drub
        Or pay their skin,
Could shake them owre the burning dub,
        Or heave them in.

Sic twa—O! do I live to see't?
Sic famous twa should disagreet,        50
An' names like 'villain,' 'hypocrite,'
        Ilk ither gi'en,
While new-light herds wi' laughin' spite
        Say neither's leein'!

A' ye wha tent the gospel fauld—
There's Duncan deep, and Peebles shaul—
But chiefly thou, apostle Auld!
        We trust in thee,
That thou wilt work them, hot and cauld,
        Till they agree.                  60

Consider, sirs, how we're beset!
There's scarce a new herd that we get,
But comes frae 'mang that cursed set
      I winna name:
I hope frae heaven to see them yet
      In fiery flame.

Dalrymple has been lang our fae,
M'Gill has wrought us meikle wae,
And that curs'd rascal ca'd M'Quhae,
      And baith the Shaws,     70
That aft hae made us black and blae
      Wi' vengefu' paws.

Auld Wodrow lang has hatch'd mischief:
We thought aye death wad bring relief,
But he has gotten, to our grief,
      Ane to succeed him,
A chiel wha'll soundly buff our beef,
      I meikle dread him.

And mony a ane that I could tell,
Wha fain would openly rebel;     80
Forby turn-coats amang oursel—
      There's Smith for ane;
I doubt he's but a grey nick quill,
      And that ye'll fin'.

O a' ye flocks, owre a' the hills,
By mosses, meadows, moors, and fells,
Come join your counsels and your skills
      To cowe the lairds,
And get the brutes the power themsels
      To choose their herds.     90

Then Orthodoxy yet may prance,
And Learning in a woody dance,
And that fell cur ca'd Common Sense,
      That bites sae sair,
Be banish'd owre the seas to France;
      Let him bark there.

Then Shaw's and D'rymple's eloquence,
M'Gill's close nervous excellence,
M'Quhae's pathetic manly sense,
            And guid M'Math,                    100
Wi' Smith, wha thro' the heart can glance,
            May a' pack aff!

---

# ON THE LATE CAPTAIN GROSE'S PEREGRINA-
## TIONS THRO' SCOTLAND.

### COLLECTING THE ANTIQUITIES OF THAT KINGDOM.

HEAR, Land o' Cakes, and brither Scots,
Frae Maidenkirk to Johnny Groats ;—
If there 's a hole in a' your coats,
            I rede you tent it :
A chield's amang you taking notes,
            And, faith, he'll prent it.


If in your bounds ye chance to light
Upon a fine, fat, fodgel wight,
O' stature short, but genius bright,
            That 's he, mark weel !                10
And wow ! he has an unco sleight
            O' cauk and keel.


By some auld houlet-haunted biggin,
Or kirk deserted by its riggin'
It 's ten to ane ye'll find him snug in
            Some eldritch part,
Wi' deils, they say, Lord save 's ! colleaguin'
            At some black art.

Ilk ghaist that haunts auld ha' or cham'er,
Ye gipsy-gang that deal in glamour,          20
And you, deep read in hell's black grammar,
          Warlocks and witches—
Ye'll quake at his conjuring hammer,
          Ye midnight bitches !


It 's tauld he was a sodger bred,
And ane wad rather fa'n than fled ;
But now he 's quat the spurtle-blade
          And dog-skin wallet,
And taen the—Antiquarian trade
          I think they call it.          30


He has a fouth o' auld nick-nackets :
Rusty airn caps and jinglin' jackets,
Wad haud the Lothians three in tackets,
          A towmont gude ;
And parritch-pats and auld saut-backets
          Before the Flood.


Of Eve's first fire he has a cinder ;
Auld Tubulcain's fire-shool and fender ;
That which distinguishèd the gender
          O' Balaam's ass ;          40
A broom-stick o' the witch of Endor,
          Weel shod wi' brass.


Forbye, he'll shape you aff fu' gleg
The cut of Adam's philibeg ;
The knife that nicket Abel's craig—
          He'll prove you fully
It was a faulding jocteleg,
          Or lang-kail gullie.


But wad ye see him in his glee,
For meikle glee and fun has he,          50
Then set him down, and twa or three
          Guid fellows wi' him ;
And port, O port ! shine thou a wee,
          And then ye'll see him !

Now, by the Pow'rs o' verse and prose!
Thou art a dainty chield, O Grose!
Whae'er o' thee shall ill suppose,
   They sair misca' thee;
I'd take the rascal by the nose,
   Wad say 'Shame fa' thee!'  60

    ———••———

## ON PASTORAL POETRY.

HAIL, Poesie! thou Nymph reserv'd!
In chase o' thee what crowds hae swerv'd
Frae common sense, or sunk enerv'd
   'Mang heaps o' clavers;
And oh! o'er aft thy joes hae starv'd,
   'Mid a' thy favours!

Say, Lassie, why, thy train amang,
While loud the trump's heroic clang,
And sock or buskin skelp alang
   To death or marriage,  10
Scarce ane has tried the shepherd-sang
   But wi' miscarriage?

In Homer's craft Jock Milton thrives;
Eschylus' pen Will Shakespeare drives;
Wee Pope, the knurlin', till him rives
   Horatian fame;
In thy sweet sang, Barbauld, survives
   Even Sappho's flame.

But thee, Theocritus, wha matches?
They're no herds' ballats, Maro's catches;  20
Squire Pope but busks his skinklin' patches
   O' heathen tatters:
I pass by hunders, nameless wretches,
   That ape their betters.

In this braw age o' wit and lear,
Will nane the Shepherd's whistle mair
Blaw sweetly in its native air
  And rural grace ;
And wi' the far-fam'd Grecian share
  A rival place ?      30


Yes ! there is ane—a Scottish callan !
There 's ane ; come forrit, honest Allan !
Thou need na jouk behint the hallan,
  A chiel sae clever ;
The teeth o' Time may gnaw Tamtallan,
  But thou 's for ever !


Thou paints auld Nature to the nines,
In thy sweet Caledonian lines ;
Nae gowden stream thro' myrtles twines,
  Where Philomel,      40
While nightly breezes sweep the vines,
  Her griefs will tell !


In gowany glens thy burnie strays,
Where bonnie lasses bleach their claes ;
Or trots by hazelly shaws and braes,
  Wi' hawthorns gray,
Where blackbirds join the shepherd's lays
  At close o' day.


Thy rural loves are nature's sel' ;
Nae bombast spates o' nonsense swell ;
Nae snap conceits ; but that sweet spell    50
  O' witchin' love—
That charm that can the strongest quell,
  The sternest move.

## THE HUMBLE PETITION OF BRUAR WATER
## TO THE NOBLE DUKE OF ATHOLE.

My Lord, I know your noble ear
  Woe ne'er assails in vain ;
Embolden'd thus, I beg you'll 'hear
  Your humble slave complain,
How saucy Phoebus' scorching beams,
  In flaming summer-pride,
Dry-withering, waste my foamy streams,
  And drink my crystal tide.

The lightly-jumping glowrin' trouts,
  That thro' my waters play,        10
If, in their random wanton spouts,
  They near the margin stray ;
If, hapless chance ! they linger lang,
  I'm scorching up so shallow,
They're left the whitening stanes amang,
  In gasping death to wallow.

Last day I grat wi' spite and teen,
  As poet Burns came by,
That to a bard I should be seen
  Wi' half my channel dry :        20
A panegyric rhyme, I ween,
  Even as I was, he shor'd me ;
But had I in my glory been,
  He, kneeling, wad ador'd me.

Here, foaming down the shelvy rocks,
  In twisting strength I rin ;
There high my boiling torrent smokes,
  Wild-roaring o'er a linn :
Enjoying large each spring and well
  As Nature gave them me,        30
I am, altho' I say 't mysel,
  Worth gaun a mile to see.

Would then my noble master please
    To grant my highest wishes,
He'll shade my banks wi' tow'ring trees,
    And bonnie spreading bushes.
Delighted doubly then, my Lord,
    You'll wander on my banks,
And listen mony a grateful bird
    Return you tuneful thanks.    40


The sober laverock, warbling wild,
    Shall to the skies aspire ;
The gowdspink, Music's gayest child,
    Shall sweetly join the choir:
The blackbird strong, the lintwhite clear,
    The mavis mild and mellow ;
The robin pensive Autumn cheer,
    In all her locks of yellow.


This, too, a covert shall ensure,
    To shield them from the storm ;    50
And coward maukin sleep secure,
    Low in her grassy form:
Here shall the shepherd make his seat,
    To weave his crown of flow'rs ;
Or find a sheltering safe retreat
    From prone-descending show'rs.


And here, by sweet endearing stealth,
    Shall meet the loving pair,
Despising worlds with all their wealth
    As empty idle care:    60
The flow'rs shall vie in all their charms
    The hour of heav'n to grace,
And birks extend their fragrant arms,
    To screen the dear embrace.


Here haply too, at vernal dawn,
    Some musing bard may stray,
And eye the smoking dewy lawn,
    And misty mountain gray ;

Or, by the reaper's nightly beam,
　　Mild-chequering thro' the trees,　　　　　7c
Rave to my darkly dashing stream,
　　Hoarse-swelling on the breeze.


Let lofty firs, and ashes cool,
　　My lowly banks o'erspread,
And view, deep-bending in the pool,
　　Their shadows' wat'ry bed!
Let fragrant birks in woodbines drest
　　My craggy cliffs adorn;
And, for the little songster's nest,
　　The close embow'ring thorn.　　　　　　　8c


So may Old Scotia's darling hope,
　　Your little angel band,
Spring, like their fathers, up to prop
　　Their honour'd native land!
So may thro' Albion's farthest ken,
　　To social-flowing glasses
The grace be—'Athole's honest men,
　　And Athole's bonnie lasses!'


＊

## TO A HAGGIS.

FAIR fa' your honest sonsie face,
Great chieftain o' the puddin'-race!
Aboon them a' ye tak your place,
　　　　　　Painch, tripe, or thairm:
Weel are ye wordy o' a grace
　　　　　　As lang's my arm.


The groaning trencher there ye fill,
Your hurdies like a distant hill;
Your pin wad help to mend a mill
　　　　　　In time o' need;　　　　　　　　　10
While thro' your pores the dews distil
　　　　　　Like amber bead.

His knife see rustic Labour dight,
An' cut you up wi' ready sleight,
Trenching your gushing entrails bright
          Like ony ditch ;
And then, O what a glorious sight,
          Warm-reekin', rich !

Then, horn for horn they stretch an' strive,
Deil tak the hindmost ! on they drive,          20
Till a' their weel-swall'd kytes belyve
          Are bent like drums ;
Then auld guidman, maist like to rive,
          Bethankit hums.

Is there that o'er his French ragout,
Or olio that wad staw a sow,
Or fricassee wad mak her spew
          Wi' perfect sconner,
Looks down wi' sneering scornfu' view
          On sic a dinner ?          30

Poor devil ! see him owre his trash,
As feckless as a wither'd rash,
His spindle shank a guid whip-lash,
          His nieve a nit :
Thro' bloody flood or field to dash,
          O how unfit !

But mark the Rustic, haggis-fed—
The trembling earth resounds his tread !
Clap in his walie nieve a blade,
          He'll mak it whissle ;          40
An' legs, an' arms, an' heads will sned,
          Like taps o' thrissle.

Ye Pow'rs, wha mak mankind your care,
And dish them out their bill o' fare,
Auld Scotland wants nae skinking ware
          That jaups in luggies ;
But, if ye wish her gratefu' prayer,
          Gie her a Haggis !

## ADDRESS TO THE TOOTHACHE.

My curse upon your venom'd stang,
That shoots my tortur'd gums alang,
And thro' my lugs gies mony a twang,
       Wi' gnawing vengeance;
Tearing my nerves wi' bitter pang,
       Like racking engines!

When fevers burn, or ague freezes,
Rheumatics gnaw, or colic squeezes;
Our neighbour's sympathy may ease us,
       Wi' pitying moan;
But thee—thou hell o' a' diseases!
       Aye mocks our groan.

Adown my beard the slavers trickle,
I throw the wee stools o'er the mickle,
As round the fire the giglets keckle
       To see me loup;
While, raving mad, I wish a heckle
       Were in their doup.

O' a' the numerous human dools,
Ill hairsts, daft bargains, cutty-stools,
Or worthy friends rak'd i' the mools—
       Sad sight to see!
The tricks o' knaves, or fash o' fools,
       Thou bear'st the gree.

Where'er that place be priests ca' hell,
Whence a' the tones o' mis'ry yell,
And rankèd plagues their numbers tell,
       In dreadfu' raw,
Thou. Toothache, surely bear'st the bell
       Amang them a'!

O thou grim mischief-making chiel,
That gars the notes of discord squeal,
Till daft mankind aft dance a reel
          In gore a shoe-thick;—
Gie a' the faes o' Scotland's weal
          A towmont's Toothache!

## ON CREECH THE BOOKSELLER.

AULD chuckie Reekie's sair distrest,
Down droops her ance weel burnish'd crest,
Nae joy her bonnie buskit nest
          Can yield ava,
Her darling bird that she lo'es best—
          Willie's awa!

O Willie was a witty wight,
And had o' things an unco sleight;
Auld Reekie aye he keepit tight,
          An' trig an' braw:      10
But now they'll busk her like a fright—
          Willie's awa!

The stiffest o' them a' he bow'd;
The bauldest o' them a' he cow'd;
They durst nae mair than he allow'd,
          That was a law:
We've lost a birkie weel worth gowd,
          Willie's awa!

Now gawkies, tawpies, gowks, and fools,
Frae colleges and boarding-schools,      20
May sprout like simmer puddock-stools
          In glen or shaw;
He wha could brush them down to mools—
          Willie's awa!

The brethren o' the Commerce-Cham'er
May mourn their loss wi' doolfu' clamour;
He was a dictionar and grammar
                Amang them a';
I fear they'll now mak mony a stammer—
                Willie's awa!                    30

Nae mair we see his levee door
Philosophers and poets pour,
And toothy critics by the score,
                In bloody raw;
The adjutant o' a' the core,
                Willie's awa!

Now worthy Gregory's Latin face,
Tytler's and Greenfield's modest grace;
Mackenzie, Stewart, sic a brace
                As Rome ne'er saw;              40
They a' maun meet some ither place—
                Willie's awa!

Poor Burns e'en Scotch drink canna quicken,
He cheeps like some bewilder'd chicken
Scar'd frae its minnie and the clockin'
                By hoodie-craw;
Grief's gien his heart an unco kickin'—
                Willie's awa!

Now ev'ry sour-mou'd grinnin' blellum,
And Calvin's folk, are fit to fell him;
Ilk self-conceited critic skellum                50
                His quill may draw;
He wha could brawlie ward their bellum,
                Willie's awa!

Up wimpling stately Tweed I've sped,
And Eden scenes on crystal Jed,
And Ettrick banks, now roaring red,
                While tempests blaw;
But every joy and pleasure's fled—
                Willie's awa!                    60

May I be Slander's common speech ;
A text for Infamy to preach ;
And, lastly, streekit out to bleach
    In winter snaw ;
When I forget thee, Willie Creech,
    Tho' far awa!

May never wicked Fortune touzle him !
May never wicked men bamboozle him !
Until a pow as auld 's Methusalem
    He canty claw !          70
Then to the blessed New Jerusalem
    Fleet wing awa !

———◆———

## TO A LOUSE,

ON SEEING ONE ON A LADY'S BONNET AT CHURCH.

HA! wh'are ye gaun, ye crowlin' ferlie !
Your impudence protects you sairly :
I canna say but ye strunt rarely,
    Owre gauze and lace ;
Tho' faith ! I fear ye dine but sparely
    On sic a place.

Ye ugly, creepin', blastit wonner,
Detested, shunn'd by saunt an' sinner !
How dare ye set your fit upon her,
    Sae fine a lady ?          10
Gae somewhere else, and seek your dinner
    On some poor body.

Swith, in some beggar's haffet squattle ;
There ye may creep, and sprawl, and sprattle
Wi' ither kindred jumping cattle,
    In shoals and nations ;
Where horn nor bane ne'er dare unsettle
    Your thick plantations.

Now haud ye there, ye're out o' sight,
Below the fatt'rels, snug an' tight;                    20
Na, faith ye yet! ye'll no be right
            Till ye've got on it,
The very tapmost tow'ring height
            O' Miss's bonnet.


My sooth! right bauld ye set your nose out,
As plump and gray as onie grozet;
O for some rank mercurial rozet,
            Or fell red smeddum!
I'd gie you sic a hearty doze o't,
            Wad dress your droddum!                    30


I wad na been surpris'd to spy
You on an auld wife's flannen toy;
Or aiblins some bit duddie boy,
            On's wyliecoat;
But Miss's fine Lunardi! fie,
            How daur ye do't?


O Jenny, dinna toss your head,
An' set your beauties a' abroad!
Ye little ken what cursèd speed
            Tho blastie's makin'!                    40
Thae winks and finger-ends, I dread,
            Are notice takin'!


O wad some Pow'r the giftie gie us
To see oursels as others see us!
It wad frae mony a blunder free us,
            And foolish notion:
What airs in dress an' gait wad lea'e us,
            And ev'n devotion!

## THE WHISTLE.

I SING of a Whistle, a Whistle of worth,
I sing of a Whistle, the pride of the North,
Was brought to the court of our good Scottish king,
And long with this Whistle all Scotland shall ring.

Old Loda, still rueing the arm of Fingal,
The god of the bottle sends down from his hall—
'This Whistle's your challenge, to Scotland get o'er,
And drink them to hell, Sir, or ne'er see me more!'

Old poets have sung, and old chronicles tell,
What champions ventur'd, what champions fell ;          10
The son of great Loda was conqueror still,
And blew on the Whistle their requiem shrill.

Till Robert, the lord of the Cairn and the Scaur,
Unmatch'd at the bottle, unconquer'd in war,
He drank his poor god-ship as deep as the sea ;
No tide of the Baltic e'er drunker than he.

Thus Robert, victorious, the trophy has gain'd,
Which now in his house has for ages remain'd ;
Till three noble chieftains, and all of his blood,
The jovial contest again have renew'd ;          20

Three joyous good fellows, with hearts clear of flaw—
Craigdarroch, so famous for wit, worth, and law,
And trusty Glenriddel, so skill'd in old coins,
And gallant Sir Robert, deep-read in old wines.

Craigdarroch began, with a tongue smooth as oil,
Desiring Glenriddel to yield up the spoil ;
Or else he would muster the heads of the clan,
And once more, in claret, try which was the man.

'By the gods of the ancients !' Glenriddel replies,
'Before I surrender so glorious a prize,          30
I'll conjure the ghost of the great Rorie More,
And bumper his horn with him twenty times o'er.'

Sir Robert, a soldier, no speech would pretend,
But he ne'er turn'd his back on his foe—or his friend ;
Said ' Toss down the Whistle, the prize of the field,'
And knee-deep in claret, he'd die ere he'd yield.


To the board of Glenriddel our heroes repair,
So noted for drowning of sorrow and care ;
But for wine and for welcome not more known to fame,
Than the sense, wit, and taste of a sweet lovely dame. 40


A bard was selected to witness the fray,
And tell future ages the feats of the day ;
A bard who detested all sadness and spleen,
And wish'd that Parnassus a vineyard had been.


The dinner being over, the claret they ply,
And ev'ry new cork is a new spring of joy ;
In the bands of old friendship and kindred so set,
And the bands grew the tighter the more they were wet.


Gay Pleasure ran riot as bumpers ran o'er ;
Bright Phoebus ne'er witness'd so joyous a core,          50
And vow'd that to leave them he was quite forlorn,
Till Cynthia hinted he'd see them next morn.


Six bottles a-piece had well wore out the night,
When gallant Sir Robert, to finish the fight,
Turn'd o'er in one bumper a bottle of red,
And swore 'twas the way that their ancestor did.


Then worthy Glenriddel, so cautious and sage,
No longer the warfare ungodly would wage ;
A high-ruling elder to wallow in wine !
He left the foul business to folks less divine.          60


The gallant Sir Robert fought hard to the end ;
But who can with Fate and quart bumpers contend ?
Though fate said, a hero should perish in light ;
So up rose bright Phoebus—and down fell the knight.

Next up rose our bard, like a prophet in drink :
'Craigdarroch, thou'lt soar when creation shall sink !
But if thou would flourish immortal in rhyme,
Come—one bottle more—and have at the sublime !

'Thy line, that have struggled for freedom with Bruce,
Shall heroes and patriots ever produce :                    70
So thine be the laurel, and mine be the bay !
The field thou hast won, by yon bright god of day ! '

———◆◆———

## THE KIRK'S ALARM.

Orthodox, Orthodox, wha believe in John Knox,
    Let me sound an alarm to your conscience :
There's a heretic blast has been blawn i' the wast,
    'That what is not sense must be nonsense.'

Dr. Mac, Dr. Mac, you should stretch on a rack,
    To strike evil-doers wi' terror ;
To join faith and sense upon ony pretence,
    Is heretic, damnable error.

Town of Ayr, town of Ayr, it was mad, I declare,
    To meddle wi' mischief a-brewing ;                      10
Provost John is still deaf to the church's relief,
    And orator Bob is its ruin.

D'rymple mild, D'rymple mild, tho' your heart's like a child,
    And your life like the new driven snaw,
Yet that winna save ye, auld Satan must have ye,
    For preaching that three's ane and twa.

Rumble John, Rumble John, mount the steps wi' a groan,
    Cry the book is wi' heresy cramm'd ;
Then lug out your ladle, deal brimstane like adle,
    And roar ev'ry note of the damn'd.                      20

Simper James, Simper James, leave the fair Killie dames
  There's a holier chase in your view;
I'll lay on your head, that the pack ye'll soon lead,
  For puppies like you there's but few.


Singet Sawney, Singet Sawney, are ye herding the penny,
  Unconscious what evils await?
Wi' a jump, yell, and howl, alarm every soul,
  For the foul thief is just at your gate.


Daddy Auld, Daddy Auld, there's a tod in the fauld,
  A tod meikle waur than the clerk;                          30
Tho' ye can do little skaith, ye'll be in at the death,
  And gif ye canna bite, ye may bark.


Davie Bluster, Davie Bluster, if for a saint ye do muster,
  The corps is no nice of recruits:
Yet to worth let's be just, royal blood ye might boast,
  If the ass was the king of the brutes.


Jamie Goose, Jamie Goose, ye hae made but toom roose,
  In hunting the wicked Lieutenant;
But the Doctor's your mark, for the Lord's haly ark,
  He has cooper'd and ca'd a wrang pin in 't.               40


Poet Willie, Poet Willie, gie the Doctor a volley,
  Wi' your 'liberty's chain' and your wit;
O'er Pegasus' side ye ne'er laid a stride,
  Ye but smelt, man, the place where he shit.


Andro Gouk, Andro Gouk, ye may slander the book,
  And the book no the waur, let me tell ye!
Ye are rich, and look big, but lay by hat and wig,
  And ye'll hae a calf's head o' sma' value


Barr Steenie, Barr Steenie, what mean ye? what mean ye?
  If ye'll meddle nae mair wi' the matter,                  50
Ye may hae some pretence to havins and sense,
  Wi' people wha ken ye nae better.

Irvine Side, Irvine Side, wi' your turkeycock pride,
  Of manhood but sma' is your share ;
Ye've the figure, 'tis true, even your faes will allow,
  And your friends they dare grant vou nae mair.

Muirland Jock, Muirland Jock, when the Lord makes a rock
  To crush common sense for her sins,
If ill manners were wit, there's no mortal so fit
  To confound the poor Doctor at ance.        60

Holy Will, Holy Will, there was wit i' your skull,
  When ye pilfer'd the alms o' the poor ;
The timmer is scant when ye're ta'en for a saint,
  Wha should swing in a rape for an hour.

Calvin's sons, Calvin's sons, seize your sp'ritual guns,
  Ammunition you never can need ;
Your hearts are the stuff will be powther enough,
  And your skulls are storehouses o' lead.

Poet Burns, Poet Burns, wi' your priest-skelping turns,
  Why desert ye your auld native shire?       70
Your muse is a gipsy, e'en tho' she were tipsy
  She cou'd ca' us nae waur than we are.

---

## LINES WRITTEN IN FRIARS-CARSE HERMITAGE,

### ON NITH-SIDE.

Thou whom chance may hither lead,
Be thou clad in russet weed,
Be thou deckt in silken stole,
Grave these counsels on thy soul.
  Life is but a day at most,
Sprung from night, in darkness lost ;
Hope not sunshine ev'ry hour,
Fear not clouds will always lour.

As Youth and Love, with sprightly dance,
Beneath thy morning star advance,                    10
Pleasure with her syren air
May delude the thoughtless pair;
Let Prudence bless Enjoyment's cup,
Then raptur'd sip, and sip it up.
As thy day grows warm and high,
Life's meridian flaming nigh,
Dost thou spurn the humble vale?
Life's proud summits wouldst thou scale?
Check thy climbing step, elate,
Evils lurk in felon wait:                            20
Dangers, eagle-pinioned, bold,
Soar around each cliffy hold,
While cheerful Peace, with linnet song,
Chants the lowly dells among.
As the shades of ev'ning close,
Beck'ning thee to long repose;
As life itself becomes disease,
Seek the chimney-nook of ease.
There ruminate with sober thought,
On all thou'st seen, and heard, and wrought;  30
And teach the sportive younkers round,
Saws of experience, sage and sound.
Say man's true genuine estimate,
The grand criterion of his fate,
Is not—Art thou high or low?
Did thy fortune ebb or flow?
Did many talents gild thy span?
Or frugal Nature grudge thee one?
Tell them, and press it on their mind,
As thou thyself must shortly find,                   40
The smile or frown of awful Heav'n
To Virtue or to Vice is giv'n.
Say to be just, and kind, and wise,—
There solid self-enjoyment lies;
That foolish, selfish, faithless ways
Lead to be wretched, vile, and base.
Thus resign'd and quiet, creep
To the bed of lasting sleep;
Sleep, whence thou shalt ne'er awake,
Night, where dawn shall never break               50

Till future life, future no more,
To light and joy and good restore,
To light and joy unknown before.
    Stranger, go! Heaven be thy guide!
Quod the Beadsman of Nith-side.

---

GLENRIDDEL HERMITAGE, *June* 28*th*, 1788.

FROM THE MS.

THOU whom chance may hither lead,
Be thou clad in russet weed,
Be thou deckt in silken stole,
Grave these maxims on thy soul.
    Life is but a day at most,                         60
Sprung from night, in darkness lost;
Hope not sunshine every hour,
Fear not clouds will always lour.
    Happiness is but a name,
Make content and ease thy aim;
Ambition is a meteor gleam,
Fame, an idle restless dream:
Peace, the tenderest flower of spring;
Pleasures, insects on the wing;
Those that sip the dew alone—                          70
Make the butterflies thy own;
Those that would the bloom devour—
Crush the locusts, save the flower.
    For the future be prepar'd,
Guard, wherever thou canst guard;
But thy utmost duly done,
Welcome what thou canst not shun.
Follies past give thou to air,
Make their consequence thy care:
Keep the name of Man in mind,                          80
And dishonour not thy kind.
Reverence, with lowly heart,
HIM whose wondrous work thou art:
Keep His goodness still in view,
Thy trust, and thy example too.
    Stranger, go! Heaven be thy guide!
Quod the Beadsman of Nith-side.

# THE LAMENT,

### OCCASIONED BY THE UNFORTUNATE ISSUE OF A FRIEND'S AMOUR.

O THOU pale Orb, that silent shines,
    While care-untroubled mortals sleep!
Thou seest a wretch that inly pines,
    And wanders here to wail and weep!
With woe I nightly vigils keep,
    Beneath thy wan, unwarming beam;
And mourn, in lamentation deep,
    How life and love are all a dream.

I joyless view thy rays adorn
    The faintly-markèd, distant hill:    10
I joyless view thy trembling horn,
    Reflected in the gurgling rill:
My fondly-fluttering heart, be still!
    Thou busy pow'r, Remembrance, cease!
Ah! must the agonizing thrill
    For ever bar returning peace!

No idly-feign'd poetic pains,
    My sad love-lorn lamentings claim;
No shepherd's pipe—Arcadian strains;
    No fabled tortures, quaint and tame:    20
The plighted faith, the mutual flame,
    The oft attested Pow'rs above,
The promis'd father's tender name—
    These were the pledges of my love!

Encircled in her clasping arms,
    How have the raptur'd moments flown!
How have I wish'd for fortune's charms,
    For her dear sake, and her's alone!
And must I think it! is she gone,
    My secret heart's exulting boast?    30
And does she heedless hear my groan?
    And is she ever, ever lost?

Oh! can she bear so base a heart,
    So lost to honour, lost to truth,
As from the fondest lover part,
    The plighted husband of her youth?
Alas! life's path may be unsmooth!
    Her way may lie thro' rough distress!
Then who her pangs and pains will soothe,
    Her sorrows share, and make them less?    40


Ye wingèd hours that o'er us past,
    Enraptur'd more, the more enjoy'd,
Your dear remembrance in my breast
    My fondly-treasur'd thoughts employ'd.
That breast, how dreary now, and void,
    For her too scanty once of room!
Ev'n ev'ry ray of hope destroy'd,
    And not a wish to gild the gloom!


The morn that warns th' approaching day
    Awakes me up to toil and woe:    50
I see the hours in long array,
    That I must suffer, lingering slow.
Full many a pang, and many a throe,
    Keen recollection's direful train,
Must wring my soul, ere Phoebus, low,
    Shall kiss the distant western main.


And when my nightly couch I try,
    Sore-harass'd out with care and grief,
My toil-beat nerves, and tear-worn eye,
    Keep watchings with the nightly thief:    60
Or if I slumber, Fancy, chief,
    Reigns, haggard-wild, in sore affright:
Ev'n day, all-bitter, brings relief
    From such a horror-breathing night.


O thou bright Queen, who o'er th' expanse
    Now highest reign'st, with boundless sway!
Oft has thy silent-marking glance
    Observ'd us, fondly-wand'ring, stray!

The time, unheeded, sped away,
    While love's luxurious pulse beat high,          70
Beneath thy silver-gleaming ray,
    To mark the mutual-kindling eye.

O scenes in strong remembrance set!
    Scenes never, never to return!
Scenes, if in stupor I forget,
    Again I feel, again I burn!
From ev'ry joy and pleasure torn,
    Life's weary vale I'll wander thro';
And hopeless, comfortless, I'll mourn
    A faithless woman's broken vow.          80

———◆◆———

## DESPONDENCY.

OPPRESS'D with grief, oppress'd with care,
A burden more than I can bear,
    I set me down and sigh;
O life! thou art a galling load,
Along a rough, a weary road,
    To wretches such as I!
Dim-backward as I cast my view,
    What sick'ning scenes appear!
What sorrows yet may pierce me thro',
    Too justly I may fear!          10
        Still caring, despairing,
            Must be my bitter doom;
        My woes here shall close ne'er,
            But with the closing tomb!

Happy, ye sons of busy life,
Who, equal to the bustling strife,
    No other view regard!
Ev'n when the wishèd end's denied,
Yet, while the busy means are plied,
    They bring their own reward:          20

Whilst I, a hope-abandon'd wight,
    Unfitted with an aim,
Meet ev'ry sad returning night,
    And joyless morn the same ;
        You, bustling, and justling,
            Forget each grief and pain ;
        I, listless, yet restless,
            Find every prospect vain.

How blest the Solitary's lot,
Who, all-forgetting, all-forgot,                    30
    Within his humble cell,
The cavern wild with tangling roots,
Sits o'er his newly-gather'd fruits,
    Beside his crystal well ?
Or, haply, to his ev'ning thought,
    By unfrequented stream,
The ways of men are distant brought,
    A faint collected dream :
        While praising, and raising
            His thoughts to Heav'n on high,    40
        As wand'ring, meand'ring,
            He views the solemn sky.

Than I, no lonely hermit plac'd
Where never human footstep trac'd,
    Less fit to play the part ;
The lucky moment to improve,
And just to stop and just to move,
    With self-respecting art :
But ah ! those pleasures, loves, and joys,
    Which I too keenly taste,                      50
The Solitary can despise,
    Can want, and yet be blest !
        He needs not, he heeds not,
            Or human love or hate,
        Whilst I here must cry here
            At perfidy ingrate !

Oh ! enviable, early days,
When dancing thoughtless pleasure's maze,
    To care, to guilt unknown !

How ill exchang'd for riper times,                    60
To see the follies, or the crimes,
    Of others, or my own!
Ye tiny elves that guiltless sport,
    Like linnets in the bush,
Ye little know the ills ye court,
    When manhood is your wish!
        The losses, the crosses,
            That active man engage!
        The fears all, the tears all,
            Of dim-declining age.                      70

## WILLIE CHALMERS.

Wi' braw new branks in mickle pride,
    And eke a braw new brechan,
My Pegasus I'm got astride,
    And up Parnassus pechin';
Whiles owre a bush wi' downward crush,
    The doited beastie stammers;
Then up he gets, and off he sets
    For sake o' Willie Chalmers.

I doubt na, lass, that weel kenn'd name
    May cost a pair o' blushes;                        10
I am nae stranger to your fame
    Nor his warm urgèd wishes.
Your bonnie face sae mild and sweet,
    His honest heart enamours,
And faith ye'll no be lost a whit,
    Tho' waired on Willie Chalmers.

Auld Truth hersel might swear ye're fair,
    Aud Honour safely back her,
And Modesty assume your air,
    And ne'er a ane mistak' her:                       20
And sic twa love-inspiring een
    Might fire even holy palmers;
Nae wonder then they've fatal been
    To honest Willie Chalmers.

I doubt na fortune may you shore
 Some mim-mou'd pouther'd priestie,
Fu' lifted up wi' Hebrew lore,
 And band upon his breastie :
But oh ! what signifies to you,
 His lexicons and grammars ;                    30
The feeling heart's the royal blue,
 And that's wi' Willie Chalmers.


Some gapin' glowrin' country laird
 May warsle for your favour ;
May claw his lug, and straik his beard,
 And host up some palaver.
My bonnie maid, before ye wed
 Sic clumsy-witted hammers,
Seek Heaven for help, and barefit skelp
 Awa' wi' Willie Chalmers.                      40


Forgive the Bard ! my fond regard
 For ane that shares my bosom
Inspires my muse to gie 'm his dues,
 For de'il a hair I roose him.
May powers aboon unite you soon,
 And fructify your amours,
And every year come in mair dear
 To you and Willie Chalmers.


——◆◆——


## A BARD'S EPITAPH.

Is there a whim-inspirèd fool,
Owre fast for thought, owre hot for rule,
Owre blate to seek, owre proud to snool,
          Let him draw near ;
And owre this grassy heap sing dool,
          And drap a tear.

Is there a bard of rustic song,
Who, noteless, steals the crowds among,
That weekly this area throng,
            O, pass not by!                10
But, with a frater-feeling strong,
            Here heave a sigh.


Is there a man whose judgment clear,
Can others teach the course to steer,
Yet runs, himself, life's mad career,
            Wild as the wave;
Here pause—and, thro' the starting tear,
            Survey this grave.


The poor inhabitant below
Was quick to learn and wise to know,       20
And keenly felt the friendly glow,
            And softer flame;
But thoughtless follies laid him low,
            And stain'd his name!


Reader, attend! whether thy soul
Soars fancy's flights beyond the pole,
Or darkling grubs this earthly hole,
            In low pursuit;
Know prudent cautious self-control
            Is wisdom's root.                30

—————*•—————

## EPISTLE TO JOHN RANKINE.

O ROUGH, rude, ready-witted Rankine,
The wale o' cocks for fun and drinkin'!
There's mony godly folks are thinkin'
            Your dreams an' tricks
Will send you, Korah-like a-sinkin',
            Straught to auld Nick's.

Ye hae sae mony cracks an' cants,
And in your wicked, drucken rants,
Ye mak a devil o' the saunts,
   An' fill them fou ;    10
And then their failings, flaws, an' wants,
   Are a' seen thro'.

Hypocrisy, in mercy spare it !
That holy robe, O dinna tear it !
Spare 't for their sakes wha aften wear it,
   The lads in black ;
But your curst wit, when it comes near it,
   Rives 't aff their back.

Think, wicked sinner, wha ye're skaithing,
It 's just the blue-gown badge an' claithing   20
O' saunts ; tak that, ye lea'e them naithing
   To ken them by,
Frae ony unregenerate heathen
   Like you or I.

I've sent you here some rhyming ware,
A' that I bargain'd for, an' mair ;
Sae, when ye hae an hour to spare,
   I will expect
Yon sang ; ye'll sen't, wi' cannie care,
   And no neglect.    30

Tho', faith, sma' heart hae I to sing !
My Muse dow scarcely spread her wing !
I've play'd mysel a bonnie spring,
   An' danc'd my fill !
I'd better gane an' sair'd the king
   At Bunker's Hill.

'Twas ae night lately, in my fun,
I gaed a roving wi' the gun,
An' brought a paitrick to the grun',
   A bonnie hen ;    40
And, as the twilight was begun,
   Thought nane would ken.

The poor wee thing was little hurt;
I straikit it a wee for sport,
Ne'er thinkin they wad fash me for't;
   But, Deil-may-care!
Somebody tells the poacher-court
   The hale affair.

Some auld us'd hands had ta'en a note,
That sic a hen had got a shot;   50
I was suspected for the plot;
   I scorn'd to lie;
So gat the whissle o' my groat,
   An' pay't the fee.

But, by my gun, o' guns the wale,
An' by my pouther an' my hail,
An' by my hen, an' by her tail,
   I vow an' swear!
The game shall pay, o'er moor an' dale,
   For this, niest year. 60

As soon 's the clockin'-time is by,
An' the wee pouts begun to cry,
Lord, I'se hae sportin by an' by,
   For my gowd guinea;
Tho' I should herd the buckskin kye
   For't, in Virginia.

Trowth, they had muckle for to blame!
'Twas neither broken wing nor limb,
But twa-three draps about the wame
   Scarce thro' the feathers; 70
An' baith a yellow George to claim,
   An' thole their blethers!

It pits me aye as mad 's a hare;
So I can rhyme nor write nae mair;
But pennyworths again is fair,
   When time 's expedient:
Meanwhile I am, respected Sir,
   Your most obedient.

## EPISTLE TO DAVIE, A BROTHER POET.

WHILE winds frae aff Ben-Lomond blaw,
And bar the doors wi' driving snaw,
  And hing us owre the ingle,
I set me down, to pass the time,
And spin a verse or twa o' rhyme,
  In hamely westlin jingle.
While frosty winds blaw in the drift,
  Ben to the chimla lug,
`I grudge a wee the great-folk's gift,
  That live sae bien an' snug ;                    10
    I tent less, and want less
      Their roomy fire-side ;
    But hanker and canker
      To see their cursèd pride.


It 's hardly in a body's pow'r,
To keep, at times, frae being sour,
  To see how things are shar'd ;
How best o' chiels are whyles in want,
While coofs on countless thousands rant,
  And ken na how to wair 't :                      20
But, Davie, lad, ne'er fash your head,
  Tho' we hae little gear,
We're fit to win our daily bread,
  As lang 's we're hale and fier :
    ' Mair spier na, nor fear na,'
      Auld age ne'er mind a feg ;
    The last o't, the warst o't,
      Is only but to beg.


To lie in kilns and barns at e'en,
When banes are craz'd, and bluid is thin,          30
  Is, doubtless, great distress !

Yet then content could mak us blest;
Ev'n then, sometimes, we'd snatch a taste
    Of truest happiness.
The honest heart that's free frae a'
    Intended fraud or guile,
However fortune kick the ba',
    Has aye some cause to smile:
        And mind still, you'll find still,
            A comfort this nae sma';
        Nae mair then, we'll care then,
            Nae farther can we fa'.


What tho', like commoners of air,
We wander out, we know not where,
    But either house or hal'?
Yet nature's charms, the hills and woods,
The sweeping vales, and foaming floods,
    Are free alike to all.
In days when daisies deck the ground,
    And blackbirds whistle clear,
With honest joy our hearts will bound,
    To see the coming year:
        On braes when we please, then,
            We'll sit and sowth a tune;
        Syne rhyme till't, we'll time till't,
            And sing't when we hae done.


It's no in titles nor in rank;
It's no in wealth like Lon'on bank,
    To purchase peace and rest;
It's no in making muckle, mair:
It's no in books, it's no in lear,
    To make us truly blest:
If happiness hae not her seat
    And centre in the breast,
We may be wise, or rich, or great,
    But never can be blest:
        Nae treasures, nor pleasures,
            Could make us happy lang;
        The heart aye's the part aye
            That makes us right or wrang.

40

50

60

70

Think ye, that sic as you and I,
Wha drudge and drive thro' wet an' dry,
  Wi' never-ceasing toil;
Think ye, are we less blest than they,
Wha scarcely tent us in their way,
  As hardly worth their while?
Alas! how oft in haughty mood,
  God's creatures they oppress!
Or else, neglecting a' that's guid,
  They riot in excess!           80
    Baith careless, and fearless,
      Of either heav'n or hell!
    Esteeming, and deeming
      It's a' an idle tale!


Then let us cheerfu' acquiesce;
Nor make our scanty pleasures less,
  By pining at our state;
And, even should misfortunes come,
I, here wha sit, hae met wi' some,
  An's thankfu' for them yet.      90
They gie the wit of age to youth;
  They let us ken oursel;
They mak us see the naked truth,
  The real guid and ill.
    Tho' losses, and crosses,
      Be lessons right severe,
    There's wit there, ye'll get there,
      Ye'll find nae other where.


But tent me, Davie, ace o' hearts!
(To say aught less wad wrang the cartes,    100
  And flatt'ry I detest)
This life has joys for you and I;
And joys that riches ne'er could buy;
  And joys the very best.
There's a' the pleasures o' the heart,
  The lover an' the frien';
Ye hae your Meg, your dearest part,
  And I my darling Jean!

It warms me, it charms me,
    To mention but her name:            110
It heats me, it beets me,
    And sets me a' on flame!


O all ye pow'rs who rule above!
O Thou, whose very self art love!
    Thou know'st my words sincere!
The life-blood streaming thro' my heart,
Or my more dear immortal part,
    Is not more fondly dear!
When heart-corroding care and grief
    Deprive my soul of rest,            120
Her dear idea brings relief
    And solace to my breast.
        Thou Being, All-seeing,
            O hear my fervent pray'r;
        Still take her, and make her
            Thy most peculiar care!


All hail, ye tender feelings dear!
The smile of love, the friendly tear,
    The sympathetic glow!
Long since this world's thorny ways      130
Had number'd out my weary days,
    Had it not been for you!
Fate still has blest me with a friend,
    In every care and ill;
And oft a more endearing band,
    A tie more tender still.
        It lightens, it brightens
            The tenebrific scene,
        To meet with, and greet with
            My Davie or my Jean.         140


O, how that name inspires my style!
The words come skelpin', rank and file,
    Amaist before I ken!
The ready measure rins as fine,
As Phoebus and the famous Nine
    Were glowrin' owre my pen.

My spavied Pegasus will limp,
     Till ance he's fairly het;
And then he'll hilch, and stilt, and jimp,
     An' rin an unco fit:                              150
          But lest then the beast then
               Should rue this hasty ride,
          I'll light now, and dight now
               His sweaty wizen'd hide.

-----

## SECOND EPISTLE TO DAVIE.

AULD NEIBOR,

I'M three times doubly o'er your debtor,
For your auld-farrant, frien'ly letter;
Tho' I maun say't, I doubt ye flatter,
          Ye speak sae fair;
For my puir. silly, rhymin' clatter
          Some less maun sair.

Hale be your heart, hale be your fiddle;
Lang may your elbuck jink and diddle,
To cheer you through the weary widdle
          O' war'ly cares,                              10
Till bairns' bairns kindly cuddle
          Your auld gray hairs.

But Davie, lad, I'm red ye're glaikit;
I'm tauld the Muse ye hae negleckit;
An' gif it's sae, ye sud be lickit
          Until ye fyke;
Sic hauns as you sud ne'er be faikit,
          Be hain't wha like.

For me, I'm on Parnassus' brink,
Rivin' the words to gar them clink;                    20
Whyles dazed wi' love, whyles dazed wi' drink,
          Wi' jads or masons;
An' whyles, but aye owre late, I think
          Braw sober lessons.

Of a' the thoughtless sons o' man,
Commend me to the Bardie clan;
Except it be some idle plan
      O' rhymin' clink,
The devil-haet, that I sud ban,
      They ever think.      30

Nae thought, nae view, nae scheme o' livin',
Nae cares to gie us joy or grievin';
But just the pouchie put the nieve in,
      An' while ought's there,
Then hiltie skiltie, we gae scrievin',
      An' fash nae mair.

Leeze me on rhyme! it's aye a treasure,
My chief, amaist my only pleasure;
At hame, a-fiel', at wark, or leisure,
      The Muse, poor hizzie!      40
Tho' rough an' raploch be her measure,
      She's seldom lazy.

Haud to the Muse, my dainty Davie:
The warl' may play you mony a shavie;
But for the Muse, she'll never leave ye,
      Tho' e'er sae puir,
Na, even tho' limpin' wi' the spavie
      Frae door to door.

---

# EPISTLE TO JOHN LAPRAIK, AN OLD
# SCOTTISH BARD.

While briors an' woodbines budding green,
An' paitricks scraichin' loud at e'en,
An' morning poussie whiddin' seen,
      Inspire my Muse,
This freedom, in an unknown frien',
      I pray excuse.

On Fasten-een we had a rockin',
To ca' the crack and weave our stockin';
And there was muckle fun and jokin',
            Ye need na doubt;                          10
At length we had a hearty yokin'
            At sang about.


There was ae sang, amang the rest,
Aboon them a' it pleas'd me best,
That some kind husband had addrest
            To some sweet wife:
It thirl'd the heart-strings thro' the breast,
            A' to the life.


I've scarce heard ought describ'd sae weel,
What gen'rous, manly bosoms feel;                       20
Thought I 'Can this be Pope, or Steele,
            Or Beattie's wark!'
They tauld me 'twas an odd kind chiel
            About Muirkirk.


It pat me fidgin' fain to hear 't,
And sae about him there I spier'd;
Then a' that kenn'd him round declar'd
            He had ingine,
That nane excell'd it, few cam near 't,
            It was sae fine.                            30


That, set him to a pint of ale,
An' either douce or merry tale,
Or rhymes an' sangs he'd made himsel,
            Or witty catches,
'Tween Inverness and Teviotdale,
            He had few matches.


Then up I gat, an' swoor an aith,
Tho' I should pawn my pleugh and graith,
Or die a cadger pownie's death,
            At some dyke-back,                          40
A pint an' gill I'd gie them baith
            To hear your crack.

But, first an' foremost, I should tell,
Amaist as soon as I could spell,
I to the crambo-jingle fell;
   Tho' rude an' rough,
Yet crooning to a body's sel,
   Does weel eneugh.


I am nae poet, in a sense,
But just a rhymer, like, by chance,   50
An' hae to learning nae pretence,
   Yet what the matter?
Whene'er my Muse does on me glance,
   I jingle at her.


Your critic-folk may cock their nose,
And say 'How can you e'er propose,
You wha ken hardly verse frae prose,
   To mak a sang?'
But, by your leaves, my learnèd foes,
   Ye're maybe wrang.   60


What's a' your jargon o' your schools,
Your Latin names for horns an' stools;
If honest nature made you fools,
   What sairs your grammars?
Ye'd better ta'en up spades and shools,
   Or knappin'-hammers.


A set o' dull conceited hashes
Confuse their brains in college classes!
They gang in stirks, and come out asses,
   Plain truth to speak;   70
An' syne they think to climb Parnassus
   By dint o' Greek!


Gie me ae spark o' Nature's fire,
That's a' the learning I desire;
Then tho' I drudge thro' dub an' mire
   At pleugh or cart,
My Muse, though hamely in attire,
   May touch the heart.

O for a spunk o' Allan's glee,
Or Fergusson's, the bauld an' slee,
Or bright Lapraik's, my friend to be,  80
    If I can hit it!
That would be lear eneugh for me,
    If I could get it.

Now, sir, if ye hae friends enow,
Tho' real friends, I b'lieve, are few,
Yet, if your catalogue be fou,
    I'se no insist,
But gif ye want ae friend that's true,
    I'm on your list.  90

I winna blaw about mysel,
As ill I like my fauts to tell;
But friends, an' folks that wish me well,
    They sometimes roose me;
Tho' I maun own, as mony still
    As far abuse me.

There's ae wee faut they whiles lay to me,
I like the lasses—Gude forgie me!
For mony a plack they wheedle frae me,
    At dance or fair;  100
Maybe some ither thing they gie me
    They weel can spare.

But Mauchline race, or Mauchline fair,
I should be proud to meet you there;
We'se gie ae night's discharge to care,
    If we forgather,
An' hae a swap o' rhymin'-ware
    Wi' ane anither.

The four-gill chap, we'se gar him clatter,
An' kirsen him wi' reekin water;  110
Syne we'll sit down an' tak our whitter,
    To cheer our heart;
An' faith, we'se be acquainted better
    Before we part.

Awa, ye selfish warly race,
Wha think that havins, sense, an' grace,
Ev'n love an' friendship, should give place
          To catch-the-plack !
I dinna like to see your face,
          Nor hear your crack.                    120

But ye whom social pleasure charms,
Whose hearts the tide of kindness warms,
Who hold your being on the terms,
          ' Each aid the others,'
Come to my bowl, come to my arms,
          My friends, my brothers !

But to conclude my lang epistle,
As my auld pen 's worn to the gristle ;
Twa lines frae you wad gar me fissle,
          Who am, most fervent,                   130
While I can either sing, or whistle,
          Your friend and servant.

———— ••  ————

## TO THE SAME.

WHILE new-ca'd kye rowte at the stake,
An' pownies reek in pleugh or braik,
This hour on e'enin's edge I take,
          To own I'm debtor,
To honest-hearted auld Lapraik,
          For his kind letter.

Forjeskit sair, with woary legs,
Rattlin' the corn out-owre the rigs,
Or dealing thro' amang the naigs
          Their ten-hours' bite,                  10
My awkwart Muse sair pleads and begs
          I would na write.

The tapetless, ramfeezl'd hizzie,
She's saft at best, and something lazy,
Quo' she 'Ye ken we've been sae busy,
   This month an' mair,
That trouth my head is grown quite dizzie,
   An' something sair.'


Her dowff excuses pat me mad;
'Conscience,' says I, 'ye thowless jad!  20
I'll write, an' that a hearty blaud,
   This very night;
So dinna ye affront your trade,
   But rhyme it right.


'Shall bauld Lapraik, the king o' hearts,
Tho' mankind were a pack o' cartes,
Roose you sae weel for your deserts,
   In terms sae friendly,
Yet ye'll neglect to shaw your parts,
   An' thank him kindly?'  30


Sae I gat paper in a blink,
An' down gaed stumpie in the ink:
Quoth I 'Before I sleep a wink,
   I vow I'll close it;
An if ye winna mak it clink,
   By Jove, I'll prose it!'


Sae I've begun to scrawl, but whether
In rhyme, or prose, or baith thegither,
Or some hotch-potch that's rightly neither,
   Let time mak proof;  40
But I shall scribble down some blether
   Just clean aff-loof.


My worthy friend, ne'er grudge an' carp,
Tho' fortune use you hard an' sharp;
Come, kittle up your moorland harp
   Wi' gleesome touch!
Ne'er mind how fortune waft an' warp;
   She's but a bitch.

She's gien me mony a jirt an' fleg,
Sin' I could striddle owre a rig;                        50
But, by the Lord, tho' I should beg
            Wi' lyart pow,
I'll laugh, an' sing, an' shake my leg,
            As lang's I dow!


Now comes the sax-an'-twentieth simmer
I've seen the bud upo' the timmer,
Still persecuted by the limmer,
            Frae year to year:
But yet, despite the kittle kimmer,
            I, Rob, am here.                             60


Do ye envy the city gent,
Behind a kist to lie an' sklent,
Or purse-proud, big wi' cent per cent
            An' muckle wame,
In some bit brugh to represent
            A bailie's name?


Or is't the paughty feudal thane,
Wi' ruffl'd sark an' glancing cane,
Wha thinks himsel nae sheep-shank bane,
            But lordly stalks,                          70
While caps and bonnets aff are taen,
            As by he walks?


'O Thou wha gies us each guid gift!
Gie me o' wit an' sense a lift,
Then turn me, if Thou please, adrift,
            Thro' Scotland wide;
Wi' cits nor lairds I wadna shift,
            In a' their pride!'


Were this the charter of our state,
'On pain o' hell be rich an' great,'                     80
Damnation then would be our fate,
            Beyond remead;
But, thanks to Heaven! that's no the gate
            We learn our creed.

For thus the royal mandate ran,
When first the human race began,
'The social, friendly, honest man,
    Whate'er he be,
'Tis he fulfils great Nature's plan,
    And none but he!'       90

O mandate glorious and divine!
The followers of the ragged Nine,
Poor, thoughtless devils! yet may shine,
    In glorious light,
While sordid sons of Mammon's line
    Are dark as night.

Tho' here they scrape, an' squeeze, an' growl,
Their worthless nievefu' of a soul
May in some future carcase howl,
    The forest's fright;      100
Or in some day-detesting owl
    May shun the light.

Then may Lapraik and Burns arise,
To reach their native kindred skies,
And sing their pleasures, hopes, an' joys,
    In some mild sphere,
Still closer knit in friendship's ties
    Each passing year!

## TO WILLIAM SIMPSON.

I GAT your letter, winsome Willie;
Wi' gratefu' heart I thank you brawlie;
Tho' I maun say't, I wad be silly,
    An' unco vain,
Should I believe, my coaxin' billie,
    Your flatterin' strain.

But I'se believe ye kindly meant it :
I sud be laith to think ye hinted
Ironic satire, sidelins sklented
        On my poor Musie ;       10
Tho' in sic phraisin' terms ye've penn'd it,
        I scarce excuse ye.

My senses wad be in a creel,
Should I but dare a hope to speel,
Wi' Allan, or wi' Gilbertfield,
        The braes o' fame ;
Or Fergusson, the writer-chiel,
        A deathless name.

(O Fergusson ! thy glorious parts
Ill suited law's dry, musty arts !       20
My curse upon your whunstane hearts,
        Ye E'nbrugh gentry !
The tythe o' what ye waste at cartes
        Wad stow'd his pantry !)

Yet when a tale comes i' my head,
Or lasses gie my heart a screed,
As whiles they're like to be my dead,
        (O sad disease !)
I kittle up my rustic rced ;
        It gies me ease.       30

Auld Coila, now, may fidge fu' fain,
She 's gotten poets o' her ain,
Chiels wha their chanters winna hain,
        But tune their lays,
Till echoes a' resound again
        Her weel-sung praise.

Nae poet thought her worth his while,
To set her name in measur'd style ;
She lay like some unkenn'd-of isle,
        Beside New Holland,       4c
Or where wild-meeting oceans boil
        Besouth Magellan.

Ramsay an' famous Fergusson
Gied Forth an' Tay a lift aboon;
Yarrow an' Tweed, to mony a tune,
  Owre Scotland rings,
While Irwin, Lugar, Ayr, an' Doon,
  Naebody sings.

Th' Ilissus, Tiber, Thames, an' Seine,
Glide sweet in mony a tunefu' line;
But, Willie, set your fit to mine,     50
  An' cock your crest,
We'll gar our streams an' burnies shine
  Up wi' the best.

We'll sing auld Coila's plains an' fells,
Her moors red-brown wi' heather bells,
Her banks an' braes, her dens an' dells,
  Where glorious Wallace
Aft bure the gree, as story tells,
  Frae Southron billies.     60

At Wallace' name, what Scottish blood
But boils up in a spring-tide flood!
Oft have our fearless fathers strode
  By Wallace' side,
Still pressing onward, red-wat-shod,
  Or glorious died.

O, sweet are Coila's haughs an' woods,
When lintwhites chant amang the buds,
And jinkin' hares, in amorous whids,
  Their loves enjoy,     70
While thro' the braes the cushat croods
  Wi' wailfu' cry!

Ev'n winter bleak has charms to me
When winds rave thro' the naked tree;
Or frost on hills of Ochiltree
  Are hoary gray;
Or blinding drifts wild-furious flee,
  Dark'ning the day!

O Nature! a' thy shews an' forms
To feeling, pensive hearts hae charms!          80
Whether the summer kindly warms,
          Wi' life an' light,
Or winter howls, in gusty storms,
          The lang, dark night!

The Muse, nae poet ever fand her,
Till by himsel he learn'd to wander
Adown some trottin' burn's meander,
          An' no think lang;
O sweet, to stray an' pensive ponder
          A heart-felt sang!          90

The warly race may drudge an' drive,
Hog-shouther, jundie, stretch, an' strive;
Let me fair Nature's face descrive,
          And I, wi' pleasure,
Shall let the busy, grumbling hive
          Bum owre their treasure.

Fareweel, 'my rhyme-composing brither!'
We've been owre lang unkenn'd to ither:
Now let us lay our heads thegither,
          In love fraternal;          100
May Envy wallop in a tether,
          Black fiend infernal!

While Highlandmen hate tolls an' taxes;
While moorlan' herds like guid fat braxies
While Terra Firma, on her axis,
          Diurnal turns,
Count on a friend, in faith an' practice,
          In Robert Burns.

#### POSTCRIPT.

My memory's no worth a preen;
I had amaist forgotten clean,          110
Ye bade me write you what they mean
          By this New-Light,
'Bout which our herds sae aft have been
          Maist like to fight.

In days when mankind were but callans
At grammar, logic, an' sic talents,
They took nae pains their speech to balance,
          Or rules to gie,
But spak their thoughts in plain, braid Lallans,
          Like you or me.          120

In thae auld times, they thought the moon,
Just like a sark, or pair o' shoon,
Wore by degrees, till her last roon,
          Gaed past their viewin',
An' shortly after she was done,
          They gat a new one.

This past for certain, undisputed ;
It ne'er cam i' their heads to doubt it,
Till chiels gat up an' wad confute it,
          An' ca'd it wrang ;          130
An' muckle din there was about it,
          Baith loud an' lang.

Some herds, weel learn'd upo' the beuk,
Wad threap auld folk the thing misteuk ;
For 'twas the auld moon turn'd a neuk,
          An' out o' sight,
An' backlins-comin, to the leuk,
          She grew mair bright.

This was deny'd, it was affirm'd ;
The herds an' hissels were alarm'd :          140
The rev'rend gray-beards rav'd an' storm'd,
          That beardless laddies
Should think they better were inform'd
          Than their auld daddies.

Frae less to mair it gaed to sticks ;
Frae words an' aiths to clours an' nicks ;
An' mony a fallow gat his licks,
          Wi' hearty crunt ;
An' some, to learn them for their tricks,
          Were hang'd an' brunt.          150

This game was play'd in mony lands,
An' auld-light caddies bure sic hands,
That, faith, the youngsters took the sands
        Wi' nimble shanks ;
The lairds forbad, by strict commands,
        Sic bluidy pranks.


But new-light herds gat sic a cowe,
Folk thought them ruin'd stick-an-stowe,
Till now amaist on ev'ry knowe
        Ye'll find ane plac'd ;          160
An' some, their new-light fair avow,
        Just quite barefac'd.


Nae doubt the auld-light flocks are bleatin' ;
Their zealous herds are vex'd an' sweatin' ;
Mysel, I've even seen them greetin'
        Wi' girnin spite,
To hear the moon sae sadly lied on
        By word an' write.


But shortly they will cowe the louns !
Some auld-light herds in neibor-touns          170
Are mind't, in things they ca' balloons,
        To tak a flight,
An' stay ae month amang the moons,
        An' see them right.


Guid observation they will gie them ;
An' when the auld moon 's gaun to lea'e them ;
The hindmost shaird, they'll fetch it wi' them,
        Just i' their pouch,
An' when the new-light billies see them,
        I think they'll crouch !          180


Sae, ye observe that a' this clatter
Is naething but a ' moonshine matter ' ;
But tho' dull-prose folk Latin splatter
        In logic tulzie,
I hope we bardies ken some better
        Than mind sic brulzie.

# LETTER TO JOHN GOUDIE, KILMARNOCK,

## ON THE PUBLICATION OF HIS ESSAYS.

O GOUDIE ! terror of the Whigs,
Dread o' blackcoats and rev'rend wigs,
Sour Bigotry, on her last legs,
      Girnin' looks back,
Wishin' the ten Egyptian plagues
      Wad seize you quick.

Poor gapin', glowrin' Superstition,
Wae 's me ! she 's in a sad condition ;
Fy, bring Black-Jock, her state physician,
      To see her water ;      10
Alas ! there 's ground for great suspicion
      She'll ne'er get better.

Auld Orthodoxy lang did grapple,
But now she 's got an unco' ripple ;
Haste, gie her name up i' the chapel,
      Nigh unto death ;
See how she fetches at the thrapple,
      An' gasps for breath.

Enthusiasm 's past redemption,
Gane in a galloping consumption ;      20
Not a' the quacks, with a' their gumption,
      Will ever mend her ;
Her feeble pulse gies strong presumption,
      Death soon will end her.

'Tis you and Taylor are the chief,
Wha are to blame for this mischief ;
But gin the Lord's ain folk get leave,
      A toom tar-barrel
An' twa red peats wad send relief,
      An' end the quarrel.      30

For me, my skill's but very sma',
An' skill in prose I've nane ava,
But, quietlins-wise, between us twa,
      Weel may ye speed !
An', tho' they sud you sair misca',
      Ne'er fash your head.

E'en swinge the dogs, an' thresh them siccar ;
The mair they squeal, aye chap the thicker ;
An' still, 'mang hands, a hearty bicker
      O' something stout ;—       40
It gars an author's pulse beat quicker,
      An' helps his wit !

There's naething like the honest nappy !
Where will ye e'er see men sae happy,
Or women sousy, saft, an' sappy,
      'Tween morn an' morn,
As them wha like to taste the drappie
      In glass or horn ?

I've seen me dazed upon a time,
I scarce cou'd wink or see a styme ;       50
Just ae half-mutchkin does me prime
      (Ought less is little) ;
Then back I rattle on the rhyme
      As gleg's a whittle !

—··—

## THIRD EPISTLE TO J. LAPRAIK.

Guid speed an' furder to you, Johnny,
Guid health, hale han's, and weather bonnie ;
Now when ye're nickin' down fu' cannie
      The staff o' bread,
May ye ne'er want a stoup o' bran'y
      To clear your head.

May Boreas never thresh your rigs,
Nor kick your rickles aff their legs,
Sendin' the stuff o'er muirs an' hags
          Like drivin' wrack ;                        10
But may the tapmast grain that wags
          Come to the sack.


I'm bizzie too, an' skelpin' at it,
But bitter, daudin showers hae wat it ;
Sae my auld stumpie pen I gat it
          Wi' muckle wark,
An' took my jocteleg an' whatt it,
          Like ony clerk.


It's now twa month that I'm your debtor,
For your braw, nameless, dateless letter,        20
Abusin' me for harsh ill-nature
          On holy men,
While Deil a hair yoursel ye're better,
          But mair profane.


But let the kirk-folk ring their bells.
Let's sing about our noble sels ;
We'll cry nae jads frae heathen hills
          To help, or roose us,
But browster wives an' whisky stills,
          They are the Muses.                          30


Your friendship, sir, I winna quat it,
An' if ye make objections at it,
Then han' in nieve some day we'll knot it,
          An' witness take,
An' when wi' usquebae we've wat it
          It winna break.


But if the beast and branks be spar'd
Till kye be gaun without the herd,
An' a' the vittel in the yard,
          An' theekit right,                           40
I mean your ingle-side to guard
          Ae winter night.

Then muse-inspirin' aqua-vitae
Shall make us baith sae blithe an' witty,
Till ye forget ye're auld an' gatty,
    An' be as canty
As ye were nine years less than thretty,—
    Sweet ane an' twenty!

But stooks are cowpit wi' the blast,
An' now the sinn keeks in the west,     50
Then I maun rin amang the rest
    An' quit my chanter;
Sae I subscribe mysel in haste,
    Yours, Rab the Ranter.

———••———

## TO THE REV. JOHN M'MATH.

ENCLOSING A COPY OF HOLY WILLIE'S PRAYER, WHICH HE
HAD REQUESTED.

WHILE at the stook the shearers cow'r
To shun the bitter blaudin' show'r,
Or in gulravage rinnin' scour;
    To pass the time,
To you I dedicate the hour
    In idle rhyme.

My Musie, tir'd wi' mony a sonnet
On gown, an' ban', an' douce black bonnet,
Is grown right eerie now she's done it,
    Lest they shou'd blame her,    10
An' rouse their holy thunder on it,
    And anathem her.

I own 'twas rash, an' rather hardy,
That I, a simple country bardie,
Shou'd meddle wi' a pack so sturdy,
    Wha, if they ken me,
Can easy, wi' a single wordie,
    Lowse hell upon me.

But I gae mad at their grimaces,
Their sighin', cantin', grace-proud faces,                    20
Their three-mile prayers, and half-mile graces,
        Their raxin' conscience,
Whase greed, revenge, an' pride disgraces
        Waur nor their nonsense.


There's Gawn, misca't waur than a beast,
Wha has mair honour in his breast
Than mony scores as guid's the priest
        Wha sae abus'd him:
An' may a bard no crack his jest
        What way they've used him?       30


See him the poor man's friend in need,
The gentleman in word an' deed,
An' shall his fame an' honour bleed
        By worthless skellums,
An' not a Muse erect her head
        To cowe the blellums?


O Pope, had I thy satire's darts
To gie the rascals their deserts,
I'd rip their rotten, hollow hearts,
        An' tell aloud                    40
Their jugglin' hocus-pocus arts
        To cheat the crowd.


God knows I'm no the thing I shou'd be,
Nor am I even the thing I could be,
But, twenty times, I rather would be
        An atheist clean,
Than under gospel colours hid be,
        Just for a screen.


An honest man may like a glass,
An honest man may like a lass,                    50
But mean revenge, an' malice fause,
        He'll still disdain,
An' then cry zeal for gospel laws,
        Like some we ken.

They tak religion in their mouth;
They talk o' mercy, grace, an' truth,
For what? to gie their malice skouth
        On some puir wight,
An' hunt him down, o'er right an' ruth,
           To ruin straight.      60


All hail, Religion, maid divine!
Pardon a muse sae mean as mine,
Who in her rough imperfect line
        Thus daurs to name thee;
To stigmatize false friends of thine
        Can ne'er defame thee.


Tho' blotcht an' foul wi' mony a stain,
An' far unworthy of thy train,
Wi' trembling voice I tune my strain
        To join wi' those,      70
Who boldly daur thy cause maintain
        In spite o' foes:


In spite o' crowds, in spite o' mobs,
In spite of undermining jobs,
In spite o' dark banditti stabs
        At worth an' merit,
By scoundrels, even wi' holy robes,
        But hellish spirit.


O Ayr, my dear, my native ground!
Within thy presbyterial bound,      80
A candid lib'ral band is found
        Of public teachers,
As men, as Christians too, renown'd,
        An' manly preachers.


Sir, in that circle you are nam'd;
Sir, in that circle you are fam'd;
An' some, by whom your doctrine 's blam'd,
        (Which gies you honour)-
Even, sir, by them your heart 's esteem'd,
        An' winning manner.      90

Pardon this freedom I have ta'en,
An' if impertinent I've been,
Impute it not, good sir, in ane
          Whase heart ne'er wrang'd ye,
But to his utmost would befriend
          Ought that belang'd ye.

            —◆—

## TO JAMES SMITH.

DEAR Smith, the sleeest pawkie thief
That e'er attempted stealth or rief,
Ye surely hae some warlock-breef
          Owre human hearts;
For ne'er a bosom yet was prief
          Against your arts.

For me, I swear by sun an' moon,
And ev'ry star that blinks aboon,
Ye've cost me twenty pair o' shoon
          Just gaun to see you;      10
And ev'ry ither pair that's done,
          Mair taen I'm wi' you.

That auld capricious carlin', Nature,
To mak amends for scrimpit stature,
She's turn'd you aff, a human creature
          On her first plan,
And in her freaks, on ev'ry feature,
          She's wrote 'The Man.'

Just now I've taen the fit o' rhyme,
My barmie noddle's working prime,      20
My fancie yerkit up sublime
          Wi' hasty summon:
Hae ye a leisure-moment's time
          To hear what's comin'?

Some rhyme a neebor's name to lash ;
Some rhyme (vain thought !) for needfu' cash ;
Some rhyme to court the country clash,
   An' raise a din ;
For me, an aim I never fash ;
    I rhyme for fun.    30


The star that rules my luckless lot,
Has fated me the russet coat,
An' damn'd my fortune to the groat :
   But, in requit,
Has blest me with a random shot
    O' country wit.


This while my notion 's taen a sklent,
To try my fate in guid, black prent ;
But still the mair I'm that way bent,
   Something cries ' Hoolie !   40
I red you, honest man, tak tent !
    Ye'll shaw your folly.


' There 's ither poets, much your betters,
Far seen in Greek, deep men o' letters,
Hae thought they had ensured their debtors
   A' future ages ;
Now moths deform in shapeless tatters
    Their unknown pages.'


Then fareweel hopes o' laurel-boughs,
To garland my poetic brows !    50
Henceforth I'll rove where busy ploughs
   Are whistling thrang,
An' teach the lanely heights an' howes
    My rustic sang.


I'll wander on, wi' tentless heed
How never-halting moments speed,
Till fate shall snap the brittle thread ;
   Then, all unknown,
I'll lay me with th' inglorious dead,
    Forgot and gone !    60

But why o' death begin a tale?
Just now we're living sound an' hale ;
Then top and maintop crowd the sail,
　　　　　Heave Care o'er side !
And large, before Enjoyment's gale,
　　　　　Let's tak the tide.


This life, sae far's I understand,
Is a' enchanted fairy-land,
Where pleasure is the magic wand,
　　　　　That, wielded right,　　　　　70
Maks hours like minutes, hand in hand,
　　　　　Dance by fu' light.


The magic wand then let us wield :
For, ance that five-an'-forty's speel'd,
See, crazy, weary, joyless Eild,
　　　　　Wi' wrinkled face,
Comes hoastin', hirplin' owre the field,
　　　　　Wi' creepin' pace.


When ance life's day draws near the gloamin',
Then fareweel vacant careless roamin' ;　　　80
An' fareweel cheerfu' tankards foamin',
　　　　　An' social noise ;
An' fareweel dear deluding woman,
　　　　　The joy of joys !


O life, how pleasant is thy morning,
Young Fancy's rays the hills adorning !
Cold-pausing Caution's lesson scorning,
　　　　　We frisk away,
Like schoolboys, at th' expected warning,
　　　　　To joy and play.　　　　　90


We wander there, we wander here,
We eye the rose upon the brier,
Unmindful that the thorn is near,
　　　　　Among the leaves :
And tho' the puny wound appear,
　　　　　Short while it grieves.

Some, lucky, find a flow'ry spot,
For which they never toil'd nor swat ;
They drink the sweet and eat the fat,
   But care or pain ;   100
And, haply, eye the barren hut
   With high disdain.


With steady aim, some Fortune chase ;
Keen hope does ev'ry sinew brace ;
Thro' fair, thro' foul, they urge the race,
   And seize the prey ;
Then cannie, in some cozie place,
   They close the day.


And others, like your humble servan',
Poor wights ! nae rules nor roads observin', 110
To right or left, eternal swervin',
   They zig-zag on ;
Till curst with age, obscure an' starvin',
   They often groan.


Alas ! what bitter toil an' straining—
But truce wi' peevish, poor complaining !
Is Fortune's fickle Luna waning?
   E'en let her gang !
Beneath what light she has remaining,
   Let's sing our sang.   120


My pen I here fling to the door,
And kneel 'Ye Pow'rs !' and warm implore,
'Tho' I should wander Terra o'er,
   In all her climes,
Grant me but this, I ask no more,
   Aye rowth o' rhymes.


'Gio drooping roasts to country lairds,
Till icicles hing frae their beards ;
Gie fine braw claes to fine life-guards,
   And maids of honour ;   130
And yill an' whisky gie to cairds,
   Until they sconner.

'A title, Dempster merits it ;
A garter gie to Willie Pitt ;
Gie wealth to some be-ledger'd cit,
          In cent per cent ;
But gie me real, sterling wit,
          And I'm content.


'While ye are pleased to keep me hale,
I'll sit down o'er my scanty meal,          140
Be 't water-brose, or muslin-kail,
          Wi' cheerfu' face,
As lang 's the Muses dinna fail
          To say the grace.'


An anxious e'e I never throws
Behint my lug, or by my nose ;
I jouk beneath misfortune's blows
          As weel 's I may ;
Sworn foe to sorrow, care, and prose,
          I rhyme away.          150


O ye douce folk, that live by rule,
Grave, tideless-blooded, calm, and cool,
Compar'd wi' you—O fool ! fool ! fool !
          How much unlike !
Your hearts are just a standing pool,
          Your lives a dyke !


Nae hare-brain'd sentimental traces,
In your unletter'd, nameless faces !
In arioso trills and graces
          Ye never stray,          160
But gravissimo, solemn basses,
          Ye hum away.


Ye are sae grave, nae doubt ye're wise ;
Nae ferly tho' ye do despise
The hairum-scairum, ram-stam boys,
          The rattlin' squad :
I see you upward cast your eyes—
          Ye ken the road.

Whilst I – but I shall haud me there—
Wi' you I'll scarce gang ony where—    170
Then, Jamie, I shall say nae mair,
      But quat my sang,
Content with You to mak a pair,
      Where'er I gang.

## TO GAVIN HAMILTON, ESQ., MAUCHLINE,

### RECOMMENDING A BOY.

I HOLD it, Sir, my bounden duty,
To warn you how that Master Tootie,
    Alias Laird M'Gaun,
Was here to lure the lad away
'Bout whom ye spak the tither day,
    An' wad hae done 't aff han' :
But lest he learn the callan tricks,
    As faith I muckle doubt him,
Like scrapin' out auld Crummie's nicks,
    An' tellin' lies about them ;    10
As lieve then I'd have then
    Your clerkship he should sair,
If sae be ye may be
    Not fitted otherwhere.

Altho' I say 't, he 's gleg enough,
An' 'bout a house that 's rude an' rough,
    The boy might learn to swear ;
But then wi' you, he'll be sae taught,
An' get sic fair example straught,
    I hae na ony fear.    20
Ye'll catechize him every quirk,
    An' shore him weel wi' hell ;
An' gar him follow to the kirk——
    Aye when ye gang yoursel.
If ye then, maun be then
    Frae hame this comin' Friday,
Then please, sir, to lea'e, sir,
    The orders wi' your lady.

My word of honour I ha'e gi'en,
In Paisley John's, that night at e'en,        30
   To meet the Warld's worm :
To try to get the twa to gree,
An' name the airles an' the fee,
   In legal mode an' form :
I ken he weel a snick can draw,
   When simple bodies let him ;
An' if a Devil be at a',
   In faith he's sure to get him.
To phrase you an' praise you
   Ye ken your Laureat scorns :        40
The pray'r still, you share still,
   Of grateful Minstrel Burns.

———◆◆———

## EPISTLE TO MR. M‘ADAM,

OF CRAIGEN-GILLAN, IN ANSWER TO AN OBLIGING LETTER HE
SENT IN THE COMMENCEMENT OF MY POETIC CAREER.

SIR, o'er a gill I gat your card,
   I trow it made me proud ;
'See wha taks notice o' the Bard !'
   I lap and cried fu' loud.

'Now deil-ma-care about their jaw,
   The senseless, gawkie million ;
I'll cock my nose aboon them a',
   I'm roos'd by Craigen-Gillan !'

'Twas noble, sir ; 'twas like yoursel,
   To grant your high protection :        10
A great man's smile, ye ken fu' weel,
   Is aye a blest infection.

Tho', by his banes wha in a tub
   Match'd Macedonian Sandy !
On my ain legs, thro' dirt and dub,
   I independent stand aye.

And when those legs to gude, warm kail,
  Wi' welcome canna bear me:
A lee dyke-side, a sybow-tail,
  And barley-scone shall cheer me.    20

Heaven spare you lang to kiss the breath
  O' mony flow'ry simmers!
And bless your bonnie lasses baith,—
  I'm tald they're loosome kimmers!

And God bless young Dunaskin's laird,
  The blossom of our gentry!
And may he wear an auld man's beard,
  A credit to his country.

———··———

## EPISTLE TO MAJOR LOGAN.

Hail, thairm-inspirin', rattlin' Willie!
Though fortune's road be rough an' hilly
To every fiddling, rhyming billie,
    We never heed,
But take it like the unback'd filly,
    Proud o' her speed.

When idly govin' whyles we saunter,
Yirr, fancy barks, awa' we canter
Uphill, down brae, till some mishanter,
    Some black bog-hole,    10
Arrests us, then the scathe an' banter
    We're forced to thole.

Hale be your heart! hale be your fiddle!
Lang may your elbuck jink and diddle,
To cheer you through the weary widdle
    O' this wild warl',
Until you on a crummock driddle
    A gray-hair'd carl.

Come wealth, come poortith, late or soon,
Heaven send your heart-strings aye in tune,     20
And screw your temper-pins aboon,
    A fifth or mair,
The melancholious lazy croon,
    O' cankrie care.


May still your life from day to day
Nae 'lente largo' in the play,
But 'allegretto forte' gay
    Harmonious flow,
A sweeping, kindling, bauld strathspey—
    Encore! Bravo!     30


A blessing on the cheery gang
Wha dearly like a jig or sang,
An' never think o' right an' wrang
    By square an' rule,
But as the clegs o' feeling stang
    Are wise or fool.


My hand-waled curse keep hard in chase
The harpy, hoodock, purse-proud race,
Wha count on poortith as disgrace—
    Their tuneless hearts!     40
May fire-side discords jar a base
    To a' their parts!


But come, your hand, my careless brither,
I' th' ither warl' if there's anither,
An' that there is I've little swither
    About the matter;
We cheek for chow shall jog thegither,
    I'se ne'er bid better.


We've faults and failings—granted clearly,
We're frail backsliding mortals merely,     50
Eve's bonnie squad priests wyte them sheerly
    For our grand fa';
But still, but still, I like them dearly—
    God bless them a'!

Ochone for poor Castalian drinkers,
When they fa' foul o' earthly jinkers,
The witching cursed delicious blinkers
          Hae put me hyte,
And gart me weet my waukrife winkers,
          Wi' girnin' spite.                    60

But by yon moon!—and that's high swearin'—
An' every star within my hearin'!
An' by her een wha was a dear ane!
          I'll ne'er forget;
I hope to gie the jads a clearin'
          In fair play yet.

My loss I mourn, but not repent it,
I'll seek my pursie where I tint it;
Ance to the Indies I were wonted,
          Some cantraip hour,                    70
By some sweet elf I'll yet be dinted,
          Then *vive l'amour!*

*Faites mes baissemains respectueuse*
To sentimental sister Susie,
An' honest Lucky; no to roose you,
          Ye may be proud
That sic a couple Fate allows ye
          To grace your blood.

Nea mair at present can I measure,
An' trowth my rhymin' ware's nae treasure;    80
But when in Ayr, some half hour's leisure,
          Be 't light, be 't dark,
Sir Bard will do himself the pleasure
          To call at Park.

*Mossgiel, October 30, 1786.*

## A POETICAL EPISTLE TO A TAILOR.

WHAT ails ye now, ye lousie bitch,
To thresh my back at sic a pitch?
Losh, man! hae mercy wi' your natch,
      Your bodkin's bauld,
I didna suffer half sae much
      Frae Daddie Auld.


What tho' at times when I grow crouse,
I gi'e their wames a random pouse,
Is that enough for you to souse
      Your servant sae?      10
Gae mind your seam, ye prick-the-louse
      An' jag-the-flae!


King David o' poetic brief,
Wrought 'mang the lasses such mischief
As fill'd his after life wi' grief
      An' bloody rants,
An' yet he's rank'd amang the chief
      O' lang-syne saunts.


And maybe, Tam, for a' my cants,
My wicked rhymes, an' drucken rants,      20
I'll gie auld cloven Clooty's haunts
      An unco slip yet,
An' snugly sit amang the saunts,
      At Davie's hip yet.


But fegs! the Session says I maun
Gae fa' upo' anither plan,
Than garrin' lasses cowp the cran
      Clean heels owre body,
And sairly thole their mither's ban
      Afore the howdy.      30

This leads me on to tell for sport
How I did wi' the Session sort—
Auld Clinkum at the Inner port
   Cried three times, ' Robin !
Come hither, lad, an' answer for't,—
   Ye're blam'd for jobbin'.'

Wi' pinch I put a Sunday's face on,
An' snoov'd awa' before the Session ;
I made an open fair confession,
   I scorn'd to lie ;    40
An' syne Mess John, beyond expression,
   Fell foul o' me.

A furnicator-loun he call'd me,
An' said my fau't frae bliss expell'd me ;
I own'd the tale was true he tell'd me,
   'But what the matter ?'
Quo' I 'I fear unless ye geld me,
   I'll ne'er be better.'

'Geld you !' quo' he, 'and whatfor no ?
If that your right hand, leg or toe,   50
Should ever prove your sp'ritual foe,
   You shou'd remember
To cut it aff, an' whatfor no
   Your dearest member ?'

'Na, na,' quo' I, ' I'm no for that,
Gelding's nae better than 'tis ca't,
I'd rather suffer for my faut
   A hearty flewit,
As sair owre hip as ye can draw 't,
   Tho' I should rue it.   60

'Or gin ye like to end the bother,
To please us a', I've just ae ither,
When next wi' yon lass I forgather,
   Whate'er betide it,
I'll frankly gi'e her 't a' thegither,
   An' let her guide it.'

But, Sir, this pleas'd them warst ava,
An' therefore, Tam, when that I saw,
I said 'Gude night,' and cam awa,
      And left the Session ;        70
I saw they were resolvèd a'
      On my oppression.

———♦———

# ANSWER TO VERSES ADDRESSED TO THE POET

### BY THE GUIDWIFE OF WAUCHOPE-HOUSE.

GUIDWIFE,
I mind it weel, in early date,
When I was beardless, young and blat
    An' first could thresh the barn,
Or haud a yokin' at the pleugh,
An' tho' forfoughten sair eneugh,
    Yet unco proud to learn, —
When first amang the yellow corn
    A man I reckon'd was,
And wi' the lave ilk merry morn
    Could rank my rig and lass,        10
      Still shearing, and clearing
        The tither stooked raw,
      Wi' claivers, an' haivers,
        Wearing the day awa,—

Ev'n then a wish ! (I mind its power)
A wish that to my latest hour
    Shall strongly heave my breast ;
That I for poor auld Scotland's sake,
Some usefu' plan or beuk could make,
    Or sing a sang at least.        20

The rough bur-thistle, spreading wide
    Amang the bearded bear,
I turn'd the weeder-clips aside,
    An' spar'd the symbol dear :

No nation, no station,
   My envy e'er could raise;
A Scot still, but blot still,
   I knew nae higher praise.


But still the elements o' sang
In formless jumble, right an' wrang,          30
   Wild floated in my brain;
Till on that hairst I said before,
My partner in the merry core,
   She rous'd the forming strain:
I see her yet, the sonsie quean,
   That lighted up my jingle,
Her witching smile, her pauky een,
   That gart my heart-strings tingle;
     I firèd, inspirèd,
       At ev'ry kindling keek,          40
     But bashing, and dashing,
       I fearèd aye to speak.


Health to the sex! ilk guid chiel says,
Wi' merry dance in winter days,
   An' we to share in common:
The gust o' joy, the balm of woe,
The saul o' life, the heav'n below,
   Is rapture-giving woman.
Ye surly sumphs, who hate the name,
   Be mindfu' o' your mither:          50
She, honest woman, may think shame
   That ye're connected with her!
     Ye're wae men, ye're nae men,
       That slight the lovely dears;
     To shame ye, disclaim ye,
       Ilk honest birkie swears.


For you, no bred to barn or byre,
Wha sweetly tune the Scottish lyre,
   Thanks to you for your line:
The marled plaid ye kindly spare,          60
By me should gratefully be ware;
   'Twad please me to the nine.

I'd be mair vauntie o' my hap,
  Douce hingin' owre my curple,
Than ony ermine ever lap,
  Or proud imperial purple.
    Farewell then, lang hale then,
      An' plenty be your fa';
    May losses and crosses
      Ne'er at your hallan ca'.                    70

———••———

## EPISTLE TO HUGH PARKER.

In this strange land, this uncouth clime,
A land unknown to prose or rhyme;
Where words ne'er crost the Muse's heckles,
Nor limpit in poetic shackles;
A land that prose did never view it,
Except when drunk he stacher't through it;
Here, ambush'd by the chimla cheek,
Hid in an atmosphere of reek,
I hear a wheel thrum i' the neuk,
I hear it—for in vain I leuk.                      10
The red peat gleams, a fiery kernel,
Enhuskèd by a fog infernal;
Here, for my wonted rhyming raptures,
I sit and count my sins by chapters;
For life and spunk like ither Christians,—
I'm dwindled down to mere existence,
Wi' nae converse but Gallowa' bodies,
Wi' nae kend face but Jenny Geddes.
Jenny, my Pegasean pride!
Dowie she saunters down Nithside,                  20
And ay a westlin leuk she throws,
While tears hap o'er her auld brown nose!
Was it for this, wi' canny care,
Thou bure the Bard through many a shire?
At howes or hillocks never stumbled,
And late or early never grumbled?

O, had I power like inclination,
I'd heeze thee up a constellation,
To canter with the Sagitarre,
Or loup the ecliptic like a bar ;                    30
Or turn the pole like any arrow ;
Or, when auld Phoebus bids good-morrow,
Down the zodiac urge the race,
And cast dirt on his godship's face ;
For I could lay my bread and kail
He'd ne'er cast saut upo' thy tail.
Wi' a' this care and a' this grief,
And sma', sma' prospect of relief,
And nought but peat reek i' my head,
How can I write what ye can read ?                   40
Tarbolton, twenty-fourth o' June,
Ye'll find me in a better tune ;
But till we meet and weet our whistle,
Tak this excuse for nae epistle.

## EPISTLE TO ROBERT GRAHAM, ESQ.,
### OF FINTRY.

When Nature her great master-piece design'd,
And fram'd her last, best work, the human mind,
Her eye intent on all the mazy plan,
She form'd of various parts the various man.
   Then first she calls the useful many forth ;
Plain plodding industry, and sober worth :
Thence peasants, farmers, native sons of earth,
And merchandise' whole genus take their birth :
Each prudent cit a warm existence finds,
And all mechanics' many-apron'd kinds.               10
Some other rarer sorts are wanted yet,
The lead and buoy are needful to the net :
The caput mortuum of gross desires
Makes a material for mere knights and squires ;

The martial phosphorus is taught to flow,
She kneads the lumpish philosophic dough,
Then marks the unyielding mass with grave designs,
Law, physic, politics, and deep divines:
Last, she sublimes th' Aurora of the poles,
The flashing elements of female souls.          20
    The order'd system fair before her stood,
Nature, well-pleas'd, pronounc'd it very good;
But ere she gave creating labour o'er,
Half-jest, she try'd one curious labour more;
Some spumy, fiery, ignis fatuus matter,
Such as the slightest breath of air might scatter;
With arch alacrity and concious glee
(Nature may have her whim as well as we,
Her Hogarth-art perhaps she meant to show it)
She forms the thing, and christens it a Poet,—          30
Creature, tho' oft the prey of care and sorrow,
When blest to-day, unmindful of to-morrow;
A being form'd t' amuse his graver friends,
Admir'd and prais'd—and there the homage ends;
A mortal quite unfit for Fortune's strife,
Yet oft the sport of all the ills of life;
Prone to enjoy each pleasure riches give,
Yet haply wanting wherewithal to live;
Longing to wipe each tear, to heal each groan,
Yet frequent all unheeded in his own.          40
    But honest Nature is not quite a Turk,
She laugh'd at first, then felt for her poor work.
Pitying the propless climber of mankind,
She cast about a standard tree to find;
And, to support his helpless woodbine state,
Attach'd him to the generous truly great—
A title, and the only one I claim,
To lay strong hold for help on bounteous Graham.
    Pity the tuneful muses' hapless train,
Weak, timid landsmen on life's stormy main!          50
Their hearts no selfish stern absorbent stuff,
That never gives—tho' humbly takes enough;
The little fate allows, they share as soon,
Unlike sage proverb'd wisdom's hard wrung boon.
The world were blest did bliss on them depend:
Ah, that 'the friendly e'er should want a friend!'

Let prudence number o'er each sturdy son,
Who life and wisdom at one race begun,
Who feel by reason, and who give by rule,
(Instinct's a brute, and sentiment a fool!)                    60
Who make poor 'will do' wait upon 'I should'—
We own they're prudent, but who feels they're good?
Ye wise ones, hence! ye hurt the social eye!
God's image rudely etch'd on base alloy!
But come ye who the godlike pleasure know,
Heaven's attribute distinguish'd—to bestow!
Whose arms of love would grasp the human race:
Come thou who giv'st with all a courtier's grace;
Friend of my life, true patron of my rhymes!
Prop of my dearest hopes for future times.                     70
Why shrinks my soul, half-blushing, half-afraid,
Backward, abash'd to ask thy friendly aid?
I know my need, I know thy giving hand,
I crave thy friendship at thy kind command;
But there are such who court the tuneful nine—
Heavens! should the branded character be mine!
Whose verse in manhood's pride sublimely flows.
Yet vilest reptiles in their begging prose.
Mark how their lofty independent spirit
Soars on the spurning wing of injur'd merit!                   80
Seek not the proofs in private life to find;
Pity the best of words should be but wind!
So to heaven's gates the lark's shrill song ascends,
But grovelling on the earth the carol ends.
In all the clam'rous cry of starving want,
They dun benevolence with shameless front;
Oblige them, patronize their tinsel lays,
They persecute you all your future days!
Ere my poor soul such deep damnation stain,
My horny fist assume the plough again;                         90
The piebald jacket let me patch once more;
On eighteen-pence a week I've liv'd before.
Tho', thanks to Heaven, I dare even that last shift,
I trust, meantime, my boon is in thy gift;
That, plac'd by thee upon the wish'd-for height,
Where, man and nature fairer in her sight,
My muse may imp her wing for some sublimer flight.

## TO DR. BLACKLOCK.

Wow, but your letter made me vauntie!
And are ye hale, and weel, and cantie?
I kenn'd it still your wee bit jauntie
      Wad bring ye to:
Lord send you aye as weel's I want ye,
      And then ye'll do.


The ill-thief blaw the Heron south!
And never drink be near his drouth!
He tauld mysel by word o' mouth,
      He'd tak my letter;      10
I lippen'd to the chiel in trouth,
      And bade nae better.


But aiblins honest Master Heron
Had at the time some dainty fair one,
To ware his theologic care on,
      And holy study;
And tir'd o' sauls to waste his lear on,
      E'en tried the body.


But what d'ye think, my trusty fier,
I'm turn'd a gauger—Peace be here!      20
Parnassian queans, I fear, I fear,
      Ye'll now disdain me!
And then my fifty pounds a year
      Will little gain me.


Ye glaiket, gleesome, dainty damies,
Wha by Castalia's wimplin' streamies,
Lowp, sing, and lave your pretty limbies,
      Ye ken, ye ken,
That strang necessity supreme is
      'Mang sons o' men.      30

I hae a wife and twa wee laddies,
They maun hae brose and brats o' duddies;
Ye ken yoursels my heart right proud is—
    I need na vaunt,
But I'll sned besoms—thraw saugh woodies,
    Before they want.


Lord help me thro' this warld o' care!
I'm weary sick o't late and air!
Not but I hae a richer share
    Than mony ithers;           40
But why should ae man better fare,
    And a' men brithers?


Come, Firm Resolve, take thou the van,
Thou stalk o' carl-hemp in man!
And let us mind, faint heart ne'er wan
    A lady fair;
Wha does the utmost that he can,
    Will whyles do mair.


But to conclude my silly rhyme
(I'm scant o' verse, and scant o' time)—    50
To make a happy fire-side clime
    To weans and wife,
That's the true pathos and sublime
    Of human life.


My compliments to sister Beckie;
And eke the same to honest Lucky,
I wat she is a daintie chuckie,
    As e'er tread clay!
And gratefully, my guid auld cockie,
    I'm yours for aye.           60

## LETTER TO JAMES TENNANT, GLENCONNER.

AULD comrade dear and brither sinner,
How's a' the folk about Glenconner?
How do you this blae eastlin wind,
That's like to blaw a body blind?
For me, my faculties are frozen,
My dearest member nearly dozen'd.
I've sent you here by Johnie Simson,
Twa sage philosophers to glimpse on;
Smith, wi' his sympathetic feeling,
An' Reid, to common sense appealing.          10
Philosophers have fought an' wrangled,
An' meikle Greek an' Latin mangled,
Till wi' their logic-jargon tir'd,
An' in the depth of Science mir'd,
To common sense they now appeal,
What wives an' wabsters see an' feel.
But, hark ye, friend, I charge you strictly,
Peruse them, an' return them quickly;
For now I'm grown sae cursèd douce,
I pray an' ponder but the house;               20
My shins, my lane, I there sit roastin',
Perusing Bunyan, Brown, an' Boston;
Till by an' by, if I haud on,
I'll grunt a real Gospel-groan:
Already I begin to try it,
To cast my een up like a pyet,
When by the gun she tumbles o'er,
Flutt'ring an' gaspin' in her gore:
Sae shortly you shall see me bright,
A burning an' a shining light.                 30
  My heart-warm love to guid auld Glen,
The ace an' wale of honest men:
When bending down wi' auld grey hairs,
Beneath the load of years and cares,
May He who made him still support him,
An' views beyond the grave comfort him.
His worthy fam'ly far and near,
God bless them a' wi' grace and gear!

My auld school-fellow, Preacher Willie,
The manly tar, my mason billie,      40
An' Auchenbay, I wish him joy;
If he's a parent, lass or boy,
May he be dad, and Meg the mither
Just five-and-forty years thegither!
An' no forgetting wabster Charlie,
I'm tauld he offers very fairly.
An' Lord, remember singing Sannock,
Wi' hale-breeks, saxpence, an' a bannock.
An' next, my auld acquaintance, Nancy,
Since she is fitted to her fancy,      50
An' her kind stars hae airted till her
A good chiel wi' a pickle siller.
My kindest, best respects I sen' it,
To cousin Kate an' sister Janet;
Tell them frae me, wi' chiels be cautious,
For, faith, they'll aiblins fin' them fashious:
To grant a heart is fairly civil,
But to grant a maidenhead's the devil.
An' lastly, Jamie, for yoursel,
May guardian angels tak a spell,      60
An' steer you seven miles south o' hell:
But first, before you see heav'n's glory,
May ye get mony a merry story,
Mony a laugh, and mony a drink,
An' aye enough o' needfu' clink.
    Now fare ye weel, an' joy be wi' you!
For my sake, this I beg it o' you,
Assist poor Simson a' ye can,
Ye'll fin' hin just an honest man;
Sae I conclude and quat my chanter,      70
Yours, saint or sinner,
                  ROB THE RANTER.

# EPISTLE TO ROBERT GRAHAM, ESQ.,
## OF FINTRY:

ON THE CLOSE OF THE DISPUTED ELECTION BETWEEN SIR JAMES
JOHNSTONE AND CAPTAIN MILLER, FOR THE DUMFRIES
DISTRICT OF BOROUGHS.

FINTRY, my stay in worldly strife,
Friend o' my Muse, friend o' my life,
      Are ye as idle 's I am?
Come then, wi' uncouth, kintra fleg,
O'er Pegasus I'll fling my leg,
      And ye shall see me try him.

But where shall I go rin a ride,
That I may splatter nane beside?
      I wad na be uncivil:
In manhood's various paths and ways    10
There 's aye some doytin' body strays,
      And *I* ride like the devil.

Thus I break off wi' a' my birr,
An' down yon dark deep alley spur,
      Where Theologics daunder:
Alas! curst wi' eternal fogs,
And damned in everlasting bogs,
      As sure 's the creed I'll blunder.

I'll stain a band, or jaup a gown,
Or rin my reckless guilty crown    20
      Against the haly door.
Sair do I rue my luckless fate
When, as the muse an' deil wad hae 't,
      I rade that road before.

Suppose I take a spurt, and mix
Amang the wilds o' Politics,
      Electors and elected;
Where dogs at Court (sad sons of bitches!)
Septennially a madness touches,
      Till all the land 's infected.    30

All hail ! Drumlanrig's haughty Grace,
Discarded remnant of a race
      Once godlike great in story ;
Thy forbears' virtues all contrasted,
The very name of Douglas blasted,
      Thine that inverted glory !

Hate, envy, oft the Douglas bore ;
But thou hast superadded more,
      And sunk them in contempt ;
Follies and crimes have stained the name,     40
But, Queensberry, thine the virgin claim—
      From all that's good exempt !

I'll sing the zeal Drumlanrig bears
Who left the all-important cares
      Of princes and their darlings ;
And, bent on winning borough towns,
Came shaking hands wi' wabster loons,
      And kissing barefit carlins.

Combustion thro' our boroughs rode
Whistling his roaring pack abroad     50
      Of mad unmuzzled lions ;
As Queensberry buff and blue unfurl'd,
And Westerha' and Hopeton hurl'd
      To every Whig defiance.

But cautious Queensberry left the war,
Th' unmanner'd dust might soil his star ;
      Besides, he hated bleeding ;
But left behind him heroes bright,
Heroes in Cæsarean fight,
      Or Ciceronian pleading.     60

O ! for a throat like huge Mons-Meg,
To muster o'er each ardent Whig
      Beneath Drumlanrig's banner !
Heroes and heroines commix,
All in the field of politics,
      To win immortal honour.

M'Murdo and his lovely spouse,
(Th' enamour'd laurels kiss her brows!)
   Led on the loves and graces:
She won each gaping burgess' heart,    70
While he, all-conquering, play'd his part
   Among their wives and lasses.

Craigdarroch led a light-arm'd corps,
Tropes, metaphors and figures pour,
   Like Hecla streaming thunder:
Glenriddel, skill'd in rusty coins,
Blew up each Tory's dark designs,
   And bared the treason under.

In either wing two champions fought,
Redoubted Staig, who set at nought    80
   The wildest savage Tory:
And Welsh, who ne'er yet flinch'd his ground,
High-waved his magnum-bonum round
   With Cyclopean fury.

Miller brought up th' artillery ranks,
The many-pounders of the Banks,
   Resistless desolation!
While Maxwelton, that baron bold,
'Mid Lawson's port entrench'd his hold,
   And threaten'd worse damnation.   90

To these what Tory hosts oppos'd,
With these what Tory warriors clos'd,
   Surpasses my descriving:
Squadrons extended long and large,
With furious speed rush to the charge,
   Like raving devils driving.

What verse can sing, what prose narrate,
The butcher deeds of bloody fate
   Amid this mighty tulzie!
Grim Horror girn'd—pale Terror roar'd,   100
As Murther at his thrapple shor'd,
   And Hell mix'd in the brulzie.

As Highland crags by thunder cleft,
When lightnings fire the stormy lift,
      Hurl down with crashing rattle;
As flames among a hundred woods;
As headlong foam a hundred floods;
      Such is the rage of battle!


The stubborn Tories dare to die;
As soon the rooted oaks would fly     110
      Before th' approaching fellers:
The Whigs come on like Ocean's roar,
When all his wintry billows pour
      Against the Buchan Bullers.


Lo, from the shades of Death's deep night,
Departed Whigs enjoy the fight,
      And think on former daring:
The muffled murtherer of Charles
The Magna Charta flag unfurls,
      All deadly gules its bearing.     120


Nor wanting ghosts of Tory fame,
Bold Scrimgeour follows gallant Graham,
      Auld Covenanters shiver.
(Forgive, forgive, much-wrong'd Montrose!
Now death and hell engulf thy foes,
      Thou liv'st on high for ever!)


Still o'er the field the combat burns,
The Tories, Whigs, give way by turns;
      But Fate the word has spoken,
For woman's wit and strength o' man     130
Alas! can do but what they can!
      The Tory ranks are broken.


O that my een were flowing burns!
My voice a lioness that mourns
      Her darling cubs' undoing;
That I might greet, that I might cry,
While Tories fall, while Tories fly,
      And furious Whigs pursuing!

What Whig but melts for good Sir James?
Dear to his country by the names            140
> Friend, patron, benefactor!
Not Pulteney's wealth can Pulteney save!
And Hopeton falls, the generous brave!
> And Stewart, bold as Hector!

Thou, Pitt, shalt rue this overthrow;
And Thurlow growl a curse of woe;
> And Melville melt in wailing!
How Fox and Sheridan rejoice!
And Burke shall sing, 'O Prince, arise,
> Thy power is all-prevailing!'     150

For your poor friend, the Bard, afar
He only hears and sees the war,
> A cool spectator purely!
So, when the storm the forest rends,
The robin in the hedge descends,
> And sober chirps securely.

Now for my friends' and brethren's sakes,
And for my dear-loved Land o' Cakes,
> I pray with holy fire—
Lord send a rough-shod troop o' hell          160
Owre a' wad Scotland buy or sell,
> To grind them in the mire!

---

## EPISTLE TO ROBERT GRAHAM, ESQ.,
## OF FINTRY.

LATE crippl'd of an arm, and now a leg,
About to beg a pass for leave to beg;
Dull, listless, teas'd, dejected, and depress'd
(Nature is adverse to a cripple's rest):
Will generous Graham list to his Poet's wail?
(It soothes poor Misery, heark'ning to her tale,)

And hear him curse the light he first survey'd,
And doubly curse the luckless rhyming trade?
  Thou, Nature, partial Nature, I arraign;
Of thy caprice maternal I complain.                    10
The lion and the bull thy care have found,
One shakes the forests, and one spurns the ground:
Thou giv'st the ass his hide, the snail his shell,
Th' envenom'd wasp, victorious, guards his cell.
Thy minions, kings defend, control, devour,
In all th' omnipotence of rule and power.
Foxes and statesmen, subtile wiles ensure;
The cit and polecat stink, and are secure.
Toads with their poison, doctors with their drug,
The priest and hedgehog in their robes, are snug.      20
Ev'n silly woman has her warlike arts,
Her tongue and eyes, her dreaded spear and darts.
  But Oh! thou bitter step-mother and hard,
To thy poor, fenceless, naked child—the Bard!
A thing unteachable in world's skill,
And half an idiot too, more helpless still.
No heels to bear him from the op'ning dun;
No claws to dig, his hated sight to shun;
No horns, but those by luckless Hymen worn,
And those, alas! not Amalthea's horn:                  30
No nerves olfact'ry, Mammon's trusty cur,
Clad in rich Dulness' comfortable fur,
In naked feeling, and in aching pride,
He bears th' unbroken blast from ev'ry side:
Vampyre booksellers drain him to the heart,
And scorpion critics cureless venom dart.
  Critics—appall'd I venture on the name,
Those cut-throat bandits in the paths of fame,
Bloody dissectors, worse than ten Monroes;
He hacks to teach, they mangle to expose.              40
  His heart by causeless, wanton malice wrung,
By blockheads' daring into madness stung;
His well-won bays, than life itself more dear,
By miscreants torn, who ne'er one sprig must wear :
Foil'd, bleeding, tortur'd in th' unequal strife,
The hapless Poet flounders on thro' life.
Till fled each hope that once his bosom fired,
And fled each Muse that glorious once inspired,

Low sunk in squalid, unprotected age,
Dead even resentment for his injur'd page,                    50
He heeds or feels no more the ruthless critic's rage!
  So, by some hedge, the generous steed deceas'd,
For half-starv'd snarling curs a dainty feast;
By toil and famine wore to skin and bone,
Lies, senseless of each tugging bitch's son.
  O Dulness! portion of the truly blest!
Calm shelter'd haven of eternal rest!
Thy sons ne'er madden at the fierce extremes
Of Fortune's polar frost, or torrid beams.
If mantling high she fills the golden cup,                    60
With sober selfish ease they sip it up;
Conscious the bounteous meed they well deserve,
They only wonder 'some folks' do not starve.
The grave sage hern thus easy picks his frog,
And thinks the mallard a sad worthless dog.
When disappointment snaps the clue of hope,
And thro' disastrous night they darkling grope,
With deaf endurance sluggishly they bear,
And just conclude that 'fools are fortune's care.'
So heavy, passive to the tempest's shocks,                    70
Strong on the sign-post stands the stupid ox.
  Not so the idle Muses' mad-cap train,
Not such the workings of their moon-struck brain;
In equanimity they never dwell,
By turns in soaring heav'n, or vaulted hell.
  I dread thee, Fate, relentless and severe,
With all a poet's, husband's, father's fear!
Already one strong-hold of hope is lost,
Glencairn, the truly noble, lies in dust;
(Fled, like the sun eclips'd as noon appears,               80
And left us darkling in a world of tears:)
Oh! hear my ardent, grateful, selfish pray'r!
Fintry, my other stay, long bless and spare!
Thro' a long life his hopes and wishes crown,
And bright in cloudless skies his sun go down!
May bliss domestic smoothe his private path;
Give energy to life; and soothe his latest breath,
With many a filial tear circling the bed of death!

## TO TERRAUGHTY, ON HIS BIRTHDAY.

HEALTH to the Maxwells' veteran Chief!
Health, aye unsour'd by care or grief:
Inspired, I turned Fate's sibyl leaf
   This natal morn,
I see thy life is stuff o' prief,
    Scarce quite half worn.

This day thou metes threescore eleven,
And I can tell that bounteous Heaven
(The second-sight, ye ken, is given
   To ilka poet)     10
On thee a tack o' seven times seven
    Will yet bestow it.

If envious buckies view wi' sorrow
Thy lengthen'd days on this blest morrow,
May desolation's lang-teeth'd harrow,
   Nine miles an hour,
Rake them, like Sodom and Gomorrah,
    In brunstane stoure.

But for thy friends,—and they are mony,
Baith honest men and lassies bonnie,—  20
May couthie fortune, kind and cannie,
   In social glee,
Wi' mornings blithe and e'enings funny
    Bless them and thee!

Fareweel, auld birkie! Lord be near ye,
And thon the Deil he daurna steer ye:
Your friends aye love, your faes aye fear ye;
   For me, shame fa' me,
If neist my heart I dinna wear ye
    While BURNS they ca' me.  30

## EPISTLE FROM ESOPUS TO MARIA.

FROM those drear solitudes and frowsy cells,
Where infamy with sad repentance dwells;
Where turnkeys make the jealous portal fast,
And deal from iron hands the spare repast;
Where truant 'prentices, yet young in sin,
Blush at the curious stranger peeping in;
Where strumpets, relics of the drunken roar,
Resolve to drink, nay, half to whore, no more;
Where tiny thieves not destin'd yet to swing,
Beat hemp for others, riper for the string:       10
From these dire scenes my wretched lines I date,
To tell Maria her Esopus' fate.
'Alas! I feel I am no actor here!'
'Tis real hangmen real scourges bear!
Prepare, Maria, for a horrid tale
Will turn thy very rouge to deadly pale;
Will make thy hair, tho' erst from gipsy poll'd,
By barber woven, and by barber sold,
Though twisted smooth with Harry's nicest care,
Like hoary bristles to erect and stare.            20
The hero of the mimic scene, no more
I start in Hamlet, in Othello roar;
Or, haughty Chieftain, 'mid the din of arms,
In Highland bonnet woo Malvina's charms;
While sans-culottes stoop up the mountain high,
And steal from me Maria's prying eye.
Bless'd Highland bonnet! once my proudest dress,
Now prouder still, Maria's temples press.
I see her wave thy towering plumes afar,
And call each coxcomb to the wordy war.            30
I see her face the first of Ireland's sons,
And even out-Irish his Hibernian bronze;
The crafty colonel leaves the tartan'd lines,
For other wars, where he a hero shines:
The hopeful youth, in Scottish senate bred,
Who owns a Bushby's heart without the head.

Comes 'mid a string of coxcombs to display
That *veni, vidi, vici,* is his way;
The shrinking bard adown an alley skulks,
And dreads a meeting worse than Woolwich hulks; 40
Though there his heresies in church and state
Might well award him Muir and Palmer's fate:
Still she undaunted reels and rattles on,
And dares the public like a noontide sun.
What scandal call'd Maria's jaunty stagger
The ricket reeling of a crooked swagger?
Whose spleen? e'en worse than Burns's venom when
He dips in gall unmix'd his eager pen,
And pours his vengeance in the burning line!
Who christen'd thus Maria's lyre divine          50
The idiot strum of vanity bemused,
And even th' abuse of poesy abused?
Who call'd her verse a parish workhouse, made
For motley, foundling fancies, stolen or stray'd?
A workhouse! ah, that sound awakes my woes,
And pillows on the thorn my rack'd repose!
In durance vile here must I wake and weep,
And all my frowsy couch in sorrow steep;
That straw where many a rogue has lain of yore,
And vermin'd gipsies litter'd heretofore.        60

Why, Lonsdale, thus thy wrath on vagrants pour?
Must earth no rascal, save thyself, endure?
Must thou alone in guilt immortal swell,
And make a vast monopoly of hell?
Thou know'st the virtues cannot hate thee worse;
The vices also, must they club their curse?
Or must no tiny sin to others fall,
Because thy guilt's supreme enough for all?

Maria, send me too thy griefs and cares;
In all of thee sure thy Esopus shares.           70
As thou at all mankind the flag unfurls,
Who on my fair one satire's vengeance hurls?
Who calls thee pert, affected, vain coquette,
A wit in folly, and a fool in wit?
Who says that fool alone is not thy due,
And quotes thy treacheries to prove it true?

Our force united on thy foes we'll turn,
And dare the war with all of woman born:
For who can write and speak as thou and I?
My periods that decyphering defy,　　　　　80
And thy still matchless tongue that conquers all reply.

———————

### EPISTLE TO COLONEL DE PEYSTER.

My honour'd Colonel, deep I feel
Your interest in the Poet's weal;
Ah! now sma' heart hae I to speel
　　　　The steep Parnassus,
Surrounded thus by bolus pill,
　　　　And potion glasses.

O what a canty warld were it,
Would pain, and care, and sickness spare it;
And fortune favour worth and merit,
　　　　As they deserve:　　　　　10
And aye a rowth, roast beef and claret:
　　　　Syne wha wad starve?

Dame Life, tho' fiction out may trick her,
And in paste gems and fripp'ry deck her,
Oh! flick'ring, feeble, and unsicker
　　　　I've found her still,
Aye wav'ring like the willow wicker,
　　　　'Tween good and ill.

Then that curst carmagnole, auld Satan,
Watches, like baudrons by a rattan,
Our sinfu' saul to get a claut on　　　　　20
　　　　Wi' felon ire;
Syne, whip! his tail ye'll ne'er cast saut on,
　　　　He's off like fire.

Ah Nick! ah Nick! it isna fair,
First showing us the tempting ware,
Bright wines and bonnie lasses rare,
   To put us daft;
Syne weave, unseen, thy spider snare
    O' hell's damn'd waft.  30

Poor man, the flee, aft bizzes by,
And aft as chance he comes thee nigh,
Thy auld damn'd elbow yeuks wi' joy,
   And hellish pleasure;
Already in thy fancy's eye,
   Thy sicker treasure.

Soon heels-o'er-gowdie! in he gangs,
And like a sheep-head on a tangs,
Thy girning laugh enjoys his pangs
   And murd'ring wrestle,  40
As, dangling in the wind, he hangs
   A gibbet's tassel.

But lest you think I am uncivil,
To plague you with this draunting drivel,
Abjuring a' intentions evil,
   I quat my pen:
The Lord preserve us frae the Devil!
   Amen! amen!

    ———◆———

# WINTER.

THE wintry wast extends his blast,
 And hail and rain does blaw;
Or the stormy north sends driving forth
 The blinding sleet and snaw:
While, tumbling brown, the burn comes down,
 And roars frae bank to brae:
And bird and beast in covert rest,
 And pass the heartless day.

'The sweeping blast, the sky o'ercast,'
　　The joyless winter-day,                              10
Let others fear, to me more dear
　　Than all the pride of May:
The tempest's howl, it soothes my soul,
　　My griefs it seems to join;
The leafless trees my fancy please,
　　Their fate resembles mine!

Thou Pow'r Supreme, whose mighty scheme
　　These woes of mine fulfil,
Here, firm, I rest,—they must be best,
　　Because they are Thy will!                            20
Then all I want (Oh! do thou grant
　　This one request of mine!)
Since to enjoy thou dost deny,
　　Assist me to resign.

———◆◆———

# A PRAYER IN THE PROSPECT OF DEATH.

O Thou unknown Almighty Cause
　　Of all my hope and fear!
In whose dread presence, ere an hour,
　　Perhaps I must appear!

If I have wander'd in those paths
　　Of life I ought to shun;
As something, loudly in my breast,
　　Remonstrates I have done;

Thou know'st that Thou hast formèd me
　　With passions wild and strong;                        10
And list'ning to their witching voice
　　Has often led me wrong.

Where human weakness has come short,
　　Or frailty stept aside,
Do thou, All-Good! for such Thou art,
　　In shades of darkness hide.

Where with intention I have err'd,
  No other plea I have,
But Thou art good ; and Goodness still
  Delighteth to forgive.                          20

## STANZAS ON THE SAME OCCASION.

WHY am I loath to leave this earthly scene?
  Have I so found it full of pleasing charms?
Some drops of joy with draughts of ill between ;
  Some gleams of sunshine 'mid renewing storms!
Is it departing pangs my soul alarms?
  Or Death's unlovely, dreary, dark abode?
For guilt, for guilt, my terrors are in arms ;
  I tremble to approach an angry God,
And justly smart beneath his sin-avenging rod.

Fain would I say, 'Forgive my foul offence!'        10
  Fain promise never more to disobey ;
But, should my Author health again dispense,
  Again I might desert fair virtue's way ;
Again in folly's path might go astray ;
  Again exalt the brute, and sink the man ;
Then how should I for Heavenly mercy pray,
  Who act so counter Heavenly mercy's plan?
Who sin so oft have mourn'd, yet to temptation ran?

O Thou, great Governor of all below!
  If I may dare a lifted eye to Thee,             20
Thy nod can make the tempest cease to blow,
  And still the tumult of the raging sea :
With that controlling pow'r assist ev'n me
  Those headlong furious passions to confine,
For all unfit I feel my powers to be,
  To rule their torrent in th' allowèd line ;
O, aid me with Thy help, Omnipotence Divine !

# THE FIRST PSALM.

The man, in life wherever plac'd,
    Hath happiness in store,
Who walks not in the wicked's way,
    Nor learns their guilty lore:

Nor from the seat of scornful pride
    Casts forth his eyes abroad,
But with humility and awe
    Still walks before his God.

That man shall flourish like the trees
    Which by the streamlets grow;      10
The fruitful top is spread on high,
    And firm the root below.

But he whose blossom buds in guilt
    Shall to the ground be cast,
And like the rootless stubble tost
    Before the sweeping blast.

For-why that God the good adore
    Hath giv'n them peace and rest,
But hath decreed that wicked men
    Shall ne'er be truly blest.      20

---

# A PRAYER, UNDER THE PRESSURE OF VIOLENT ANGUISH.

O Thou great Being! what Thou art
    Surpasses me to know:
Yet sure I am, that known to Thee
    Are all Thy works below.

Thy creature here before Thee stands,
    All wretched and distrest;
Yet sure those ills that wring my soul
    Obey Thy high behest.

Sure Thou, Almighty, canst not act
  From cruelty or wrath !                                    10
O free my weary eyes from tears,
  Or close them fast in death !

But if I must afflicted be,
  To suit some wise design ;
Then man my soul with firm resolves
  To bear and not repine !

———•———

# THE FIRST SIX VERSES OF THE NINETIETH PSALM.

O Thou, the first, the greatest friend
  Of all the human race !
Whose strong right hand has ever been
  Their stay and dwelling-place !

Before the mountains heav'd their heads
  Beneath Thy forming hand,
Before this ponderous globe itself
  Arose at Thy command ;

That pow'r which rais'd and still upholds
  This universal frame,                                    10
From countless unbeginning time
  Was ever still the same.

Those mighty periods of years
  Which seem to us so vast,
Appear no more before Thy sight
  Than yesterday that 's past.

Thou giv'st the word ; Thy creature, man,
  Is to existence brought ;
Again Thou say'st, 'Ye sons of men,
  Return ye into nought !'                                  20

Thou layest them, with all their cares,
    In everlasting sleep ;
As with a flood thou tak'st them off
    With overwhelming sweep.

They flourish like the morning flow'r,
    In beauty's pride array'd ;
But long ere night cut down it lies
    All wither'd and decay'd.

————••————

# THE POET'S WELCOME TO HIS LOVE-
## BEGOTTEN DAUGHTER.

Thou 's welcome, wean ! mishanter fa' me,
If ought of thee, or of thy mammy,
Shall ever daunton me, or awe me,
        My sweet wee lady,
Or if I blush when thou shalt ca' me
        Tit-ta or daddy.

Wee image of my bonnie Betty,
I fatherly will kiss and daut thee,
As dear an' near my heart I set thee
        Wi' as guid will,                          10
As a' the priests had seen me get thee
        That 's out o' hell.

What tho' they ca' me fornicator,
An' tease my name in kintra clatter :
The mair they talk I'm kent the better,
        E'en let them clash ;
An auld wife's tongue 's a feckless matter
        To gie ane fash.

Welcome, my bonnie, sweet wee dochter—
Tho' ye come here a wee unsought for,        20
An' tho' your comin' I hae fought for
        Baith kirk an' queir ;
Yet, by my faith, ye're no unwrought for !
        That I shall swear !

Sweet fruit o' mony a merry dint,
My funny toil is now a' tint,
Sin' thou came to the warl asklent,
   Which fools may scoff at;
In my last plack thy part 's be in't—
   The better half o't.   30

An' if thou be what I wad hae thee,
An' tak the counsel I shall gie thee,
A lovin' father I'll be to thee,
   If thou be spar'd;
Thro' a' thy childish years I'll ee thee,
   An' think't weel war'd.

Tho' I should be the waur bested,
Thou's be as braw an' bienly clad,
An' thy young years as nicely bred
   Wi' education,   40
As ony brat o' wedlock's bed
   In a' thy station.

Gude grant that thou may aye inherit
Thy mither's person, grace, an' merit,
An' thy poor worthless daddy's spirit,
   Without his failins;
'Twill please me mair to see and hear o't,
   Than stockit mailins.

---

# ELEGY ON THE DEATH OF ROBERT RUISSEAUX.

Now Robin lies in his last lair,
He'll gabble rhyme, nor sing nae mair,
Cauld poverty, wi' hungry stare,
   Nae mair shall fear him;
Nor anxious fear, nor cankert care,
   E'er mair come near him.

To tell the truth, they seldom fasht him,
Except the moment that they crusht him;
For sune as chance or fate had husht 'em,
　　　　Tho' e'er sae short,　　　　　　　10
Then wi' a rhyme or sang he lasht 'em,
　　　　And thought it sport.

Tho' he was bred to kintra wark,
And counted was baith wight and stark,
Yet that was never Robin's mark
　　　　To mak a man;
But tell him he was learn'd and clark,
　　　　Ye roos'd him than!

---

## A DEDICATION TO GAVIN HAMILTON, ESQ.

EXPECT na, Sir, in this narration,
A fleechin', fleth'rin' Dedication,
To roose you up, an' ca' you guid,
An' sprung o' great an' noble bluid,
Because ye're sirnam'd like his Grace,
Perhaps related to the race;
Then when I'm tir'd—and sae are ye,
Wi' mony a fulsome, sinfu' lie,
Set up a face how I stop short
For fear your modesty be hurt.　　　　　　10

　　This may do—maun do, Sir, wi' them wha
Maun please the great folk for a wamefou;
For me! sae laigh I needna bow,
For, Lord be thankit, I can plough;
And when I downa yoke a naig,
Then, Lord be thankit, I can beg;
Sae I shall say, an' that's nae flatt'rin',
It's just sic Poet an' sic Patron.

　　The Poet, some guid angel help him,
Or else, I fear, some ill ane skelp him!　　　　20

He may do weel for a' he's done yet,
But only—he's no just begun yet.

　The Patron (Sir, ye maun forgie me,
I winna lie, come what will o' me)—
On ev'ry hand it will allow'd be,
He's just—nae better than he should be.

　I readily and freely grant,
He downa see a poor man want;
What's no his ain he winna tak it,
What ance he says he winna break it;　　　　　30
Ought he can lend he'll not refus't,
Till aft his guidness is abus'd;
And rascals whyles that do him wrang,
Ev'n that, he does na mind it lang:
As master, landlord, husband, father,
He does na fail his part in either.

　But then, nae thanks to him for a' that;
Nae godly symptom ye can ca' that;
It's naething but a milder feature
Of our poor, sinfu', corrupt nature:　　　　　40
Ye'll get the best o' moral works,
'Mang black Gentoos and pagan Turks,
Or hunters wild on Ponotaxi,
Wha never heard of orthodoxy.
That he's the poor man's friend in need,
The gentleman in word and deed,
It's no thro' terror of damnation;
It's just a carnal inclination.

　Morality, thou deadly bane,
Thy tens o' thousands thou hast slain!　　　　　50
Vain is his hope, whase stay and trust is
In moral mercy, truth, and justice!

　No—stretch a point to catch a plack;
Abuse a brother to his back;
Steal thro' the winnock frae a whore,
But point the rake that taks the door:
Be to the poor like ony whunstane,
And haud their noses to the grunstane,

Ply ev'ry art o' legal thieving ;
No matter—stick to sound believing.                     6c

Learn three-mile pray'rs, an' half-mile graces,
Wi' weel-spread looves, an' lang, wry faces ;
Grunt up a solemn, lengthen'd groan,
And damn a' parties but your own ;
I'll warrant then ye're nae deceiver,
A steady, sturdy, staunch believer.

O ye wha leave the springs of Calvin,
For gumlie dubs of your ain delvin !
Ye sons of heresy and error,
Ye'll some day squeal in quaking terror !          70
When vengeance draws the sword in wrath,
And in the fire throws the sheath ;
When Ruin, with his sweeping besom,
Just frets till Heav'n commission gies him :
While o'er the harp pale mis'ry moans, ⎫
And strikes the ever-deep'ning tones,     ⎬
Still louder shrieks, and heavier groans ! ⎭

Your pardon, Sir, for this digression,
I maist forgat my Dedication ;
But when divinity comes 'cross me,                     80
My readers still are sure to lose me.

So, Sir, ye see 'twas nae daft vapour.
But I maturely thought it proper,
When a' my works I did review,
To dedicate them, Sir, to You :
Because (ye need na tak it ill)
I thought them something like yoursel'.

Then patronize them wi' your favour,
And your petitioner shall ever—
I had amaist said ever pray :
But that 's a word I need na say :                     90
For prayin' I hae little skill o't ;
I'm baith dead-sweer, an wretched ill o't ;
But I'se repeat each poor man's pray'r,
That kens or hears about you, Sir.

'May ne'er misfortune's gowling bark
Howl thro' the dwelling o' the Clerk!
May ne'er his gen'rous, honest heart,
For that same gen'rous spirit smart!
May Kennedy's far-honour'd name                    100
Lang beet his hymeneal flame,
Till Hamiltons, at least a dizen,
Are frae their nuptial labours risen!
Five bonnie lasses round their table,
And seven braw fellows, stout an' able,
To serve their King and Country weel,
By word, or pen, or pointed steel!
May health and peace, in mutual rays,
Shine on the evening o' his days;
Till his wee, curlie John's ier-oe,               110
When ebbing life nae mair shall flow,
The last, sad, mournful rites bestow!'

I will not wind a lang conclusion
Wi' complimentary effusion:
But whilst your wishes and endeavours
Are blest with Fortune's smiles and favours,
I am, dear Sir, with zeal most fervent,
Your much indebted, humble servant.

But if (which Pow'rs above prevent)
That iron-hearted carl, Want,                      120
Attended in his grim advances,
By sad mistakes, and black mischances,
While hopes, and joys, and pleasures fly him,
Make you as poor a dog as I am,
Your humble servant then no more;
For who would humbly serve the poor?
But, by a poor man's hopes in Heav'n!
While recollection's pow'r is given,
If, in the vale of human life,
The victim sad of fortune's strife,               130
I, thro' the tender gushing tear,
Should recognize my Master dear,
If friendless, low, we meet together,
Then, Sir, your hand—my Friend and Brother!

# THE INVENTORY,

IN ANSWER TO THE USUAL MANDATE SENT BY A SURVEYOR OF
THE TAXES, REQUIRING A RETURN OF THE NUMBER OF
HORSES, SERVANTS, CARRIAGES, ETC. KEPT.

Sir, as your mandate did request,
I send you here a faithfu' list
O' gudes an' gear, an' a' my graith,
To which I'm clear to gi'e my aith.
Imprimis then, for carriage cattle,
I have four brutes o' gallant mettle,
As ever drew before a pettle ;
My han' afore 's a gude auld has-been,
An' wight an' wilfu' a' his days been ;
My han' ahin 's a weel gaun fillie,　　　　10
That aft has borne me hame frae Killie,
An' your auld burrough mony a time,
In days when riding was nae crime—
But ance whan in my wooing pride
I like a blockhead boost to ride,
The wilfu' creature sae I pat to,
(Lord, pardon a' my sins an' that too !)
I play'd my fillie sic a shavie,
She 's a' bedevil'd wi' the spavie.
My furr-ahin 's a wordy beast,　　　　20
As e'er in tug or tow was trac'd.
The fourth 's, a Highland Donald hastie,
A damn'd red-wud Kilburnie blastie.
Foreby a Cowte, o' Cowte 's the wale,
As ever ran afore a tail ;
If he be spar'd to be a beast,
He'll draw me fifteen pun at least.
Wheel carriages I ha'e but few,
Three carts, an' twa are feckly new ;
An auld wheel barrow, mair for token,　　　　30
Ae leg, an' baith the trams, are broken ;
I made a poker o' the spin'le,
An' my auld mother burnt the trin'le.
For men, I've three mischievous boys,
Run de'ils for rantin' an' for noise ;

A gaudsman ane, a thrasher t'other,
Wee Davock hauds the nowte in fother.
I rule them as I ought discreetly,
An' often labour them completely.
An' aye on Sundays duly nightly, 40
I on the questions tairge them tightly ;
Till faith, wee Davock's grown sae gleg,
Tho' scarcely langer than my leg
He'll screed you aff Effectual Calling,
As fast as ony in the dwalling.
  I've nane in female servan' station,
(Lord keep me aye frae a' temptation!)
I ha'e nae wife, and that my bliss is,
An' ye have laid nae tax on misses ;
An' then if kirk folks dinna clutch me, 50
I ken the devils dare na touch me.
Wi' weans I'm mair than weel contented,
Heav'n sent me ane mae than I wanted.
My sonsie smirking dear-bought Bess,
She stares the daddy in her face,
Enough of ought ye like but grace.
But her, my bonnie sweet wee lady,
I've paid enough for her already,
An' gin ye tax her or her mither,
B' the Lord, ye'se get them a' thegither. 60
  And now, remember, Mr. Aiken,
Nae kind of license out I'm takin' ;
Frae this time forth, I do declare,
I'se ne'er ride horse nor hizzie mair ;
Thro' dirt and dub for life I'll paidle,
Ere I sae dear pay for a saddle ;
My travel a' on foot I'll shank it,
I've sturdy bearers, Gude be thankit !
The Kirk an' you may tak' you that,
It puts but little in your pat ; 70
Sae dinna put me in your buke,
Nor for my ten white shillings luke.
  This list wi' my ain han' I wrote it,
The day an' date as under notit :
Then know all ye whom it concerns,
Subscripsi huic—ROBERT BURNS.

  *Mossgiel, February 22, 1786.*

## ADDRESS OF BEELZEBUB

TO THE PRESIDENT OF THE HIGHLAND SOCIETY.

Long life, my Lord, an' health be yours,
Unskaith'd by hunger'd Highland boors ;
Lord grant nae duddie desperate beggar,
Wi' dirk, claymore, or rusty trigger,
May twin auld Scotland o' a life
She likes—as lambkins like a knife.
Faith, you and Applecross were right
To keep the Highland hounds in sight !
I doubt na', they wad bid nae better
Than let them ance out owre the water ;        10
Then up amang thae lakes and seas
They'll mak' what rules and laws they please ;
Some daring Hancock, or a Franklin,
May set their Highland bluid a ranklin' ;
Some Washington again may head them,
Or some Montgomery fearless lead them,
Till God knows what may be effected
When by such heads and hearts directed ;
Poor dunghill sons of dirt and mire
May to Patrician rights aspire !        20
Nae sage North, now, nor sager Sackville,
To watch and premier o'er the pack vile ;
An' where will ye get Howes and Clintons
To bring them to a right repentance,
To cowe the rebel generation,
An' save the honour o' the nation ?
They an' be d—d ! what right hae they
To meat or sleep, or light o' day !
Far less to riches, pow'r, or freedom,
But what your lordship likes to gie them ?        30

But hear, my lord ! Glengarry, hear !
Your hand 's owre light on them, I fear ;
Your factors, grieves, trustees, and bailies,
I canna' say but they do gaylies ;
They lay aside a' tender mercies,
An' tirl the hallions to the birses ;

Yet while they're only poind't and herriet,
They'll keep their stubborn Highland spirit;
But smash them! crash them a' to spails!
An' rot the dyvors i' the jails!                    40
The young dogs, swinge them to the labour!
Let wark an' hunger mak' them sober!
The hizzies, if they're aughtlins fawsont,
Let them in Drury Lane be lesson'd!
An' if the wives an' dirty brats
Come thiggin' at your doors an' yetts,
Flaffin' wi' duds an' grey wi' beas',
Frightin' awa your deucks an' geese,
Get out a horsewhip or a jowler,
The langest thong, the fiercest growler,            50
An' gar the tatter'd gypsies pack
Wi' a' their bastards on their back!
Go on, my lord! I lang to meet you,
An' in my house at hame to greet you;
Wi' common lords ye shanna mingle,
The benmost neuk beside the ingle,
At my right han' assign'd your seat
'Tween Herod's hip an' Polycrate;
Or (if you on your station tarrow)
Between Almagro and Pizarro,—                        60
A seat, I'm sure, ye're weel deservin't;
An' till ye come—Your humble servant,
                                        BEELZEBUB.

*June 1, Anno Mundi* 5790.

---

## NATURE'S LAW.

LET other heroes boast their scars,
    The marks of sturt and strife;
And other poets sing of wars,
    The plagues of human life;
Shame fa' the fun; wi' sword and gun
    To slap mankind like lumber!
I sing his name and nobler fame,
    Wha multiplies our number.

Great Nature spoke, with air benign,
   'Go on, ye human race!      10
This lower world I you resign;
   Be fruitful and increase.
The liquid fire of strong desire
   I've pour'd it in each bosom;
Here, on this hand, does mankind stand,
   And there is Beauty's blossom!'


The Hero of these artless strains,
   A lowly Bard was he,
Who sung his rhymes in Coila's plains
   With meikle mirth an' glee;     20
Kind Nature's care had given his share,
   Large, of the flaming current;
And, all devout, he never sought
   To stem the sacred torrent.


He felt the powerful, high behest,
   Thrill, vital, thro' and thro';
And sought a correspondent breast
   To give obedience due;
Propitious Powers screen'd the young flow'rs,
   From mildews of abortion;     30
And lo! the bard, a great reward,
   Has got a double portion!


Auld, cantie Coil may count the day,
   As annual it returns,
The third of Libra's equal sway,
   That gave another Burns,
With future rhymes, in other times,
   To emulate his sire;
To sing auld Coil in nobler style
   With more poetic fire.     40


Ye Powers of peace, and peaceful song,
   Look down with gracious eyes;
And bless auld Coila, large and long,
   With multiplying joys.

Long may she stand to prop the land,
  The flow'r of ancient nations;
And Burnses spring, her fame to sing,
  To endless generations!

———✦———

## TO MR. JOHN KENNEDY.

Now Kennedy, if foot or horse
E'er bring you in by Mauchline Corss,
Lord! man, there's lasses there wad force
      A hermit's fancy,
And down the gate in faith they're worse
      And mair unchancy.

But, as I'm sayin', please step to Dow's
And taste sic gear as Johnny brews,
Till some bit callan brings me news
      That you are there,          10
And if we dinna had a bouze
      I'se ne'er drink mair.

It's no I like to sit an' swallow,
Then like a swine to puke an' wallow,
But gie me just a true good fallow
      Wi' right ingine,
And spunkie ance to make us mellow,
      And then we'll shine.

Now if ye're ane o' warl's folk,
Wha rate the wearer by the cloak,
An' sklent on poverty their joke,          20
      Wi' bitter sneer,
Wi' you no friendship I will troke,
      Nor cheap nor dear.

But if, as I'm informèd weel,
Ye hate as ill's the very deil,
The flinty hearts that canna feel—
      Come, Sir, here's tae you ;
Hae ! there's my haun' ; I wiss you weel,
      And gude be wi' you.      30

## THE CALF.

TO THE REV. MR. JAMES STEVEN, ON HIS TEXT,

'*And ye shall go forth, and grow up as calves of the stall.*'—Mal. iv. 2.

RIGHT, Sir ! your text I'll prove it true,
    Tho' Heretics may laugh ;
For instance, there's yoursel just now,
    God knows, an unco Calf !

And should some Patron be so kind,
    As bless you wi' a kirk,
I doubt na, Sir, but then we'll find,
    Ye're still as great a Stirk.

But, if the Lover's raptur'd hour,
    Shall ever be your lot,      10
Forbid it, ev'ry heavenly Power,
    You e'er should be a Stot !

Tho', when some kind, connubial Dear,
    Your but-and-ben adorns,
The like has been that you may wear
    A noble head of horns.

And, in your lug, most reverend James,
    To hear you roar and rowte,
Few men o' sense will doubt your claims
    To rank amang the Nowte.      20

And when ye're number'd wi' the dead,
  Below a grassy hillock,
Wi' justice they may mark your head—
  'Here lies a famous Bullock!'

———•———

# LINES ON AN INTERVIEW WITH LORD DAER.

THIS wot ye all whom it concerns,
I, Rhymer Robin, alias Burns,
    October twenty-third,
A ne'er to be forgotten day,
Sae far I sprachled up the brae,
    I dinner'd wi' a Lord.

I've been at drunken writers' feasts,
Nay, been bitch-fou 'mang godly priests,
    Wi' rev'rence be it spoken!
I've even join'd the honour'd jorum,            10
When mighty Squireships of the quorum
    Their hydra drouth did sloken.

But wi' a Lord—stand out my shin;
A Lord—a Peer—an Earl's son,
    Up higher yet, my bonnet!
And sic a Lord!—lang Scotch ells twa,
Our Peerage he o'erlooks them a',
    As I look o'er my sonnet.

But O for Hogarth's magic pow'r!
To show Sir Bardie's willyart glow'r,           20
    And how he star'd and stammer'd,
When govin', as if led wi' branks,
An' stumpin' on his ploughman shanks,
    He in the parlour hammer'd.

I sidling shelter'd in a nook,
An' at his Lordship steal't a look,
    Like some portentous omen ;
Except good sense and social glee,
An' (what surprisèd me) modesty,
    I markèd nought uncommon.     30

I watch'd the symptoms o' the Great,
The gentle pride, the lordly state,
    The arrogant assuming ;
The fient a pride, nae pride had he,
Nor sauce, nor state that I could see,
    Mair than an honest ploughman.

Then from his lordship I shall learn
Henceforth to meet with unconcern
    One rank as weel's another ;
Nae honest worthy man need care     40
To meet with noble youthful Daer,
    For he but meets a brother.

---

# LYING AT A REVEREND FRIEND'S HOUSE
## ONE NIGHT

THE AUTHOR LEFT THE FOLLOWING VERSES IN THE ROOM
WHERE HE SLEPT.

O Thou dread Pow'r, who reign'st above,
    I know Thou wilt me hear
When for this scene of peace and love,
    I make my pray'r sincere.

The hoary sire—the mortal stroke,
    Long, long be pleas'd to spare ;
To bless his little filial flock,
    And show what good men are.

She, who her lovely offspring eyes
  With tender hopes and fears,         10
O bless her with a mother's joys,
  But spare a mother's tears!

Their hope, their stay, their darling youth,
  In manhood's dawning blush—
Bless him, thou God of love and truth,
  Up to a parent's wish.

The beauteous, seraph sister-band,
  With earnest tears I pray,
Thou know'st the snares on ev'ry hand,
  Guide Thou their steps alway.       20

When soon or late they reach that coast,
  O'er life's rough ocean driven,
May they rejoice, no wand'rer lost,
  A family in Heaven!

---

## THE FAREWELL.

FAREWELL, old Scotia's bleak domains,
Far dearer than the torrid plains
  Where rich ananas blow!
Farewell, a mother's blessing dear!
A brother's sigh! a sister's tear!
  My Jean's heart-rending throe!
Farewell, my Bess! tho' thou'rt bereft
  Of my parental care,
A faithful brother I have left,
  My part in him thou'lt share!      10
    Adieu too, to you too,
      My Smith, my bosom frien';
    When kindly you mind me,
      O then befriend my Jean!

When bursting anguish tears my heart,
From thee, my Jeany, must I part?
    Thou weeping answ'rest 'no!'
Alas! misfortune stares my face,
And points to ruin and disgrace;
    I for thy sake must go!                    20
Thee, Hamilton, and Aiken dear,
    A grateful, warm adieu!
I, with a much-indebted tear,
    Shall still remember you!
        All-hail then the gale then,
            Wafts me from thee, dear shore!
        It rustles, and whistles,
            I'll never see thee more!

---

## INSCRIPTION ON THE TOMBSTONE

ERECTED BY BURNS TO THE MEMORY OF FERGUSSON.

No sculptur'd marble here, nor pompous lay,
    'No storied urn nor animated bust;'
This simple stone directs pale Scotia's way
    To pour her sorrows o'er her Poet's dust.

She mourns, sweet tuneful youth, thy hapless fate:
    Tho' all the powers of song thy fancy fir'd,
Yet Luxury and Wealth lay by in State,
    And thankless starv'd what they so much admir'd.

This humble tribute with a tear he gives,
    A brother Bard, who can no more bestow:      10
But dear to fame thy Song immortal lives,
    A nobler monument than Art can show.

# VERSES WRITTEN UNDER THE PORTRAIT OF FERGUSSON THE POET,

### IN A COPY OF THAT AUTHOR'S WORKS PRESENTED TO A YOUNG LADY IN EDINBURGH, MARCH 19, 1787.

CURSE on ungrateful man, that can be pleas'd,
And yet can starve the author of the pleasure!
O thou, my elder brother in misfortune,
By far my elder brother in the Muses,
With tears I pity thy unhappy fate!
Why is the Bard unpitied by the world,
Yet has so keen a relish of its pleasures?

———◆◆———

# ON SCARING SOME WATER FOWL

### IN LOCH-TURIT, A WILD SCENE AMONG THE HILLS OF OCHTERTYRE.

WHY, ye tenants of the lake,
For me your wat'ry haunt forsake?
Tell me, fellow-creatures, why
At my presence thus you fly?
Why disturb your social joys,
Parent, filial, kindred ties?—
Common friend to you and me,
Nature's gifts to all are free:
Peaceful keep your dimpling wave,
Busy feed, or wanton lave;                    10
Or, beneath the sheltering rock,
Bide the surging billow's shock.
Conscious, blushing for our race,
Soon, too soon, your fears I trace.
Man, your proud, usurping foe,
Would be lord of all below;

Plumes himself in Freedom's pride,
Tyrant stern to all beside.
　　The eagle, from the cliffy brow,
Marking you his prey below,　　　　　　　　　20
In his breast no pity dwells,
Strong Necessity compels.
But Man, to whom alone is giv'n
A ray direct from pitying Heav'n,
Glories in his heart humane—
And creatures for his pleasure slain.
　　In these savage, liquid plains,
Only known to wand'ring swains,
Where the mossy riv'let strays,
Far from human haunts and ways ;　　　　30
All on Nature you depend,
And life's poor season peaceful spend.
　　Or, if man's superior might
Dare invade your native right,
On the lofty ether borne,
Man with all his pow'rs you scorn ;
Swiftly seek, on clanging wings,
Other lakes and other springs ;
And the foe you cannot brave,
Scorn at least to be his slave.　　　　　　40

---

## WRITTEN WITH A PENCIL

OVER THE CHIMNEY-PIECE IN THE PARLOUR OF THE INN AT
KENMORE, TAYMOUTH.

ADMIRING Nature in her wildest grace,
These northern scenes with weary feet I trace ;
O'er many a winding dale and painful steep,
Th' abodes of covey'd grouse and timid sheep,
My savage journey, curious, I pursue,
Till fam'd Breadalbane opens to my view.
The meeting cliffs each deep-sunk glen divides,
The woods, wild scatter'd, clothe their ample sides ;

Th' outstretching lake, embosom'd 'mong the hills,
The eye with wonder and amazement fills;　　　10
The Tay meand'ring sweet in infant pride,
The palace rising on his verdant side;
The lawns wood-fringed in Nature's native taste,
The hillocks dropt in Nature's careless haste;
The arches striding o'er the new-born stream;
The village, glittering in the noontide beam—

　　*　　*　　*　　*　　*　　*

Poetic ardours in my bosom swell,
Lone wand'ring by the hermit's mossy cell:
The sweeping theatre of hanging woods;
Th' incessant roar of headlong tumbling floods—　　20

　　*　　*　　*　　*　　*　　*

Here Poesy might wake her heav'n-taught lyre,
And look through Nature with creative fire;
Here, to the wrongs of Fate half reconcil'd,
Misfortune's lighten'd steps might wander wild;
And Disappointment, in these lonely bounds,
Find balm to soothe her bitter, rankling wounds:
Here heart-struck Grief might heav'nward stretch her scan,
And injur'd Worth forget and pardon man.

　　*　　*　　*　　*　　*　　*

———◆———

## WRITTEN WITH A PENCIL

STANDING BY THE FALL OF FYERS, NEAR LOCH-NESS.

AMONG the heathy hills and ragged woods
The roaring Fyers pours his mossy floods;
Till full he dashes on the rocky mounds,
Where, thro' a shapeless breach, his stream resounds.
As high in air the bursting torrents flow,
As deep recoiling surges foam below,
Prone down the rock the whitening sheet descends,
And viewless Echo's ear, astonished, rends.

Dim-seen, thro' rising mists and ceaseless show'rs,
The hoary cavern, wide-surrounding, lours.　　　　10
Still thro' the gap the struggling river toils,
And still, below, the horrid cauldron boils—

\*　　　\*　　　\*　　　\*　　　\*　　　\*

## ON THE DEATH OF ROBERT DUNDAS, ESQ.

OF ARNISTON, LATE LORD PRESIDENT OF THE COURT OF
SESSION.

Lone on the bleaky hills the straying flocks
Shun the fierce storms among the sheltering rocks;
Down from the rivulets, red with dashing rains,
The gathering floods burst o'er the distant plains;
Beneath the blasts the leafless forests groan;
The hollow caves return a sullen moan.

Ye hills, ye plains, ye forests, and ye caves,
Ye howling winds, and wintry swelling waves!
Unheard, unseen, by human ear or eye,
Sad to your sympathetic glooms I fly;　　　　10
Where to the whistling blast and water's roar,
Pale Scotia's recent wound I may deplore.

O heavy loss, thy country ill could bear!
A loss these evil days can ne'er repair!
Justice, the high vicegerent of her God,
Her doubtful balance eyed, and sway'd her rod;
Hearing the tidings of the fatal blow,
She sunk, abandon'd to the wildest woe.

Wrongs, injuries, from many a darksome den,
Now gay in hope explore the paths of men:　　　　20
See from his cavern grim Oppression rise,
And throw on Poverty his cruel eyes;
Keen on the helpless victim see him fly,
And stifle, dark, the feebly bursting cry:

Mark ruffian Violence, distain'd with crimes,
Rousing elate in these degenerate times ;
View unsuspecting Innocence a prey,
As guileful Fraud points out the erring way :
While subtile Litigation's pliant tongue
The life-blood equal sucks of Right and Wrong :    30
Hark, injured Want recounts th' unlisten'd tale,
And much-wrong'd Mis'ry pours th' unpitied wail !

Ye dark waste hills, and brown unsightly plains,
To you I sing my grief-inspirèd strains :
Ye tempests, rage ! ye turbid torrents, roll !
Ye suit the joyless tenor of my soul.
Life's social haunts and pleasures I resign ;
Be nameless wilds and lonely wanderings mine,
To mourn the woes my country must endure,
That wound degenerate ages cannot cure.    40

—••—

# ON THE DEATH OF SIR JAMES HUNTER BLAIR.

THE lamp of day, with ill-presaging glare,
    Dim, cloudy, sunk beneath the western wave ;
Th' inconstant blast howl'd thro' the dark'ning air,
    And hollow whistled in the rocky cave.

Lone as I wander'd by each cliff and dell,
    Once the lov'd haunts of Scotia's royal train ;
Or mus'd where limpid streams, once hallow'd, well ;
    Or mould'ring ruins mark the sacred fane.

Th' increasing blast roar'd round the beetling rocks,
    The clouds swift-wing'd flew o'er the starry sky,    10
The groaning trees untimely shed their locks,
    And shooting meteors caught the startled eye.

The paly moon rose in the livid east,
    And 'mong the cliffs disclos'd a stately Form,
In weeds of woe, that frantic beat her breast,
    And mix'd her wailings with the raving storm.

Wild to my heart the filial pulses glow,
   'Twas Caledonia's trophied shield I view'd:
Her form majestic droop'd in pensive woe,
   The lightning of her eye in tears imbued.    20

Revers'd that spear, redoubtable in war,
   Reclin'd that banner, erst in fields unfurl'd,
That like a deathful meteor gleam'd afar,
   And brav'd the mighty monarchs of the world.

'My patriot son fills an untimely grave!'
   With accents wild and lifted arms she cried;
'Low lies the hand that oft was stretch'd to save,
   Low lies the heart that swell'd with honest pride!

'A weeping country joins a widow's tear,
   The helpless poor mix with the orphan's cry;    30
The drooping arts surround their patron's bier,
   And grateful science heaves the heartfelt sigh.

'I saw my sons resume their ancient fire;
   I saw fair Freedom's blossoms richly blow;
But, ah! how hope is born but to expire!
   Relentless fate has laid their guardian low.

'My patriot falls: but shall he lie unsung,
   While empty greatness saves a worthless name?
No; every Muse shall join her tuneful tongue,
   And future ages hear his growing fame.    40

'And I will join a mother's tender cares,
   Thro' future times to make his virtues last,
That distant years may boast of other Blairs,'—
   She said, and vanish'd with the sweeping blast.

## PROLOGUE,

WHEN by a generous public's kind acclaim,
That dearest meed is granted—honest fame ;
When here your favour is the actor's lot,
Nor even the man in private life forgot ;
What breast so dead to heav'nly virtue's glow,
But heaves impassion'd with the grateful throe ?
   Poor is the task to please a barb'rous throng,
It needs no Siddons' power in Southern's song :
But here an ancient nation, fam'd afar
For genius, learning high, as great in war—          10
Hail, Caledonia ! name for ever dear !
Before whose sons I'm honour'd to appear !
Where every science, every nobler art,
That can inform the mind, or mend the heart,
Is known ; as grateful nations oft have found,
Far as the rude barbarian marks the bound.
Philosophy, no idle, pedant dream,
Here holds her search, by heaven-taught Reason's beam ;
Here History paints with elegance and force,
The tide of Empire's fluctuating course ;          20
Here Douglas forms wild Shakespeare into plan,
And Harley rouses all the god in man.
When well-form'd taste and sparkling wit unite,
With manly love, or female beauty bright
(Beauty, where faultless symmetry and grace
Can only charm us in the second place)—
Witness my heart, how oft with panting fear,
As on this night, I've met these judges here !
But still the hope Experience taught to live,
Equal to judge—you're candid to forgive.          30
No hundred-headed Riot here we meet,
With decency and law beneath his feet,
Nor Insolence assumes fair Freedom's name ;
Like Caledonians, you applaud or blame.

O Thou, dread Power! whose empire-giving hand
Has oft been stretch'd to shield the honour'd land,
Strong may she glow with all her ancient fire;
May every son be worthy of his sire;
Firm may she rise with generous disdain
At Tyranny's, or direr Pleasure's chain;            40
Still self-dependent in her native shore,
Bold may she brave grim Danger's loudest roar,
Till Fate the curtain drop on worlds to be no more.

---

## PROLOGUE

SPOKEN AT THE THEATRE, DUMFRIES, ON NEW YEAR'S DAY
EVENING [1790].

No song nor dance I bring from yon great city
That queens it o'er our taste—the more's the pity;
Tho', by-the-by, abroad why will you roam?
Good sense and taste are natives here at home:
But not for panegyric I appear,
I come to wish you all a good New-Year!
Old Father Time deputes me here before ye,
Not for to preach, but tell his simple story:
The sage grave Ancient cough'd, and bade me say,
'You're one year older this important day.'       10
If wiser too—he hinted some suggestion,
But 'twould be rude, you know, to ask the question;
And with a would-be roguish leer and wink,
Said, 'Sutherland, in one word, bid them *think*!'
  Ye sprightly youths quite flush with hope and spirit,
Who think to storm the world by dint of merit,
To you the dotard has a deal to say,
In his sly, dry, sententious, proverb way!
He bids you mind, amid your thoughtless rattle,
That the first blow is ever half the battle;     20
That tho' some by the skirt may try to snatch him;
Yet by the forelock is the hold to catch him;
That whether doing, suffering, or forbearing,
You may do miracles by persevering.

Last, tho' not least in love, ye youthful fair,
Angelic forms, high Heaven's peculiar care!
To you old Bald-pate smoothes his wrinkled brow,
And humbly begs you'll mind the important—*Now!*
To crown your happiness he asks your leave,
And offers bliss to give and to receive.　　　　30
　　For our sincere, tho' haply weak endeavours,
With grateful pride we own your many favours;
And howsoe'er our tongues may ill reveal it,
Believe our glowing bosoms truly feel it.

---

# PROLOGUE

FOR MR. SUTHERLAND'S BENEFIT-NIGHT, DUMFRIES.

WHAT needs this din about the town o' Lon'on,
How this new play an' that new sang is comin'?
Why is outlandish stuff sae meikle courted?
Does nonsense mend like brandy, when imported?
Is there nae poet, burning keen for fame,
Will try to gie us sangs and plays at hame?
For comedy abroad he need na toil,
A fool and knave are plants of every soil;
Nor need he hunt as far as Rome and Greece
To gather matter for a serious piece;　　　　10
There's themes enow in Caledonian story,
Would show the tragic muse in a' her glory.
　　Is there no daring Bard will rise, and tell
How glorious Wallace stood, how hapless fell?
Where are the Muses fled that could produce
A drama worthy o' the name o' Bruce;
How here, even here, he first unsheath'd the sword
'Gainst mighty England and her guilty lord;
And after mony a bloody, deathless doing,
Wrench'd his dear country from the jaws of ruin?　　20
O for a Shakespeare or an Otway scene,
To draw the lovely, hapless Scottish Queen!
Vain all th' omnipotence of female charms
'Gainst headlong, ruthless, mad Rebellion's arms.

She fell, but fell with spirit truly Roman,
To glut the vengeance of a rival woman;
A woman, tho' the phrase may seem uncivil,
As able and as wicked as the devil!
One Douglas lives in Home's immortal page,
But Douglases were heroes every age:                    30
And tho' your fathers, prodigal of life,
A Douglas follow'd to the martial strife,
Perhaps, if bowls row right, and Right succeeds,
Ye yet may follow where a Douglas leads!
  As ye hae generous done, if a' the land
Would tak the Muses' servants by the hand;
Not only hear, but patronize, befriend them,
And where ye justly can commend, commend them;
And aiblins when they winna stand the test,
Wink hard, and say the folks hae done their best!      40
Would a' the land do this, then I'll be cation
Ye'll soon hae poets o' the Scottish nation
Will gar Fame blaw until her trumpet crack,
And warsle time, an' lay him on his back!
  For us and for our stage should ony spier,
'Whase aught thae chiels maks a' this bustle here?
My best leg foremost, I'll set up my brow.
We hae the honour to belong to you!
We're your ain bairns, e'en guide us as ye like,
But like good mithers, shore before ye strike—          50
And gratefu' still I hope ye'll ever find us,
For a' the patronage and meikle kindness
We've got frae a' professions, sets and ranks:
God help us! we're but poor—ye'se get but thanks.

---

## THE RIGHTS OF WOMAN.

PROLOGUE SPOKEN BY MISS FONTENELLE ON HER BENEFIT-
NIGHT.  [NOV. 26, 1792.]

WHILE Europe's eye is fix'd on mighty things,
The fate of Empires, and the fall of Kings;
While quacks of State must each produce his plan,
And even children lisp the Rights of Man;

Amid the mighty fuss just let me mention,
The Rights of Woman merit some attention.
First, in the Sexes' intermix'd connexion,
One sacred Right of Woman is, Protection.
The tender flower that lifts its head, elate,
Helpless, must fall before the blasts of Fate,　　　10
Sunk on the earth, defac'd its lovely form,
Unless your shelter ward th' impending storm.
Our second Right—but needless here is caution,
To keep that Right inviolate 's the fashion,
Each man of sense has it so full before him,
He'd die before he'd wrong it—'tis Decorum.
There was, indeed, in far less polished days,
A time, when rough rude man had naughty ways;
Would swagger, swear, get drunk, kick up a riot,
Nay, even thus invade a Lady's quiet!　　　20
Now, thank our stars! those Gothic times are fled;
Now, well-bred men—and you are all well-bred!
Most justly think (and we are much the gainers)
Such conduct neither spirit, wit, nor manners.
For Right the third, our last, our best, our dearest,
That Right to fluttering female hearts the nearest,
Which even the Rights of Kings in low prostration
Most humbly own—'tis dear, dear admiration!
In that blest sphere alone we live and move;
There taste that life of life—immortal love.　　　30
Sighs, tears, smiles, glances, fits, flirtations, airs,
'Gainst such an host what flinty savage dares?
When awful Beauty joins with all her charms,
Who is so rash as rise in rebel arms?
Then truce with kings, and truce with constitutions,
With bloody armaments and revolutions!
Let Majesty your first attention summon,
Ah! ça ira! The Majesty of Woman!

## ADDRESS, SPOKEN BY MISS FONTENELLE,

ON HER BENEFIT-NIGHT, DECEMBER 4, 1793, AT THE
THEATRE, DUMFRIES.

STILL anxious to secure your partial favour,
And not less anxious, sure, this night, than ever,
A Prologue, Epilogue, or some such matter,
'Twould vamp my bill, said I, if nothing better;
So sought a Poet, roosted near the skies,
Told him I came to feast my curious eyes;
Said nothing like his works was ever printed;
And last, my Prologue-business slily hinted.
'Ma'am, let me tell you,' quoth my man of rhymes,
'I know your bent—these are no laughing times:    10
Can you—but, Miss, I own I have my fears—
Dissolve in pause, and sentimental tears?
With laden sighs, and solemn-rounded sentence,
Rouse from his sluggish slumbers fell Repentance,
Paint Vengeance as he takes his horrid stand,
Waving on high the desolating brand,
Calling the storms to bear him o'er a guilty land?'
    I could no more—askance the creature eyeing,
D'ye think, said I, this face was made for crying?
I'll laugh, that's poz—nay, more, the world shall know it;
And so, your servant! gloomy Master Poet!    21
    Firm as my creed, Sirs, 'tis my fix'd belief,
That Misery's another word for Grief;
I also think—so may I be a bride!
That so much laughter, so much life enjoy'd.
    Thou man of crazy care and ceaseless sigh,
Still under bleak Misfortune's blasting eye;
Doom'd to that sorest task of man alive—
To make three guineas do the work of five:
Laugh in Misfortune's face—the beldam witch!    30
Say you'll be merry, tho' you can't be rich.
    Thou other man of care, the wretch in love,
Who long with jiltish arts and airs hast strove;
Who, as the boughs all temptingly project,
Measur'st in desperate thought—a rope—thy neck—

Or, where the beetling cliff o'erhangs the deep,
Peerest to meditate the healing leap:
Would'st thou be cur'd, thou silly, moping elf?
Laugh at her follies—laugh e'en at thyself:
Learn to despise those frowns now so terrific,       40
And love a kinder: that's your grand specific.
  To sum up all, be merry, I advise;
And as we're merry, may we still be wise.

# ON SEEING MISS FONTENELLE

### IN A FAVOURITE CHARACTER.

SWEET naïveté of feature,
  Simple, wild, enchanting elf,
Not to thee, but thanks to Nature,
  Thou art acting but thyself.

Wert thou awkward, stiff, affected,
  Spurning nature, torturing art;
Loves and graces all rejected,
  Then indeed thou'dst act a part.

# ODE, SACRED TO THE MEMORY OF
# MRS. OSWALD.

DWELLER in yon dungeon dark,
Hangman of creation! mark
Who in widow-weeds appears,
Laden with unhonour'd years,
Noosing with care a bursting purse,
Baited with many a deadly curse!

### STROPHE.

View the wither'd beldam's face—
Can thy keen inspection trace
Aught of humanity's sweet melting grace?

Note that eye, 'tis rheum o'erflows,                    10
Pity's flood there never rose.
See those hands, ne'er stretch'd to save
Hands that took—but never gave.
Keeper of Mammon's iron chest,
Lo, there she goes, unpitied and unblest;
She goes, but not to realms of everlasting rest!

### ANTISTROPHE.

Plunderer of armies, lift thine eyes
(Awhile forbear, ye torturing fiends!)—
Seest thou whose step unwilling hither bends?
No fallen angel, hurl'd from upper skies;                20
'Tis thy trusty quondam mate,
Doom'd to share thy fiery fate,
She, tardy, hell-ward plies.

### EPODE.

And are they of no more avail,
Ten thousand glitt'ring pounds a year?
In other worlds can Mammon fail,
Omnipotent as he is here?
O, bitter mock'ry of the pompous bier,
While down the wretched vital part is driv'n!
The cave-lodg'd beggar, with a conscience clear,       30
Expires in rags, unknown, and goes to Heav'n.

———•———

## ELEGY ON THE YEAR 1788.

For Lords or Kings I dinna mourn,
E'en let them die—for that they're born:
But oh! prodigious to reflec'!
A Towmont, Sirs, is gane to wreck!
O Eighty-eight, in thy sma' space
What dire events hae taken place!
Of what enjoyments thou hast reft us!
In what a pickle thou hast left us!

The Spanish empire's tint a head,
And my auld teethless Bawtie's dead!                    10
The tulzie's sair 'tween Pitt an' Fox,
An' our gudewife's wee birdy cocks;
The tane is game, a bludie devil,
But to the hen-birds unco civil;
The tither's something dour o' treadin,
But better stuff ne'er claw'd a midden.

Ye ministers, come mount the poupit,
An' cry till ye be hearse an' roupet,
For Eighty-eight he wish'd you weel,
And gied you a' baith gear an' meal;                    20
E'en mony a plack, and mony a peck,
Ye ken yoursels, for little feck.

Ye bonnie lasses, dight your een,
For some o' you hae tint a frien';
In Eighty-eight, ye ken, was ta'en
What ye'll ne'er hae to gie again.

Observe the very nowt an' sheep,
How dowf and daviely they creep;
Nay, even the yirth itsel does cry,
For E'mbrugh wells are grutten dry.                     30

O Eighty-nine, thou's but a bairn,
An' no owre auld, I hope, to learn!
Thou beardless boy, I pray tak care,
Thou now hast got thy daddie's chair,
Nae hand-cuff'd, mizzl'd, hap-shackl'd Regent,
But, like himsel, a full free agent.
Be sure ye follow out the plan
Nae waur than he did, honest man:
As muckle better as you can.

*January 1, 1789.*

## ON SEEING A WOUNDED HARE LIMP BY ME,

### WHICH A FELLOW HAD JUST SHOT AT.

INHUMAN man! curse on thy barb'rous art,
 And blasted be thy murder-aiming eye;
 May never pity soothe thee with a sigh,
Nor ever pleasure glad thy cruel heart!

Go, live, poor wanderer of the wood and field,
 The bitter little that of life remains;
 No more the thickening brakes and verdant plains
To thee shall home, or food, or pastime yield.

Seek, mangled wretch, some place of wonted rest,
 No more of rest, but now thy dying bed!   10
 The sheltering rushes whistling o'er thy head,
The cold earth with thy bloody bosom prest.

Perhaps a mother's anguish adds its woe;
 The playful pair crowd fondly by thy side:
 Ah, helpless nurslings! who will now provide
That life a mother only can bestow?

Oft as by winding Nith, I, musing, wait
 The sober eve, or hail the cheerful dawn,
 I'll miss thee sporting o'er the dewy lawn,
And curse the ruffian's aim, and mourn thy hapless fate.

---

## SKETCH

### INSCRIBED TO THE RIGHT HON. C. J. FOX.

How Wisdom and Folly meet, mix, and unite;
How Virtue and Vice blend their black and their white;
How Genius, th' illustrious father of fiction,
Confounds rule and law, reconciles contradiction—
I sing; If these mortals, the Critics, should bustle,
I care not, not I—let the Critics go whistle!

But now for a Patron, whose name and whose glory
At once may illustrate and honour my story.
Thou first of our orators, first of our wits ;　　9
Yet whose parts and acquirements seem just lucky hits ;
With knowledge so vast, and with judgment so strong,
No man with the half of 'em e'er could go wrong ;
With passions so potent, and fancies so bright,
No man with the half of 'em e'er could go right ;
A sorry, poor, misbegot son of the Muses,
For using thy name offers fifty excuses.
Good Lord, what is man ! for as simple he looks,
Do but try to develop his hooks and his crooks,
With his depths and his shallows, his good and his evil,
All in all, he 's a problem must puzzle the devil.　　20
On his one ruling passion Sir Pope hugely labours,
That, like th' old Hebrew walking-switch, eats up its
　　neighbours :
Mankind are his show-box—a friend, would you know him ?
Pull the string, Ruling Passion : the picture will show him.
What pity, in rearing so beauteous a system,
One trifling particular, Truth, should have miss'd him !
For, spite of his fine theoretic positions,
Mankind is a science defies definitions.

Some sort all our qualities each to its tribe,
And think Human-nature they truly describe ;　　30
Have you found this, or t'other ? there 's more in the
　　wind ;
As by one drunken fellow his comrades you'll find.
But such is the flaw, or the depth of the plan,
In the make of the wonderful creature call'd Man ;
No two virtues, whatever relation they claim,
Nor even two different shades of the same,
Though like as was ever twin-brother to brother
Possessing the one shall imply you've the other.

But truce with abstraction, and truce with a muse　　39
Whose rhymes you'll perhaps, Sir, ne'er deign to peruse :
Will you leave your justings, your jars, and your quarrels,
Contending with Billy for proud-nodding laurels !
My much-honour'd Patron, believe your poor Poet,
Your courage much more than your prudence you show it

In vain with Squire Billy for laurels you struggle,
He'll have them by fair trade, if not, he will smuggle;
Not cabinets even of kings would conceal 'em,
He'd up the back-stairs, and, by God, he would steal 'em.
Then feats like Squire Billy's you ne'er can achieve 'em,
It is not, outdo him—the task is, out-thieve him.　　50

---

## NEW-YEAR DAY.

### TO MRS. DUNLOP.

THIS day Time winds th' exhausted chain,
To run the twelvemonth's length again:
I see the old, bald-pated fellow,
With ardent eyes, complexion sallow,
Adjust the unimpair'd machine
To wheel the equal, dull routine.
The absent lover, minor heir,
In vain assail him with their prayer,
Deaf as my friend, he sees them press,
Nor makes the hour one moment less.　　10
Will you (the Major's with the hounds,
The happy tenants share his rounds;
Coila's fair Rachel's care to-day,
And blooming Keith's engaged with Gray)
From housewife cares a minute borrow—
That grandchild's cap will do to-morrow—
And join with me a moralizing?
This day's propitious to be wise in.
First, what did yesternight deliver?
'Another year has gone for ever.'　　20
And what is this day's strong suggestion?
'The passing moment's all we rest on!'
Rest on—for what? what do we here?
Or why regard the passing year?
Will Time, amus'd with proverb'd lore,
Add to our date one minute more?
A few days may, a few years must,
Repose us in the silent dust.
Then is it wise to damp our bliss?
Yes—all such reasonings are amiss!　　30

The voice of Nature loudly cries,
And many a message from the skies,
That something in us never dies ;
That on this frail, uncertain state
Hang matters of eternal weight ;
That future-life in worlds unknown
Must take its hue from this alone ;
Whether as heavenly glory bright,
Or dark as misery's woeful night.
    Since then, my honour'd, first of friends,    40
On this poor being all depends ;
Let us th' important Now employ,
And live as those that never die.
    Tho' you, with days and honours crown'd,
Witness that filial circle round
(A sight life's sorrows to repulse ;
A sight pale Envy to convulse)—
Others now claim your chief regard ;
Yourself, you wait your bright reward.

---

# POETICAL ADDRESS TO MR. WILLIAM TYTLER,

WITH THE PRESENT OF THE POET'S PICTURE.

REVERÈD defender of beauteous Stuart,
    Of Stuart, a name once respected,
A name which to love was the mark of a true heart,
    But now 'tis despis'd and neglected.


Tho' something like moisture conglobes in my eye,
    Let no one misdeem me disloyal ;
A poor friendless wand'rer may well claim a sigh,
    Still more if that wand'rer were royal.


My fathers that name have rever'd on a throne ;
    My fathers have fallen to right it ;    10
Those fathers would spurn their degenerate son,
    That name should he scoffingly slight it.

Still in prayers for King George I most heartily join,
  The Queen, and the rest of the gentry;
Be they wise, be they foolish, is nothing of mine;
  Their title's avow'd by my country.

But why of this epocha make such a fuss,
  That gave us the Hanover stem?
If bringing them over was lucky for us,
  I'm sure 'twas as lucky for them.                    20

But, Royalty, truce! we're on dangerous ground;
  Who knows how the fashions may alter?
The doctrine to-day that is loyalty sound.
  To-morrow may bring us a halter.

I send you a trifle, a head of a bard,
  A trifle scarce worthy your care;
But accept it, good Sir, as a mark of regard,
  Sincere as a saint's dying prayer.

Now life's chilly evening dim shades in your eye,
  And ushers the long dreary night;                    30
But you, like the star that athwart gilds the sky,
  Your course to the latest is bright.

----•----

## ELEGY ON THE LATE MISS BURNET,

### OF MONBODDO.

LIFE ne'er exulted in so rich a prize
As Burnet, lovely from her native skies;
Nor envious death so triumph'd in a blow,
As that which laid th' accomplish'd Burnet low.

Thy form and mind, sweet maid, can I forget?
In richest ore the brightest jewel set!
In thee high Heaven above was truest shown,
And by his noblest work the Godhead best is known.

In vain ye flaunt in summer's pride, ye groves;
   Thou crystal streamlet with thy flowery shore,    10
Ye woodland choir that chant your idle loves,
   Ye cease to charm—Eliza is no more!

Ye heathy wastes, inmix'd with reedy fens;
   Ye mossy streams, with sedge and rushes stor'd;
Ye rugged cliffs o'erhanging dreary glens,
   To you I fly, ye with my soul accord.

Princes, whose cumbrous pride was all their worth,—
   Shall venal lays their pompous exit hail?
And thou, sweet excellence! forsake our earth,
   And not a Muse in honest grief bewail?    20

We saw thee shine in youth and beauty's pride,
   And virtue's light, that beams beyond the spheres;
But like the sun eclips'd at morning tide,
   Thou left'st us darkling in a world of tears.

The parent's heart that nestled fond in thee,
   That heart how sunk, a prey to grief and care;
So deckt the woodbine sweet yon agèd tree,
   So from it ravish'd, leaves it bleak and bare.

—————◆◆—————

# VERSES

ON THE DESTRUCTION OF THE WOODS NEAR DRUMLANRIG.

As on the banks o' wandering Nith,
   Ae smiling simmer-morn I stray'd,
And traced its bonnie howes and haughs,
   Where linties sang and lambkins play'd,
I sat me down upon a craig,
   And drank my fill o' fancy's dream,
When, from the eddying deep below,
   Uprose the genius of the stream.

Dark, like the frowning rock, his brow,
  And troubled, like his wintry wave,    10
And deep, as soughs the boding wind
  Amang his eaves, the sigh he gave—
'And came ye here, my son,' he cried,
  'To wander in my birken shade?
To muse some favourite Scottish theme,
  Or sing some favourite Scottish maid?


'There was a time, it's nae lang syne,
  Ye might hae seen me in my pride,
When a' my banks sae bravely saw
  Their woody pictures in my tide;    20
When hanging beech and spreading elm
  Shaded my stream sae clear and cool,
And stately oaks their twisted arms
  Threw broad and dark across the pool;


'When glinting, through the trees, appear'd
  The wee white cot aboon the mill,
And peacefu' rose its ingle reek,
  That slowly curling clamb the hill.
But now the cot is bare and cauld,
  Its branchy shelter's lost and gane,    30
And scarce a stinted birk is left
  To shiver in the blast its lane.'


'Alas!' quoth I, 'what ruefu' chance
  Has twined ye o' your stately trees?
Has laid your rocky bosom bare?
  Has stripp'd the cleeding o' your braes?
Was it the bitter eastern blast,
  That scatters blight in early spring?
Or was't the wil'fire scorch'd their boughs,
  Or canker-worm wi' secret sting?'    40


'Nae eastlin blast,' the sprite replied;
  'It blew na here sae fierce and fell,
And on my dry and halesome banks
  Nae canker-worms get leave to dwell:

Man ! cruel man !' the genius sigh'd
  As through the cliffs he sank him down—
'The worm that gnaw'd my bonnie trees,
  That reptile wears a ducal crown.'

---

## ADDRESS TO THE SHADE OF THOMSON,

ON CROWNING HIS BUST AT EDNAM, ROXBURGH-SHIRE,

WITH BAYS.

WHILE virgin Spring, by Eden's flood,
  Unfolds her tender mantle green,
Or pranks the sod in frolic mood,
  Or tunes Eolian strains between ;

While Summer with a matron grace
  Retreats to Dryburgh's cooling shade,
Yet oft, delighted, stops to trace
  The progress of the spiky blade ;

While Autumn, benefactor kind,
  By Tweed erects his agèd head,                    10
And sees, with self-approving mind,
  Each creature on his bounty fed ;

While maniac Winter rages o'er
  The hills whence classic Yarrow flows,
Rousing the turbid torrent's roar,
  Or sweeping, wild, a waste of snows ;

So long, sweet poet of the year,
  Shall bloom that wreath thou well hast won ;
While Scotia, with exulting tear,
  Proclaims that Thomson was her son.               20

## ON A CERTAIN COMMEMORATION.

Dost thou not rise, indignant Shade!
    And smile with spurning scorn,
When they wha would hae starved thy life
    Thy senseless turf adorn?

Helpless, alone, thou clamb the brae,
    Wi' meikle honest toil,
And claught th' unfading garland there,
    Thy sair-won rightful spoil.

And wear it thou! And call aloud
    This axiom undoubted—                          10
'Wouldst thou hae nobles' patronage?
    First learn to live without it!'

To whom hae much, more shall be given,
    Is every great man's faith;
But he, the helpless needy wretch,
    Shall lose the mite he hath.

---

## SONNET

ON HEARING A THRUSH SING IN A MORNING WALK IN
JANUARY, WRITTEN JANUARY 25, 1793, THE
BIRTH-DAY OF THE AUTHOR.

Sing on, sweet Thrush, upon the leafless bough;
    Sing on, sweet bird, I listen to thy strain:
    See agèd Winter, 'mid his surly reign,
At thy blythe carol clears his furrow'd brow.

So in lone Poverty's dominion drear
    Sits meek Content with light unanxious heart,
    Welcomes the rapid moments, bids them part,
Nor asks if they bring aught to hope or fear.

I thank thee, Author of this opening day!
  Thou whose bright sun now gilds the orient skies! 10
  Riches denied, thy boon was purer joys,
What wealth could never give nor take away!

Yet come, thou child of poverty and care;
The mite high Heaven bestow'd, that mite with thee I'll
    share.

————••————

## SONNET ON THE DEATH OF
## ROBERT RIDDEL, ESQ. OF GLENRIDDEL.

No more ye warblers of the wood—no more!
  Nor pour your descant, grating on my soul;
  Thou young-eyed Spring, gay in thy verdant stole,
More welcome were to me grim Winter's wildest roar.

How can ye charm, ye flow'rs, with all your dyes?
  Ye blow upon the sod that wraps my friend:
  How can I to the tuneful strain attend?
That strain flows round th' untimely tomb where Riddel
    lies.

Yes, pour, ye warblers, pour the notes of woe!
  And soothe the Virtues weeping o'er his bier:     10
  The Man of Worth, and has not left his peer,
Is in his 'narrow house' for ever darkly low.

Thee, Spring, again with joys shall others greet;
Me, mem'ry of my loss will only meet.

————••————

## LIBERTIE—A VISION.

As I stood by yon roofless tower,
  Where the wa'flower scents the dewy air,
Where the howlet mourns in her ivy bower,
  And tells the midnight moon her care;

The winds were laid, the air was still,
  The stars they shot alang the sky;
The fox was howling on the hill,
  And the distant echoing glens reply;

The stream adown the hazelly path
  Was rushing by the ruined wa's         10
To join yon river on the strath,
  Whase distant roaring swells an' fa's;

The cauld blue north was streaming forth
  Her lights wi' hissing eerie din;
Athwart the lift they start an' shift,
  Like fortune's favours, tint as win;

By heedless chance I turned mine eyes,
  And, by the moonbeam, shook to see
A stern and stalwart ghaist arise,
  Attired as minstrels wont to be;       20

Had I statue been o' stane,
  His daring look had daunted me;
And, on his bonnet graved was, plain,
  The sacred posy—LIBERTIE!

And frae his harp sic strains did flow
  Might roused the slumbering dead to hear;
But oh! it was a tale of woe
  As ever met a Briton's ear.

He sang wi' joy his former day,
  He weeping wailed his latter times;     30
But what he said it was nae play,
  I winna venture 't in my rhymes. . . .

'No Spartan tube, no Attic shell,
  No lyre Aeolian I awake;
'Tis liberty's bold note I swell;
  Thy harp, Columbia, let me take!

See gathering thousands, while I sing,
A broken chain exulting bring,
  And dash it in a tyrant's face !
And dare him to his very beard,                              40
And tell him he no more is feared,
  No more the despot of Columbia's race !
A tyrant's proudest insults braved,
They shout, a people freed ; they hail an empire saved !


'Where is man's godlike form ?
  Where is that brow erect and bold,
  That eye that can unmoved behold
The wildest rage, the loudest storm,
That e'er created fury dared to raise ?
  Avaunt, thou caitiff ! servile, base,                      50
  That tremblest at a despot's nod,
  Yet, crouching under the iron rod,
Canst laud the hand that struck the insulting blow !
  Art thou of man's imperial line ?
  Dost boast that countenance divine ?
Each skulking feature answers No !
  But come, ye sons of Libertie,
  Columbia's offspring, brave as free !
In danger's hour still flaming in the van,
Ye know and dare maintain the royalty of Man !  60


    ' Alfred ! on the starry throne,
Surrounded by the tuneful choir,
The bards that erst have struck the patriot lyre,
And roused the freeborn Briton's soul of fire—
  No more thy England own !
Dare injured nations form the great design
  To make detested tyrants bleed ?
  Thy England execrates the glorious deed !
  Beneath her hostile banners waving,
  Every pang of honour braving,                             70
England in thunder calls—"The tyrant's cause is mine ! "


'That hour accurst how did the fiends rejoice,
And hell thro' all her confines raise the exulting voice !
That hour which saw the generous English name
Linked with such damnèd deeds of everlasting shame !

Thee, Caledonia, thy wild heaths among,
Thee, famed for martial deed and heaven-taught song,
  To thee I turn with swimming eyes ;
Where is that soul of Freedom fled?
Immingled with the mighty dead !                     80
  Beneath the hallow'd turf where Wallace lies !
Hear it not, Wallace, in thy bed of death !
  Ye babbling winds, in silence sweep ;
  Disturb not ye the hero's sleep,
Nor give the coward secret breath.

Is this the ancient Caledonian form,
Firm as the rock, resistless as the storm ?
The eye which shot immortal hate,
  Crushing the despot's proudest bearing?
The arm which, nerved with thundering fate,            90
  Brav'd usurpation's boldest daring?
Dark-quenched as yonder sinking star,
No more that glance lightens afar ;
That palsied arm no more whirls on the waste of war !'

---

## FRAGMENT OF AN ODE

### TO THE MEMORY OF PRINCE CHARLES EDWARD STUART.

FALSE flatterer, Hope, away !
Nor think to lure us as in days of yore ;
  We solemnise this sorrowing natal-day
To prove our loyal truth ; we can no more ;
  And owning Heaven's mysterious sway,
    Submissive low adore.

Ye honour'd mighty dead !
Who nobly perish'd in the glorious cause,
Your king, your country, and her laws !
  From great Dundee who smiling victory led,          10
And fell a martyr in her arms
(What breast of northern ice but warms ?)
  To bold Balmerino's undying name,
Whose soul of fire, lighted at heaven's high flame,
Deserves the proudest wreath departed heroes claim.

Nor unavenged your fate shall be,
  It only lags the fatal hour;
Your blood shall with incessant cry
  Awake at last th' unsparing power;
As from the cliff, with thundering course,     20
  The snowy ruin smokes along,
With doubling speed and gathering force,
Till deep it crashing whelms the cottage in the vale!
  So Vengeance' arm ensanguined, strong,
Shall with resistless might assail,
  Usurping Brunswick's pride shall lay,
And Stewart's wrongs, and yours, with tenfold weight repay.

---

## MONODY ON A LADY FAMED FOR HER CAPRICE.

How cold is that bosom which folly once fired,
  How pale is that cheek where the rouge lately glisten'd!
How silent that tongue which the echoes oft tir'd,
  How dull is that ear which to flattery so listen'd!

If sorrow and anguish their exit await,
  From friendship and dearest affection remov'd;
How doubly severer, Maria, thy fate,
  Thou diedst unwept, as thou livedst unlov'd.

Loves, Graces, and Virtues, I call not on you;
  So shy, grave, and distant, ye shed not a tear:    10
But come, all ye offspring of Folly so true,
  And flowers let us cull for Maria's cold bier.

We'll search thro' the garden for each silly flower,
  We'll roam through the forest for each idle weed;
But chiefly the nettle, so typical, shower,
  For none e'er approach'd her but rued the rash deed.

We'll sculpture the marble, we'll measure the lay;
  Here Vanity strums on her idiot lyre;
There keen Indignation shall dart on his prey,    19
  Which spurning Contempt shall redeem from his ire.

### THE EPITAPH.

HERE lies, now a prey to insulting neglect,
    What once was a butterfly, gay in life's beam :
Want only of wisdom denied her respect,
    Want only of goodness denied her esteem.

————•◦————

## POEM, ADDRESSED TO MR. MITCHELL,

#### COLLECTOR OF EXCISE, DUMFRIES.

FRIEND of the Poet, tried and leal,
Wha, wanting thee, might beg or steal ;
Alake, alake, the meikle Deil
        Wi' a' his witches
Are at it, skelpin' ! jig and reel,
        In my poor pouches.

I modestly fu' fain wad hint it,
That one pound one, I sairly want it :
If wi' the hizzie down ye sent it,
        It would be kind ;      10
And while my heart wi' life-blood dunted,
        I'd bear't in mind.

So may the auld year gang out moaning
To see the new come laden, groaning,
Wi' double plenty o'er the loaning
        To thee and thine ;
Domestic peace and comforts crowning
        The haill design.

#### POSTSCRIPT.

Ye've heard this while how I've been lickit,
And by fell death was nearly nickit :      20
Grim loon ! he gat me by the fecket,
        And sair me sheuk ;
But by guid luck I lap a wicket,
        And turn'd a neuk.

But by that health, I've got a share o't,
And by that life, I'm promis'd mair o't,
My heal and weal I'll take a care o't
  A tentier way:
Then fareweel folly, hide and hair o't,
   For ance and aye!  30

———•———

## TO MISS LOGAN, WITH BEATTIE'S POEMS,

### FOR A NEW YEAR'S GIFT.

AGAIN the silent wheels of time
 Their annual round have driven,
And you, tho' scarce in maiden prime,
 Are so much nearer Heaven.

No gifts have I from Indian coasts
 The infant year to hail;
I send you more than India boasts,
 In Edwin's simple tale.

Our sex with guile and faithless love
 Is charg'd, perhaps too true;  10
But may, dear Maid, each lover prove
 An Edwin still to you!

———•———

## LINES SENT TO SIR JOHN WHITEFORD,
## OF WHITEFORD, BART.

### WITH THE LAMENT ON THE DEATH OF THE EARL OF GLENCAIRN.

THOU, who thy honour as thy God reverest,
Who, save thy mind's reproach, nought earthly fearest,
To thee this votive offering I impart,
The tearful tribute of a broken heart.

The friend thou valued'st, I the Patron lov'd ;
His worth, his honour, all the world approv'd.
We'll mourn till we too go as he has gone,
And tread the shadowy path to that dark world unknown.

————◆◆————

## TO MISS CRUIKSHANK,

A VERY YOUNG LADY, WRITTEN ON THE BLANK LEAF OF A
BOOK, PRESENTED TO HER BY THE AUTHOR.

BEAUTEOUS rose-bud, young and gay,
Blooming in thy early May,
Never may'st thou, lovely flow'r,
Chilly shrink in sleety show'r !
Never Boreas' hoary path,
Never Eurus' pois'nous breath,
Never baleful stellar lights,
Taint thee with untimely blights !
Never, never reptile thief
Riot on thy virgin leaf !                          10
Nor even Sol too fiercely view
Thy bosom blushing still with dew !
    May'st thou long, sweet crimson gem,
Richly deck thy native stem ;
Till some evening, sober, calm,
Dropping dews, and breathing balm,
While all around the woodland rings,
And every bird thy requiem sings ;
Thou, amid the dirgeful sound,
Shed thy dying honours round,                      20
And resign to parent earth
The loveliest form she e'er gave birth.

————◆◆————

## VERSES TO A YOUNG LADY,

MISS GRAHAM OF FINTRY, WITH A PRESENT OF SONGS.

HERE, where the Scottish Muse immortal lives,
　　In sacred strains and tuneful numbers join'd,
Accept the gift; tho' humble he who gives,
　　Rich is the tribute of the grateful mind.

So may no ᐧruffian-feeling in thy breast
　　Discordant jar thy bosom-chords among!
But Peace attune thy gentle soul to rest,
　　Or Love, ecstatic, wake his seraph song!

Or Pity's notes, in luxury of tears,
　　As modest Want the tale of woe reveals;          10
While conscious Virtue all the strain endears,
　　And heaven-born Piety her sanction seals!

## WRITTEN ON THE BLANK LEAF OF THE LAST
## EDITION OF HIS POEMS,

PRESENTED TO THE LADY WHOM HE HAD OFTEN CELEBRATED
UNDER THE NAME OF CHLORIS.

'TIS Friendship's pledge, my young, fair friend,
　　Nor thou the gift refuse,
Nor with unwilling ear attend
　　The moralizing Muse.

Since thou, in all thy youth and charms,
　　Must bid the world adieu
(A world 'gainst peace in constant arms)
　　To join the friendly few;

Since, thy gay morn of life o'ercast,
  Chill came the tempest's lower                        10
(And ne'er misfortune's eastern blast
  Did nip a fairer flower) ;

Since life's gay scenes must charm no more,—
  Still much is left behind ;
Still nobler wealth hast thou in store—
  The comforts of the mind !

Thine is the self-approving glow,
  Of conscious honour's part ;
And, dearest gift of heaven below,
  Thine friendship's truest heart.                      20

The joys refin'd of sense and taste,
  With every muse to rove :
And doubly were the poet blest,
  These joys could he improve.

---

## TO A YOUNG LADY, MISS JESSY LEWARS,
## DUMFRIES,

#### WITH BOOKS WHICH THE BARD PRESENTED HER.

THINE be the volumes, Jessy fair,
And with them take the Poet's prayer—
That fate may in her fairest page,
With every kindliest, best presage
Of future bliss, enrol thy name ;
With native worth, and spotless fame,
And wakeful caution still aware
Of ill—but chief, man's felon snare.
All blameless joys on earth we find,
And all the treasures of the mind—                      10
These be thy guardian and reward ;
So prays thy faithful friend, the Bard.

THE FOLLOWING POEM WAS WRITTEN

# TO A GENTLEMAN WHO HAD SENT HIM A NEWSPAPER,

AND OFFERED TO CONTINUE IT FREE OF EXPENSE.

KIND Sir, I've read your paper through,
And, faith, to me, 'twas really new!
How guess'd ye, Sir, what maist I wanted?
This mony a day I've grain'd and gaunted,
To ken what French mischief was brewin';
Or what the drumlie Dutch were doin';
That vile doup-skelper, Emperor Joseph,
If Venus yet had got his nose off;
Or how the collieshangie works
Atween the Russians and the Turks;                    10
Or if the Swede, before he halt,
Would play anither Charles the Twalt:
If Denmark, any body spak o't;
Or Poland, wha had now the tack o't;
How cut-throat Prussian blades were hingin';
How libbet Italy was singin';
If Spaniard, Portuguese or Swiss,
Were sayin' or takin' aught amiss:
Or how our merry lads at hame,
In Britain's court, kept up the game:                 20
How royal George, the Lord leuk o'er him!
Was managing St. Stephen's quorum;
If sleekit Chatham Will was livin',
Or glaikit Charlie got his nieve in;
How daddie Burke the plea was cookin',
If Warren Hastings' neck was yeukin';
How cesses, stents, and fees were rax'd,
Or if bare arses yet were tax'd;
The news o' princes, dukes, and earls,
Pimps, sharpers, bawds, and opera-girls;              30
If that daft buckie, Geordie Wales,
Was threshin' still at hizzies' tails;
Or if he was grown oughtlins doucer,
And no a perfect kintra cooser.

A' this and mair I never heard of;
And, but for you, I might despair'd of.
So gratefu' back your news I send you,
And pray a' guid things may attend you!

*Ellisland, Monday Morning, 1790.*

*Remonstrance to the Gentleman to whom the foregoing
Poem was addressed.*

Dear Peter, dear Peter,
    We poor sons of metre                                    40
Are often negleckit, ye ken;
    For instance, your sheet, man,
    (Though glad I'm to see't, man,)
I get it no ae day in ten.

---

# SENT TO A GENTLEMAN WHOM HE HAD
## OFFENDED.

THE friend whom wild from wisdom's way
    The fumes of wine infuriate send
(Not moony madness more astray)—
    Who but deplores that hapless friend?

Mine was th' insensate frenzied part,
    Ah! why should I such scenes out-live?
Scenes so abhorrent to my heart!
    'Tis thine to pity and forgive.

---

ON READING IN A NEWSPAPER

## THE DEATH OF JOHN M‘LEOD, ESQ.,

BROTHER TO A YOUNG LADY, A PARTICULAR FRIEND OF THE
AUTHOR'S.

SAD thy tale, thou idle page,
  And rueful thy alarms:
Death tears the brother of her love
  From Isabella's arms.

Sweetly deckt with pearly. dew
  The morning rose may blow;
But cold successive noontide blasts
  May lay its beauties low.

Fair on Isabella's morn
  The sun propitious smil'd;        10
But, long ere noon, succeeding clouds
  Succeeding hopes beguil'd.

Fate oft tears the bosom chords
  That Nature finest strung:
So Isabella's heart was form'd,
  And so that heart was wrung.

Dread Omnipotence alone
  Can heal the wound He gave;
Can point the brimful grief-worn eyes
  To scenes beyond the grave.        20

Virtue's blossoms there shall blow,
  And fear no withering blast;
There Isabella's spotless worth
  Shall happy be at last.

# ON THE BIRTH OF A POSTHUMOUS CHILD,

### BORN IN PECULIAR CIRCUMSTANCES OF FAMILY DISTRESS.

SWEET flow'ret, pledge o' meikle love,
    And ward o' mony a prayer,
What heart o' stane wad thou na move,
    Sae hapless, sweet, and fair?

November hirples o'er the lea,
    Chill, on thy lovely form;
And gane, alas! the shelt'ring tree,
    Should shield thee frae the storm.

May He who gives the rain to pour,
    And wings the blast to blaw,                    10
Protect thee frae the driving show'r,
    The bitter frost and snaw.

May He, the friend of woe and want,
    Who heals life's various stounds,
Protect and guard the mother plant,
    And heal her cruel wounds.

But late she flourish'd, rooted fast,
    Fair in the summer morn:
Now feebly bends she in the blast,
    Unshelter'd and forlorn.                        20

Blest be thy bloom, thou lovely gem,
    Unscath'd by ruffian hand!
And from thee many a parent stem
    Arise to deck our land.

## EPITAPH ON THE POET'S DAUGHTER.

HERE lies a rose, a budding rose,
    Blasted before its bloom;
Whose innocence did sweets disclose
    Beyond that flower's perfume.

To those who for her loss are grieved,
    This consolation 's given—
She 's from a world of woe relieved,
    And blooms a rose in heaven.

———◆———

## VERSES

### WRITTEN UNDER VIOLENT GRIEF.

ACCEPT the gift a friend sincere
    Wad on thy worth be pressin';
Remembrance oft may start a tear,
But oh! that tenderness forbear,
    Though 'twad my sorrows lessen.

My morning raise sae clear and fair,
    I thought sair storms wad never
Bedew the scene; but grief and care
In wildest fury hae made bare
    My peace, my hope, for ever!    10

You think I'm glad; oh, I pay weel
    For a' the joy I borrow,
In solitude—then, then I feel
I canna to mysel' conceal
    My deeply-ranklin' sorrow.

Farewell! within thy bosom free
    A sigh may whiles awaken;
A tear may wet thy laughin' ee,
For Scotia's son—ance gay like thee—
    Now hopeless, comfortless, forsaken!    20

## TO A LADY,

WITH A PRESENT OF A PAIR OF DRINKING GLASSES.

FAIR Empress of the Poet's soul,
 And Queen of Poetesses;
Clarinda, take this little boon,
 This humble pair of glasses.

And fill them high with generous juice,
 As generous as your mind;
And pledge me in the generous toast—
 'The whole of human kind!'

'To those who love us!'—second fill;
 But not to those whom *we* love;    10
Lest we love those who love not us!
 A third—'To thee and me, Love!'

—— ·•· ——

## TO MISS FERRIER,

ENCLOSING THE ELEGY ON SIR J. H. BLAIR.

NAE heathen name shall I prefix
 Frae Pindus or Parnassus;
Auld Reekie dings them a' to sticks,
 For rhyme-inspiring lasses.

Jove's tunefu' dochters three times three
 Made Homer deep their debtor;
But, gi'en the body half an ee,
 Nine Ferriers wad done better!

Last day my mind was in a bog,
 Down George's Street I stoited;    10
A creeping cauld prosaic fog
 My very senses doited.

Do what I dought to set her free,
  My saul lay in the mire ;
Ye turned a neuk—I saw your ee—
  She took the wing like fire !

The mournfu' sang I here enclose,
  In gratitude I send you ;
And wish and pray in rhyme and prose,
  A' gude things may attend you !            20

---

## WRITTEN ON THE BLANK LEAF

#### OF A COPY OF THE FIRST EDITION OF HIS POEMS,
#### PRESENTED TO AN OLD SWEETHEART, THEN MARRIED.

ONCE fondly lov'd, and still remember'd dear,
  Sweet early object of my youthful vows,
Accept this mark of friendship warm, sincere ;
  Friendship ! 'tis all cold duty now allows.

And when you read the simple artless rhymes,
  One friendly sigh for him—he asks no more,
Who distant burns in flaming torrid climes.
  Or haply lies beneath th' Atlantic roar.

---

## INSCRIPTION FOR AN ALTAR TO INDEPENDENCE,

#### AT KERROUGHTRY, SEAT OF MR. HERON,
#### WRITTEN IN SUMMER, 1795.

THOU of an independent mind,
With soul resolv'd, with soul resign'd ;
Prepar'd Power's proudest frown to brave,
Who wilt not be, nor have a slave ;
Virtue alone who dost revere,
Thy own reproach alone dost fear,—
Approach this shrine, and worship here.

## VERSES

INTENDED TO BE WRITTEN BELOW A NOBLE EARL'S PICTURE.

Whose is that noble, dauntless brow?
   And whose that eye of fire?
And whose that generous princely mien
   Even rooted foes admire?

Stranger, to justly shew that brow,
   And mark that eye of fire,
Would take His hand, whose vernal tints
   His other works inspire.

Bright as a cloudless summer sun,
   With stately port he moves;                    10
His guardian seraph eyes with awe
   The noble ward he loves.

Among the illustrious Scottish sons
   That chief thou may'st discern,
Mark Scotia's fond returning eye,—
   It dwells upon Glencairn.

## SKETCH.

A little, upright, pert, tart, tripping wight,
And still his precious self his dear delight;
Who loves his own smart shadow in the streets
Better than e'er the fairest she he meets:
A man of fashion too, he made his tour,
Learn'd vive la bagatelle, and vive l'amour;
So travell'd monkeys their grimace improve,
Polish their grin, nay, sigh for ladies' love!
Much specious lore, but little understood;
Veneering oft outshines the solid wood:            10
His solid sense—by inches you must tell,
But mete his cunning by the old Scots ell;
His meddling vanity, a busy fiend,
Still making work his selfish craft must mend.

## TO ROBERT GRAHAM, ESQ. OF FINTRY,

### ON RECEIVING A FAVOUR.

I CALL no Goddess to inspire my strains,
A fabled Muse may suit a Bard that feigns ;
Friend of my life ! my ardent spirit burns,
And all the tribute of my heart returns,
For boons recorded, goodness ever new,
The gift still dearer as the giver you.
Thou orb of day ! thou other paler light !
And all ye many sparkling stars of night !
If aught that giver from my mind efface ;
If I that giver's bounty e'er disgrace ;          10
Then roll to me, along your wand'ring spheres,
Only to number out a villain's years !
I lay my hand upon my swelling breast,
And grateful would, but cannot, speak the rest.

——•+——

## IMPROMPTU, ON MRS. RIDDEL'S BIRTHDAY,
## IN NOVEMBER.

OLD Winter, with his frosty beard,
Thus once to Jove his prayer preferr'd—
'What have I done of all the year,
To bear this hated doom severe ?
My cheerless suns no pleasure know ;
Night's horrid car drags, dreary slow ;
My dismal months no joys are crowning,
But spleeny English hanging, drowning.
Now, Jove, for once be mighty civil,
To counterbalance all this evil ;          10
Give me, and I've no more to say,
Give me Maria's natal day !
That brilliant gift will so enrich me,
Spring, Summer, Autumn, cannot match me.'
' 'Tis done ! ' says Jove ; so onds my story,
And Winter once rejoic'd in glory.

## TO CAPTAIN RIDDEL, GLENRIDDEL.

EXTEMPORE LINES ON RETURNING A NEWSPAPER.

YOUR News and Review, Sir, I've read through and
      through, Sir,
  With little admiring or blaming ;
The papers are barren of home-news or foreign,
  No murders or rapes worth the naming.

Our friends the Reviewers, those chippers and hewers,
  Are judges of mortar and stone, Sir ;
But of meet or unmeet in a fabric complete,
  I'll boldly pronounce they are none, Sir.

My goose-quill too rude is to tell all your goodness
  Bestow'd on your servant, the Poet ;                    10
Would to God I had one like a beam of the sun,
  And then all the world, Sir, should know it !

## 'IN VAIN WOULD PRUDENCE.'

IN vain would Prudence, with decorous sneer,
Point out a cens'ring world, and bid me fear ;
Above that world on wings of love I rise,
I know its worst—and can that worst despise.
'Wrong'd, injured, shunn'd, unpitied, unredrest,
The mock'd quotation of the scorner's jest—'
Let Prudence' direst bodements on me fall,
Clarinda, rich reward, o'erpays them all !

## 'THOUGH FICKLE FORTUNE.'

THOUGH fickle Fortune has deceiv'd me,—
 She promis'd fair and perform'd but ill;
Of mistress, friends, and wealth bereav'd me,—
 Yet I bear a heart shall support me still.
I'll act with prudence as far's I'm able,
 But if success I must never find,
Then come misfortune, I bid thee welcome,
 I'll meet thee with an undaunted mind.

———◆◆———

## 'I BURN, I BURN.'

'I BURN, I burn, as when thro' ripen'd corn
By driving winds the crackling flames are borne.'
Now raving-wild, I curse that fatal night;
Now bless the hour which charm'd my guilty sight.
In vain the laws their feeble force oppose:
Chain'd at his feet they groan, Love's vanquish'd foes;
In vain religion meets my sinking eye;
I dare not combat—but I turn and fly;
Conscience in vain upbraids th' unhallow'd fire;
Love grasps his scorpions—stifled they expire!      10
Reason drops headlong from his sacred throne,
Your dear idea reigns and reigns alone:
Each thought intoxicated homage yields,
And riots wanton in forbidden fields!

By all on high adoring mortals know!
By all the conscious villain fears below!
By your dear self!—the last great oath I swear;
Nor life nor soul were ever half so dear!

## TRAGIC FRAGMENT.

ALL devil as I am, a damnèd wretch,
A harden'd, stubborn, unrepenting villain,
Still my heart melts at human wretchedness ;
And with sincere tho' unavailing sighs
I view the helpless children of distress.
With tears indignant I behold th' oppressor
Rejoicing in the honest man's destruction,
Whose unsubmitting heart was all his crime.
Even you, ye helpless crew, I pity you ;
Ye, whom the seeming good think sin to pity ;        10
Ye poor, despis'd, abandon'd vagabonds,
Whom Vice, as usual, has turn'd o'er to Ruin.
O but for kind, tho' ill-requited friends,
I had been driven forth like you forlorn,
The most detested, worthless wretch among you !
O injur'd God ! Thy goodness has endow'd me
With talents passing most of my compeers,
Which I in just proportion have abus'd,
As far surpassing other common villains,
As Thou in natural parts hadst given me more.        20


## THE HENPECK'D HUSBAND.

CURS'D be the man, the poorest wretch in life,
The crouching vassal to the tyrant wife !
Who has no will but by her high permission ;
Who has not sixpence but in her possession ;
Who must to her his dear friend's secret tell ;
Who dreads a curtain lecture worse than hell.
Were such the wife had fallen to my part,
I'd break her spirit, or I'd break her heart :
I'd charm her with the magic of a switch,
I'd kiss her maids, and kick the perverse bitch.        10

## EPIGRAM CN SAID OCCASION.

O Death, hadst thou but spar'd his life
    Whom we, this day, lament!
We freely wad exchang'd the wife,
    And a' been weel content.

Ev'n as he is, cauld in his graff,
    The swap we yet will do't;
Take thou the carlin's carcase aff,
    Thou'se get the saul o' boot.

## ANOTHER.

One Queen Artemisia, as old stories tell,
When depriv'd of her husband she lovèd so well,
In respect for the love and affection he'd show'd her,
She reduc'd him to dust and she drank up the powder.

But Queen Netherplace, of a diff'rent complexion,
When call'd on to order the funeral direction,
Would have eat her dead lord, on a slender pretence,
Not to shew her respect, but—to save the expense.

## EPITAPH ON HOLY WILLIE.

Here Holy Willie's sair worn clay
    Taks up its last abode;
His saul has taen some other way,
    I fear the left-hand road.

Stop ! there he is, as sure 's a gun,
   Poor silly body, see him ;
Nae wonder he 's as black 's the grun,
   Observe wha 's standing wi' him.


Your brunstane devilship, I see,
   Has got him there before ye ;
But haud your nine-tail cat a-wee,
   Till ance you've heard my story.                    10


Your pity I will not implore,
   For pity ye have nane ;
Justice, alas ! has gien him o'er,
   And mercy's day is gane.


But hear me, Sir, deil as ye are,
   Look something to your credit ;
A coof like him wad stain your name,
   If it were kent ye did it.                              20


---


## A JEREMIAD.


Ah, woe is me ! my mother dear ;
   A man of strife ye've born me ;
For sair contention I maun bear,—
   They hate, revile, and scorn me.


I ne'er could lend on bill or bond
   That, five per cent, might blest me ;
And borrowing, on the t'other hand—
   The deil a ane wad trust me.

Yet I, a coin-denièd wight,
   By fortune quite discarded—                    10
Ye see how I am, day and night,
   By lad and lass blackguarded.

---

## ON STIRLING.

HERE Stuarts once in glory reign'd,
And laws for Scotland's weal ordain'd ;
But now unroof'd their palace stands,
Their sceptre 's sway'd by other hands ;
The injured Stuart line is gone,
A race outlandish fills their throne.
An idiot race to honour lost,
Who know them best, despise them most.

---

## LINES

ON BEING TOLD THAT THE ABOVE VERSES WOULD AFFECT

HIS PROSPECTS.

RASH mortal, and slanderous poet, thy name
Shall no longer appear in the records of fame ;
Dost not know that old Mansfield, who writes like the
   Bible,
Says the more 'tis a truth, sir, the more 'tis a libel ?

---

## REPLY TO THE MINISTER OF GLADSMUIR.

LIKE Esop's lion, Burns says, sore I feel
All others scorn—but damn that ass's heel !

## LINES

WRITTEN AND PRESENTED TO MRS. KEMBLE, ON SEEING HER
IN THE CHARACTER OF YARICO IN THE DUMFRIES
THEATRE, 1794.

KEMBLE, thou cur'st my unbelief
  Of Moses and his rod;
At Yarico's sweet notes of grief
  The rock with tears had flow'd.

---

## LINES.

I MURDER hate by field or flood,
  Tho' glory's name may screen us;
In wars at hame I'll spend my blood,
  Life-giving wars of Venus.

The deities that I adore
  Are social Peace and Plenty;
I'm better pleased to make one more,
  Than be the death of twenty.

---

## LINES

WRITTEN ON A WINDOW, AT THE KING'S ARMS TAVERN,
DUMFRIES.

YE men of wit and wealth, why all this sneering
'Gainst poor Excisemen! give the cause a hearing;
What are your landlords' rent-rolls? taxing ledgers:
What premiers, what? even Monarchs' mighty gaugers:
Nay, what are priests, those seeming godly wise men?
What are they, pray, but spiritual Excisemen?

# EXTEMPORE IN THE COURT OF SESSION.

### LORD ADVOCATE.

He clench'd his pamphlets in his fist,
    He quoted and he hinted,
Till in a declamation-mist,
    His argument he tint it:
He gapèd for't, he grapèd for't,
    He fand it was awa, man;
But what his common sense came short,
    He ekèd out wi' law, man.

### MR. ERSKINE.

Collected Harry stood awee,
    Then open'd out his arm, man;      10
His lordship sat wi' ruefu' e'e,
    And eyed the gathering storm, man:
Like wind-driv'n hail it did assail,
    Or torrents owre a linn, man;
The Bench sae wise, lift up their eyes,
    Half-wauken'd wi' the din, man.

---

# A GRACE BEFORE DINNER.

O Thou, who kindly dost provide
    For every creature's want!
We bless thee, God of Nature wide,
    For all thy goodness lent:
And, if it please thee, Heavenly Guide,
    May never worse be sent;
But whether granted, or denied,
    Lord, bless us with content!
                    Amen!

## A FAREWELL.

Farewell, dear Friend! may guid luck hit you,
And, mang her favourites admit you!
If e'er Detraction shore to smit you,
              May nane believe him!
And ony De'il that thinks to get you,
              Good Lord, deceive him!

---

## ON A FRIEND.

An honest man here lies at rest,
As e'er God with his image blest;
The friend of man, the friend of truth,
The friend of age, and guide of youth:
Few hearts like his, with virtue warm'd,
Few heads with knowledge so inform'd:
If there's another world, he lives in bliss;
If there is none, he made the best of this.

---

## A VERSE

COMPOSED AND REPEATED BY BURNS, TO THE MASTER OF THE
HOUSE, ON TAKING LEAVE AT A PLACE IN THE HIGHLANDS,
WHERE HE HAD BEEN HOSPITABLY ENTERTAINED.

When death's dark stream I ferry o'er,
    A time that surely shall come,
In Heaven itself I'll ask no more
    Than just a Highland welcome.

# VERSES

WRITTEN ON A WINDOW OF THE INN AT CARRON.

We came na here to view your warks
 In hopes to be mair wise,
But only, lest we gang to hell,
 It may be nae surprise.

But when we tirled at your door,
 Your porter dought na hear us ;
Sae may, shou'd we to hell's yetts come,
 Your billy Satan sair us !

---

# LINES

WRITTEN ON A PANE OF GLASS IN THE INN AT MOFFAT.

Ask why God made the gem so small,
 An' why so huge the granite ?
Because God meant mankind should set
 That higher value on it.

---

# EPIGRAM

WRITTEN AT INVERARY.

Whoe'er he be that sojourns here,
 I pity much his case,
Unless he come to wait upon
 The Lord their God, his Grace.
There 's naething here but Highland pride,
 And Highland scab and hunger ;
If Providence has sent me here,
 'Twas surely in his anger.

# A TOAST

GIVEN AT A MEETING OF THE DUMFRIES-SHIRE VOLUNTEERS,
HELD TO COMMEMORATE THE ANNIVERSARY OF RODNEY'S
VICTORY, APRIL 12, 1782.

INSTEAD of a Song, boys, I'll give you a Toast—
Here's the memory of those on the twelfth that we lost:
That we lost, did I say? nay, by heav'n, that we found,
For their fame it shall last while the world goes round.
The next in succession, I'll give you the King,
Whoe'er would betray him, on high may he swing!
And here's the grand fabric, our free Constitution,
As built on the base of the great Revolution;
And longer with Politics, not to be cramm'd,
Be Anarchy curs'd, and Tyranny damn'd;          10
And who would to Liberty e'er prove disloyal,
May his son be a hangman, and he his first trial!

---

# EXTEMPORE, ON MR. WILLIAM SMELLIE,

AUTHOR OF THE PHILOSOPHY OF NATURAL HISTORY, AND
MEMBER OF THE ANTIQUARIAN AND ROYAL
SOCIETIES OF EDINBURGH.

CROCHALLAN came,
The old cock'd hat, the grey surtout—the same;
His bristling beard just rising in its might,—
'Twas four long nights and days to shaving night;
His uncomb'd grizzly locks wild staring, thatch'd
A head for thought profound and clear, unmatch'd;
Yet, tho' his caustic wit was biting rude,
His heart was warm, benevolent, and good.

## EXTEMPORE TO MR. SYME,

ON REFUSING TO DINE WITH HIM, AFTER HAVING BEEN
PROMISED THE FIRST OF COMPANY, AND THE
FIRST OF COOKERY.

No more of your guests, be they titled or not,
   And cookery the first in the nation ;
Who is proof to thy personal converse and wit,
   Is proof to all other temptation.

## TO MR. SYME,

WITH A PRESENT OF A DOZEN OF PORTER.

O, HAD the malt thy strength of mind,
   Or hops the flavour of thy wit,
'Twere drink for first of human kind,
   A gift that e'en for Syme were fit.

*Jerusalem Tavern, Dumfries.*

## TO JOHN M'MURDO, ESQ.

O, COULD I give thee India's wealth,
   As I this trifle send !
Because thy joy in both would be
   To share them with a friend.

But golden sands did never grace
   The Heliconian stream ;
Then take what gold could never buy—
   An honest Bard's esteem.

## ON MISS JESSY LEWARS.

WRITTEN IN PENCIL ON THE BACK OF A MENAGERIE BILL.

TALK not to me of savages
  From Afric's burning sun,
No savage e'er could rend my heart,
  As, Jessy, thou hast done.

But Jessy's lovely hand in mine,
  A mutual faith to plight,
Not ev'n to view the heavenly choir
  Would be so blest a sight.

---

## EPITAPH ON MISS JESSY LEWARS.

SAY, Sages, what's the charm on earth
  Can turn Death's dart aside?
It is not purity and worth,
  Else Jessy had not died.

---

## THE RECOVERY OF MISS JESSY LEWARS.

BUT rarely seen since Nature's birth,
  The natives of the sky;
Yet still one seraph's left on earth,
  For Jessy did not die.

---

## TO DR. MAXWELL,

ON MISS JESSY STAIG'S RECOVERY.

MAXWELL, if merit here you crave,
  That merit I deny:
*You* save fair Jessy from the grave?
  An Angel could not die.

## THE TOAST.

FILL me with the rosy wine,
Call a toast, a toast divine;
Give the Poet's darling flame,
Lovely Jessy be the name;
Then thou mayest freely boast,
Thou hast given a peerless toast.

## THE KIRK OF LAMINGTON.

As cauld a wind as ever blew,
A caulder kirk, and in't but few;
A caulder preacher never spak;—
Ye'se a' be het ere I come back.

## WRITTEN ON A BLANK LEAF

### OF ONE OF MISS HANNAH MORE'S WORKS, WHICH A LADY HAD GIVEN HIM.

THOU flattering mark of friendship kind,
Still may thy pages call to mind
    The dear, the beauteous donor:
Though sweetly female every part,
Yet such a head, and more—the heart
    Does both the sexes honour.
She show'd her taste refined and just
    When she selected thee,
Yet deviating own I must,
    For so approving me.                        10
        But kind still I'll mind still
            The giver in the gift;
        I'll bless her and wiss her
            A Friend aboon the lift.

## ON THE DEATH OF A LAP-DOG.

### NAMED ECHO.

In wood and wild, ye warbling throng,
  Your heavy loss deplore;
Now half-extinct your powers of song,
  Sweet Echo is no more.

Ye jarring, screeching things around,
  Scream your discordant joys;
Now half your din of tuneless sound
  With Echo silent lies.

---

## LINES WRITTEN AT LOUDON MANSE.

The night was still, and o'er the hill
  The moon shone on the castle wa';
The mavis sang, while dew-drops hang
  Around her, on the castle wa'.

Sae merrily they danced the ring,
  Frae eenin' till the cock did craw;
And aye the o'erword o' the spring
  Was Irvine's bairns are bonnie a'.

---

## THE SOLEMN LEAGUE AND COVENANT.

The Solemn League and Covenant
  Now brings a smile, now brings a tear;
But sacred Freedom, too, was theirs:
  If thou'rt a slave, indulge thy sneer.

## INSCRIPTION ON A GOBLET.

WRITTEN IN THE HOUSE OF MR. SYME.

There's death in the cup—sae beware!
  Nay, more—there is danger in touching;
But wha can avoid the fell snare?
  The man and his wine's sae bewitching!

----◆----

## THE BOOK-WORMS.

Through and through the inspired leaves,
  Ye maggots, make your windings;
But, oh! respect his lordship's taste,
  And spare his golden bindings.

----◆----

## ON ROBERT RIDDELL.

To Riddel, much-lamented man,
  This ivied cot was dear;
Wanderer, dost value matchless worth?
  This ivied cot revere.

----◆----

## FRAGMENT.

Now health forsakes that angel face,
  Nae mair my Dearie smiles;
Pale sickness withers ilka grace,
  And a' my hopes beguiles.
The cruel powers reject the prayer
  I hourly mak' for thee;
Ye heavens, how great is my despair,
  How can I see him dee!

## [THE LOYAL NATIVES' VERSES.

YE sons of sedition, give ear to my song,
Let Syme, Burns, and Maxwell pervade every throng,
With Cracken the attorney, and Mundell the quack,
Send Willie the monger to hell with a smack.]

*These verses were handed over the table to Burns at a convivial meeting, and he
endorsed the subjoined reply :*

## BURNS—EXTEMPORE.

YE true 'Loyal Natives,' attend to my song,
In uproar and riot rejoice the night long ;
From envy and hatred your corps is exempt ;
But where is your shield from the darts of contempt ?

————◆————

## REMORSE.

OF all the numerous ills that hurt our peace,
That press the soul, or wring the mind with anguish,
Beyond comparison the worst are those
That to our folly or our guilt we owe.
In every other circumstance, the mind
Has this to say—'It was no deed of mine ;'
But when to all the evil of misfortune
This sting is added—'Blame thy foolish self !'
Or worser far, the pangs of keen Remorse,
The torturing, gnawing consciousness of guilt—                    10
Of guilt, perhaps, where we've involvèd others,
The young, the innocent, who fondly lov'd us,
Nay, more, that very love their cause of ruin !
O burning hell ! in all thy store of torments,
There's not a keener lash !
Lives there a man so firm, who, while his heart
Feels all the bitter horrors of his crime,
Can reason down its agonizing throbs ;
And, after proper purpose of amendment,
Can firmly force his jarring thoughts to peace ?                  20
O, happy, happy, enviable man !
O glorious magnanimity of soul !

## THE TOAD-EATER.

WHAT of earls with whom you have supt,
  And of dukes that you dined with yestreen?
Lord! an insect's an insect at most,
  Though it crawl on the curls of a Queen.

---

## EXTEMPORE.

### ON PASSING A LADY'S CARRIAGE.

IF you rattle along like your mistress's tongue,
  Your speed will out-rival the dart:
But, a fly for your load, you'll break down on the road,
  If your stuff be as rotten's her heart.

---

## EPIGRAM.

WHEN ——, deceased, to the devil went down,
'Twas nothing would serve him but Satan's own crown;
'Thy fool's head,' quoth Satan, 'that crown shall wear never,
I grant thou'rt as wicked, but not quite so clever.'

---

## LINES INSCRIBED ON A PLATTER.

MY blessings on ye, honest wife,
  I ne'er was here before:
Ye've wealth o' gear for spoon and knife—
  Heart could not wish for more.

Heaven keep you clear of sturt and strife,
  Till far ayont four score,
And while I toddle on thro' life,
  I'll ne'er gae by your door!

## TO MR. RENTON, BERWICK.

Your billet, sir, I grant receipt;
Wi' you I'll canter ony gate,
Though 'twere a trip to yon blue warl',
Where birkies march on burning marl:
Then, sir, God willing, I'll attend ye,
And to his goodness I commend ye.
                                R. Burns.

---

## ON MR. M'MURDO,

### CHAMBERLAIN TO THE DUKE OF QUEENSBERRY.

Blest be M'Murdo to his latest day,
No envious cloud o'ercast his evening ray;
No wrinkle furrow'd by the hand of care,
Nor ever sorrow add one silver hair!
Oh, may no son the father's honour stain,
Nor ever daughter give the mother pain.

---

## TO A LADY

### WHO WAS LOOKING UP THE TEXT DURING SERMON.

Fair maid, you need not take the hint,
    Nor idle texts pursue:
'Twas *guilty sinners* that he meant—
    Not *angels* such as you!

---

## IMPROMPTU.

How daur ye ca' me howlet-face,
    Ye ugly, glowering spectre?
My face was but the keekin' glass,
    An' there ye saw your picture.

## THE SELKIRK GRACE.

Some hae meat, and canna eat,
 And some wad eat that want it ,
But we hae meat and we can eat,
 And sae the Lord be thankit.

———•·•———

## ELEGY ON THE DEATH OF PEG NICHOLSON.

Peg Nicholson was a gude bay mare,
 As ever trode on airn ;
But now she 's floating down the Nith,
 An' past the mouth o' Cairn.

Peg Nicholson was a gude bay mare,
 An' rode thro' thick an' thin ;
But now she 's floating down the Nith,
 An' wanting even the skin.

Peg Nicholson was a gude bay mare,
 An' ance she bare a priest ;   10
But now she 's floating down tho Nith,
 For Solway fish a feast.

Peg Nicholson was a gude bay mare,
 An' the priest he rode her sair ;
An' meikle oppress'd an' bruised she was,
 As priest-rid cattle are.

———•·•———

## TO JOHN TAYLOR.

With Pegasus upon a day,
 Apollo, weary flying,—
Through frosty hills the journey lay,—
 On foot the way was plying.

Poor slip-shod giddy Pegasus
  Was but a sorry walker;
To Vulcan then Apollo goes
  To get a frosty calker.

Obliging Vulcan fell to work,
  Threw by his coat and bonnet,                    10
And did Sol's business in a crack;
  Sol paid him with a sonnet.

Ye Vulcan's sons of Wanlockhead,
  Pity my sad disaster;
My Pegasus is poorly shod—
  I'll pay you like my master.

---

## LINES WRITTEN ON A BANK-NOTE.

WAE worth thy power, thou cursed leaf!
Fell source o' a' my woe and grief!
For lack o' thee I've lost my lass!
For lack o' thee I scrimp my glass!
I see the children of affliction
Unaided, thro' thy curs'd restriction.
I've seen the oppressor's cruel smile
Amid his hapless victim's spoil,
And for thy potence vain have wuss'd
To crush the villain in the dust.                   10
For lack o' thee I leave this much-lov'd shore,
Never, perhaps, to greet old Scotland more.

## EPIGRAM ON A NOTED COXCOMB.

LIGHT lay the earth on Billy's breast,
　　His chicken heart so tender;
But build a castle on his head,
　　His skull will prop it under.

＊＊

## TAM THE CHAPMAN.

As Tam the Chapman on a day
Wi' Death forgather'd by the way,
Weel pleas'd, he greets a wight sae famous,
And Death was nae less pleased wi' Thomas,
Wha cheerfully lays down the pack,
And there blaws up a hearty crack;
His social, friendly, honest heart,
Sae tickled Death they could na part:
Sae after viewing knives and garters,
Death takes him hame to gie him quarters.　　10

＊＊

## VERSES ADDRESSED TO J. RANKINE.

I AM a keeper of the law
In some sma' points, altho' not a';
Some people tell me gin I fa',
　　　Ae way or ither,
The breaking of ae point, tho' sma',
　　　Breaks a' thegither.

I hae been in for't ance or twice,
And winna say owre far for thrice,
Yet never met with that surprise
　　　That broke my rest;　　　　10
But now a rumour's like to rise,
　　　A whaup's i' the nest.

# LINES

SUPPOSED TO HAVE BEEN WRITTEN BY BURNS, AND FORWARDED
TO JOHN RANKINE, AYRSHIRE, IMMEDIATELY
AFTER THE POET'S DECEASE.

HE who of Rankine sang, lies stiff and dead,
And a green grassy hillock hides his head;
Alas! alas! a devilish change indeed!

## ON HIMSELF.

HERE comes Burns
On Rosinante;
She's damn'd poor,
But he's damn'd canty!

## GRACE BEFORE MEAT.

O LORD, when hunger pinches sore,
Do thou stand us in need,
And send us from thy bounteous store,
A tup or wether head! Amen.

## ON COMMISSARY GOLDIE'S BRAINS.

LORD, to account who dares thee call,
Or e'er dispute thy pleasure?
Else why within so thick a wall
Enclose so poor a treasure?

# IMPROMPTU

## ON AN INNKEEPER NAMED BACON, WHO INTRUDED HIMSELF INTO ALL COMPANIES.

At Brownhill we always get dainty good cheer,
And plenty of bacon each day in the year;
We've all things that's nice, and mostly in season,
But why always *Bacon*—come, give me a reason?

# ADDRESSED TO A LADY

## WHOM THE AUTHOR FEARED HE HAD OFFENDED.

Rusticity's ungainly form
  May cloud the highest mind;
But when the heart is nobly warm,
  The good excuse will find.

Propriety's cold cautious rules
  Warm fervour may o'erlook;
But spare poor sensibility
  The ungentle, harsh rebuke.

# ON MARIA.

'Praise Woman still,' his lordship roars;
  'Deserved or not, no matter!'
But thee, whom all my soul adores,
  Even Flattery cannot flatter.
Maria, all my thought and dream,
  Inspires my vocal shell;
The more I praise my lovely theme,
  The more the truth I tell.

## TO THE BEAUTIFUL ELIZA J——N.

How, Liberty! girl, can it be by thee named?
And Equality too! hussey, art not ashamed?
Free and Equal, indeed? while mankind thou enchainest,
And over their hearts a proud despot thou reignest!

---

## ON A REQUEST OF CHLORIS.

FROM a white-blossom'd sloe my dear Chloris requested
　　A sprig her fair breast to adorn;
No, by heavens! I exclaimed, let me perish if ever
　　I plant in that bosom a thorn!

---

## TO MR. MACKENZIE, SURGEON, MAUCHLINE.

FRIDAY first's the day appointed
By the Right Worshipful anointed,
　　To hold our grand procession;
To get a blad o' Johnie's morals,
And taste a swatch o' Manson's barrels
　　I' the way of our profession.

The Master and the Brotherhood
　　Would a' be glad to see you;
For me I would be mair than proud
　　To share the mercies wi' you.　　　　10
　　　　If Death, then, wi' skaith, then,
　　　　　　Some mortal heart is hechtin',
　　　　Inform him, and storm him,
　　　　　　That Saturday you'll fecht him.
　　　　　　　　　　ROBERT BURNS.

*Mossgiel, An. M.* 5790.

## TO AN ARTIST.

DEAR —, I'll gie ye some advice
  You'll tak it no uncivil:
You shouldna paint at angels mair,
  But try and paint the devil.
To paint an angel's kittle wark,
  Wi' auld Nick there's less danger;
You'll easy draw a weel-kent face,
  But no sae weel a stranger.

————

## LINES WRITTEN ON A TUMBLER.

YOU'RE welcome, Willie Stewart;
  You're welcome, Willie Stewart;
There's ne'er a flower that blooms in May,
  That's half sae welcome's thou art.

Come, bumpers high, express your joy,
  The bowl we maun renew it;
The tappit-hen, gae bring her ben,
  To welcome Willie Stewart.

May foes be strang. and friends be slack,
  Ilk action may he rue it;                    10
May woman on him turn her back,
  That wrangs thee, Willie Stewart!

————

## ON MR. W. CRUIKSHANK

### OF THE HIGH SCHOOL, EDINBURGH.

HONEST Will to heaven is gane,
  And mony shall lament him;
His faults they a' in Latin lay,
  In English nane e'er kent them.

## INSCRIBED ON A TAVERN WINDOW.

THOU Greybeard, old Wisdom, mayst boast of thy treasures ;
   Give me with young Folly to live :
I grant thee thy calm-blooded, time-settled pleasures ;
   But Folly has raptures to give.

## LINES

### WRITTEN EXTEMPORE IN A LADY'S POCKET-BOOK.
[MISS KENNEDY, SISTER-IN-LAW OF GAVIN HAMILTON.]

GRANT me, indulgent Heav'n, that I may live
To see the miscreants feel the pains they give ;
Deal Freedom's sacred treasures free as air,
Till slave and despot be but things which were.

## A FRAGMENT.

No cold approach, no altered mien ;
   Just what would make suspicion start ;
No pause the dire extremes between,—
   He made me blest, and broke my heart.

## ON MARIA DANCING.

How gracefully Maria leads the dance !
She's life itself.  I never saw a foot
So nimble and so elegant ; it speaks,
And the sweet whispering poetry it makes
Shames the musician.
              *Adriano, or The First of June.*

## THANKSGIVING FOR VICTORY.

Ye hypocrites! are these your pranks?
To murder men, and give God thanks?
Desist for shame! proceed no further!
God won't accept your thanks for murther!

———••———

## TO ———.

Sir,
    Yours this moment I unseal,
      And, faith! I am gay and hearty!
    To tell the truth an' shame the Deil,
      I am as fu' as Bartie:

    But Foorsday, Sir, my promise leal,
      Expect me o' your party,
    If on a beastie I can speel,
      Or hurl in a cartie.

———••———

## TO ALEX. CUNNINGHAM, WRITER.

My godlike friend—nay! do not stare;
    You think the phrase is odd-like!
But God is love the Saints declare,
    Then surely thou art God-like!

And is thy ardour still the same?
    And kindled still at Auna?
Others may boast a partial flame,
    But thou art a volcano!

Ev'n Wedlock asks not love beyond
    Death's tie-dissolving portal!
But thou, omnipotently fond,
    Mayst promise love immortal.

## GRACE AFTER MEAT.

O Thou, in whom we live and move,
  Who mad'st the sea and shore;
Thy goodness constantly we prove,
  And grateful would adore.
And if it please thee, Pow'r above,
  Still grant us, with such store,
The friend we trust, the fair we love,
  And we desire no more.

———+———

## ANOTHER.

Lord, we thank an' thee adore
  For temp'ral gifts we little merit;
At present we will ask no more,
  Let William Hyslop give the spirit.

———+———

## ANOTHER.

O Lord, since we have feasted thus,
  Which we so little merit,
Let Meg now take away the flesh
  And Jock bring in the spirit!

———+———

## EXTEMPORE LINES,

IN ANSWER TO A CARD FROM AN INTIMATE FRIEND OF BURNS,
WISHING HIM TO SPEND AN HOUR AT A TAVERN.

The King's most humble servant, I
  Can scarcely spare a minute;
But I'll be wi' ye by an' bye;
  Or else the Deil's be in it.

## MY BOTTLE.

My bottle is my holy pool,
That heals the wounds o' care an' dool,
And pleasure is a wanton trout,
An' ye drink it a' ye'll find him out.

## ON A SWEARING COXCOMB.

Here cursing swearing Burton lies,
A buck, a bean, or *Dem-my-eyes!*
Who in this life did little good,
And whose last words were *Dem-my-blood!*

## ON ANDREW TURNER.

In se'enteen hunder an' forty-nine,
The deil gat stuff to mak a swine,
 An' cuist it in a corner;
But by and by he changed his plan,
An' made it something like a man,
 An' ca'd it Andrew Turner.

## ON JAMES GRACIE

### DEAN OF GUILD FOR DUMFRIES.

Gracie, thou art a man of worth,
 O be thou dean for ever!
May he be damned to hell henceforth
 Who fauts thy weight or measure.

## LINES

WRITTEN UNDER THE PICTURE OF MISS BURNS.

CEASE, ye prudes, your envious railing,
    Lovely Burns has charms—confess :
True it is, she had one failing,
    Had a woman ever less ?

## ON MISS J. SCOTT, OF AYR.

OH ! had each Scot of ancient times
Been, Jeanie Scott, as thou art,
The bravest heart on English ground
Had yielded like a coward.

## EPIGRAM ON CAPTAIN FRANCIS GROSE,

### THE CELEBRATED ANTIQUARY.

THE Devil got notice that Grose was a-dying,
So whip ! at the summons, old Satan came flying ;
But when he approach'd where poor Francis lay moaning,
And saw each bed-post with its burden a-groaning,
Astonish'd, confounded, cried Satan, 'By God,
I'll want 'im, ere I take such a damnable load.'

## EPIGRAM ON ELPHINSTONE'S TRANSLATION

## OF MARTIAL'S EPIGRAMS.

O THOU whom Poetry abhors,
Whom Prose has turnèd out of doors,
Heard'st thou yon groan ?—proceed no further,
'Twas laurel'd Martial calling murther.

## REPLY TO A NOTE FROM CAPT. RIDDELL.

DEAR Sir, at ony time or tide,
I'd rather sit with you than ride,
    Tho' 'twere wi' royal Geordie;
And troth! your kindness, soon and late,
Aft gars me to mysel look blate;
    The Lord in Heaven reward ye!

## ON A COUNTRY LAIRD.

BLESS Jesus Christ, O Cardoness,
    With grateful lifted eyes,
Who said that not the soul alone,
    But body too, shall rise:
For had he said 'The soul alone
    From death I will deliver,'
Alas, alas! O Cardoness,
    Then hadst thou lain for ever!

## ON BEING SHEWN A BEAUTIFUL COUNTRY SEAT.

WE grant they're thine, those beauties all,
    So lovely in our eye;
Keep them, thou eunuch, Cardoness,
    For others to enjoy!

## ON SEEING THE BEAUTIFUL SEAT OF LORD GALLOWAY.

WHAT dost thou in that mansion fair?
    Flit, Galloway, and find
Some narrow, dirty, dungeon cave,
    The picture of thy mind!

## ON THE SAME.

No Stewart art thou, Galloway,
  The Stewarts all were brave ;
Besides, the Stewarts were but fools,
  Not one of them a knave.

————•+——

## ON THE SAME.

BRIGHT ran thy line, O Galloway,
  Thro' many a far-fam'd sire ;
So ran the far-fam'd Roman way,
  So ended in a mire !

————•+——

## TO THE SAME,

### ON THE AUTHOR BEING THREATENED WITH HIS RESENTMENT.

SPARE me thy vengeance, Galloway,
  In quiet let me live :
I ask no kindness at thy hand,
  For thou hast none to give.

————•+——

## VERSES TO J. RANKINE.

AE day, as Death, that grusome carl,
Was driving to the tither warl'
A mixtie-maxtie motley squad,
And mony a guilt-bespotted lad ;
Black gowns of each denomination,
And thieves of every rank and station,
From him that wears the star and garter,
To him that wintles in a halter ;
Asham'd himsel to see the wretches,
He mutters, glowrin' at the bitches,       10

' By God ! I'll not be seen behint them,
Nor 'mang the sp'ritual core present them,
Without at least ae honest man
To grace this damn'd infernal clan.'
By Adamhill a glance he threw,
'Lord God !' quoth he, 'I have it now,
There 's just the man I want, i' faith !'
And quickly stoppit Rankine's breath.

———••———

## EXTEMPORANEOUS EFFUSION,

### ON BEING APPOINTED TO THE EXCISE.

SEARCHING auld wives' barrels,—
    Ochone the day !
That clarty barm should stain my laurels ;
    But—what'll ye say ?
These movin' things, ca'd wives and weans,
Wad move the very hearts o' stanes !

———••———

## ON HEARING THAT THERE WAS FALSEHOOD IN
## THE REV. DR. BABINGTON'S VERY LOOKS.

THAT there is falsehood in his looks
    I must and will deny ;
They say their master is a knave—
    And sure they do not lie.

———••———

## POVERTY.

IN politics if thou wouldst mix,
    And mean thy fortunes be ;
Bear this in mind,—be deaf and blind,
    Let great folks hear and see.

## EPITAPH ON A SCHOOLMASTER.

IN CLEISH PARISH, KINROSS-SHIRE.

HERE lie Willie Michie's banes;
O Satan, when ye tak him,
Gie him the schoolin' of your weans,
For clever deils he'll mak them!

---

## EPITAPH ON WILLIAM NICOL,

OF THE HIGH SCHOOL, EDINBURGH.

YE maggots, feed on Nicol's brain,
For few sic feasts ye've gotten,
And fix your claws in Nicol's heart,
For deil a bit o't's rotten.

---

## EPITAPH ON A HENPECKED COUNTRY SQUIRE.

As father Adam first was fooled
(A case that's still too common),
Here lies a man a woman ruled,
—The Devil ruled the woman.

---

## EPITAPH ON A SUICIDE.

EARTHED up, here lies an imp of hell
Planted by Satan s dibble:
Poor silly wretch, he's damned himsel
To save the Lord the trouble.

## EPITAPH ON MY FATHER.

O YE, whose cheek the tear of pity stains,
    Draw near with pious rev'rence and attend!
Here lie the loving husband's dear remains,
    The tender father, and the gen'rous friend.

The pitying heart that felt for human woe;
    The dauntless heart that fear'd no human pride;
The friend of man, to vice alone a foe;
    For ' ev'n his failings lean'd to virtue's side.'

---

## EPITAPH ON JOHN DOVE,

### INNKEEPER, MAUCHLINE.

HERE lies Johnny Pidgeon;
What was his religion?
    Wha e'er desires to ken,
To some other warl'
Maun follow the carl,
    For here Johnny Pidgeon had nane!
Strong ale was ablution,
Small beer persecution,
    A dram was memento mori;
But a full flowing bowl                        10
Was the saving his soul,
    And port was celestial glory.

---

## EPITAPH ON JOHN BUSHBY,

### WRITER, DUMFRIES.

HERE lies John Bushby, honest man!
Cheat him, Devil, if you can.

## EPITAPH ON A WAG IN MAUCHLINE.

LAMENT him, Mauchline husbands a',
    He aften did assist ye ;
For had ye staid whole weeks awa,
    Your wives they ne'er had miss'd ye.

Ye Mauchline bairns, as on ye pass
    To school in bands thegither,
O tread ye lightly on his grass ;
    Perhaps he was your father.

---

## EPITAPH ON A PERSON NICKNAMED
### 'THE MARQUIS,'

#### WHO DESIRED BURNS TO WRITE ONE ON HIM.

HERE lies a mock Marquis whose titles were shamm'd,
If ever he rise, it will be to be damn'd.

---

## EPITAPH ON WALTER RIDDELL.

SIC a reptile was Wat,
    Sic a miscreant slave,
That the worms ev'n damn'd him
    When laid in his grave.
'In his flesh there's a famine,'
    A starv'd reptile cries ;
'An' his heart is rank poison,'
    Another replies.

## EPITAPH ON GABRIEL RICHARDSON.

HERE brewer Gabriel's fire's extinct,
   And empty are his barrels;
He's blest, if as he brewed he drink,—
   This man of honest morals!

## EPITAPH FOR GAVIN HAMILTON, ESQ.

THE poor man weeps—here Gavin sleeps,
   Whom canting wretches blam'd:
But with such as he, where'er he be,
   May I be sav'd or damn'd!

## EPITAPH FOR ROBERT AIKEN, ESQ.

KNOW thou, O stranger to the fame
Of this much lov'd, much honour'd name,
(For none that knew him need be told)
A warmer heart death ne'er made cold.

## EPITAPH ON A CELEBRATED RULING ELDER.

HERE souter Hood in Death does sleep;
   To Hell, if he's gone thither,
Satan, gie him thy gear to keep,
   He'll haud it weel thegither.

## EPITAPH ON WEE JOHNNY.

*Hic jacet wee Johnny.*

WHOE'ER thou art, O reader, know
  That death has murder'd Johnny!
An' here his body lies fu' low;
  For saul—he ne'er had ony.

———◆◆———

## EPITAPH ON A NOISY POLEMIC.

BELOW thir stanes lie Jamie's banes:
  O Death, it's my opinion,
Thou ne'er took such a bleth'rin' bitch
  Into thy dark dominion!

———◆◆———

## EPITAPH ON JAMES GRIEVE, LAIRD OF
## BOGHEAD.

HERE lies Boghead amang the dead
  In hopes to get salvation;
But if such as he in Heaven may be,
  Then welcome—hail! damnation.

# II.

# SONGS AND BALLADS

---

### MARY MORISON.

O MARY, at thy window be,
   It is the wish'd, the trysted hour!
Those smiles and glances let me see,
   That make the miser's treasure poor:
How blythely wad I bide the stoure,
   A weary slave frae sun to sun,
Could I the rich reward secure,
   The lovely Mary Morison.

Yestreen, when to the trombling string
   The dance gaed thro' the lighted ha',       10
To thee my fancy took its wing,
   I sat, but neither heard nor saw:
Tho' this was fair, and that was braw,
   And yon the toast of a' the town,
I sigh'd, and said amang them a',
   'Ye are na Mary Morison.'

O Mary, canst thou wreck his peace,
   Wha for thy sake wad gladly die?
Or canst thou break that heart of his,
   Whase only faut is loving thee?       20
If love for love thou wilt na gie,
   At least be pity to me shown!
A thought ungentle canna be
   The thought o' Mary Morison.

## MY LOVE IS LIKE A RED RED ROSE.

My love is like a red red rose
    That's newly sprung in June :
My love is like the melodie
    That's sweetly play'd in tune.

So fair art thou, my bonnie lass,
    So deep in love am I :
And I will love thee still, my dear,
    Till a' the seas gang dry.

Till a the seas gang dry. my dear,
    And the rocks melt wi' the sun :      10
And I will love thee still, my dear,
    While the sands o' life shall run.

And fare thee weel, my only love,
    And fare thee weel awhile !
And I will come again, my love,
    Tho' it were ten thousand mile.

——*——

## AFTON WATER.

Flow gently, sweet Afton, among thy green braes,
Flow gently, I'll sing thee a song in thy praise ;
My Mary's asleep by thy murmuring stream,
Flow gently, sweet Afton, disturb not her dream.

Thou stock-dove whose echo resounds thro' the glen.
Ye wild whistling blackbirds in yon thorny den,
Thou green-crested lapwing, thy screaming forbear,
I charge you disturb not my slumbering fair.

How lofty, sweet Afton, thy neighbouring hills,
Far mark'd with the courses of clear winding rills;     10
There daily I wander as noon rises high,
My flocks and my Mary's sweet cot in my eye.

How pleasant thy banks and green valleys below,
Where wild in the woodlands the primroses blow;
There oft as mild ev'ning weeps over the lea,
The sweet-scented birk shades my Mary and me.

Thy crystal stream, Afton, how lovely it glides,
And winds by the cot where my Mary resides;
How wanton thy waters her snowy feet lave,
As gathering sweet flow'rets she stems thy clear wave.     20

Flow gently, sweet Afton, among thy green braes,
Flow gently, sweet river, the theme of my lays;
My Mary's asleep by thy murmuring stream,
Flow gently, sweet Afton, disturb not her dream.

———◆———

## GO FETCH TO ME A PINT O' WINE.

Go fetch to me a pint o' wine,
    An' fill it in a silver tassie;
That I may drink, before I go,
    A service to my bonnie lassie.
The boat rocks at the pier o' Leith,
    Fu' loud the wind blaws frae the ferry,
The ship rides by the Berwick-law,
    And I maun leave my bonnie Mary.

The trumpets sound, the banners fly,
    The glittering spears are rankèd ready;     10
The shouts o' war are heard afar,
    The battle closes thick and bloody;
But it's no the roar o' sea or shore
    Wad mak me langer wish to tarry;
Nor shout o' war that's heard afar,
    It's leaving thee, my bonnie Mary.

### HIGHLAND MARY.

YE banks, and braes, and streams around
   The castle o' Montgomery,
Green be your woods, and fair your flowers,
   Your waters never drumlie!
There simmer first unfauld her robes,
   And there the langest tarry;
For there I took the last fareweel
   O' my sweet Highland Mary.

How sweetly bloom'd the gay green birk,
   How rich the hawthorn's blossom,      10
As underneath their fragrant shade
   I clasp'd her to my bosom!
The golden hours on angel wings
   Flew o'er me and my dearie;
For dear to me as light and life
   Was my sweet Highland Mary.

Wi' mony a vow, and lock'd embrace,
   Our parting was fu' tender;
And, pledging aft to meet again,
   We tore oursels asunder;      20
But oh! fell death's untimely frost,
   That nipt my flower sae early!
Now green's the sod, and cauld's the clay,
   That wraps my Highland Mary!

O pale, pale now, those rosy lips,
   I aft have kiss'd sae fondly!
And closed for aye the sparkling glance,
   That dwelt on me sae kindly!
And mould'ring now in silent dust,
   That heart that lo'ed me dearly!      30
But still within my bosom's core
   Shall live my Highland Mary.

## TO MARY IN HEAVEN.

THOU lingering star, with lessening ray,
  That lov'st to greet the early morn,
Again thou usherest in the day
  My Mary from my soul was torn.
O Mary! dear departed shade!
  Where is thy place of blissful rest?
Seest thou thy lover lowly laid?
  Hear'st thou the groans that rend his breast?

That sacred hour can I forget?
  Can I forget the hallow'd grove,         10
Where by the winding Ayr we met,
  To live one day of parting love?
Eternity will not efface
  Those records dear of transports past;
Thy image at our last embrace—
  Ah! little thought we 'twas our last!

Ayr gurgling kiss'd his pebbled shore,
  O'erhung with wild woods, thickening green;
The fragrant birch, and hawthorn hoar,
  Twin'd amorous round the raptur'd scene.    20
The flowers sprang wanton to be prest,
  The birds sang love on ev'ry spray,
Till too too soon, the glowing west
  Proclaim'd the speed of wingèd day.

Still o'er these scenes my memory wakes,
  And fondly broods with miser care!
Time but the impression deeper makes,
  As streams their channels deeper wear.
My Mary, dear departed shade!
  Where is thy blissful place of rest?        30
Seest thou thy lover lowly laid?
  Hear'st thou the groans that rend his breast?

## MY NANNIE O.

BEHIND yon hills where Lugar flows,
  'Mang moors an' mosses many O,
The wintry sun the day has clos'd,
  And I'll awa' to Nannie O.

The westlin wind blaws loud an' shill,
  The night's baith mirk and rainy O ;
But I'll get my plaid, an' out I'll steal,
  An' owre the hill to Nannie O.

My Nannie's charming, sweet, an' young :
  Nae artfu' wiles to win ye O :          10
May ill befa' the flattering tongue
  That wad beguile my Nannie O.

Her face is fair, her heart is true,
  As spotless as she's bonnie O :
The opening gowan, wat wi' dew,
  Nae purer is than Nannie O.

A country lad is my degree,
  An' few there be that ken me O ;
But what care I how few they be,
  I'm welcome aye to Nannie O.          20

My riches a's my penny-fee,
  An' I maun guide it cannie O ;
But warl's gear ne'er troubles me,
  My thoughts are a' my Nannie O.

Our auld Guidman delights to view
  His sheep an' kye thrive bonnie O ;
But I'm as blythe that hauds his pleugh,
  An' has nae care but Nannie O.

Come weel, come woe, I care na by,
  I'll tak what Heav'n will send me O ;          30
Nae ither care in life have I,
  But live, an' love my Nannie O.

## AE FOND KISS.

AE fond kiss, and then we sever!
Ae fareweel, alas, for ever!
Deep in heart-wrung tears I'll pledge thee,
Warring sighs and groans I'll wage thee.
Who shall say that fortune grieves him
While the star of hope she leaves him?
Me, nae cheerfu' twinkle lights me,
Dark despair around benights me.

I'll ne'er blame my partial fancy,
Naething could resist my Nancy;                     10
But to see her was to love her,
Love but her, and love for ever.
Had we never lov'd sae kindly,
Had we never lov'd sae blindly,
Never met—or never parted,
We had ne'er been broken-hearted.

Fare thee weel, thou first and fairest!
Fare thee weel, thou best and dearest!
Thine be ilka joy and treasure,
Peace, enjoyment, love, and pleasure.               20
Ae fond kiss, and then we sever;
Ae fareweel, alas, for ever!
Deep in heart-wrung tears I'll pledge thee,
Warring sighs and groans I'll wage thee.

---

## MY NANNIE'S AWA.

Now in her green mantle blythe Nature arrays,
And listens the lambkins that bleat o'er the braes,
While birds warble welcomes in ilka green shaw;
But to me it's delightless—my Nannie's awa.

The snaw-drap and primrose our woodlands adorn,
And violets bathe in the weet o' the morn:
They pain my sad bosom, sae sweetly they blaw,
They mind me o' Nannie—and Nannie's awa.

Thou laverock that springs frae the dews o' the lawn
The shepherd to warn o' the grey-breaking dawn,      10
And thou, mellow mavis, that hails the night-fa',
Gie over for pity—my Nannie's awa.

Come autumn sae pensive, in yellow and gray,
And soothe me wi' tidings o' nature's decay;
The dark, dreary winter, and wild-driving snaw,
Alane can delight me—now Nannie's awa.

## YE BANKS AND BRAES.

YE banks and braes o' bonnie Doon,
    How can ye bloom sae fresh and fair?
How can ye chant, ye little birds,
    And I sae weary fu' o' care?
Thou'lt break my heart, thou warbling bird,
    That wantons thro' the flowering thorn:
Thou minds me o' departed joys,
    Departed never to return.

Aft hae I rov'd by bonnie Doon,
    To see the rose and woodbine twine;      10
And ilka bird sang o' its love,
    And fondly sae did I o' mine.
Wi' lightsome heart I pu'd a rose,
    Fu' sweet upon its thorny tree;
And my fause lover stole my rose,
    But ah! he left the thorn wi' me.

### (EARLIER VERSION.)

YE flowery banks o' bonnie Doon,
    How can ye blume sae fair?
How can ye chant, ye little birds,
    And I sae fu' o' care?

Thou'll break my heart, thou bonnie bird,
  That sings upon the bough ;
Thou minds me o' the happy days,
  When my fause luve was true.

Thou'll break my heart, thou bonnie bird,
  That sings beside thy mate ;        10
For sae I sat, and sae I sang,
  And wist na o' my fate.

Aft hae I rov'd by bonnie Doon,
  To see the wood-bine twine,
And ilka bird sang o' its love,
  And sae did I o' mine.

Wi' lightsome heart I pu'd a rose
  Frae off its thorny tree :
But my fause luver staw my rose,
  And left the thorn wi' me.        20

Wi' lightsome heart I pu'd a rose
  Upon a morn in June ;
And sae I flourish'd on the morn,
  And sae was pu'd ere noon.

---

## OF A' THE AIRTS.

Of a' the airts the wind can blaw,
  I dearly like the west,
For there the bonnie lassie lives,
  The lassie I lo'e best :
There's wild woods grow, and rivers row,
  And mony a hill between ;
But day and night my fancy's flight
  Is ever wi' my Jean.

I see her in the dewy flowers,
  I see her sweet and fair:          10
I hear her in the tunefu' birds,
  I hear her charm the air:
There 's not a bonnie flower that springs
  By fountain, shaw, or green;
There 's not a bonnie bird that sings,
  But minds me o' my Jean.

———••———

## THERE WAS A LAD.

THERE was a lad was born in Kyle,
But what'n a day o' what'n a style
I doubt it 's hardly worth the while
    To be sae nice wi' Robin.

    Robin was a rovin' boy,
      Rantin' rovin', rantin' rovin';
    Robin was a rovin' boy,
      Rantin' rovin' Robin.

Our monarch's hindmost year but ane
Was five-and-twenty days begun,          10
'Twas then a blast o' Janwar win'
  Blew hansel in on Robin.

The gossip keekit in his loof,
Quo' scho, Wha lives will see the proof,
This waly boy will be nae coof,
    I think we'll ca' him Robin.

He'll hae misfortunes great and sma',
But aye a heart aboon them a';
He'll be a credit till us a',
    We'll a' be proud o' Robin.          20

But sure as three times three mak nine,
I see by ilka score and line,
This chap will dearly like our kin',
    So leeze me on thee, Robin.

Guid faith, quo' scho, I doubt you, Sir,
Ye gar the lasses lie aspar,
But twenty fauts ye may hae waur,
  So blessings on thee, Robin!

    Robin was a rovin' boy,
      Rantin' rovin', rantin' rovin';     30
    Robin was a rovin' boy,
      Rantin' rovin' Robin.

## GREEN GROW THE RASHES.

GREEN grow the rashes O,
  Green grow the rashes O;
The sweetest hours that e'er I spend,
  Are spent amang the lasses O!

There's nought but care on ev'ry han',
  In ev'ry hour that passes O;
What signifies the life o' man,
  An' 'twere na for the lasses O.

The warly race may riches chase,
  An' riches still may fly them O;     10
An' tho' at last they catch them fast,
  Their hearts can ne'er enjoy them O.

But gie me a canny hour at e'en,
  My arms about my dearie O;
An' warly cares, an' warly men,
  May a' gae tapsalteerie O!

For you sae douce, ye sneer at this,
  Ye're nought but senseless asses O:
The wisest man the warl' saw,
  He dearly lov'd the lasses O.     20

Auld nature swears, the lovely dears
  Her noblest work she classes O;
Her prentice han' she tried on man,
  An' then she made the lasses O.

## FOR A' THAT AND A' THAT.

Is there, for honest poverty,
  That hangs his head, and a' that ?
The coward-slave, we pass him by,
  We dare be poor for a' that !
    For a' that, and a' that,
      Our toils obscure, and a' that ;
    The rank is but the guinea stamp ;
      The man's the gowd for a' that.

What tho' on hamely fare we dine,
  Wear hodden-gray, and a' that ;         10
Gie fools their silks, and knaves their wine,
  A man's a man for a' that.
    For a' that, and a' that,
      Their tinsel show, and a' that ;
    The honest man, tho' e'er sae poor,
      Is King o' men for a' that.

Ye see yon birkie, ca'd a lord,
  Wha struts, and stares, and a' that ;
Tho' hundreds worship at his word,
  He's but a coof for a' that :         20
    For a' that, and a' that,
      His riband, star, and a' that,
    The man of independent mind,
      He looks and laughs at a' that.

A prince can mak a belted knight,
  A marquis, duke, and a' that ;
But an honest man's aboon his might,
  Guid faith he mauna fa' that !
    For a' that, and a' that,
      Their dignities, and a' that,         30
    The pith o' sense, and pride o' worth,
      Are higher rank than a' that.

Then let us pray that come it may,
  As come it will for a' that;
That sense and worth, o'er a' the earth,
  May bear the gree, and a' that.
    For a' that and a' that,
      It's coming yet, for a' that,
    That man to man the warld o'er
      Shall brothers be for a' that.                    40

## AULD LANG SYNE.

SHOULD auld acquaintance be forgot,
  And never brought to min'?
Should auld acquaintance be forgot,
  And auld lang syne?

    For auld lang syne, my dear,
      For auld lang syne,
    We'll tak a cup o' kindness yet,
      For auld lang syne.

We twa hae run about the braes,
  And pu'd the gowans fine;                              10
But we've wander'd mony a weary foot
  Sin' auld lang syne.

We twa hae paidled i' the burn,
  From morning sun till dine;
But seas between us braid hae roar'd
  Sin' auld lang syne.

And there's a hand, my trusty fiere,
  And gie's a hand o' thine;
And we'll tak a right guid-willie waught,
  For auld lang syne.                                    20

And surely ye'll be your pint-stowp,
  And surely I'll be mine;
And we'll tak a cup o' kindness yet
  For auld lang syne.

## SCOTS WHA HAE.

ROBERT BRUCE'S ADDRESS TO HIS ARMY, BEFORE
THE BATTLE OF BANNOCKBURN.

Scots, wha hae wi' Wallace bled,
Scots, wham Bruce has aften led,
Welcome to your gory bed,
　　　Or to victorie.

Now's the day, and now's the hour;
See the front o' battle lour!
See approach proud Edward's power—
　　　Chains and slaverie!

Wha will be a traitor knave?
Wha can fill a coward's grave?　　　　　10
Wha sae base as be a slave?
　　　Let him turn and flee!

Wha for Scotland's King and law
Freedom's sword will strongly draw,
Freeman stand, or freeman fa'?
　　　Let him follow me!

By oppression's woes and pains!
By your sons in servile chains!
We will drain our dearest veins,
　　　But they shall be free!　　　　　20

Lay the proud usurpers low!
Tyrants fall in every foe!
Liberty's in every blow!
　　　Let us do or die!

# IT WAS A' FOR OUR RIGHTFU' KING.

It was a' for our rightfu' King,
  We left fair Scotland's strand ;
It was a' for our rightfu' King,
  We e'er saw Irish land,
          My dear,
  We e'er saw Irish land.

Now a' is done that men can do,
  And a' is done in vain ;
My love and native land farewell,
  For I maun cross the main,          10
          My dear,
  For I maun cross the main.

He turn'd him right and round about
  Upon the Irish shore ;
And gae his bridle-reins a shake,
  With adieu for evermore,
          My dear,
  Adieu for evermore.

The sodger from the wars returns,
  The sailor frae the main ;          20
But I hae parted frae my love,
  Never to meet again,
          My dear,
  Never to meet again.

When day is gane, and night is come,
  And a' folk boune to sleep,
I think on him that 's far awa',
  The lee-lang night, and weep,
          My dear,
  The lee-lang night, and weep.          30

## MACPHERSON'S FAREWELL.

FAREWELL, ye dungeons dark and strong,
　　The wretch's destinie :
Macpherson's time will not be long
　　On yonder gallows tree.

　　Sae rantingly, sae wantonly,
　　　　Sae dauntingly gaed he ;
　　He played a spring and danced it round,
　　　　Below the gallows tree.

Oh, what is death but parting breath ?
　　On mony a bloody plain　　　　　　　　10
I've dared his face, and in this place
　　I scorn him yet again !

Untie these bands from off my hands,
　　And bring to me my sword,
And there's no a man in all Scotland,
　　But I'll brave him at a word.

I've lived a life of sturt and strife ;
　　I die by treacherie :
It burns my heart I must depart
　　And not avengèd be.　　　　　　　　　20

Now farewell light, thou sunshine bright,
　　And all beneath the sky !
May coward shame distain his name,
　　The wretch that dares not die !

———＋·———

## WANDERING WILLIE.

HERE awa, there awa, wandering Willie,
　　Here awa, there awa, haud awa hame ;
Come to my bosom, my ain only dearie,
　　Tell me thou bring'st me my Willie the same.

Winter winds blew loud and cauld at our parting,
  Fears for my Willie brought tears to my ee;
Welcome now, Simmer, and welcome, my Willie,
  The Simmer to nature, my Willie to me!

Rest, ye wild storms, in the cave of your slumbers;
  How your dread howling a lover alarms!                    10
Wauken, ye breezes, row gently, ye billows,
  And waft my dear laddie ance mair to my arms.

But oh, if he's faithless, and minds na his Nannie,
  Flow still between us, thou wide roaring main;
May I never see it, may I never trow it,
  But, dying, believe that my Willie's my ain!

———•◦•———

## BRAW LADS.

Braw braw lads on Yarrow braes,
  Ye wander thro' the blooming heather;
But Yarrow braes nor Ettrick shaws
  Can match the lads o' Gala Water.

But there is ane, a secret ane,
  Aboon them a' I lo'e him better;
And I'll be his, and he'll be mine,
  The bonnie lad o' Gala Water.

Altho' his daddie was nae laird,
  And tho' I hae nae meikle tocher,                         10
Yet rich in kindest, truest love,
  We'll tent our flocks by Gala Water.

It ne'er was wealth, it ne'er was wealth,
  That coft contentment, peace or pleasure;
The bands and bliss o' mutual love,
  O that's the chiefest warld's treasure!

## CA' THE YOWES.

Ca' the yowes to the knowes,
Ca' them where the heather grows,
Ca' them where the burnie rows,
  My bonnie dearie.

Hark! the mavis' evening sang
Sounding Clouden's woods amang;
Then a-faulding let us gang,
  My bonnie dearie.

We'll gae down by Clouden side,
Thro' the hazels spreading wide                    10
O'er the waves that sweetly glide
  To the moon sae clearly.

Yonder's Clouden's silent towers,
Where at moonshine midnight hours,
O'er the dewy-bending flowers,
  Fairies dance sae cheery.

Ghaist nor bogle shalt thou fear;
Thou'rt to love and Heaven sae dear,
Nocht of ill may come thee near,
  My bonnie dearie.                              20

Fair and lovely as thou art,
Thou hast stown my very heart;
I can die—but canna part,
  My bonnie dearie.

## JOHN ANDERSON MY JO.

JOHN ANDERSON my jo, John,
　When we were first acquent,
Your locks were like the raven,
　Your bonnie brow was brent;
But now your brow is beld, John,
　Your locks are like the snow;
But blessings on your frosty pow,
　John Anderson, my jo.

John Anderson my jo, John,
　We clamb the hill thegither;　　　　10
And mony a canty day, John,
　We've had wi' ane anither:
Now we maun totter down, John,
　And hand in hand we'll go,
And sleep thegither at the foot,
　John Anderson, my jo.

## THE BIRKS OF ABERFELDY.

BONNIE lassie, will ye go,
Will ye go, will ye go,
Bonnie lassie, will ye go
　To the Birks of Aberfeldy?

Now simmer blinks on flowery braes,
And o'er the crystal streamlet plays,
Come let us spend the lightsome days
　In the Birks of Aberfeldy.

While o'er their heads the hazels hing,
The little birdies blythely sing,　　　　10
Or lightly flit on wanton wing
　In the Birks of Aberfeldy.

The braes ascend like lofty wa's,
The foaming stream deep-roaring fa's,
O'erhung wi' fragrant spreading shaws—
    The Birks of Aberfeldy.

The hoary cliffs are crown'd wi' flowers,
White o'er the linns the burnie pours,
And rising, weets wi' misty showers
    The Birks of Aberfeldy.      20

Let fortune's gifts at random flee,
They ne'er shall draw a wish frae me,
Supremely blest wi' love and thee,
    In the Birks of Aberfeldy.

——◆——

# O, WERT THOU IN THE CAULD BLAST.

O, WERT thou in the cauld blast,
    On yonder lea, on yonder lea,
My plaidie to the angry airt,
    I'd shelter thee, I'd shelter thee.
Or did misfortune's bitter storms
    Around thee blaw, around thee blaw,
Thy bield should be my bosom,
    To share it a', to share it a'.

Or were I in the wildest waste,
    Sae black and bare, sae black and bare,    10
The desert were a paradise,
    If thou wert there, if thou wert there.
Or were I monarch o' the globe,
    Wi' thee to reign, wi' thee to reign,
The brightest jewel in my crown
    Wad be my queen, wad be my queen.

## UP IN THE MORNING.

Up in the morning's no' for me,
  Up in the morning early;
When a' the hills are covered wi' snaw,
  I'm sure it's winter fairly.

Cauld blaws the wind frae east to wast,
  The drift is driving sairly;
Sae loud and shrill's I hear the blast,
  I'm sure it's winter fairly.

The birds sit chittering in the thorn,
  A' day they fare but sparely;                    10
And lang's the night frae e'en to morn,
  I'm sure it's winter fairly.

----

## MY HEART'S IN THE HIGHLANDS.

My heart's in the Highlands, my heart is not here;
My heart's in the Highlands a-chasing the deer;
Chasing the wild deer, and following the roe,
My heart's in the Highlands, wherever I go.
Farewell to the Highlands, farewell to the North,
The birth-place of valour, the country of worth;
Wherever I wander, wherever I rove,
The hills of the Highlands for ever I love.

Farewell to the mountains, high cover'd with snow;
Farewell to the straths and green valleys below;    10
Farewell to the forests and wild-hanging woods;
Farewell to the torrents and loud-pouring floods.
My heart's in the Highlands, my heart is not here;
My heart's in the Highlands a-chasing the deer;
Chasing the wild deer, and following the roe,
My heart's in the Highlands, wherever I go.

## DUNCAN GRAY.

DUNCAN GRAY came here to woo,
    Ha, ha, the wooing o't,
On blythe Yule night when we were fou,
    Ha, ha, the wooing o't.
Maggie coost her head fu' heigh,
Look'd asklent and unco skeigh,
Gart poor Duncan stand abeigh;
    Ha, ha, the wooing o't.


Duncan fleech'd, and Duncan pray'd;
    Ha, ha, the wooing o't,                    10
Meg was deaf as Ailsa Craig,
    Ha, ha, the wooing o't.
Duncan sigh'd baith out and in,
Grat his een baith bleer't and blin',
Spak o' lowpin o'er a linn;
    Ha, ha, the wooing o't.


Time and chance are but a tide,
    Ha, ha, the wooing o't,
Slighted love is sair to bide,
    Ha, ha, the wooing o't.                    20
Shall I, like a fool, quoth he,
For a haughty hizzie die?
She may gae to—France for me!
    Ha, ha, the wooing o't.


How it comes let doctors tell,
    Ha, ha, the wooing o't,
Meg grew sick as he grew haill,
    Ha, ha, the wooing o't.
Something in her bosom wrings,
For relief a sigh she brings;
And O, her een they spak sic things!                    30
    Ha, ha, the wooing o't.

Duncan was a lad o' grace,
     Ha, ha, the wooing o't,
Maggie's was a piteous case,
     Ha, ha, the wooing o't.
Duncan couldna be her death,
Swelling pity smoor'd his wrath ;
Now they're crouse and cantie baith !
     Ha, ha, the wooing o't.     40

---

## POORTITH CAULD.

O POORTITH cauld, and restless love,
   Ye wreck my peace between ye ;
Yet poortith a' I could forgive,
   An' 'twerena for my Jeanie.

    O why should fate sic pleasure have,
      Life's dearest bands untwining?
    Or why sae sweet a flower as love
      Depend on Fortune's shining?

This warld's wealth when I think on,
   Its pride, and a' the lave o't,—     10
O fie on silly coward man,
   That he should be the slave o't.

Her een sae bonnie blue betray
   How she repays my passion ;
But prudence is her o'erword aye,
   She talks of rank and fashion.

O wha can prudence think upon,
   And sic a lassie by him ?
O wha can prudence think upon,
   And sae in love as I am ?     20

How blest the simple cotter's fate!
 He woos his artless dearie;
The silly bogles, wealth and state,
 Can never make him eerie.

O why should fate sic pleasure have
 Life's dearest bands untwining?
Or why sae sweet a flower as love
 Depend on Fortune's shining?

———◆◆———

## BANKS OF DEVON.

How pleasant the banks of the clear-winding Devon,
 With green-spreading bushes, and flowers blooming fair!
But the bonniest flower on the banks of the Devon
 Was once a sweet bud on the braes of the Ayr.

Mild be the sun on this sweet blushing flower,
 In the gay rosy morn as it bathes in the dew!
And gentle the fall of the soft vernal shower,
 That steals on the evening each leaf to renew.

O, spare the dear blossom, ye orient breezes,
 With chill hoary wing as ye usher the dawn!    10
And far be thou distant, thou reptile that seizes
 The verdure and pride of the garden and lawn!

Let Bourbon exult in his gay gilded lilies,
 And England triumphant display her proud rose;
A fairer than either adorns the green valleys
 Where Devon, sweet Devon, meandering flows.

## THE RIGS O' BARLEY.

It was upon a Lammas night,
  When corn rigs are bonnie,
Beneath the moon's unclouded light
  I held awa to Annie:
The time flew by wi' tentless heed,
  Till 'tween the late and early,
Wi' sma' persuasion she agreed
  To see me thro' the barley.

The sky was blue, the wind was still,
  The moon was shining clearly;                    10
I set her down wi' right good will
  Amang the rigs o' barley;
I kent her heart was a' my ain;
  I loved her most sincerely;
I kissed her owre and owre again
  Amang the rigs o' barley.

I locked her in my fond embrace;
  Her heart was beating rarely;
My blessings on that happy place,
  Amang the rigs o' barley!                        20
But by the moon and stars so bright,
  That shone that hour so clearly,
She aye shall bless that happy night
  Amang the rigs o' barley.

I hae been blythe wi' comrades dear;
  I hae been merry drinking;
I hae been joyfu' gatherin' gear;
  I hae been happy thinking:
But a' the pleasures e'er I saw,
  Tho' three times doubled fairly,               30
That happy night was worth them a',
  Amang the rigs o' barley.

  Corn rigs, an' barley rigs,
    An' corn rigs are bonnie:
  I'll ne'er forget that happy night,
    Amang the rigs wi' Annie.

## THE GLOOMY NIGHT.

THE gloomy night is gathering fast,
Loud roars the wild inconstant blast,
Yon murky cloud is foul with rain,
I see it driving o'er the plain ;
The hunter now has left the moor,
The scatter'd coveys meet secure,
While here I wander, prest with care,
Along the lonely banks of Ayr.

The Autumn mourns her ripening corn
By early Winter's ravage torn ;                              10
Across her placid azure sky,
She sees the scowling tempest fly :
Chill runs my blood to hear it rave,
I think upon the stormy wave,
Where many a danger I must dare,
Far from the bonnie banks of Ayr.

'Tis not the surging billow's roar,
'Tis not that fatal, deadly shore ;
Tho' death in ev'ry shape appear,
The wretched have no more to fear :                          20
But round my heart the ties are bound,
That heart transpierc'd with many a wound :
These bleed afresh, those ties I tear,
To leave the bonnie banks of Ayr.

Farewell, old Coila's hills and dales,
Her heathy moors and winding vales ;
The scenes where wretched fancy roves,
Pursuing past unhappy loves !
Farewell, my friends ! Farewell, my foes !
My peace with these, my love with those ;                   30
The bursting tears my heart declare,
Farewell, the bonnie banks of Ayr !

## THE FAREWELL.

TO THE BRETHREN OF ST. JAMES'S LODGE, TARBOLTON.

Adieu! a heart-warm fond adieu!
  Dear brothers of the mystic tie!
Ye favour'd, ye enlighten'd few,
  Companions of my social joy!
Tho' I to foreign lands must hie,
  Pursuing Fortune's slidd'ry ba',
With melting heart, and brimful eye,
  I'll mind you still, tho' far awa'.

Oft have I met your social band,
  And spent the cheerful festive night;          10
Oft, honour'd with supreme command,
  Presided o'er the sons of light:
And by that hieroglyphic bright,
  Which none but craftsmen ever saw!
Strong memory on my heart shall write
  Those happy scenes when far awa'!

May freedom, harmony, and love
  Unite you in the grand design,
Beneath th' Omniscient eye above,
  The glorious Architect Divine!                 20
That you may keep th' unerring line,
  Still rising by the plummet's law,
Till Order bright completely shine,
  Shall be my pray'r when far awa'.

And You, farewell! whose merits claim,
  Justly, that highest badge to wear!
Heav'n bless your honour'd noble name,
  To Masonry and Scotia dear!
A last request permit me here:
  When yearly ye assemble a',—                    30
One round, I ask it with a tear,
  To him, the Bard that's far awa'.

## AND MAUN I STILL ON MENIE DOAT.

AGAIN rejoicing nature sees
  Her robe assume its vernal hues,
Her leafy locks wave in the breeze,
  All freshly steep'd in morning dews.

And maun I still on Menie doat,
  And bear the scorn that 's in her e'e?
For it 's jet, jet black, an' it 's like a hawk,
  An' it winna let a body be!

In vain to me the cowslips blaw,
  In vain to me the violets spring;                    10
In vain to me, in glen or shaw,
  The mavis and the lintwhite sing.

The merry ploughboy cheers his team,
  Wi' joy the tentie seedsman stalks,
But life to me 's a weary dream,
  A dream of ane that never wauks.

The wanton coot the water skims,
  Amang the reeds the ducklings cry,
The stately swan majestic swims,
  And every thing is blest but I.                      20

The shepherd steeks his faulding slap,
  And owre the moorlands whistles shill.
Wi' wild, unequal, wand'ring step
  I meet him on the dewy hill.

And when the lark, 'tween light and dark,
  Blythe waukens by the daisy's side,
And mounts and sings on flittering wings,
  A woe-worn ghaist I hameward glide.

Come, Winter, with thine angry howl,
   And raging bend the naked tree;     30
Thy gloom will soothe my cheerless soul,
   When Nature all is sad like me!

And maun I still on Menie doat,
   And bear the scorn that's in her e'e?
For it's jet, jet black, an' it's like a hawk,
   An' it winna let a body be!

## THE BRAES O' BALLOCHMYLE.

THE Catrine woods were yellow seen,
   The flowers decayed on Catrine lee,
Nae lav'rock sang on hillock green,
   But nature sickened on the ee.
Thro' faded groves Maria sang,
   Hersel in beauty's bloom the whyle,
And aye the wild-wood echoes rang,
   Fareweel the braes o' Ballochmyle.

Low in your wintry beds, ye flowers,
   Again ye'll flourish fresh and fair;     10
Ye birdies dumb, in withering bowers,
   Again ye'll charm the vocal air.
But here, alas! for me nae mair
   Shall birdie charm, or floweret smile;
Fareweel, the bonnie banks of Ayr,
   Fareweel, fareweel, sweet Ballochmyle.

## THE BLUE-EYED LASSIE.

I GAED a waefu' gate yestreen,
   A gate, I fear, I'll dearly rue;
I gat my death frae twa sweet een,
   Twa lovely een o' bonnie blue.

'Twas not her golden ringlets bright,
   Her lips like roses wat wi' dew,
Her heaving bosom lily-white;
   It was her een sae bonnie blue.

She talk'd, she smil'd, my heart she wyl'd,
   She charm'd my soul I wist na how;    10
And aye the stound, the deadly wound,
   Cam frae her een sae bonnie blue.
But spare to speak, and spare to speed;
   She'll aiblins listen to my vow:
Should she refuse, I'll lay my dead
   To her twa een sae bonnie blue.

————•◦•————

## TIBBIE, I HAE SEEN THE DAY.

O TIBBIE, I hae seen the day,
   Ye would na been sae shy;
For laik o' gear ye lightly me,
   But, trowth, I care na by.

Yestreen I met you on the moor,
Ye spak na, but gaed by like stoure:
Ye geck at me because I'm poor,
   But fient a hair care I.

I doubt na, lass, but ye may think,
Because ye hae the name o' clink,    10
That ye can please me at a wink,
   Whene'er ye like to try.

But sorrow tak him that's sae mean,
Altho' his pouch o' coin were clean,
Wha follows ony saucy quean
   That looks sae proud and high.

Altho' a lad were e'er sae smart,
If that he want the yellow dirt,
Ye'll cast your head anither airt,    20
   And answer him fu' dry.

But if he hae the name o' gear,
Ye'll fasten to him like a brier,
Tho' hardly he, for sense or lear,
    Be better than the kye.

But, Tibbie, lass, tak my advice,
Your daddy's gear maks you sae nice ;
The deil a ane wad spier your price.
    Were ye as poor as I.

There lives a lass in yonder park,                 30
I would na gie her in her sark,
For you wi' a' your thousand mark ;
    Ye need na look sae high.

---

## TAM GLEN.

My heart is a breaking, dear Tittie,
    Some counsel unto me come len',
To anger them a' is a pity ;
    But what will I do wi' Tam Glen ?

I'm thinking, wi' sic a braw fellow,
    In poortith I might mak a fen' ;
What care I in riches to wallow,
    If I maunna marry Tam Glen ?

There 's Lowrie the laird o' Dumeller,
    'Guid-day to you, brute !' he comes ben :      10
He brags and he blaws o' his siller,
    But when will he dance like Tam Glen?

My minnie does constantly deave me,
    And bids me beware o' young men ;
They flatter, she says, to deceive me ;
    But wha can think sae o' Tam Glen ?

My daddie says, gin I'll forsake him,
    He'll gie me guid hunder marks ten :
But, if it 's ordain'd I maun take him,
    O wha will I get but Tam Glen?                  20

Yestreen at the Valentines' dealing,
   My heart to my mou gied a sten :
For thrice I drew ane without failing,
   And thrice it was written, Tam Glen.

The last Halloween I was waukin'
   My droukit sark-sleeve, as ye ken ;
His likeness cam up the house stalkin'—
   And the very grey breeks o' Tam Glen !

Come, counsel, dear Tittie, don't tarry ;
   I'll gie you my bonnie black hen,                    30
Gif ye will advise me to marry
   The lad I lo'e dearly, Tam Glen.

———•✦•———

## CONTENTED WI' LITTLE.

CONTENTED wi' little, and cantie wi' mair,
Whene'er I forgather wi' sorrow and care,
I gie them a skelp, as they're creepin' alang,
Wi' a cog o' gude swats, and an auld Scottish sang.

I whyles claw the elbow o' troublesome thought ;
But man is a soger, and life is a faught :
My mirth and gude humour are coin in my pouch,
And my freedom's my lairdship nae monarch dare touch.

A towmond o' trouble, should that be my fa',
A night o' gude fellowship sowthers it a' ;                    10
When at the blythe end of our journey at last,
Wha the deil ever thinks o' the road he has past ?

Blind Chance, let her snapper and stoyte on her way,
Be't to me, be't frae me, e'en let the jad gae :
Come ease or come travail, come pleasure or pain,
My warst word is—'Welcome, and welcome again !'

## WHISTLE, AND I'LL COME TO YOU, MY LAD.

O WHISTLE, and I'll come to you, my lad;
O whistle, and I'll come to you, my lad:
Tho' father and mither and a' should gae mad,
O whistle, and I'll come to you, my lad.

But warily tent, when ye come to court me,
And come na unless the back-yett be a-jee;
Syne up the back-stile, and let naebody see,
And come as ye were na comin' to me.
And come as ye were na comin' to me.

At kirk, or at market, whene'er ye meet me,      10
Gang by me as tho' that ye car'd na a flee:
But steal me a blink o' your bonnie black ee,
Yet look as ye were na lookin' at me.
Yet look as ye were na lookin' at me.

Aye vow and protest that ye care na for me,
And whiles ye may lightly my beauty a wee;
But court na anither, tho' jokin' ye be,
For fear that she wyle your fancy frae me.
For fear that she wyle your fancy frae me.

———••———

## TRUE HEARTED WAS HE.

TRUE hearted was he, the sad swain o' the Yarrow,
    And fair are the maids on the banks o' the Ayr,
But by the sweet side o' the Nith's winding river,
    Are lovers as faithful, and maidens as fair:
To equal young Jessie seek Scotland all over;
    To equal young Jessie you seek it in vain;
Grace, beauty, and elegance, fetter her lover,
    And maidenly modesty fixes the chain.

O, fresh is the rose in the gay, dewy morning,
    And sweet is the lily at evening close;      10
But in the fair presence o' lovely young Jessie,
    Unseen is the lily, unheeded the rose.

Love sits in her smile, a wizard ensnaring;
   Enthron'd in her een he delivers his law:
And still to her charms she alone is a stranger!
   Her modest demeanour's the jewel of a'.

---

## MEG O' THE MILL.

O KEN ye what Meg o' the Mill has gotten,
An' ken ye what Meg o' the Mill has gotten?
She has gotten a coof wi' a claut o' siller,
And broken the heart o' the barley Miller.

The Miller was strappin, the Miller was ruddy;
A heart like a lord, and a hue like a lady;
The Laird was a widdiefu', bleerit knurl;
She's left the guid fellow and ta'en the churl.

The Miller he hecht her a heart leal and loving;
The Laird did address her wi' matter mair moving,  10
A fine pacing horse wi' a clear chained bridle,
A whip by her side, and a bonnie side-saddle.

O wae on the siller, it is sae prevailing;
And wae on the love that is fix'd on a mailen!
A tocher's nae word in a true lover's parle,
But gie me my love, and a fig for the warl!

---

## OPEN THE DOOR TO ME, OH!

OH, open the door, some pity to shew,
   Oh, open the door to me, oh!
Tho' thou hast been false, I'll ever prove true,
   Oh, open the door to me, oh!

Cauld is the blast upon my pale cheek,
   But caulder thy love for me, oh!
The frost that freezes the life at my heart,
   Is nought to my pains frae thee, oh!

The wan moon is setting ayont the white wave,
  And time is setting with me, oh!                    10
False friends, false love, farewell! for mair
  I'll ne'er trouble them, nor thee, oh!

She has open'd the door, she has open'd it wide;
  She sees his pale corse on the plain, oh!
My true love, she cried, and sank down by his side,
  Never to rise again, oh!

———••———

## MY AIN KIND DEARIE O.

WHEN o'er the hill the eastern star
  Tells bughtin-time is near, my jo;
And owsen frae the furrow'd field
  Return sae dowf and wearie O;
Down by the burn, where scented birks
  Wi' dew are hanging clear, my jo,
I'll meet thee on the lea-rig,
  My ain kind dearie O.

In mirkest glen, at midnight hour,
  I'd rove, and ne'er be eerie O,               10
If thro' that glen I gaed to thee,
  My ain kind dearie O.
Altho' the night were ne'er sae wild,
  And I were ne'er sae wearie O,
I'd meet thee on the lea-rig,
  My ain kind dearie O.

The hunter lo'es the morning sun,
  To rouse the mountain deer, my jo;
At noon the fisher seeks the glen,
  Along the burn to steer, my jo;              20
Gie me the hour o' gloamin grey,
  It maks my heart sae cheery O,
To meet thee on the lea-rig,
  My ain kind dearie O.

## AULD ROB MORRIS.

There's auld Rob Morris that wons in yon glen,
He's the king o' gude fellows and wale of auld men,
He has gowd in his coffers, he has owsen and kine,
And ae bonnie lassie, his darling and mine.

She's fresh as the morning, the fairest in May;
She's sweet as the ev'ning amang the new hay;
As blythe and as artless as the lamb on the lea,
And dear to my heart as the light to my ee.

But oh ! she's an heiress, auld Robin's a laird,
And my daddie has nought but a cot-house and yard; 10
A wooer like me maunna hope to come speed,
The wounds I must hide that will soon be my dead.

The day comes to me, but delight brings me nane ;
The night comes to me, but my rest it is gane:
I wander my lane, like a night-troubled ghaist,
And I sigh as my heart it wad burst in my breast.

O had she but been of a lower degree,
I then might hae hoped she wad smiled upon me ;
O how past descriving had then been my bliss,
As now my distraction no words can express! 20

---

## O, FOR ANE AN' TWENTY, TAM!

An' O for ane an' twenty, Tam!
  An' hey, sweet ane an' twenty, Tam !
I'll learn my kin a rattlin' sang,
  An' I saw ane an' twenty, Tam.

They snool me sair, and haud me down,
  An' gar me look like bluntie, Tam !
But three short years will soon wheel roun',
  An' then comes ane an' twenty, Tam.

A gleib o' lan', a claut o' gear,
    Was left me by my auntie, Tam ;                    10
At kith or kin I need na spier,
    An I saw ane and twenty, Tam.

They'll hae me wed a wealthy coof,
    Tho' I mysel' hae plenty, Tam ;
But hear'st thou, laddie ? there 's my loof,
    I'm thine at ane and twenty, Tam !

------◆------

## FAIR ELIZA.

TURN again, thou fair Eliza—
    Ae kind blink before we part !
Rue on thy despairing lover !
    Canst thou break his faithfu' heart ?
Turn again, thou fair Eliza ;
    If to love thy heart denies,
For pity hide the cruel sentence
    Under friendship's kind disguise !

Thee, dear maid, hae I offended ?
    The offence is loving thee ;                       10
Canst thou wreck his peace for ever,
    Wha for thine would gladly die ?
While the life beats in my bosom,
    Thou shalt mix in ilka throe :
Turn again, thou lovely maiden—
    Ae sweet smile on me bestow.

Not the bee upon the blossom,
    In the pride o' sunny noon ;
Not the little sporting fairy,
    All beneath the simmer moon ;                      20
Not the poet in the moment
    Fancy lightens in his ee,
Kens the pleasure, feels the rapture,
    That thy presence gies to me.

N

## GLOOMY DECEMBER.

Ance mair I hail thee, thou gloomy December!
  Ance mair I hail thee wi' sorrow and care;
Sad was the parting thou makes me remember,
  Parting wi' Nancy, oh! ne'er to meet mair.
Fond lovers' parting is sweet painful pleasure,
  Hope beaming mild on the soft parting hour;
But the dire feeling, O farewell for ever!
  Is anguish unmingled and agony pure.

Wild as the winter now tearing the forest,
  Till the last leaf o' the summer is flown,     10
Such is the tempest has shaken my bosom,
  Till my last hope and last comfort is gone;
Still as I hail thee, thou gloomy December,
  Still shall I hail thee wi' sorrow and care;
For sad was the parting thou makes me remember,
  Parting wi' Nancy, oh! ne'er to meet mair.

———••———

## CLARINDA.

Clarinda, mistress of my soul,
  The measured time is run!
The wretch beneath the dreary pole
  So marks his latest sun.

To what dark cave of frozen night
  Shall poor Sylvander hie,
Depriv'd of thee, his life and light,
  The sun of all his joy?

We part—but by these precious drops
  That fill thy lovely eyes!     10
No other light shall guide my steps
  Till thy bright beams arise.

She, the fair sun of all her sex,
  Has blest my glorious day;
And shall a glimmering planet fix
  My worship to its ray?

## FOR THE SAKE OF SOMEBODY.

My heart is sair, I dare na tell,
　　My heart is sair for somebody ;
I could wake a winter night,
　　For the sake o' somebody !
　　　　Oh-hon ! for somebody !
　　　　Oh-hey ! for somebody !
I could range the world around,
　　For the sake o' somebody.

Ye powers that smile on virtuous love,
　　O, sweetly smile on somebody !　　　　　10
Frae ilka danger keep him free,
　　And send me safe my somebody.
　　　　Oh-hon ! for somebody !
　　　　Oh-hey ! for somebody !
I wad do—what wad I not ?
　　For the sake o' somebody !

---

## SONG OF DEATH.

SCENE—*A field of battle. Time of the day—Evening. The wounded and
dying of the victorious army are supposed to join in the song.*

FAREWELL, thou fair day, thou green earth, and ye skies,
　　Now gay with the broad setting sun !
Farewell, loves and friendships, ye dear tender ties,—
　　Our race of existence is run !

Thou grim King of Terrors, thou life's gloomy foe,
　　Go, frighten the coward and slave !
Go, teach them to tremble, fell Tyrant ! but know,
　　No terrors hast thou for the brave !

Thou strik'st the dull peasant—he sinks in the dark,
　　Nor saves e'en the wreck of a name :　　　　　10
Thou strik'st the young hero—a glorious mark !
　　He falls in the blaze of his fame !

In the field of proud honour—our swords in our hands,
  Our King and our Country to save—
While victory shines on life's last ebbing sands,
  O! who would not die with the brave!

———◆———

## KENMURE'S ON AND AWA.

O KENMURE's on and awa, Willie!
  O Kenmure's on and awa!
And Kenmure's lord's the bravest lord
  That ever Galloway saw.

Success to Kenmure's band, Willie!
  Success to Kenmure's band;
There's no a heart that fears a Whig
  That rides by Kenmure's hand.

Here's Kenmure's health in wine, Willie!
  Here's Kenmure's health in wine;                10
There ne'er was a coward o' Kenmure's blude,
  Nor yet o' Gordon's line.

O Kenmure's lads are men, Willie!
  O Kenmure's lads are men;
Their hearts and swords are metal true—
  And that their faes shall ken.

They'll live or die wi' fame, Willie!
  They'll live or die wi' fame;
But soon, wi' sounding victorie,
  May Kenmure's lord come hame!                   20

Here's him that's far awa, Willie!
  Here's him that's far awa;
And here's the flower that I love best—
  The rose that's like the snaw!

## THE CAPTAIN'S LADY

O MOUNT and go,
    Mount and make you ready;
O mount and go,
    And be the Captain's Lady.

When the drums do beat,
    And the cannons rattle,
Thou shalt sit in state,
    And see thy love in battle.

When the vanquish'd foe
    Sues for peace and quiet,        10
To the shades we'll go,
    And in love enjoy it.

    O mount and go,
        Mount and make you ready;
    O mount and go,
        And be the Captain's Lady.

---

## NOW WESTLIN WINDS.

Now westlin winds and slaughtering guns
    Bring autumn's pleasant weather;
The moorcock springs, on whirring wings,
    Amang the blooming heather:
Now waving grain, wide o'er the plain,
    Delights the weary farmer;
And the moon shines bright, when I rove at night
    To muse upon my charmer.

The partridge loves the fruitful fells;
    The plover loves the mountains;        10
The woodcock haunts the lonely dells;
    The soaring hern the fountains:

Thro' lofty groves the cushat roves,
　The path of man to shun it;
The hazel bush o'erhangs the thrush,
　The spreading thorn the linnet.

Thus ev'ry kind their pleasure find,
　The savage and the tender;
Some social join, and leagues combine;
　Some solitary wander;　　　　　　　　　　　　20
Avaunt, away! the cruel sway,
　Tyrannic man's dominion;
The sportsman's joy, the murdering cry,
　The fluttering, gory pinion!

But, Peggy dear, the ev'ning's clear,
　Thick flies the skimming swallow;
The sky is blue, the fields in view,
　All fading-green and yellow:
Come let us stray our gladsome way,
　And view the charms of nature;　　　　　　　　30
The rustling corn, the fruited thorn,
　And every happy creature.

We'll gently walk, and sweetly talk,
　Till the silent moon shine clearly;
I'll grasp thy waist, and, fondly prest,
　Swear how I love thee dearly:
Not vernal show'rs to budding flow'rs,
　Not autumn to the farmer,
So dear can be as thou to me,
　My fair, my lovely charmer!　　　　　　　　　40

————♦————

## HERE'S A HEALTH TO ANE I LO'E DEAR.

### CHORUS.

HERE's a health to ane I lo'e dear,
Here's a health to ane I lo'e dear;
Thou art sweet as the smile when fond lovers meet,
And soft as their parting tear, Jessy!

Altho' thou maun never be mine,
  Altho' even hope is denied ;
'Tis sweeter for thee despairing,
  Than aught in the world beside, Jessy !

I mourn thro' the gay, gaudy day,
  As, hopeless, I muse on thy charms :          10
But welcome the dream o' sweet slumber,
  For then I am lockt in thy arms, Jessy !

I guess by the dear angel smile,
  I guess by the love-rolling ee ;
But why urge the tender confession
  'Gainst fortune's fell cruel decree, Jessy !

---

## BANKS OF CREE.

HERE is the glen, and here the bower,
  All underneath the birchen shade ;
The village-bell has toll'd the hour,
  O what can stay my lovely maid ?

'Tis not Maria's whispering call ;
  'Tis but the balmy breathing gale,
Mixt with some warbler's dying fall,
  The dewy star of eve to hail.

It is Maria's voice I hear !
  So calls the woodlark in the grove           10
His little faithful mate to cheer ;
  At once 'tis music—and 'tis love.

And art thou come ? and art thou true ?
  O welcome, dear, to love and me !
And let us all our vows renew,
  Along the flowery banks of Cree.

## HOW LANG AND DREARY.

How lang and dreary is the night,
  When I am frae my dearie!
I restless lie frae e'en to morn,
  Tho' I were ne'er sae weary.

    For oh, her lanely nights are lang;
      And oh, her dreams are eerie;
    And oh, her widow'd heart is sair,
      That's absent frae her dearie.

When I think on the lightsome days
  I spent wi' thee, my dearie,          10
And now that seas between us roar,
  How can I be but eerie!

How slow ye move, ye heavy hours;
  The joyless day how drearie!
It wasna sae ye glinted by,
  When I was wi' my dearie.

———✦———

## LOGAN BRAES.

O Logan, sweetly didst thou glide
That day I was my Willie's bride;
And years sinsyne hae o'er us run,
Like Logan to the simmer sun.
But now thy flow'ry banks appear
Like drumlie winter, dark and drear,
While my dear lad maun face his faes,
Far, far frae me and Logan Braes.

Again the merry month o' May
Has made our hills and valleys gay;     10
The birds rejoice in leafy bowers,
The bees hum round the breathing flowers;

Blithe morning lifts his rosy eye,
And evening's tears are tears of joy:
My soul, delightless, a' surveys,
While Willie's far frae Logan Braes.

Within yon milk-white hawthorn bush,
Amang her nestlings, sits the thrush;
Her faithfu' mate will share her toil,
Or wi' his song her cares beguile:                          20
But I wi' my sweet nurslings here,
Nae mate to help, nae mate to cheer,
Pass widow'd nights and joyless days,
While Willie's far frae Logan Braes.

O wae upon you, men o' state,
That brethren rouse to deadly hate!
As ye mak mony a fond heart mourn,
Sae may it on your heads return!
How can your flinty hearts enjoy
The widow's tears, the orphan's cry?                       30
But soon may peace bring happy days,
And Willie hame to Logan Braes!

———◆◆———

## I'LL AYE CA' IN BY YON TOWN.

I'LL aye ca' in by yon town,
    And by yon garden green again;
I'll aye ca' in by yon town,
    And see my bonnie Jean again.

There's nane sall ken, there's nane sall guess,
    What brings me back the gate again,
But she, my fairest faithfu' lass,
    And stownlins we sall meet again.

She'll wander by the aiken tree
    When trystin-time draws near again;                     10
And when her lovely form I see,
    O haith, she's doubly dear again!

## I'LL KISS THEE YET.

I'LL kiss thee yet, yet,
    And I'll kiss thee o'er again,
An' I'll kiss thee yet, yet,
    My bonnie Peggy Alison!

Ilk care and fear, when thou art near,
    I ever mair defy them, O;
Young Kings upon their hansel throne
    Are no sae blest as I am, O!

When in my arms, wi' a' thy charms,
    I clasp my countless treasure, O;      10
I seek nae mair o' Heaven to share,
    Than sic a moment's pleasure, O!

And by thy een sae bonnie blue,
    I swear I'm thine for ever, O;
And on thy lips I seal my vow,
    And break it shall I never, O!

———◆◆———

## A BOTTLE AND A FRIEND.

HERE's a bottle and an honest friend!
    What wad ye wish for mair, man?
Wha kens, before his life may end,
    What his share may be o' care, man?
Then catch the moments as they fly,
    And use them as ye ought, man:
Believe me, happiness is shy,
    And comes not aye when sought, man.

## WILLIE BREWED.

O WILLIE brew'd a peck o' maut,
    And Rob and Allan cam to see;
Three blyther hearts, that lee-lang night,
    Ye wad na found in Christendie.

We are na fou', we're no that fou,
    But just a drappie in our ee;
The cock may craw, the day may daw,
    And aye we'll taste the barley bree.

Here are we met, three merry boys,
    Three merry boys, I trow, are we;
And mony a night we've merry been,    10
    And mony mae we hope to be!

It is the moon, I ken her horn,
    That 's blinkin' in the lift sae hie;
She shines sae bright to wyle us hame,
    But, by my sooth! she'll wait a wee.

Wha first shall rise to gang awa,
    A cuckold, coward loun is he!
Wha first beside his chair shall fa',
    He is the King among us three!    20

---

## O GUID ALE COMES.

O GUID ale comes, and guid ale goes,
Guid ale gars me sell my hose,
Sell my hose, and pawn my shoon;
Guid ale keeps my heart aboon.

I had sax owsen in a pleugh,
And they drew a' weel eneugh,
I sell'd them a' just ane by ane;
Guid ale keeps the heart aboon.

Guid ale hauds me bare and busy,
Gars me moop wi' the servant hizzie,        10
Stand i' the stool when I hae done ;
Guid ale keeps the heart aboon.

---- • • ----

## NO CHURCHMAN AM I.

No churchman am I for to rail and to write,
No statesman nor soldier to plot or to fight,
No sly man of business contriving a snare,
For a big-bellied bottle 's the whole of my care.

The peer I don't envy, I give him his bow ;
I scorn not the peasant, tho' ever so low ;
But a club of good fellows, like those that are there,
And a bottle like this, are my glory and care.

Here passes the squire on his brother—his horse ;
There centum per centum, the cit with his purse ;        10
But see you the Crown how it waves in the air?
There a big-bellied bottle still eases my care.

The wife of my bosom, alas ! she did die :
For sweet consolation to church I did fly ;
I found that old Solomon provèd it fair,
That the big-bellied bottle 's a cure for all care.

I once was persuaded a venture to make ;
A letter inform'd me that all was to wreck ;
But the pursy old landlord just waddled up stairs
With a glorious bottle that ended my cares.        20

'Life's cares they are comforts,' a maxim laid down
By the bard, what d'ye call him ? that wore the black gown,
And, faith, I agree with th' old prig to a hair,
For a big-bellied bottle 's a heav'n of a care.

### (*Added in a Mason Lodge*).

Then fill up a bumper, and make it o'erflow,
And honours masonic prepare for to throw ;
May every true brother of the compass and square
Have a big-bellied bottle when harass'd with care.

## COUNT THE LAWIN.

GANE is the day, and mirk's the night,
But we'll ne'er stray for faut o' light,
For ale and brandy's stars and moon,
And bluid-red wine's the risin' sun.

   Then guidwife count the lawin, the lawin, the lawin,
   Then guidwife count the lawin, and bring a coggie mair.

There's wealth and ease for gentlemen,
And semple-folk maun fecht and fen',
But here we're a' in ae accord,
For ilka man that's drunk's a lord.       10

My coggie is a haly pool,
That heals the wounds o' care and dool;
And pleasure is a wanton trout,
An' ye drink it a' ye'll find him out.

---

## DELUDED SWAIN.

DELUDED swain, the pleasure
   The fickle Fair can give thee,
Is but a fairy treasure,
   Thy hopes will soon deceive thee.

The billows on the ocean,
   The breezes idly roaming.
The clouds' uncertain motion,
   They are but types of woman.

O! art thou not ashamed
   To doat upon a feature?      10
If man thou wouldst be named,
   Despise the silly creature.

Go, find an honest fellow;
   Good claret set before thee;
Hold on till thou art mellow,
   And then to bed in glory.

## THE DE'IL 'S AWA' WI' THE EXCISEMAN.

The De'il cam fiddling thro' the town,
  And danced awa wi' the Exciseman ;
And ilka wife cried 'Auld Mahoun,
  We wish you luck o' your prize, man.'

We'll mak our maut, and brew our drink,
  We'll dance, and sing, and rejoice, man ;
And mony thanks to the muckle black De'il
  That danced awa wi' the Exciseman.

There 's threesome reels, and foursome reels,
  There 's hornpipes and strathspeys, man :        10
But the ae best dance e'er cam to our lan',
  Was—the De'il 's awa wi' the Exciseman.

—◦—

## THERE WAS A BONNIE LASS.

There was a bonnie lass, and a bonnie, bonnie lass,
  And she lo'ed her bonnie laddie dear ;
Till war's loud alarms tore her laddie frae her arms,
  Wi' mony a sigh and tear.

Over sea, over shore, where the cannons loudly roar,
  He still was a stranger to fear :
And nocht could him quell, or his bosom assail,
  But the bonnie lass he lo'ed sae dear.

—◦—

## RATTLIN', ROARIN' WILLIE.

O rattlin', roarin' Willie,
  O, he held to the fair,
An' for to sell his fiddle,
  An' buy some other ware ;

But parting wi' his fiddle,
　The saut tear blin't his ee ;
And rattlin', roarin' Willie,
　Ye're welcome hame to me !

O Willie, come sell your fiddle,
　O sell your fiddle sae fine ;　　　　10
O Willie, come sell your fiddle,
　And buy a pint o' wine !
If I should sell my fiddle,
　The warl' would think I was mad ;
For mony a rantin' day
　My fiddle and I hae had.

As I cam by Crochallan,
　I cannily keekit ben —
Rattlin', roarin' Willie
　Was sitting at yon board en' ;　　　20
Sitting at yon board en',
　And amang guid companie ;
Rattlin', roarin' Willie,
　Ye're welcome hame to me !

———◦◦———

## LANDLADY, COUNT THE LAWIN.

LANDLADY, count the lawin,
The day is near the dawin ;
Ye're a' blind drunk, boys,
　And I'm but jolly fou.
　　Hey tutti, taiti,
　　How tutti, taiti —
　　Wha 's fou now ?

Cog, an' ye were aye fou,
Cog, an' ye were aye fou,
I wad sit and sing to you　　　　10
　If ye were aye fou.

Weel may ye a' be!
Ill may we never see!
God bless the King, boys,
And the companie!
Hey tutti, taiti,
How tutti, taiti—
Wha's fou now?

---

## MY LOVE SHE'S BUT A LASSIE YET.

My love she's but a lassie yet;
  My love she's but a lassie yet;
We'll let her stand a year or twa,
  She'll no be half sae saucy yet.
I rue the day I sought her, O,
  I rue the day I sought her, O;
Wha gets her needs na say she's woo'd,
  But he may say he's bought her, O!

Come, draw a drap o' the best o't yet;
  Come, draw a drap o' the best o't yet;      10
Gae seek for pleasure where ye will,
  But here I never miss'd it yet.
We're a' dry wi' drinking o't,
  We're a' dry wi' drinking o't;
The minister kiss'd the fiddler's wife,
  An' could na preach for thinkin' o't.

---

## DOES HAUGHTY GAUL.

Does haughty Gaul invasion threat?
  Then let the loons beware, Sir,
There's wooden walls upon our seas,
  And volunteers on shore, Sir.
The Nith shall run to Corsincon,
  And Criffel sink in Solway,
Ere we permit a foreign foe
  On British ground to rally!

O let us not like snarling tykes
   In wrangling be divided,          10
Till, slap! come in an unco loon
   And wi' a rung decide it.
Be Britain still to Britain true,
   Amang oursels united;
For never but by British hands
   Maun British wrangs be righted!

The kettle o' the kirk and state,
   Perhaps a clout may fail in't;
But deil a foreign tinkler loon
   Shall ever ca' a nail in't.        20
Our father's blude the kettle bought,
   An' wha wad dare to spoil it?
By heavens! the sacrilegious dog
   Shall fuel be to boil it!

The wretch that would a tyrant own,
   And the wretch, his true-born brother,
Who'd set the mob aboon the throne,—
   May they be damned together!
Who will not sing *God save the King!*
   Shall hang as high 's the steeple;    30
But while we sing *God save the King!*
   We'll not forget the people!

---

## THE DAY RETURNS.

THE day returns, my bosom burns,
   The blissful day we twa did meet;
Tho' winter wild in tempest toil'd,
   Ne'er summer-sun was half sae sweet.
Than a' the pride that loads the tide,
   And crosses o'er the sultry line;
Than kingly robes, than crowns and globes,
   Heaven gave me more, it made thee mine!

While day and night can bring delight,
  Or nature aught of pleasure give;                    10
While joys above my mind can move,
  For thee, and thee alone, I live!
When that grim foe of life below
  Comes in between to make us part;
The iron hand that breaks our band,
  It breaks my bliss—it breaks my heart!

———◆———

## O MAY, THY MORN.

O MAY, thy morn was ne'er sae sweet,
  As the mirk night o' December:
For sparkling was the rosy wine,
  And private was the chamber;
And dear was she I dare na name,
  But I will aye remember.

And here's to them, that, like oursel,
  Can push about the jorum!
And here's to them that wish us weel,
  May a' that's guid watch o'er them!      10
And here's to them we dare na tell,
  The dearest o' the quorum!

———◆———

## THERE'LL NEVER BE PEACE TILL JAMIE
## COMES HAME.

BY yon castle wa', at the close of the day,
I heard a man sing, tho' his head it was grey:
And as he was singing, the tears down came—
There'll never be peace till Jamie comes hame.

The church is in ruins, the state is in jars,
Delusions, oppressions, and murderous wars;
We dare na weel say't, but we ken wha's to blame—
There'll never be peace till Jamie comes hame.

My seven braw sons for Jamie drew sword,     9
And now I greet round their green beds in the yerd;
It brak the sweet heart o' my faithfu' auld dame—
There'll never be peace till Jamie comes hame.

Now life is a burden that bows me down,
Sin' I tint my bairns, and he tint his crown;
But till my last moment my words are the same—
There'll never be peace till Jamie comes hame.

———•———

## FAREWEEL TO A' OUR SCOTTISH FAME.

FAREWEEL to a' our Scottish fame,
   Fareweel our ancient glory!
Fareweel even to the Scottish name,
   Sae fam'd in martial story!
Now Sark rins o'er the Solway sands,
   And Tweed rins to the ocean,
To mark where England's province stands;
   Such a parcel of rogues in a nation!

What guile or force could not subdue,
   Through many warlike ages,     10
Is wrought now by a coward few,
   For hireling traitors' wages.
The English steel we could disdain,
   Secure in valour's station,
But English gold has been our bane;
   Such a parcel of rogues in a nation!

O would, ere I had seen the day
   That treason thus could sell us,
My auld grey head had lien in clay,
   Wi' Bruce and loyal Wallace!     20
But pith and power, till my last hour
   I'll mak this declaration,
We're bought and sold for English gold:
   Such a parcel of rogues in a nation!

## WILL YE GO TO THE INDIES, MY MARY.

WILL ye go to the Indies, my Mary,
  And leave auld Scotia's shore?
Will ye go to the Indies, my Mary,
  Across the Atlantic's roar?

O sweet grows the lime and the orange,
  And the apple on the pine;
But a' the charms o' the Indies
  Can never equal thine.

I hae sworn by the Heavens to my Mary,
  I hae sworn by the Heavens to be true;          10
And sae may the Heavens forget me,
  When I forget my vow!

O plight me your faith, my Mary,
  And plight me your lily-white hand;
O plight me your faith, my Mary,
  Before I leave Scotia's strand.

We hae plighted our troth, my Mary,
  In mutual affection to join;
And curst be the cause that shall part us!
  The hour, and the moment o' time!               20

---

## THE BONNIE LAD THAT'S FAR AWA'.

O HOW can I be blithe and glad,
  Or how can I gang brisk and braw,
When the bonnie lad that I lo'e best
  Is o'er the hills and far awa?

It's no the frosty winter wind,
  It's no the driving drift and snaw;
But aye the tear comes in my ee,
  To think on him that's far awa.

My father pat me frae his door,
   My friends they hae disown'd me a':     10
But I hae ane will tak my part,
   The bonnie lad that's far awa.

A pair o' gloves he bought to me,
   And silken snoods he gae me twa;
And I will wear them for his sake,
   The bonnie lad that's far awa.

O weary winter soon will pass,
   And spring will cleed the birken shaw:
And my young babie will be born,
   And he'll be hame that's far awa.     20

---

## YESTREEN I HAD A PINT O' WINE.

YESTREEN I had a pint o' wine,
   A place where body saw na';
Yestreen lay on this breast o' mine
   The gowden locks of Anna.
The hungry Jew in wilderness
   Rejoicing o'er his manna,
Was naething to my hinny bliss
   Upon the lips of Anna.

Ye monarchs, tak the east and west,
   Frae Indus to Savannah!     10
Gie me within my straining grasp
   The melting form of Anna.
There I'll despise imperial charms,
   An Empress or Sultana,
While dying raptures in her arms
   I give and take with Anna!

Awa, thou flaunting god o' day!
   Awa, thou pale Diana!
Ilk star, gae hide thy twinkling ray
   When I'm to meet my Anna.     20

Come, in thy raven plumage, night !
　Sun, moon, and stars withdrawn a' ;
And bring an angel pen to write
　My transports wi' my Anna !

(*Postscript.*)

The kirk and state may join, and tell
　To do such things I mauna :
The kirk and state may gae to hell,
　And I'll gae to my Anna.
She is the sunshine o' my ee,
　To live but her I canna ;　　　　　　　　30
Had I on earth but wishes three,
　The first should be my Anna.

———••———

## MY TOCHER'S THE JEWEL.

O MEIKLE thinks my luve o' my beauty,
　And meikle thinks my luve o' my kin ;
But little thinks my luve I ken brawlie
　My tocher's the jewel has charms for him.
It's a' for the apple he'll nourish the tree ;
　It's a' for the hiney he'll cherish the bee ;
My laddie's sae meikle in love wi' the siller,
　He canna hae luve to spare for me.

Your proffer o' luve's an airle-penny,
　My tocher's the bargain ye wad buy ;　　　10
But an ye be crafty, I am cunnin',
　Sae ye wi' anither your fortune may try.
Ye're like to the timmer o' yon rotten wood ;
　Ye're like to the bark o' yon rotten tree ;
Ye'll slip frae me like a knotless thread,
　And ye'll crack your credit wi' mae nor me.

# WHAT CAN A YOUNG LASSIE DO WI' AN AULD MAN?

WHAT can a young lassie, what shall a young lassie,
  What can a young lassie do wi' an auld man?
Bad luck on the penny that tempted my minnie
  To sell her poor Jenny for siller an' lan'!

He's always compleenin' frae mornin to e'enin',
  He hosts and he hirples the weary day lang:
He's doylt and he's dozin, his bluid it is frozen,
  O, dreary's the night wi' a crazy auld man!

He hums and he hankers, he frets and he cankers,
  I never can please him do a' that I can;          10
He's peevish, and jealous of a' the young fellows:
  O, dool on the day I met wi' an auld man!

My auld auntie Katie upon me takes pity,
  I'll do my endeavour to follow her plan;
I'll cross him and rack him, until I heart-break him,
  And then his auld brass will buy me a new pan.

———••———

# BLYTHE AND MERRY.

BLYTHE, blythe and merry was she,
  Blythe was she but and ben:
Blythe by the banks of Earn,
  And blythe in Glenturit glen.

By Ochtertyre there grows the aik,
  On Yarrow banks the birken shaw;
But Phemie was a bonnier lass
  Than braes o' Yarrow ever saw.

Her looks were like a flower in May,
  Her smile was like a simmer morn;          10
She trippèd by the banks of Earn
  As light's a bird upon a thorn.

Her bonnie face it was as meek
    As ony lamb's upon a lea;
The evening sun was ne'er sae sweet
    As was the blink o' Phemie's ee.

The Highland hills I've wander'd wide,
    And o'er the Lowlands I hae been;
But Phemie was the blythest lass
    That ever trod the dewy green.                    20

------

## PEGGY'S CHARMS.

WHERE, braving angry winter's storms,
    The lofty Ochils rise,
Far in their shade my Peggy's charms
    First blest my wondering eyes;
As one who, by some savage stream,
    A lovely gem surveys,
Astonish'd doubly, marks it beam
    With art's most polish'd blaze.

Blest be the wild, sequester'd shade,
    And blest the day and hour,                       10
Where Peggy's charms I first survey'd,
    When first I felt their power!
The tyrant death with grim control
    May seize my fleeting breath;
But tearing Peggy from my soul
    Must be a stronger death.

------

## THE LAZY MIST.

THE lazy mist hangs from the brow of the hill,
Concealing the course of the dark-winding rill;
How languid the scenes, late so sprightly, appear,
As autumn to winter resigns the pale year!
The forests are leafless, the meadows are brown,
And all the gay foppery of summer is flown:

Apart let me wander, apart let me muse,
How quick time is flying, how keen fate pursues ;
How long I have lived, but how much lived in vain ;
How little of life's scanty span may remain :      10
What aspects old Time, in his progress, has worn ;
What ties cruel fate in my bosom has torn.
How foolish, or worse, till our summit is gain'd !
And downward, how weaken'd, how darken'd, how pain'd !
This life 's not worth having with all it can give ;
For something beyond it poor man sure must live.

———+·———

## STRATHALLAN'S LAMENT.

Thickest night, o'erhang my dwelling!
    Howling tempests, o'er me rave !
Turbid torrents, wintry swelling,
    Still surround my lonely cave !

Crystal streamlets gently flowing,
    Busy haunts of base mankind,
Western breezes softly blowing,
    Suit not my distracted mind.

In the cause of right engagèd,
    Wrongs injurious to redress,
Honour's war we strongly wagèd,      10
    But the heavens denied success.

Ruin's wheel has driven o'er us,
    Not a hope that dare attend ;
The wide world is all before us—
    But a world without a friend !

———+·———

## RAVING WINDS AROUND HER BLOWING.

RAVING winds around her blowing,
Yellow leaves the woodlands strowing,
By a river hoarsely roaring,
Isabella stray'd deploring:
'Farewell, hours that late did measure
Sunshine days of joy and pleasure;
Hail, thou gloomy night of sorrow,
Cheerless night that knows no morrow!

'O'er the past too fondly wandering,
On the hopeless future pondering;                    10
Chilly grief my life-blood freezes,
Fell despair my fancy seizes.
Life, thou soul of every blessing,
Load to misery most distressing,
O, how gladly I'd resign thee,
And to dark oblivion join thee!'

---

## MUSING ON THE ROARING OCEAN.

MUSING on the roaring ocean
    Which divides my love and me;
Wearying Heaven in warm devotion,
    For his weal where'er he be;

Hope and fear's alternate billow
    Yielding late to nature's law;
Whispering spirits round my pillow
    Talk of him that's far awa.

Ye whom sorrow never wounded,
    Ye who never shed a tear,                         10
Care-untroubled, joy-surrounded,
    Gaudy day to you is dear.

Gentle night, do thou befriend me ;
    Downy sleep, the curtain draw ;
Spirits kind, again attend me,
    Talk of him that 's far awa !

## LORD GREGORY.

O MIRK, mirk is this midnight hour,
    And loud the tempest's roar ;
A waefu' wanderer seeks thy tow'r,
    Lord Gregory, ope thy door.

An exile frae her father's ha',
    And a' for loving thee ;
At least some pity on me shaw,
    If love it mayna be.

Lord Gregory, mind'st thou not the grove,
    By bonnie Irwine side,          10
Where first I own'd that virgin love
    I lang lang had denied ?

How aften didst thou pledge and vow
    Thou wad for aye be mine !
And my fond heart, itsel sae true,
    It ne'er mistrusted thine.

Hard is thy heart, Lord Gregory,
    And flinty is thy breast :
Thou bolt of heaven that flashest by,
    O wilt thou give me rest !          20

Ye mustering thunders from above,
    Your willing victim see !
But spare, and pardon my fause love,
    His wrangs to heaven and me !

## STAY, MY CHARMER.

STAY, my charmer, can you leave me?
Cruel, cruel to deceive me!
Well you know how much you grieve me;
　　Cruel charmer, can you go?

By my love so ill requited;
By the faith you fondly plighted;
By the pangs of lovers slighted;
　　Do not, do not leave me so!

## FAIREST MAID ON DEVON BANKS.

FAIREST maid on Devon banks,
　　Crystal Devon, winding Devon,
Wilt thou lay that frown aside,
　　And smile as thou wert wont to do?

Full well thou know'st I love thee dear;
Couldst thou to malice lend an ear?
O did not love exclaim 'Forbear,
　　Nor use a faithful lover so?'

Then come, thou fairest of the fair,
Those wonted smiles, O let me share;　　　10
And by thy beauteous self I swear,
　　No love but thine my heart shall know.

## YOUNG JOCKEY.

YOUNG Jockey was the blithest lad
　　In a' our town or here awa;
Fu' blithe he whistled at the gaud,
　　Fu' lightly danced he in the ha'!

He roos'd my een sae bonnie blue,
  He roos'd my waist sae genty sma';
An' aye my heart came to my mou,
  When ne'er a body heard or saw.

My Jockey toils upon the plain,
  Thro' wind and weet, thro' frost and snaw;    10
And o'er the lea I look fu' fain
  When Jockey's owsen hameward ca'.
An' aye the night comes round again,
  When in his arms he takes me a';
An' aye he vows he'll be my ain
  As lang's he has a breath to draw.

## JOCKEY'S TA'EN THE PARTING KISS.

JOCKEY's ta'en the parting kiss,
  O'er the mountains he is gane;
And with him is a' my bliss,
  Nought but griefs with me remain.

Spare my luve, ye winds that blaw,
  Plashy sleets and beating rain!
Spare my luve, thou feathery snaw,
  Drifting o'er the frozen plain!

When the shades of evening creep
  O'er the day's fair, gladsome ee,    10
Sound and safely may he sleep,
  Sweetly blithe his waukening be!

He will think on her he loves,
  Fondly he'll repeat her name;
For where'er he distant roves,
  Jockey's heart is still the same.

## O WHA IS SHE THAT LO'ES ME?

O WHA is she that lo'es me,
 And has my heart a-keeping?
O sweet is she that lo'es me,
 As dews o' simmer weeping,
 In tears the rose-buds steeping.

 O that's the lassie o' my heart,
 My lassie ever dearer;
 O that's the queen o' womankind,
 And ne'er a ane to peer her.

If thou shalt meet a lassie,    10
 In grace and beauty charming,
That e'en thy chosen lassie,
 Erewhile thy breast sae warming,
 Had ne'er sic powers alarming;

If thou hadst heard her talking,
 And thy attentions plighted,
That ilka body talking,
 But her by thee is slighted,
 And thou art all delighted;

If thou hast met this fair one;    20
 When frae her thou hast parted,
If every other fair one,
 But her, thou hast deserted,
 And thou art broken-hearted;

 O that's the lassie, &c.

---

## BLITHE HAE I BEEN ON YON HILL.

BLITHE hae I been on yon hill,
 As the lambs before me;
Careless ilka thought and free,
 As the breeze flew o'er me:
Now nae langer sport and play,
 Mirth or sang can please me;
Lesley is sae fair and coy,
 Care and anguish seize me.

Heavy, heavy is the task,
  Hopeless love declaring:                    10
Trembling, I dow nocht but glowr,
  Sighing, dumb, despairing!
If she winna ease the thraws
  In my bosom swelling,
Underneath the grass-green sod
  Soon maun be my dwelling.

———◆◆———

## O WERE MY LOVE YON LILAC FAIR.

O WERE my love yon lilac fair,
  Wi' purple blossoms to the spring;
And I, a bird to shelter there,
  When wearied on my little wing;

How I wad mourn, when it was torn
  By autumn wild, and winter rude!
But I wad sing on wanton wing,
  When youthfu' May its bloom renew'd.

O gin my love were yon red rose
  That grows upon the castle wa',          10
And I mysel' a drap o' dew,
  Into her bonnie breast to fa'!

Oh, there beyond expression blest,
  I'd feast on beauty a' the night;
Seal'd on her silk-saft faulds to rest,
  Till fley'd awa' by Phoebus' light.

———◆◆———

## COME, LET ME TAKE THEE.

COME, let me take thee to my breast,
  And pledge we ne'er shall sunder;
And I shall spurn as vilest dust
  The warld's wealth and grandeur:

And do I hear my Jeanie own
  That equal transports move her?
I ask for dearest life alone
  That I may live to love her.

Thus in my arms, wi' all thy charms,
  I clasp my countless treasure;    10
I'll seek nae mair o' heaven to share,
  Than sic a moment's pleasure:
And by thy een, sae bonnie blue,
  I swear I'm thine for ever!
And on thy lips I seal my vow,
  And break it shall I never.

## WHERE ARE THE JOYS.

Where are the joys I hae met in the morning,
  That danced to the lark's early sang?
Where is the peace that awaited my wand'ring,
  At evening the wild woods amang?

No more a-winding the course of yon river,
  And marking sweet flow'rets so fair:
No more I trace the light footsteps of pleasure,
  But sorrow and sad sighing care.

Is it that summer's forsaken our valleys,
  And grim, surly winter is near?    10
No, no, the bees humming round the gay roses
  Proclaim it the pride of the year.

Fain would I hide what I fear to discover,
  Yet long, long too well have I known:
All that has caus'd this wreck in my bosom,
  Is Jenny, fair Jenny alone.

Time cannot aid me, my griefs are immortal,
  Nor hope dare a comfort bestow:
Come, then, enamour'd and fond of my anguish,
  Enjoyment I'll seek in my woe.    20

## O SAW YE MY DEAR.

O saw ye my dear, my Phely?
O saw ye my dear, my Phely?
She's down i' the grove, she's wi' a new love,
    She winna come hame to her Willy.

What says she, my dearest, my Phely?
What says she, my dearest, my Phely?
She lets thee to wit that she has thee forgot,
    And for ever disowns thee, her Willy.

O had I ne'er seen thee, my Phely!
O had I ne'er seen thee, my Phely!         10
As light as the air, and fause as thou's fair,
    Thou'st broken the heart o' thy Willy.

————◆————

## THOU HAST LEFT ME EVER, JAMIE.

Thou hast left me ever, Jamie,
    Thou hast left me ever;
Thou hast left me ever, Jamie,
    Thou hast left me ever.
Aften hast thou vow'd that death
    Only should us sever;
Now thou'st left thy lass for aye—
    I maun see thee never, Jamie,
      I'll see thee never!

Thou hast me forsaken, Jamie,        10
    Thou hast me forsaken;
Thou hast me forsaken, Jamie,
    Thou hast me forsaken.
Thou canst love anither jo,
    While my heart is breaking;
Soon my weary een I'll close—
    Never mair to waken, Jamie,
      Ne'er mair to waken!

## MY CHLORIS.

My Chloris, mark how green the groves,
  The primrose banks how fair:
The balmy gales awake the flowers,
  And wave thy flaxen hair.

The lav'rock shuns the palace gay,
  And o'er the cottage sings:
For Nature smiles as sweet, I ween,
  To shepherds as to kings.

Let minstrels sweep the skilfu' string
  In lordly lighted ha': 10
The shepherd stops his simple reed,
  Blythe, in the birken shaw.

The princely revel may survey
  Our rustic dance wi' scorn;
But are their hearts as light as ours
  Beneath the milk-white thorn?

The shepherd, in the flowery glen,
  In shepherd's phrase will woo:
The courtier tells a finer tale,
  But is his heart as true? 20

These wild-wood flowers I've pu'd, to deck
  That spotless breast o' thine:
The courtier's gems may witness love—
  But 'tis na love like mine.

———◆———

## 'TWAS NA HER BONNIE BLUE EE.

'Twas na her bonnie blue ee was my ruin;
Fair tho' she be, that was ne'er my undoing;
'Twas the dear smile when naebody did mind us,
'Twas the bewitching, sweet, stown glance o' kindness.

Sair do I fear that to hope is denied me,
Sair do I fear that despair maun abide me ;
But tho' fell fortune should fate us to sever,
Queen shall she be in my bosom for ever.

Chloris, I'm thine wi' a passion sincerest,
And thou hast plighted me love o' the dearest !    10
And thou'rt the angel that never can alter,
Sooner the sun in his motion would falter.

## TO THE WOODLARK.

O STAY, sweet warbling woodlark, stay,
Nor quit for me the trembling spray ;
A hapless lover courts thy lay,
   Thy soothing fond complaining.

Again, again that tender part,
That I may catch thy melting art ;
For surely that wad touch her heart,
   Wha kills me wi' disdaining.

Say, was thy little mate unkind,
And heard thee as the careless wind ?    10
Oh, nocht but love and sorrow join'd
   Sic notes o' wae could wauken.

Thou tells o' never-ending care,
O' speechless grief, and dark despair ;
For pity's sake, sweet bird, nae mair !
   Or my poor heart is broken !

## HOW CRUEL ARE THE PARENTS.

How cruel are the parents
  Who riches only prize,
And to the wealthy booby
  Poor woman sacrifice.

Meanwhile the hapless daughter
  Has but a choice of strife;
To shun a tyrant father's hate,
  Become a wretched wife.

The ravening hawk pursuing,
  The trembling dove thus flies,          10
To shun impelling ruin
  A while her pinions tries;
Till of escape despairing,
  No shelter or retreat,
She trusts the ruthless falconer,
  And drops beneath his feet.

———◆———

# JOHN BARLEYCORN.

### A BALLAD.

THERE was three Kings into the east,
  Three Kings both great and high,
And they hae sworn a solemn oath
  John Barleycorn should die.

They took a plough and plough'd him down,
  Put clods upon his head,
And they hae sworn a solemn oath
  John Barleycorn was dead.

But the cheerfu' Spring came kindly on,
  And show'rs began to fall;            10
John Barleycorn got up again,
  And sore surpris'd them all.

The sultry suns of Summer came,
  And he grew thick and strong,
His head weel arm'd wi' pointed spears,
  That no one should him wrong.

The sober Autumn enter'd mild,
   When he grew wan and pale ;
His bending joints and drooping head
   Show'd he began to fail.           25

His colour sicken'd more and more,
   He faded into age ;
And then his enemies began
   To shew their deadly rage.

They've ta'en a weapon, long and sharp,
   And cut him by the knee ;
Then tied him fast upon a cart,
   Like a rogue for forgerie.

They laid him down upon his back,
   And cudgell'd him full sore ;         30
They hung him up before the storm,
   And turn'd him o'er and o'er.

They fillèd up a darksome pit
   With water to the brim,
They heavèd in John Barleycorn,
   There let him sink or swim.

They laid him out upon the floor,
   To work him farther woe,
And still, as signs of life appear'd,
   They toss'd him to and fro.         40

They wasted, o'er a scorching flame,
   The marrow of his bones ;
But a miller us'd him worst of all,
   For he crush'd him between two stones.

And they hae ta'en his very heart's blood,
   And drank it round and round ;
And still the more and more they drank,
   Their joy did more abound.

John Barleycorn was a hero bold,
  Of noble enterprise,          50
For if you do but taste his blood,
  'Twill make your courage rise ;

'Twill make a man forget his woe ;
  'Twill heighten all his joy :
'Twill make the widow's heart to sing,
  Tho' the tear were in her eye.

Then let us toast John Barleycorn,
  Each man a glass in hand ;
And may his great posterity
  Ne'er fail in old Scotland !        60

———••———

## THE SODGER'S RETURN.

WHEN wild war's deadly blast was blawn,
  And gentle peace returning,
Wi' mony a sweet babe fatherless,
  And mony a widow mourning,—
I left the lines and tented field,
  Where lang I'd been a lodger,
My humble knapsack a' my wealth,
  A poor and honest sodger.

A leal light heart was in my breast,
  My hand unstain'd wi' plunder ;      10
And for fair Scotia hame again
  I cheery on did wander.
I thought upon the banks o' Coil,
  I thought upon my Nancy,
I thought upon the witching smile
  That caught my youthful fancy.

At length I reach'd the bonnie glen,
  Where early life I sported ;
I pass'd the mill, and trysting thorn,
  Where Nancy aft I courted :      20

Wha spied I but my ain dear maid,
  Down by her mother's dwelling!
And turn'd me round to hide the flood
  That in my een was swelling.


Wi' alter'd voice quoth I, Sweet lass,
  Sweet as yon hawthorn blossom,
O! happy, happy may he be,
  That's dearest to thy bosom!
My purse is light, I've far to gang,
  And fain wad be thy lodger;                30
I've serv'd my King and Country lang—
  Take pity on a sodger!


Sae wistfully she gazed on me,
  And lovelier was than ever:
Quo' she, a sodger ance I lo'ed,
  Forget him shall I never:
Our humble cot, and hamely fare,
  Ye freely shall partake it;
That gallant badge, the dear cockade,
  Ye're welcome for the sake o't.          40


She gaz'd—she redden'd like a rose—
  Syne pale like ony lily;
She sank within my arms, and cried,
  Art thou my ain dear Willie?
By Him who made yon sun and sky,
  By whom true love's regarded,
I am the man; and thus may still
  True lovers be rewarded!


The wars are o'er, and I'm come hame,
  And find thee still true-hearted;          50
Tho' poor in gear, we're rich in love,
  And mair we'se ne'er be parted.
Quo' she, My grandsire left me gowd,
  A mailen plenish'd fairly;
And come, my faithful sodger lad,
  Thou'rt welcome to it dearly!

For gold the merchant ploughs the main,
    The farmer ploughs the manor;
But glory is the sodger's prize;
    The sodger's wealth is honour:                    60
The brave poor sodger ne'er despise,
    Nor count him as a stranger;
Remember he 's his Country's stay
    In day and hour o' danger.

---

## LAST MAY A BRAW WOOER.

LAST May a braw wooer cam down the lang glen,
    And sair wi' his love he did deave me:
I said there was naething I hated like men—
    The deuce gae wi'm to believe me, believe me,
    The deuce gae wi'm to believe me.

He spak o' the darts in my bonnie black een,
    And vow'd for my love he was dying;
I said he might die when he liked for Jean:
    The Lord forgie me for lying, for lying,
    The Lord forgie me for lying!                     10

A weel-stockèd mailen, himsel' for the laird,
    And marriage aff-hand, were his proffers:
I never loot on that I kend it, or car'd;
    But thought I might hae waur offers, waur offers,
    But thought I might hae waur offers.

But what wad ye think? in a fortnight or less,
    The deil tak his taste to gae near her!
He up the lang loan to my black cousin Bess,
    Guess ye how, the jad! I could bear her, could bear her,
    Guess ye how, the jad! I could bear her.         20

But a' the niest week as I fretted wi' care,
    I gaed to the tryst o' Dalgarnock;
And wha but my fine fickle lover was there?
    I glowr'd as I'd seen a warlock, a warlock,
    I glowr'd as I'd seen a warlock.

But owre my left shouther I gae him a blink,
  Lest neebors might say I was saucy;
My wooer he caper'd as he'd been in drink,
  And vow'd I was his dear lassie, dear lassie,
  And vow'd I was his dear lassie.                    30

I spier'd for my cousin fu' couthy and sweet,
  Gin she had recover'd her hearin',
And how her new shoon fit her auld shachl't feet—
  But, heavens! how he fell a swearin' a swearin',
  But, heavens! how he fell a swearin'.

He beggèd for Gudesake I wad be his wife
  Or else I wad kill him wi' sorrow:
So e'en to preserve the poor body in life,
  I think I maun wed him to-morrow, to-morrow,
  I think I maun wed him to-morrow.                  40

———◆◆———

## THERE WAS A LASS.

There was a lass, and she was fair,
  At kirk and market to be seen;
When a' the fairest maids were met,
  The fairest maid was bonnie Jean.

And aye she wrought her mammie's wark,
  And aye she sang sae merrily:
The blythest bird upon the bush
  Had ne'er a lighter heart than she.

But hawks will rob the tender joys
  That bless the little lintwhite's nest;            10
And frost will blight the fairest flowers,
  And love will break the soundest rest.

Young Robie was the brawest lad,
  The flower and pride of a' the glen;
And he had owsen, sheep and kye,
  And wanton naigies nine or ten.

He gaed wi' Jeanie to the tryst,
    He danc'd wi' Jeanie on the down ;
And lang ere witless Jeanie wist,
    Her heart was tint, her peace was stown.    20

As in the bosom o' the stream
    The moon-beam dwells at dewy e'en ;
So trembling, pure, was tender love
    Within the breast o' bonnie Jean.

And now she works her mammie's wark,
    And aye she sighs wi' care and pain ;
Yet wistna what her ail might be,
    Or what wad mak her weel again.

But didna Jeanie's heart loup light,
    And didna joy blink in her ee,    30
As Robie tauld a tale o' love,
    Ae e'enin' on the lily lea?

The sun was sinking in the west,
    The birds sang sweet in ilka grove ;
His cheek to hers he fondly prest,
    And whisper'd thus his tale o' love :

O Jeanie fair, I lo'e thee dear ;
    O canst thou think to fancy me ?
Or wilt thou leave thy mammie's cot,
    And learn to tent the farms wi' me ?    40

At barn or byre thou shaltna drudge,
    Or naething else to trouble thee ;
But stray amang the heather-bells,
    And tent the waving corn wi' me.

Now what could artless Jeanie do ?
    She had nae will to say him na :
At length she blush'd a sweet consent,
    And love was aye between them twa.

## COUNTRY LASSIE.

IN simmer when the hay was mawn,
  And corn wav'd green in ilka field,
While claver blooms white o'er the lea ;
  And roses blaw in ilka bield ;
Blythe Bessie in the milking shiel
  Says 'I'll be wed, come o't what will ;'
Out spak a dame in wrinkled eild,
  'O' guid advisement comes nae ill.

'It's ye hae wooers mony ane,
  And, lassie, ye're but young ye ken ;    10
Then wait a wee, and cannie wale
  A routhie butt, a routhie ben ;
There's Johnie o' the Buskie-glen,
  Fu' is his barn, fu' is his byre ;
Tak this frae me, my bonnie hen,
  It's plenty beets the luver's fire.'

'For Johnie o' the Buskie-glen
  I dinna care a single flie ;
He lo'es sae weel his craps and kye,
  He has nae love to spare for me :    20
But blithe's the blink o' Robie's ee,
  And weel I wat he lo'es me dear :
Ae blink o' him I wad nae gie
  For Buskie-glen and a' his gear.'

'O thoughtless lassie, life's a faught !
  The canniest gate, the strife is sair ;
But aye fu' han't is fechtin' best,
  A hungry care's an unco care ;
But some will spend, and some will spare,
  An' wilfu' folk maun hae their will ;    30
Syne as ye brew, my maiden fair,
  Keep mind that ye maun drink the yill.'

'O, gear will buy me rigs o' land,
  And gear will buy me sheep and kye ;
But the tender heart o' leesome love
  The gowd and siller canna buy :

> We may be poor—Robie and I,
> Light is the burden love lays on ;
> Content and love brings peace and joy,—
> What mair hae queens upon a throne ? '   40

———◆◆———

## MY FATHER WAS A FARMER.

My Father was a Farmer upon the Carrick border O,
And carefully he bred me in decency and order O ;
He bade me act a manly part, though I had ne'er a farthing O,
For without an honest manly heart, no man was worth
  regarding O.

Then out into the world my course I did determine O ;
Tho' to be rich was not my wish, yet to be great was
  charming O :
My talents they were not the worst ; nor yet my education O ;
Resolv'd was I, at least to try, to mend my situation O.

In many a way, and vain essay, I courted fortune's favour O :
Some cause unseen still stept between, to frustrate each
  endeavour O ;                               10
Sometimes by foes I was o'erpower'd ; sometimes by friends
  forsaken O ;
And when my hope was at the top, I still was worst
  mistaken O.

Then sore harass'd, and tir'd at last, with fortune's vain
  delusion O,
I dropt my schemes, like idle dreams, and came to this
  conclusion O—
The past was bad, and the future hid ; its good or ill untried O ;
But the present hour was in my pow'r, and so I would
  enjoy it O.

No help, nor hope, nor view had I : nor person to befriend
  me O ;
So I must toil, and sweat and broil, and labour to sustain
  me O ;

To plough and sow, to reap and mow, my father bred me
    early O ;
For one, he said, to labour bred, was a match for fortune
    fairly O.                         20

Thus all obscure, unknown, and poor, thro' life I'm doom'd
    to wander O,
Till down my weary bones I lay in everlasting slumber O ;
No view nor care, but shun whate'er might breed me pain
    or sorrow O,
I live to-day as well's I may, regardless of to-morrow O.

But cheerful still, I am as well as a monarch in a palace O,
Tho' fortune's frown still hunts me down, with all her
    wonted malice O ;
I make indeed my daily bread, but ne'er can make it farther O ;
But as daily bread is all I need, I do not much regard her O.

When sometimes by my labour I earn a little money O,
Some unforeseen misfortune comes generally upon me O—
Mischance, mistake, or by neglect, or my good-natur'd
    folly O ;                         31
But come what will, I've sworn it still, I'll ne'er be
    melancholy O.

All you who follow wealth and power, with unremitting
    ardour O,
The more in this you look for bliss, you leave your view
    the farther O ;
Had you the wealth Potosi boasts, or nations to adore
    you O,
A cheerful honest-hearted clown I will prefer before you O.

---

## THE LASS THAT MADE THE BED TO ME.

WHEN Januar' wind was blawing cauld,
    As to the north I took my way,
The mirksome night did me enfauld,
    I knew na where to lodge till day.

By my good luck a maid I met,
  Just in the middle o' my care;
And kindly she did me invite
  To walk into a chamber fair.


I bow'd fu' low unto this maid,
  And thank'd her for her courtesie ;                    10
I bow'd fu' low unto this maid,
  And bade her mak a bed to me.


She made the bed baith large and wide,
  Wi' twa white hands she spread it down ;
She put the cup to her rosy lips,
  And drank, 'Young man, now sleep ye soun.'


She snatch'd the candle in her hand,
  And frae my chamber went wi' speed ;
But I call'd her quickly back again
  To lay some mair below my head.                        20


A cod she laid below my head,
  And servèd me wi' due respect ;
And to salute her wi' a kiss,
  I put my arms about her neck.


'Haud aff your hands, young man,' she says,
  'And dinna sae uncivil be :
If ye hae ony love for me,
  O wrang na my virginitie !'


Her hair was like the links o' gowd,
  Her teeth were like the ivorie ;                       30
Her cheeks like lilies dipt in wine,
  The lass that made the bed to me.


Her bosom was the driven snaw,
  Twa drifted heaps sae fair to see ;
Her limbs the polish'd marble stane,
  The lass that made the bed to me.

I kiss'd her owre and owre again,
  And aye she wist na what to say ;
I laid her between me and the wa',—
  The lassie thought na lang till day.                    40

Upon the morrow when we rose,
  I thank'd her for her courtesie ;
But aye she blush'd, and aye she sigh'd
  And said 'Alas ! ye've ruin'd me.'

I clasp'd her waist, and kiss'd her syne,
  While the tear stood twinkling in her ee ,
I said 'My lassie, dinna cry,
  For ye aye shall make the bed to me.'

She took her mither's Holland sheets,
  And made them a' in sarks to me :                       50
Blythe and merry may she be,
  The lass that made the bed to me.

The bonnie lass made the bed to me,
  The braw lass made the bed to me :
I'll ne'er forget till the day I die,
  The lass that made the bed to me !

——•——

## CALEDONIA.

THERE was once a day, but old Time then was young,
  That brave Caledonia, the chief of her line,
From some of your northern deities sprung :
  (Who knows not that brave Caledonia's divine ?)
From Tweed to the Orcades was her domain,
  To hunt, or to pasture, or do what she would :
Her heavenly relations there fix'd her reign,
  And pledg'd her their godheads to warrant it good.

A lambkin in peace, but a lion in war,
  The pride of her kindred the heroine grew ;            10
Her grandsire, old Odin, triumphantly swore,
  'Whoe'er shall provoke thee, th' encounter shall rue !'

With tillage or pasture at times she would sport,
  To feed her fair flocks by her green rustling corn;
But chiefly the woods were her fav'rite resort,
  Her darling amusement, the hounds and the horn.

Long quiet she reign'd; till thitherward steers
  A flight of bold eagles from Adria's strand;
Repeated, successive, for many long years,
  They darken'd the air, and they plunder'd the land.     20
Their pounces were murder, and terror their cry,
  They conquer'd and ruin'd a world beside;
She took to her hills, and her arrows let fly,—
  The daring invaders they fled or they died.

The fell Harpy-raven took wing from the north,
  The scourge of the seas, and the dread of the shore;
The wild Scandinavian boar issued forth
  To wanton in carnage and wallow in gore:
O'er countries and kingdoms their fury prevail'd,
  No arts could appease them, no arms could repel:     30
But brave Caledonia in vain they assail'd,
  As Largs well can witness, and Loncartie tell.

The Cameleon-savage disturb'd her repose,
  With tumult, disquiet, rebellion, and strife;
Provok'd beyond bearing, at last she arose,
  And robb'd him at once of his hopes and his life:
The Anglian lion, the terror of France,
  Oft prowling, ensanguin'd the Tweed's silver flood;
But, taught by the bright Caledonian lance,
  He learnèd to fear in his own native wood.     40

Thus bold, independent, unconquer'd, and free,
  Her bright course of glory for ever shall run:
For brave Caledonia immortal must be;
  I'll prove it from Euclid as clear as the sun:
Rectangle-triangle, the figure we'll choose,
  The upright is Chance, and old Time is the base;
But brave Caledonia's the hypothenuse;
  Then ergo, she'll match them, and match them always.

## ON THE BATTLE OF SHERIFFMUIR,

### BETWEEN THE DUKE OF ARGYLE AND THE EARL OF MAR.

'O CAM ye here the fight to shun,
    Or herd the sheep wi' me, man?
Or were you at the Sherra-muir,
    And did the battle see, man?'
I saw the battle, sair and teugh,
And reeking-red ran mony a sheugh;
My heart, for fear, gae sough for sough,
To hear the thuds, and see the cluds
O' clans frae woods, in tartan duds,
    Wha glaum'd at kingdoms three, man.    10

The red-coat lads, wi' black cockades,
    To meet them were na slaw, man;
They rush'd and push'd, and blude out-gush'd,
    And mony a bouk did fa', man:
The great Argyle led on his files,
I wat they glancèd twenty miles:
They hough'd the clans like nine-pin kyles,
They hack'd and hash'd, while broadswords clash'd,
And thro' they dash'd, and hew'd and smash'd,
    Till fey men died awa, man.    20

But had you seen the philibegs,
    And skyrin tartan trews, man,
When in the teeth they dar'd our whigs,
    And covenant true blues, man;
In lines extended lang and large,
When baig'nets overpower'd the targe,
And thousands hasten'd to the charge,
Wi' Highland wrath they frae the sheath
Drew blades o' death, till, out of breath,
    They fled like frighted doos, man.    30

'O how deil, Tam, can that be true?
    The chase gaed frae the north, man:
I saw mysel, they did pursue
    The horsemen back to Forth, man;

And at Dumblane, in my ain sight,
They took the brig wi' a' their might,
And straught to Stirling wing'd their flight;
But, cursèd lot! the gates were shut,
And mony a huntit, poor red-coat,
   For fear amaist did swarf, man.'        40

My sister Kate cam up the gate
   Wi' crowdie unto me, man;
She swore she saw some rebels run
   Frae Perth unto Dundee, man:
Their left-hand general had nae skill,
The Angus lads had nae guid-will,
That day their neibors' blood to spill;
For fear, by foes, that they should lose
Their cogs o' brose, they scared at blows,
   And hameward fast did flee, man.        50

They've lost some gallant gentlemen
   Amang the Highland clans, man;
I fear my lord Panmure is slain,
   Or fallen in whiggish hands, man:
Now wad ye sing this double fight,
Some fell for wrang, and some for right;
But mony bade the world guid-night;
Then ye may tell, how pell and mell,
By red claymores, and muskets' knell,
Wi' dying yell, the tories fell,        60
   And whigs to hell did flee, man.

---

# THE FIVE CARLINS,

## AN ELECTION BALLAD OF 1789.

THERE was five Carlins in the south,
   They fell upon a scheme,
To send a lad to Lon'on town
   To bring us tidings hame.

Not only bring us tidings hame,
  But do our errands there,
And aiblins gowd and honour baith
  Might be that laddie's share.


There was Maggie by the banks o' Nith,
  A dame wi' pride eneugh ;                    10
And Marjorie o' the mony Lochs,
  A Carlin auld an' teugh.


And blinkin Bess o' Annandale,
  That dwells near Solway side ;
And whisky Jean, that took her gill,
  In Galloway so wide.


And auld black Joan frae Creighton peel,
  O' gipsy kith an' kin ;
Five wighter Carlins were na foun'
  The south countree within.                   20


To send a lad to Lon'on town
  They met upon a day ;
And mony a Knight and mony a Laird,
  That errand fain would gae.


O ! mony a Knight and mony a Laird,
  This errand fain would gae ;
But nae ane could their fancy please,
  O ! ne'er a ane but twae.


The first ane was a belted Knight,
  Bred o' a border clan,                        30
An' he wad gae to Lon'on town,
  Might nae man him withstan'.


And he wad do their errands weel,
  And meikle he wad say,
And ilka ane at Lon'on court
  Wad bid to him guid day.

Then neist came in a sodger youth,
  And spak wi' modest grace,
An' he wad gae to Lon'on town,
  If sae their pleasure was.                    40

He wad na hecht them courtly gift,
  Nor meikle speech pretend;
But he wad hecht an honest heart
  Wad ne'er desert his friend.

Now wham to choose and wham refuse,
  To strife thae Carlins fell;
For some had gentle folk to please,
  And some wad please themsel.

Then out spak mim-mou'd Meg o' Nith,
  An' she spak out wi' pride,              50
An' she wad send the sodger youth
  Whatever might betide.

For the auld guidman o' Lon'on court
  She didna care a pin,
But she wad send the sodger youth
  To greet his eldest son.

Then up sprang Bess o' Annandale:
  A deadly aith she 's ta'en,
That she wad vote the border Knight,
  Tho' she should vote her lane.             60

For far aff fowls hae feathers fair,
  An' fools o' change are fain:
But I hae tried the border Knight,
  And I'll try him yet again.

Says auld black Joan frae Creighton peel,
  A Carlin stoor and grim,
The auld guidman or young guidman,
  For me may sink or swim!

For fools will prate o' right and wrang,
    While knaves laugh them to scorn:          70
But the sodgers' friends hae blawn the best,
    Sae he shall bear the horn.

Then whisky Jean spak o'er her drink,
    Ye weel ken, kimmers a',
The auld guidman o' Lon'on court,
    His back's been at the wa';

And mony a friend that kiss'd his caup,
    Is now a fremmit wight;
But it's ne'er be said o' whisky Jean,—
    We'll send the border Knight.          80

Then slow raise Marjorie o' the Lochs,
    And wrinkled was her brow;
Her ancient weed was russet gray,
    Her auld Scots bluid was true.

There's some great folks set light by me,
    I set as light by them;
But I will send to Lon'on town,
    Wha I lo'e best at hame.

So how this weighty plea will end,
    Nae mortal wight can tell;          90
God grant the King and ilka man
    May look weel to himsel'!

---

# WHEN GUILDFORD GOOD OUR PILOT STOOD.

### A FRAGMENT.

WHEN Guildford good our Pilot stood,
    An' did our hellim thraw, man,
Ae night, at tea, began a plea,
    Within America, man:
Then up they gat the maskin-pat,
    And in the sea did jaw, man;
An' did nae less, in full Congress,
    Than quite refuse our law, man.

Then thro' the lakes Montgomery takes,
  I wat he was na slaw, man ;      10
Down Lowrie's burn he took a turn,
  And Carleton did ca', man :
But yet, what-reck, he, at Quebec,
  Montgomery-like did fa', man,
Wi' sword in hand, before his band,
  Amang his en'mies a', man.


Poor Tammy Gage, within a cage
  Was kept at Boston ha', man ;
Till Willie Howe took o'er the knowe
  For Philadelphia, man :      20
Wi' sword an' gun he thought a sin
  Guid Christian bluid to draw, man ;
But at New York, wi' knife an' fork,
  Sir Loin he hackèd sma', man.


Burgoyne gaed up, like spur an' whip,
  Till Fraser brave did fa', man ;
Then lost his way, ae misty day,
  In Saratoga shaw, man.
Cornwallis fought as lang 's he dought,
  An' did the Buckskins claw, man ;      30
But Clinton's glaive frae rust to save,
  He hung it to the wa', man.


Then Montague, an' Guildford too,
  Began to fear a fa', man ;
And Sackville doure, wha stood the stoure,
  The German Chief to thraw, man :
For Paddy Burke, like ony Turk,
  Nae mercy had at a', man ;
An' Charlie Fox threw by the box,
  An' lows'd his tinkler jaw, man.      40


Then Rockingham took up the game,
  Till death did on him ca', man ;
When Shelburne meek held up his cheek,
  Conform to gospel law, man,

Saint Stephen's boys, wi' jarring noise,
  They did his measures thraw, man,
For North an' Fox united stocks,
  An' bore him to the wa', man.


Then Clubs an' Hearts were Charlie's cartes,
  He swept the stakes awa', man,        50
Till the Diamond's Ace, of Indian race,
  Led him a sair *faux pas*, man:
The Saxon lads, wi' loud placads,
  On Chatham's boy did ca', man;
An' Scotland drew her pipe, an' blew
  'Up, Willie, waur them a', man!'


Behind the throne then Grenville's gone,
  A secret word or twa, man;
While slee Dundas arous'd the class
  Be-north the Roman wa', man:        60
An' Chatham's wraith, in heavenly graith,
  (Inspirèd Bardies saw, man,)
Wi' kindling eyes cried, 'Willie, rise!
  Would I hae fear'd them a', man?'


But, word an' blow, North, Fox, and Co.
  Gowff'd Willie like a ba', man,
Till Suthron raise, an' coost their claise
  Behind him in a raw, man;
An' Caledon threw by the drone,
  An' did her whittle draw, man;       70
An' swoor fu' rude, thro' dirt an' blood,
  To make it guid in law, man.


    *     *     *     *     *     *     *

## THE CARLE OF KELLYBURN BRAES.

THERE lived a carle on Kellyburn braes
  (Hey, and the rue grows bonnie wi' thyme),
And he had a wife was the plague o' his days;
  And the thyme it is wither'd, and rue is in prime.

Ae day as the carle gaed up the lang glen
  (Hey, and the rue grows bonnie wi' thyme),
He met wi' the Devil; says, 'How do you fen?'
  And the thyme it is wither'd, and rue is in prime.

'I've got a bad wife, sir; that's a' my complaint'
  (Hey, and the rue grows bonnie wi' thyme),     10
'For, saving your presence, to her ye're a saint;'
  And the thyme it is wither'd, and rue is in prime.

'It's neither your stot nor your staig I shall crave
  (Hey, and the rue grows bonnie wi' thyme),
'But gie me your wife, man, for her I must have;'
  And the thyme it is wither'd, and rue is in prime.

'O welcome, most kindly,' the blythe carle said
  (Hey, and the rue grows bonnie wi' thyme),
'But if ye can match her, ye're waur nor ye're ca'd;'
  And the thyme it is wither'd, and rue is in prime.  20

The Devil has got the auld wife on his back
  (Hey, and the rue grows bonnie wi' thyme),
And, like a poor pedlar, he's carried his pack;
  And the thyme it is wither'd, and rue is in prime.

He's carried her hame to his ain hallan-door
  (Hey, and the rue grows bonnie wi' thyme),
Syne bade her gae in, for a bitch and a whore;
  And the thyme it is wither'd, and rue is in prime.

Then straight he makes fifty, the pick o' his band
  (Hey, and the rue grows bonnie wi' thyme),     30
Turn out on her guard in the clap of a hand;
  And the thyme it is wither'd, and rue is in prime.

The carlin gaed thro' them like ony wud bear
  (Hey, and the rue grows bonnie wi' thyme),
Whae'er she gat hands on came near her nae mair ;
  And the thyme it is wither'd, and rue is in prime.

A reekit wee Devil looks over the wa'
  (Hey, and the rue grows bonnie wi' thyme),
' O, help, master, help, or she'll ruin us a' ;'
  And the thyme it is wither'd, and rue is in prime. 40

The Devil he swore by the edge o' his knife
  (Hey, and the rue grows bonnie wi' thyme),
He pitied the man that was tied to a wife ;
  And the thyme it is wither'd, and rue is in prime.

The Devil he swore by the kirk and the bell
  (Hey, and the rue grows bonnie wi' thyme),
He was not in wedlock, thank heav'n, but in hell ;
  And the thyme it is wither'd, and rue is in prime.

Then Satan has travell'd again wi' his pack
  (Hey, and the rue grows bonnie wi' thyme),     50
And to her auld husband he 's carried her back ;
  And the thyme it is wither'd, and rue is in prime.

' I hae been a Devil the feck o' my life '
  (Hey, and the rue grows bonnie wi' thyme),
' But ne'er was in hell, till I met wi' a wife ;'
  And the thyme it is wither'd, and rue is in prime.

---

## THERE WAS A LASS.

There was a lass, they ca'd her Meg,
  And she held o'er the moors to spin ;
There was a lad that follow'd her,
  They ca'd him Duncan Davison.
The moor was driegh, and Meg was skiegh,
  Her favour Duncan could na win ;
For wi' the rock she wad him knock,
  And ay she shook the temper-pin.

As o'er the moor they lightly foor,
 A burn was clear, a glen was green,  10
Upon the banks they eased their shanks,
 And aye she set the wheel between:
But Duncan swore a haly aith,
 That Meg should be a bride the morn;
Then Meg took up her spinnin' graith,
 And flung them a' out o'er the burn.

We'll big a house—a wee, wee house,
 And we will live like King and Queen,
Sae blythe and merry we will be
 When ye set by the wheel at e'en.  20
A man may drink and no be drunk;
 A man may fight and no be slain;
A man may kiss a bonnie lass,
 And aye be welcome back again.

## THE HERON BALLADS.

### FIRST BALLAD.

Whom will you send to London town,
 To Parliament and a' that?
Or wha in a' the country round
 The best deserves to fa' that?
   For a' that, an' a' that,
   Thro' Galloway an' a' that!
   Where is the laird or belted knight
   That best deserves to fa' that?

Wha sees Kerroughtree's open yett,
 And wha is 't never saw that?  10
Wha ever wi' Kerroughtree meets
 And has a doubt of a' that?
   For a' that, an' a' that,
   Here's Heron yet for a' that!
   The independent patriot,
   The honest man, an' a' that.

Tho' wit and worth in either sex,
  St. Mary's Isle can shaw that;
Wi' dukes an' lords let Selkirk mix,
  And weel does Selkirk fa' that.        20
      For a' that, an' a' that,
      Here's Heron yet for a' that!
      The independent commoner
      Shall be the man for a' that.

But why should we to nobles jouk,
  And is't against the law that?
For why, a lord may be a gouk,
  Wi' ribbon, star, an' a' that.
      For a' that, an' a' that,
      Here's Heron yet for a' that!     30
      A lord may be a lousy loun,
      Wi' ribbon, star, an' a' that.

A beardless boy comes o'er the hills,
  Wi' uncle's purse an' a' that;
But we'll hae ane frae 'mang oursels,
  A man we ken, an' a' that.
      For a' that, an' a' that,
      Here's Heron yet for a' that!
      For we're not to be bought an' sold
      Like naigs, an' nowt, an' a' that.    40

Then let us drink the Stewartry,
  Kerroughtree's laird, an' a' that,
Our representative to be,
  For weel he's worthy a' that.
      For a' that, an' a' that,
      Here's Heron yet for a' that!
      A House of Commons such as he,
      They would be blest that saw that.

# THE ELECTION.

### SECOND BALLAD.

Fy, let us a' to Kirkcudbright,
    For there will be bickerin' there ;
For Murray's light-horse are to muster,
    And O, how the heroes will swear !
An' there will be Murray commander,
    And Gordon the battle to win ;
Like brothers they'll stand by each other,
    Sae knit in alliance an' kin.

An' there will be black-nebbit Johnnie,
    The tongue o' the trump to them a' ;    10
An' he get na hell for his haddin'
    The Deil gets na justice ava' ;
An' there will be Kempleton's birkie,
    A boy no sae black at the bane,
But, as for his fine nabob fortune,
    We'll e'en let the subject alane.

An' there will be Wigton's new sheriff,
    Dame Justice fu' brawlie has sped,
She 's gotten the heart of a Bushby,
    But, Lord, what 's become o' the head ?    20
An' there will be Cardoness, Esquire,
    Sae mighty in Cardoness' eyes ;
A wight that will weather damnation,
    For the Devil the prey will despise.

An' there will be Douglasses doughty,
    New christ'ning towns far and near !
Abjuring their democrat doings,
    By kissing the arse o' a peer ;
An' there will be Kenmure sae gen'rous
    Whose honour is proof to the storm,    30
To save them from stark reprobation
    He lent them his name in the firm.

But we winna mention Redcastle,
  The body e'en let him escape!
He'd venture the gallows for siller,
  An' 'twere na the cost o' the rape.
An' where is our King's lord lieutenant,
  Sae fam'd for his gratefu' return?
The billie is gettin' his questions,
  To say in St. Stephen's the morn.          40


An' there will be lads o' the gospel,
  Muirhead wha 's as good as he 's true;
An' there will be Buittle's apostle,
  Wha 's more o' the black than the blue;
An' there will be folk from St. Mary's,
  A house o' great merit and note,
The deil ane but honours them highly,—
  The deil ane will gie them his vote!


An' there will be wealthy young Richard,
  Dame Fortune should hing by the neck;   50
For prodigal, thriftless bestowing—
  His merit had won him respect:
An' there will be rich brother nabobs,
  Though nabobs, yet men not the worst;
An' there will be Collieston's whiskers,
  An' Quintin, a lad o' the first.


An' there will be stamp-office Johnnie,
  Tak tent how ye purchase a dram!
An' there will be gay Cassencarrie,
  An' there will be gleg Colonel Tam;      60
An' there will be trusty Kerroughtree,
  Whose honour was ever his law,
If the virtues were pack'd in a parcel,
  His worth might be sample for a'.


An' can we forget the auld major,
  Wha'll ne'er be forgot in the Greys;
Our flatt'ry we'll keep for some other,
  Him only 'tis justice to praise.

An' there will be maiden Kilkerran,
 And also Barskimming's gude knight;  70
An' there will be roarin' Birtwhistle,
 Wha, luckily, roars in the right.

An' there, frae the Niddisdale's borders,
 Will mingle the Maxwells in droves;
Teugh Jockie, staunch Geordie, an' Walie,
 That griens for the fishes an' loaves;
An' there will be Logan MacDowall,
 Sculdudd'ry an' he will be there,
An' also the wild Scot o' Galloway,
 Sodgerin', gunpowder Blair.  80

Then hey the chaste interest o' Broughton,
 An' hey for the blessings 'twill bring!
It may send Balmaghie to the Commons,
 In Sodom 'twould make him a King;
An' hey for the sanctified Murray,
 Our land who wi' chapels has stor'd;
He founder'd his horse among harlots,
 But gied the auld naig to the Lord.

---

## JOHN BUSHBY'S LAMENTATION.

### THIRD BALLAD.

'TWAS in the seventeen hunder year
 O' grace and ninety-five,
That year I was the wae'est man
 O' ony man alive.

In March the three-and-twentieth morn
 The sun raise clear and bright;
But oh I was a waefu' man
 Ere to-fa' o' the night.

Yerl Galloway lang did rule this land,
 Wi' equal right and fame,  10
And thereto was his kinsman join'd
 The Murray's noble name.

Yerl Galloway lang did rule the land,
  Made me the judge o' strife ;
But now Yerl Galloway's sceptre 's broke,
  And eke my hangman's knife.


'Twas by the banks o' bonnie Dee,
  Beside Kirkcudbright's towers,
The Stewart and the Murray there
  Did muster a' their powers.                    20


The Murray, on the auld gray yaud,
  Wi' wingèd spurs did ride,
That auld gray yaud a' Nidsdale rade,
  He staw upon Nidside.


An' there had na been the yerl himsel',
  O there had been nae play ;
But Garlies was to London gane,
  And sae the kye might stray.


And there was Balmaghie, I ween,
  In front rank he wad shine ;                   30
But Balmaghie had better been
  Drinking Madeira wine.


Frae the Glenkens came to our aid,
  A chief o' doughty deed ;
In case that worth should wanted be,
  O' Kenmure we had need.


And by our banners march'd Muirhead,
  And Buittle was na slack ;
Whase haly priesthood nane can stain,
  For wha can dye the black ?                    40


And there sae grave Squire Cardoness,
  Look'd on till a' was done ;
Sae, in the tower o' Cardoness,
  A howlet sits at noon.

And there led I the Bushby clan,
　My gamesome billie, Will ;
And my son Maitland, wise as brave,
　My footsteps follow'd still.

The Douglas and the Heron's name
　We set nought to their score ;                     50
The Douglas and the Heron's name
　Had felt our weight before.

But Douglases o' weight had we,
　The pair o' lusty lairds,
For building cot-houses sae famed,
　And christening kail-yards.

And there Redcastle drew his sword,
　That ne'er was stained wi' gore,
Save on a wanderer lame and blind,
　To drive him frae his door.                        60

And last came creeping Collieston,
　Was mair in fear than wrath ;
Ae knave was constant in his mind,
　To keep that knave frae scaith.

　　*　　*　　*　　*　　*　　*　　*

―――・・―――

## AN EXCELLENT NEW SONG.

FOURTH BALLAD.　(MAY 1796.)

WHA will buy my troggin,
　Fine election ware ;
Broken trade o' Broughton,
　A' in high repair ?
　　Buy braw troggin,
　　　Frae the banks o' Dee ;
　　Wha wants troggin
　　　Let him come to me.

There's a noble Earl's
   Fame and high renown                        10
For an auld sang—
   It's thought the gudes were stown.

Here's the worth o' Broughton
   In a needle's ee ;
Here's a reputation
   Tint by Balmaghie.

Here's an honest conscience
   Might a prince adorn ;
Frae the downs o' Tinwald,
   So was never worn.                              20

Here's its stuff and lining,
   Cardoness's head ;
Fine for a sodger
   A' the wale o' lead.

Here's a little wadset,
   Buittle's scrap o' truth,
Pawn'd in a gin-shop
   Quenching holy drouth.

Here's armorial bearings
   Frae the manse o' Urr ;                         30
The crest, a sour crab-apple
   Rotten at the core.

Here is Satan's picture,
   Like a bizzard gled,
Pouncing poor Redcastle
   Sprawlin' like a taed.

Here's the worth and wisdom
   Collieston can boast ;
By a thievish midge
   They had been nearly lost.                      40

Here is Murray's fragments
　　O' the ten commands;
Gifted by black Jock
　　To get them aff his hands.

Saw ye e'er sic troggin?
　　If to buy ye're slack,
Hornie's turnin' chapman,—
　　He'll buy a' the pack.

———••———

## THE FÊTE CHAMPÊTRE.

O WHA will to Saint Stephen's house,
　　To do our errands there, man?
O wha will to Saint Stephen's house,
　　O' th' merry lads of Ayr, man?
Or will we send a man-o'-law?
　　Or will we send a sodger?
Or him wha led o'er Scotland a'
　　The meikle Ursa-Major?

Come, will ye court a noble lord,
　　Or buy a score o' lairds, man?　　　10
For worth and honour pawn their word,
　　Their vote shall be Glencaird's, man.
Ane gies them coin, ane gies them wine,
　　Anither gies them clatter;
Annbank, wha guess'd the ladies' taste,
　　He gies a Fête Champêtre.

When Love and Beauty heard the news,
　　The gay green-woods amang, man;
Where, gathering flowers and busking bowers,
　　They heard the blackbird's sang, man;　　20
A vow, they seal'd it with a kiss
　　Sir Politics to fetter,
As their's alone, the patent-bliss,
　　To hold a Fête Champêtre.

Then mounted Mirth, on gleesome wing,
   O'er hill and dale she flew, man;
Ilk wimpling burn, ilk crystal spring,
   Ilk glen and shaw she knew, man:
She summon'd every social sprite,
   That sports by wood or water,        30
On th' bonnie banks of Ayr to meet,
   And keep this Fête Champêtre.

Cauld Boreas, wi' his boisterous crew,
   Were bound to stakes like kye, man;
And Cynthia's car, o' silver fu',
   Clamb up the starry sky, man:
Reflected beams dwell in the streams,
   Or down the current shatter;
The western breeze steals through the trees,
   To view this Fête Champêtre.       40

How many a robe sae gaily floats!
   What sparkling jewels glance, man!
To Harmony's enchanting notes,
   As moves the mazy dance, man!
The echoing wood, the winding flood,
   Like Paradise did glitter,
When angels met, at Adam's yett,
   To hold their Fête Champêtre.

When Politics came there to mix
   And make his ether-stane, man!       50
He circled round the magic ground,
   But entrance found he nane, man:
He blush'd for shame, he quat his name,
   Forswore it every letter,
Wi' humble prayer to join and share
   This festive Fête Champêtre.

## WHISTLE OWRE THE LAVE O'T.

FIRST when Maggy was my care,
Heaven, I thought, was in her air;
Now we're married—spier nae mair—
   Whistle owre the lave o't.

Meg was meek, and Meg was mild,
Bonnie Meg was nature's child—
Wiser men than me's beguil'd;
   Whistle owre the lave o't.

How we live, my Meg and me,
How we love and how we 'gree,       10
I care na by how few may see—
   Whistle owre the lave o't.

Wha I wish were maggots' meat,
Dish'd up in her winding sheet,
I could write—but Meg may see't;
   Whistle owre the lave o't.

## DAINTY DAVIE.

Now rosy May comes in wi' flowers,
To deck her gay, green spreading bowers;
And now comes in my happy hours,
   To wander wi' my Davie.

Meet me on the warlock knowe,
   Dainty Davie, dainty Davie,
There I'll spend the day wi' you,
   My ain dear dainty Davie.

The crystal waters round us fa',
The merry birds are lovers a',       10
The scented breezes round us blaw,
   A wandering wi' my Davie.

When purple morning starts the hare,
To steal upon her early fare,
Then through the dews I will repair,
  To meet my faithfu' Davie.

When day, expiring in the west,
The curtain draws o' Nature's rest,
I flee to his arms I lo'e best,
  And that's my ain dear Davie.          20

---

## THE GALLANT WEAVER.

WHERE Cart rins rowin' to the sea,
By mony a flower and spreading tree,
There lives a lad, the lad for me,
  He is a gallant weaver.

Oh I had wooers aught or nine,
They gied me rings and ribbons fine;
And I was fear'd my heart would tine,
  And I gied it to the weaver.

My daddie sign'd my tocher-band,
To gie the lad that has the land;          10
But to my heart I'll add my hand,
  And gie it to the weaver.

While birds rejoice in leafy bowers;
While bees rejoice in opening flowers;
While corn grows green in simmer showers,
  I'll love my gallant weaver.

---

## ANNA, THY CHARMS.

ANNA, thy charms my bosom fire,
  And waste my soul with care;
But ah! how bootless to admire,
  When fated to despair!

Yet in thy presence, lovely fair,
  To hope may be forgiven ;
For sure, 'twere impious to despair
  So much in sight of heaven.

———◆◆———

## WHY, WHY TELL THY LOVER ?

WHY, why tell thy lover,
  Bliss he never must enjoy ?
Why, why undeceive him,
  And give all his hopes the lie ?

O why, while fancy raptured slumbers,
  Chloris, Chloris all the theme !
Why, why wouldst thou, cruel,
  Wake thy lover from his dream ?

———◆◆———

## NOW SPRING HAS CLAD.

Now spring has clad the groves in green,
  And strew'd the lea wi' flowers ;
The furrow'd waving corn is seen
  Rejoice in fostering showers.
While ilka thing in nature join
  Their sorrows to forego,
O why thus all alone are mine
  The weary steps of woe !

The trout in yonder wimpling burn
  Glides swift, a silver dart,
And safe beneath the shady thorn
  Defies the angler's art :
My life was once that careless stream,
  That wanton trout was I ;
But love, wi' unrelenting beam,
  Has scorch'd my fountain dry.

10

The little floweret's peaceful lot,
  In yonder cliff that grows,
Which, save the linnet's flight, I wot,
  Nae ruder visit knows,       20
Was mine ; till love has o'er me past,
  And blighted a' my bloom ;
And now beneath the withering blast
  My youth and joy consume.

The waken'd lav'rock warbling springs,
  And climbs the early sky,
Winnowing blithe her dewy wings
  In morning's rosy eye ;
As little reckt I sorrow's power,
  Until the flowery snare       30
O' witching love, in luckless hour,
  Made me the thrall o' care.

O had my fate been Greenland's snows
  Or Afric's burning zone,
Wi' man and nature leagued my foes,
  So Peggy ne'er I'd known !
The wretch whase doom is 'Hope nae mair !'
  What tongue his woes can tell !
Within whase bosom, save despair,
  Nae kinder spirits dwell.       40

## FORLORN, MY LOVE.

Forlorn, my love, no comfort near,
Far, far from thee, I wander here ;
Far, far from thee, the fate severe
  At which I most repine, love.

  O wert thou, love, but near me,
  But near, near, near me ;
  How kindly thou wouldst cheer me,
    And mingle sighs with mine, love !

Around me scowls a wintry sky,
That blasts each bud of hope and joy;    10
And shelter, shade, nor home have I,
    Save in those arms of thine, love.

Cold alter'd friendship's cruel part,
To poison fortune's ruthless dart—
Let me not break thy faithful heart,
    And say that fate is mine, love.

But dreary tho' the moments fleet,
O let me think we yet shall meet!
That only ray of solace sweet
    Can on thy Chloris shine, love.    20

———◆◆———

## YOUNG HIGHLAND ROVER.

LOUD blaw the frosty breezes,
    The snaws the mountains cover;
Like winter on me seizes,
    Since my young Highland Rover
    Far wanders nations over.
Where'er he go, where'er he stray,
    May Heaven be his warden,
Return him safe to fair Strathspey,
    And bonnie Castle-Gordon!

The trees, now naked groaning,    10
    Shall soon wi' leaves be hinging,
The birdies, dowie moaning,
    Shall a' be blythely singing,
    And every flower be springing:
Sae I'll rejoice the lee-lang day,
    When, by his mighty warden,
My youth 's return'd to fair Strathspey
    And bonnie Castle-Gordon.

## HEY FOR A LASS WI' A TOCHER.

Awa wi' your witchcraft o' beauty's alarms,
The slender bit beauty you grasp in your arms:
O, gie me the lass that has acres o' charms,
O, gie me the lass wi' the weel-stockit farms.

> Then hey, for a lass wi' a tocher, then hey, for
>     a lass wi' a tocher,
> Then hey, for a lass wi' a tocher—the nice yellow
>     guineas for me!

Your beauty 's a flower in the morning that blows,
And withers the faster, the faster it grows;
But the rapturous charm o' the bonnie green knowes!
Ilk spring they're new deckit wi' bonnie white yowes.

And e'en when this beauty your bosom has blest,
The brightest o' beauty may cloy, when possest;
But the sweet yellow darlings wi' Geordie imprest—
The langer ye hae them, the mair they're carest.

———••———

## BEHOLD THE HOUR.

Behold the hour, the boat arrive!
    Thou goest, thou darling of my heart:
Sever'd from thee can I survive?
    But fate has will'd, and we must part!
I'll often greet this surging swell;
    Yon distant isle will often hail:
'E'en here I took the last farewell;
    There latest mark'd her vanish'd sail.'

Along the solitary shore.
    While flitting sea-fowls round me cry,      10
Across the rolling dashing roar,
    I'll westward turn my wistful eye:
'Happy, thou Indian grove,' I'll say,
    'Where now my Nancy's path may be!
While thro' thy sweets she loves to stray,
    O tell me, does she muse on me?'

## O MALLY'S MEEK, MALLY'S SWEET.

As I was walking up the street,
　A barefit maid I chanced to meet;
But O the road was very hard
　For that fair maiden's tender feet.


It were mair meet that those fine feet
　Were weel laced up in silken shoon,
And 'twere more fit that she should sit
　Within yon chariot gilt aboon.


Her yellow hair, beyond compare,
　Comes trinkling down her swan-like neck,　　10
And her two eyes, like stars in skies,
　Would keep a sinking ship frae wreck.


O Mally's meek, Mally's sweet,
　Mally's modest and discreet,
Mally's rare, Mally's fair,
　Mally's every way complete.


## LADY MARY ANN.

O Lady Mary Ann
　Looks o'er the castle wa',
She saw three bonnie boys
　Playing at the ba';
The youngest he was
　The flower amang them a';
My bonnie laddie's young,
　But he's growin' yet.

O father! O father!
  An' ye think it fit,       10
We'll send him a year
  To the college yet:
We'll sew a green ribbon
  Round about his hat,
And that will let them ken
  He's to marry yet.


Lady Mary Ann
  Was a flower i' the dew,
Sweet was its smell,
  And bonnie was its hue!       20
And the langer it blossom'd
  The sweeter it grew;
For the lily in the bud
  Will be bonnier yet.


Young Charlie Cochran
  Was the sprout of an aik;
Bonnie and bloomin'
  And straught was its make:
The sun took delight
  To shine for its sake,       30
And it will be the brag
  O' the forest yet.


The simmer is gane
  When the leaves they were green,
And the days are awa
  That we hae seen:
But far better days
  I trust will come again,
For my bonnie laddie's young,
  But he's growin' yet.       40

# O, WAT YE WHA'S IN YON TOWN?

O, wat ye wha's in yon town,
    Ye see the e'enin sun upon?
The dearest maid's in yon town,
    That e'enin sun is shining on.

Now haply down yon gay green shaw,
    She wanders by yon spreading tree:
How blest ye flow'rs that round her blaw,
    Ye catch the glances o' her e'e!

How blest ye birds that round her sing,
    And welcome in the blooming year!     10
And doubly welcome be the spring,
    The season to my Jeanie dear!

The sun blinks blithe on yon·town,
    And on yon bonnie braes sae green;
But my delight in yon town,
    And dearest pleasure, is my Jean.

Without my love, not a' the charms
    O' Paradise could yield me joy;
But gie me Jeanie in my arms,
    And welcome Lapland's dreary sky!     20

My cave wad be a lover's bower,
    Tho' raging winter rent the air;
And she a lovely little flower,
    That I wad tent and shelter there.

O sweet is she in yon town,
    Yon sinkin sun's gane down upon;
A fairer than's in yon town,
    His setting beam ne'er shone upon.

If angry fate is sworn my foe,
  And suffering I am doom'd to bear;          30
I careless quit all else below,
  But spare, O spare me Jeanie dear.


For while life's dearest blood is warm,
  Ae thought frae her shall ne'er depart,
And she—as fairest is her form,
  She has the truest, kindest heart.


# A VISION.

As I stood by yon roofless tower,
  Where the wa'-flower scents the dewy air,
Where the howlet mourns in her ivy bower,
  And tells the midnight moon her care;

A lassie, all alone was making her moan,
  Lamenting our lads beyond the sea:
In the bluidy wars they fa', and our honour's gane an' a,
  And broken-hearted we maun die.

The winds were laid, the air was still,
  The stars they shot alang the sky;          10
The fox was howling on the hill,
  And the distant-echoing glens reply.


The stream, adown its hazelly path,
  Was rushing by the ruin'd wa's,
Hasting to join the sweeping Nith,
  Whase distant roaring swells and fa's


The cauld blue north was streaming forth
  Her lights, wi' hissing, eerie din;
Athort the lift they start and shift,
  Like fortune's favours, tint as win.          20

Now, looking over firth and fauld,
  Her horn the pale-faced Cynthia reared,
When lo! in guise of Minstrel auld,
  A stern and stalwart ghaist appeared.


And frae his harp sic strains did flow,
  Might rous'd the slumbering dead to hear;
But oh, it was a tale of woe,
  As ever met a Briton's ear!


He sang wi' joy his former day,
  He weeping wail'd his latter times;        30
But what he said it was nae play,
  I winna venture't in my rhymes.

— ◆ —

## THE HIGHLAND LASSIE.

NAE gentle dames, tho' ne'er sae fair,
Shall ever be my Muse's care;
Their titles a' are empty show;
Gie me my Highland lassie, O.

  Within the glen sae bushy, O,
  Aboon the plain sae rushy, O,
  I set me down wi' right good will
  To sing my Highland lassie, O


Oh, were yon hills and valleys mine,
Yon palace and yon gardens fine!          10
The world then the love should know
I bear my Highland lassie, O.

But fickle fortune frowns on me,
And I maun cross the raging sea ;
But while my crimson currents flow
I'll love my Highland lassie, O.

Altho' thro' foreign climes I range,
I know her heart will never change,
For her bosom burns with honour's glow,
My faithful Highland lassie, O.                    20

For her I'll dare the billow's roar,
For her I'll trace a distant shore,
That Indian wealth may lustre throw
Around my Highland lassie, O.

She has my heart, she has my hand,
By sacred truth and honour's band !
Till the mortal stroke shall lay me low,
I'm thine, my Highland lassie, O.

   Fareweel the glen sae bushy, O !
   Fareweel the plain sae rushy, O !              30
   To other lands I now must go,
   To sing my Highland lassie, O !

---

## MARK YONDER POMP.

Mark yonder pomp of costly fashion
   Round the wealthy titled bride :
But when compar'd with real passion,
   Poor is all that princely pride.
   What are their showy treasures ?
   What are their noisy pleasures ?
The gay gaudy glare of vanity and art :
   The polish'd jewel's blaze
   May draw the wond'ring gaze,
   And courtly grandeur bright          10
   The fancy may delight,
But never never can come near the heart.

But did you see my dearest Chloris,
  In simplicity's array;
Lovely as yonder sweet opening flower is,
  Shrinking from the gaze of day.
  O then, the heart alarming,
  And all resistless charming,
In Love's delightful fetters she chains the willing soul!
  Ambition would disown                                        20
  The world's imperial crown;
  Even Avarice would deny
  His worshipp'd deity,
And feel thro' every vein Love's raptures roll.

———◆———

## I SEE A FORM, I SEE A FACE.

O THIS is no my ain lassie,
  Fair tho' the lassie be;
O weel ken I my ain lassie,
  Kind love is in her ee.

I see a form, I see a face,
Ye weel may wi' the fairest place:
It wants, to me, the witching grace,
  The kind love that's in her ee.

She's bonnie, blooming, straight, and tall,
And lang has had my heart in thrall;                           10
And aye it charms my very saul,
  The kind love that's in her ee.

A thief sae pawkie is my Jean,
To steal a blink, by a' unseen;
But gleg as light are lovers' een,
  When kind love is in the ee.

It may escape the courtly sparks,
It may escape the learnèd clerks;
But weel the watching lover marks
  The kind love that's in her ee.                              20

## O BONNIE WAS YON ROSY BRIER.

O BONNIE was yon rosy brier,
   That blooms sae fair frae haunt o' man ;
And bonnie she, and ah, how dear !
   It shaded frae the e'enin sun.

Yon rosebuds in the morning dew,
   How pure amang the leaves sae green ;
But purer was the lover's vow
   They witness'd in their shade yestreen.

All in its rude and prickly bower,
   That crimson rose, how sweet and fair !    10
But love is far a sweeter flower
   Amid life's thorny path o' care.

The pathless wild, and wimpling burn,
   Wi' Chloris in my arms, be mine ;
And I the world nor wish nor scorn,
   Its joys and griefs alike resign.

---

## SWEET FA'S THE EVE.

SWEET fa's the eve on Craigie-burn,
   And blythe awakes the morrow,
But a' the pride o' spring's return
   Can yield me nocht but sorrow.

I see the flowers and spreading trees,
   I hear the wild birds singing ;
But what a weary wight can please,
   And care his bosom wringing ?

Fain, fain would I my griefs impart,
   Yet dare na for your anger ;    10
But secret love will break my heart,
   If I conceal it langer.

If thou refuse to pity me,
    If thou shalt love anither,
When yon green leaves fa' frae the tree,
    Around my grave they'll wither.

---

## O LASSIE, ART THOU SLEEPING YET?

O LASSIE, art thou sleeping yet?
Or art thou wakin', I would wit?
For love has bound me hand and foot,
    And I would fain be in, jo.

        O let me in this ae night,
            This ae, ae, ae night;
        For pity's sake this ae night,
            O rise and let me in, jo.

Thou hear'st the winter wind and weet,
Nae star blinks thro' the driving sleet;      10
Tak pity on my weary feet,
    And shield me frae the rain, jo.

The bitter blast that round me blaws,
Unheeded howls, unheeded fa's;
The cauldness o' thy heart's the cause
    Of a' my grief and pain, jo.

### HER ANSWER.

O TELL na me o' wind and rain,
Upbraid na me wi' cauld disdain!
Gae back the gait ye cam again,
    I winna let you in, jo.                   20

        I tell you now this ae night,
            This ae, ae, ae night;
        And ance for a' this ae night,
            I winna let you in, jo.

The snellest blast, at mirkest hours,
That round the pathless wand'rer pours,
Is nocht to what poor she endures,
    That's trusted faithless man, jo.

The sweetest flower that deck'd the mead,
Now trodden like the vilest weed ;          30
Let simple maid the lesson read,
    The weird may be her ain, jo.

The bird that charm'd his summer-day
Is now the cruel fowler's prey ;
Let witless, trusting woman say
    How aft her fate's the same, jo.

———◆◆———

## THEIR GROVES O' SWEET MYRTLE.

THEIR groves o' sweet myrtles let foreign lands reckon,
    Where bright-beaming summers exalt the perfume ;
Far dearer to me yon lone glen o' green breckan,
    Wi' the burn stealing under the lang yellow broom.

Far dearer to me are yon humble broom bowers,
    Where the blue-bell and gowan lurk lowly unseen :
For there, lightly tripping amang the wild flowers,
    A-listening the linnet, aft wanders my Jean.

Tho' rich is the breeze in their gay sunny valleys,
    And cauld Caledonia's blast on the wave ;          10
Their sweet-scented woodlands that skirt the proud palace,
    What are they? The haunt of the tyrant and slave !

The slave's spicy forests, and gold-bubbling fountains,
    The brave Caledonian views wi' disdain ;
He wanders as free as the winds of his mountains,
    Save love's willing fetters, the chains o' his Jean.

## THE BANKS OF NITH.

THE Thames flows proudly to the sea,
  Where royal cities stately stand ;
But sweeter flows the Nith to me,
  Where Comyns ance had high command :
When shall I see that honour'd land,
  That winding stream I love so dear !
Must wayward fortune's adverse hand
  For ever, ever keep me here ?

How lovely, Nith, thy fruitful vales,
  Where bounding hawthorns gaily bloom ;    10
How sweetly spread thy sloping dales,
  Where lambkins wanton thro' the broom !
Tho' wandering, now, must be my doom,
  Far from thy bonnie banks and braes,
May there my latest hours consume,
  Amang the friends of early days !

## THE BONNIE WEE THING.

BONNIE wee thing, cannie wee thing,
  Lovely wee thing, wert thou mine,
I wad wear thee in my bosom,
  Lest my jewel it should tine.

Wishfully I look and languish
  In that bonnie face o' thine ;
And my heart it stounds wi' anguish,
  Lest my wee thing be na mine.

Wit, and grace, and love, and beauty,
  In ae constellation shine ;
To adore thee is my duty,
  Goddess o' this soul o' mine !    10

## SHE'S FAIR AND FAUSE.

She 's fair and fause that causes my smart,
  I lo'ed her meikle and lang :
She 's broken her vow, she 's broken my heart,
  And I may e'en gae hang.
A coof cam in wi' rowth o' gear,
And I hae tint my dearest dear ;
But woman is but warld's gear,
  Sae let the bonnie lass gang.

Whae'er ye be that woman love,
  To this be never blind,                            10
Nae ferlie 'tis tho' fickle she prove,
  A woman has't by kind :
O Woman lovely, Woman fair !
An angel form 's fa'en to thy share ;
'Twad been o'er meikle to gi'en thee mair,
  I mean an Angel mind.

———◆◆———

## BESSY AND HER SPINNIN' WHEEL.

O leeze me on my spinnin' wheel,
O leeze me on my rock and reel ;
Frae tap to tae that cleeds me bien,
And haps me fiel and warm at e'en !
I'll set me down and sing and spin,
While laigh descends the simmer sun,
Blest wi' content, and milk and meal—
O leeze me on my spinnin' wheel.

On ilka hand the burnies trot,
And meet below my theekit cot ;                      10
The scented birk and hawthorn white
Across the pool their arms unite,
Alike to screen the birdie's nest,
And little fishes' caller rest :
The sun blinks kindly in the biel',
Where blythe I turn my spinnin' wheel.

On lofty aiks the cushats wail,
And echo cons the doolfu' tale;
The lintwhites in the hazel braes,
Delighted, rival ither's lays :                    20
The craik amang the claver hay,
The paitrick whirrin' o'er the ley,
The swallow jinkin' round my shiel,
Amuse me at my spinnin' wheel.

Wi' sma' to sell, and less to buy,
Aboon distress, below envy,
O wha wad leave this humble state,
For a' the pride of a' the great?
Amid their flaring, idle toys,
Amid their cumbrous, dinsome joys,                 30
Can they the peace and pleasure feel
Of Bessy at her spinnin' wheel?

———◆◆———

## I HAE A WIFE.

I HAE a wife o' my ain,
   I'll partake wi' naebody;
I'll tak cuckold frae nane,
   I'll gie cuckold to naebody.

I hae a penny to spend,
   There—thanks to naebody;
I hae naething to lend,
   I'll borrow frae naebody.

I am naebody's lord,
   I'll be slave to naebody;                    10
I hae a guid braid sword,
   I'll tak dunts frae naebody.

I'll be merry and free,
   I'll be sad for naebody;
Naebody cares for me,
   I care for naebody.

## MY WIFE'S A WINSOME WEE THING.

SHE is a winsome wee thing,
She is a handsome wee thing,
She is a bonnie wee thing,
    This sweet wee wife o' mine.

I never saw a fairer,
I never lo'ed a dearer,
And neist my heart I'll wear her,
    For fear my jewel tine.

She is a winsome wee thing,
She is a handsome wee thing,      10
She is a bonnie wee thing,
    This sweet wee wife o' mine.

The warld's wrack, we share o't,
The warstle and the care o't ;
Wi' her I'll blythely bear it,
    And think my lot divine.

---

## THE LASS O' BALLOCHMYLE.

'TWAS even—the dewy fields were green,
    On every blade the pearls hang ;
The Zephyrs wanton'd round the bean,
    And bore its fragrant sweets alang :
In every glen the Mavis sang,
    All nature listening seem'd the while :
Except where green-wood echoes rang,
    Amang the braes o' Ballochmyle.

With careless step I onward stray'd,
    My heart rejoiced in nature's joy,    10
When musing in a lonely glade,
    A maiden fair I chanced to spy ;

Her look was like the morning's eye,
　　Her hair like nature's vernal smile ;
Perfection whisper'd, passing by,
　　Behold the lass o' Ballochmyle !

Fair is the morn in flowery May,
　　And sweet is night in Autumn mild,
When roving thro' the garden gay,
　　Or wandering in the lonely wild :          20
But Woman, Nature's darling child !
　　There all her charms she does compile ;
Ev'n there her other works are foil'd
　　By the bonnie lass o' Ballochmyle.

O had she been a country maid,
　　And I the happy country swain,
Tho' shelter'd in the lowest shed
　　That ever rose on Scotland's plain !
Thro' weary winter's wind and rain,
　　With joy, with rapture, I would toil ;          30
And nightly to my bosom strain
　　The bonnie lass o' Ballochmyle.

Then pride might climb the slippery steep,
　　Where fame and honours lofty shine ;
And thirst of gold might tempt the deep,
　　Or downward seek the Indian mine :
Give me the cot below the pine,
　　To tend the flocks or till the soil,
And every day have joys divine,
　　With the bonnie lass o' Ballochmyle.          40

———•———

## BUT LATELY SEEN.

But lately seen in gladsome green
　　The woods rejoiced the day,
Thro' gentle showers the laughing flowers
　　In double pride were gay :

But now our joys are fled,
  On winter blasts awa!
Yet maiden May, in rich array,
  Again shall bring them a'.

But my white pow, nae kindly thowe
  Shall melt the snaws of age;        10
My trunk of eild, but buss or bield,
  Sinks in time's wintry rage.
Oh, age has weary days,
  And nights o' sleepless pain!
Thou golden time o' youthfu' prime,
  Why com'st thou not again?

## FAREWELL, THOU STREAM.

FAREWELL, thou stream that winding flows
  Around Eliza's dwelling!
O Mem'ry! spare the cruel throes
  Within my bosom swelling:
Condemn'd to drag a hopeless chain,
  And yet in secret languish,
To feel a fire in ev'ry vein,
  Nor dare disclose my anguish.

Love's veriest wretch, unseen, unknown,
  I fain my griefs would cover:        10
The bursting sigh, th' unweeting groan,
  Betray the hapless lover.
I know thou doom'st me to despair,
  Nor wilt nor canst relieve me;
But oh, Eliza, hear one prayer,—
  For pity's sake forgive me!

The music of thy voice I heard,
  Nor wist while it enslav'd me;
I saw thine eyes, yet nothing fear'd,
  Till fears no more had sav'd me:        20

Th' unwary sailor thus aghast,
    The wheeling torrent viewing,
'Mid circling horrors sinks at last
    In overwhelming ruin.

---

## LASSIE WI' THE LINT-WHITE LOCKS.

LASSIE wi' the lint-white locks,
    Bonnie lassie, artless lassie,
Wilt thou wi' me tent the flocks?
    Wilt thou be my dearie O?

Now nature cleeds the flowery lea,
And a' is young and sweet like thee;
O wilt thou share its joys wi' me,
    And say thou'lt be my dearie O?

The primrose bank, the wimpling burn,
The cuckoo on the milk-white thorn,          10
The wanton lambs at early morn
    Shall welcome thee, my dearie O.

And when the welcome simmer-shower
Has cheer'd ilk drooping little flower,
We'll to the breathing woodbine bower
    At sultry noon, my dearie O.

When Cynthia lights, wi' silver ray,
The weary shearer's hameward way,
Thro' yellow waving fields we'll stray,
    And talk o' love, my dearie O.          20

And when the howling wintry blast
Disturbs my lassie's midnight rest;
Enclaspèd to my faithfu' breast,
    I'll comfort thee, my dearie O.

## WILT THOU BE MY DEARIE?

WILT thou be my dearie?
When sorrow wrings thy gentle heart,
Wilt thou let me cheer thee?
By the treasure of my soul,
That's the love I bear thee!
I swear and vow that only thou
Shalt ever be my dearie—
Only thou, I swear and vow,
Shalt ever be my dearie.

Lassie, say thou lo'es me;                                    10
Or if thou wilt na be my ain,
Say na thou'lt refuse me:
If it winna, canna be,
Thou for thine may choose me,
Let me, lassie, quickly die,
Trusting that thou lo'es me—
Lassie, let me quickly die,
Trusting that thou lo'es me.

———•———

## HUSBAND, HUSBAND, CEASE YOUR STRIFE

HUSBAND, husband, cease your strife,
    Nor longer idly rave, sir;
Tho' I am your wedded wife,
    Yet I am not your slave, sir.

'One of two must still obey,
    Nancy, Nancy;
Is it man or woman, say,
    My spouse Nancy?'

If 'tis still the lordly word,
    Service and obedience;                                   10
I'll desert my sov'reign lord,
    And so good-bye allegiance!

'Sad shall I be, so bereft,
  Nancy, Nancy!
Yet I'll try to make a shift,
  My spouse Nancy.'

My poor heart then break it must,
  My last hour I'm near it:
When you lay me in the dust,
  Think how you will bear it.                    20

'I will hope and trust in Heaven,
  Nancy, Nancy;
Strength to bear it will be given,
  My spouse Nancy.'

Well, sir, from the silent dead
  Still I'll try to daunt you;
Ever round your midnight bed
  Horrid sprites shall haunt you.

'I'll wed another, like my dear
  Nancy, Nancy;                                  30
Then all hell will fly for fear,
  My spouse Nancy.'

———••———

## THINE AM I.

THINE am I, my faithful fair,
  Thine, my lovely Nancy;
Every pulse along my veins,
  Every roving fancy.

To thy bosom lay my heart,
  There to throb and languish:
Tho' despair had wrung its core,
  That would heal its anguish.

Take away these rosy lips,
    Rich with balmy treasure!                    10
Turn away thine eyes of love,
    Lest I die with pleasure!

What is life when wanting love?
    Night without a morning!
Love's the cloudless summer sun,
    Nature gay adorning.

------◆◆------

## ON THE SEAS AND FAR AWAY.

How can my poor heart be glad,
When absent from my Sailor lad?
How can I the thought forego,
He's on the seas to meet the foe?
Let me wander, let me rove,
Still my heart is with my love;
Nightly dreams and thoughts by day
Are with him that's far away.

    On the seas and far away,
    On stormy seas and far away;              10
    Nightly dreams and thoughts by day
    Are aye with him that's far away.

When in summer's noon I faint,
As weary flocks around me pant,
Haply in this scorching sun
My Sailor's thund'ring at his gun:
Bullets, spare my only joy!
Bullets, spare my darling boy!
Fate, do with me what you may,
Spare but him that's far away!                20

At the starless midnight hour,
When winter rules with boundless power;
As the storms the forest tear,
And thunders rend the howling air,

Listening to the doubling roar,
Surging on the rocky shore,
All I can—I weep and pray,
For his weal that's far away.

Peace, thy olive wand extend,
And bid wild War his ravage end,                    30
Man with brother man to meet,
And as a brother kindly greet:
Then may heaven with prosp'rous gales
Fill my Sailor's welcome sails,
To my arms their charge convey,
My dear lad that's far away.

———◆◆———

## BONNIE ANN.

YE gallants bright, I rede you right,
  Beware o' bonnie Ann:
Her comely face sae fu' o' grace,
  Your heart she will trepan.
Her een sae bright, like stars by night,
  Her skin sae like the swan;
Sae jimply laced her genty waist,
  That sweetly ye might span.

Youth, grace, and love, attendant move,
  And pleasure leads the van;                    10
In a' their charms, and conquering arms,
  They wait on bonnie Ann.
The captive bands may chain the hands,
  But love enslaves the man:
Ye gallants braw, I rede you a',
  Beware o' bonnie Ann.

———◆◆———

## MY PEGGY'S FACE.

My Peggy's face, my Peggy's form,
The frost of hermit age might warm ;
My Peggy's worth, my Peggy's mind.
Might charm the first of human kind.
I love my Peggy's angel air,
Her face so truly, heavenly fair,
Her native grace so void of art ;
But I adore my Peggy's heart.

The lily's hue, the rose's dye,
The kindling lustre of an eye ;                    10
Who but owns their magic sway,
Who but knows they all decay !
The tender thrill, the pitying tear,
The generous purpose, nobly dear,
The gentle look that rage disarms.
These are all immortal charms.

## THO' CRUEL FATE.

Tho' cruel fate should bid us part,
    Wide as the pole and line ;
Her dear idea round my heart
    Should tenderly entwine.

Tho' mountains rise and deserts howl,
    And oceans roar between ;
Yet, dearer than my deathless soul,
    I still would love my Jean.

# I DREAM'D I LAY WHERE FLOWERS WERE SPRINGING.

I DREAM'D I lay where flowers were springing
  Gaily in the sunny beam;
List'ning to the wild birds singing,
  By a falling crystal stream:
Straight the sky grew black and daring;
  Thro' the woods the whirlwinds rave;
Trees with agèd arms were warring,
  O'er the swelling drumlie wave.

Such was my life's deceitful morning,
  Such the pleasures I enjoy'd;                    10
But lang or noon, loud tempests storming
  A' my flowery bliss destroy'd.
Tho' fickle fortune has deceiv'd me,—
  She promised fair, and perform'd but ill;
Of mony a joy and hope bereav'd me,—
  I bear a heart shall support me still.

---

# HAD I A CAVE.

HAD I a cave on some wild distant shore,
Where the winds howl to the waves' dashing roar;
  There would I weep my woes,
  There seek my lost repose,
  Till grief my eyes should close,
    Ne'er to wake more.

Falsest of womankind, canst thou declare
All thy fond plighted vows—fleeting as air?
  To thy new lover hie,
  Laugh o'er thy perjury,                          10
  Then in thy bosom try
    What peace is there!

# WHA IS THAT AT MY BOWER DOOR?

WHA is that at my bower door?
O wha is it but Findlay?
Then gae your gate, ye'se nae be here!
Indeed maun I, quo' Findlay.
What mak ye sae like a thief?
O come and see, quo' Findlay;
Before the morn ye'll work mischief;
Indeed will I, quo' Findlay.

Gif I rise and let you in;
Let me in, quo' Findlay;                         10
Ye'll keep me waukin wi' your din;
Indeed will I, quo' Findlay.
In my bower if ye should stay;
Let me stay, quo' Findlay;
I fear ye'll bide till break o' day;
Indeed will I, quo' Findlay.

Here this night if ye remain;
I'll remain, quo' Findlay;
I dread ye'll learn the gate again;
Indeed will I, quo' Findlay.                      20
What may pass within this bower—
Let it pass, quo' Findlay;
Ye maun conceal till your last hour;
Indeed will I, quo' Findlay.

---

## THE BLINK O' MARY'S EE.

Now bank an' brae are claith'd in green,
An' scatter'd cowslips sweetly spring,
By Girvan's fairy haunted stream
The birdies flit on wanton wing.
To Cassillis' banks when e'ening fa's,
There wi' my Mary let me flee,
There catch her ilka glance o' love,
The bonnie blink o' Mary's ee!

The chield wha boasts o' warld's wealth,
  Is aften laird o' meikle care ;         10
But Mary she is a' my ain,
  Ah, fortune canna gie me mair !
Then let me range by Cassillis' banks
  Wi' her the lassie dear to me,
And catch her ilka glance o' love,
  The bonnie blink o' Mary's ee !

---

## OUT OVER THE FORTH.

Out over the Forth I look to the north,
  But what is the north and its Highlands to me
The south nor the east gie ease to my breast,
  The far foreign land, or the wild rolling sea.

But I look to the west, when I gae to rest,
  That happy my dreams and my slumbers may be ;
For far in the west lives he I lo'e best,
  The lad that is dear to my babie and me.

---

## PHILLIS THE FAIR.

While larks with little wing
  Fann'd the pure air,
Tasting the breathing spring,
  Forth I did fare :
Gay the sun's golden eye
Peep'd o'er the mountains high ;
Such thy morn ! did I cry,
  Phillis the fair.

In each bird's careless song
  Glad did I share ;        10
While yon wild flowers among,
  Chance led me there :

Sweet to the opening day,
Rosebuds bent the dewy spray;
Such thy bloom! did I say,
    Phillis the fair.

Down in a shady walk,
    Doves cooing were,
I mark'd the cruel hawk
    Caught in a snare:              20
So kind may Fortune be,
Such make his destiny,
He who would injure thee,
    Phillis the fair.

## BY ALLAN STREAM.

By Allan stream I chanced to rove,
    While Phœbus sank behind Benledi;
The winds were whispering thro' the grove,
    The yellow corn was waving ready:
I listen'd to a lover's sang,
    And thought on youthfu' pleasures mony;
And aye the wildwood echoes rang—
    O, dearly do I love thee, Annie!

O, happy be the woodbine bower,
    Nae nightly bogle mak it eerie;        10
Nor ever sorrow stain the hour,
    The place and time I met my dearie!
Her head upon my throbbing breast,
    She, sinking, said 'I'm thine for ever!'
While mony a kiss the seal imprest,
    The sacred vow, we ne'er should sever.

The haunt o' spring's the primrose brae,
    The simmer joys the flocks to follow;
How cheery thro' her shortening day
    Is autumn, in her weeds o' yellow!       20

But can they melt the glowing heart,
  Or chain the soul in speechless pleasure,
Or thro' each nerve the rapture dart,
  Like meeting her, our bosom's treasure?

————••————

# A MOTHER'S LAMENT FOR THE DEATH OF HER SON.

FATE gave the word, the arrow sped,
  And pierced my darling's heart;
And with him all the joys are fled
  Life can to me impart!
By cruel hands the sapling drops,
  In dust dishonour'd laid:
So fell the pride of all my hopes,
  My age's future shade.

The mother-linnet in the brake
  Bewails her ravish'd young;
So I, for my lost darling's sake,      10
  Lament the live-day long.
Death, oft I've fear'd thy fatal blow;
  Now, fond, I bare my breast;
O, do thou kindly lay me low
  With him I love, at rest!

————••————

# BONNIE LESLEY.

O SAW ye bonnie Lesley
  As she gaed o'er the border?
She's gane, like Alexander,
  To spread her conquests farther.

To see her is to love her,
  And love but her for ever;
For Nature made her what she is,
  And never made anither!

Thou art a queen, fair Lesley,
  Thy subjects we, before thee:          10
Thou art divine, fair Lesley,
  The hearts o' men adore thee.

The Deil he could na scaith thee,
  Or aught that wad belang thee;
He'd look into thy bonnie face,
  And say, 'I canna wrang thee.'

The Powers aboon will tent thee;
  Misfortune sha'na steer thee;
Thou'rt like themselves sae lovely,
  That ill they'll ne'er let near thee.   20

Return again, fair Lesley,
  Return to Caledonie!
That we may brag we hae a lass
  There's nane again sae bonnie.

---◆◆---

## AMANG THE TREES.

AMANG the trees where humming bees
  At buds and flowers were hinging O,
Auld Caledon drew out her drone,
  And to her pipe was singing O:
'Twas Pibroch, Sang, Strathspey, or Reels,
  She dirl'd them aff fu' clearly, O,
When there cam a yell o' foreign squeals,
  That dang her tapsalteerie O.

Their capon craws and queer ha ha's,
  They made our lugs grow eerie O;          10
The hungry bike did scrape and fyke
  Till we were wae and wearie O:
But a royal ghaist, wha ance was cas'd,
  A prisoner aughteen year awa,
He fir'd a fiddler in the north
  That dang them tapsalteerie O.

# WHEN FIRST I CAME TO STEWART KYLE.

WHEN first I came to Stewart Kyle,
  My mind it was na steady ;
Where'er I gaed, where'er I rade,
  A mistress still I had aye :
But when I came roun' by Mauchline town,
  Not dreadin' ony body,
My heart was caught before I thought,
  And by a Mauchline lady.

\*   \*   \*   \*   \*   \*   \*   \*

# ON SENSIBILITY.

SENSIBILITY, how charming,
  Thou, my friend, canst truly tell ;
But distress, with horrors arming,
  Thou hast also known too well !

Fairest flower, behold the lily,
  Blooming in the sunny ray :
Let the blast sweep o'er the valley,
  See it prostrate in the clay.

Hear the wood-lark charm the forest,
  Telling o'er his little joys ;
Hapless bird ! a prey the surest
  To each pirate of the skies.

        10

Dearly bought the hidden treasure
  Finer feelings can bestow ;
Chords that vibrate sweetest pleasure
  Thrill the deepest notes of woe.

## MONTGOMERIE'S PEGGY.

ALTHO' my bed were in yon muir,
  Amang the heather, in my plaidie,
Yet happy, happy would I be,
  Had I my dear Montgomerie's Peggy.

When o'er the hill beat surly storms,
  And winter nights were dark and rainy,
I'd seek some dell, and in my arms
  I'd shelter dear Montgomerie's Peggy.

Were I a Baron proud and high,
  And horse and servants waiting ready,          10
Then a' 'twad gie o' joy to me,
  The sharin't wi' Montgomerie's Peggy.

\*    \*    \*    \*    \*    \*    \*    \*

## ON A BANK OF FLOWERS.

ON a bank of flowers, in a summer day,
  For summer lightly drest,
The youthful blooming Nelly lay,
  With love and sleep opprest;

When Willie, wand'ring thro' the wood,
Who for her favour oft had sued;
He gaz'd, he wish'd, he fear'd, he blush'd,
  And trembled where he stood.

Her closed eyes, like weapons sheath'd,
  Were seal'd in soft repose;                    10
Her lips, still as she fragrant breath'd,
  It richer dyed the rose.

The springing lilies sweetly prest,
Wild-wanton kiss'd her rival breast;
He gaz'd, he wish'd, he fear'd, he blush'd,
  His bosom ill at rest.

Her robes, light waving in the breeze,
　　Her tender limbs embrace!
Her lovely form, her native ease,
　　All harmony and grace!　　　　　　　20

Tumultuous tides his pulses roll,
A faltering ardent kiss he stole;
He gaz'd, he wish'd, he fear'd, he blush'd,
　　And sigh'd his very soul.

As flies the partridge from the brake
　　On fear-inspirèd wings;
So Nelly, starting, half awake,
　　Away affrighted springs:

But Willie follow'd—as he should,
He overtook her in the wood:　　　　　30
He vow'd, he pray'd, he found the maid
　　Forgiving all, and good.

———◆◆———

## O RAGING FORTUNE'S WITHERING BLAST.

O RAGING fortune's withering blast
　　Has laid my leaf full low!
O raging fortune's withering blast
　　Has laid my leaf full low!

My stem was fair, my bud was green,
　　My blossom sweet did blow;
The dew fell fresh, the sun rose mild,
　　And made my branches grow;

But luckless fortune's northern storms
　　Laid a' my blossoms low,　　　　　　10
But luckless fortune's northern storms
　　Laid a' my blossoms low!

## EVAN BANKS.

Slow spreads the gloom my soul desires,
The sun from India's shore retires:
To Evan banks with temp'rate ray,
Home of my youth, he leads the day.

Oh banks to me for ever dear!
Oh stream, whose murmurs still I hear!
All, all my hopes of bliss reside
Where Evan mingles with the Clyde.

And she, in simple beauty drest,
Whose image lives within my breast;                    10
Who trembling heard my parting sigh,
And long pursued me with her eye:

Does she, with heart unchang'd as mine,
Oft in the vocal bowers recline?
Or, where yon grot o'erhangs the tide,
Muse while the Evan seeks the Clyde?

Ye lofty banks that Evan bound,
Ye lavish woods that wave around,
And o'er the stream your shadows throw,
Which sweetly winds so far below;                      20

What secret charm to mem'ry brings
All that on Evan's border springs!
Sweet banks! ye bloom by Mary's side:
Blest stream! she views thee haste to Clyde.

Can all the wealth of India's coast
Atone for years in absence lost!
Return, ye moments of delight,
With richer treasures bless my sight!

Swift from this desert let me part,
And fly to meet a kindred heart!                       30
No more may aught my steps divide
From that dear stream which flows to Clyde!

## PRAYER FOR MARY.

Powers celestial, whose protection
　　Ever guards the virtuous fair,
While in distant climes I wander,
　　Let my Mary be your care:
Let her form sae fair and faultless,
　　Fair and faultless as your own:
Let my Mary's kindred spirit
　　Draw your choicest influence down.

Make the gales you waft around her
　　Soft and peaceful as her breast;　　　10
Breathing in the breeze that fans her,
　　Soothe her bosom into rest:
Guardian angels, O protect her,
　　When in distant lands I roam;
To realms unknown while fate exiles me,
　　Make her bosom still my home.

## YOUNG PEGGY.

Young Peggy blooms our bonniest lass,
　　Her blush is like the morning,
The rosy dawn the springing grass
　　With early gems adorning.
Her eyes outshine the radiant beams
　　That gild the passing shower,
And glitter o'er the crystal streams,
　　And cheer each fresh'ning flower.

Her lips more than the cherries bright,
　　A richer dye has graced them;　　　10
They charm th' admiring gazer's sight,
　　And sweetly tempt to taste them.
Her smile is as the ev'ning mild,
　　When feather'd pairs are courting,
And little lambkins wanton wild,
　　In playful bands disporting.

Were Fortune lovely Peggy's foe,
  Such sweetness would relent her,
As blooming Spring unbends the brow
  Of surly, savage Winter.       20
Detraction's eye no aim can gain
  Her winning powers to lessen ;
And fretful envy grins in vain,
  The poison'd tooth to fasten.

Ye Pow'rs of Honour, Love, and Truth,
  From ev'ry ill defend her ;
Inspire the highly favour'd youth
  The destinies intend her ;
Still fan the sweet connubial flame
  Responsive in each bosom ;     30
And bless the dear parental name
  With many a filial blossom.

---

## ON CESSNOCK BANKS.

On Cessnock banks a lassie dwells ;
  Could I describe her shape and mien ;
Our lasses a' she far excels,
  An' she has twa sparkling rogueish een.

She's sweeter than the morning dawn
  When rising Phœbus first is seen,
And dew-drops twinkle o'er the lawn ;
  An' she has twa sparkling rogueish een.

She's stately like yon youthful ash
  That grows the cowslip braes between,   10
And drinks the stream with vigour fresh ;
  An' she has twa sparkling rogueish een.

She's spotless like the flow'ring thorn
  With flow'rs so white and leaves so green,
When purest in the dewy morn ;
  An' she has twa sparkling rogueish een.

Her looks are like the vernal May,
　　When ev'ning Phœbus shines serene,
While birds rejoice on every spray ;
　　An' she has twa sparkling rogueish een.　　20

Her hair is like the curling mist
　　That climbs the mountain-sides at e'en,
When flow'r-reviving rains are past ;
　　An' she has twa sparkling rogueish een.

Her forehead 's like the show'ry bow,
　　When gleaming sunbeams intervene
And gild the distant mountain's brow ;
　　An' she has twa sparkling rogueish een.

Her cheeks are like yon crimson gem,
　　The pride of all the flowery scene,　　30
Just opening on its thorny stem ;
　　An' she has twa sparkling rogueish een.

Her bosom 's like the nightly snow
　　When pale the morning rises keen,
While hid the murmuring streamlets flow :
　　An' she has twa sparkling rogueish een.

Her lips are like yon cherries ripe,
　　That sunny walls from Boreas screen ;
They tempt the taste and charm the sight ;
　　An' she has twa sparkling rogueish een.　　40

Her teeth are like a flock of sheep,
　　With fleeces newly washen clean,
That slowly mount the rising steep :
　　An' she has twa sparkling rogueish een.

Her breath is like the fragrant breeze
　　That gently stirs the blossom'd bean,
When Phœbus sinks behind the seas ;
　　An' she has twa sparkling rogueish een.

Her voice is like the ev'ning thrush
   That sings on Cessnock banks unseen,     50
While his mate sits nestling in the bush;
   An' she has twa sparkling rogueish een.

But it's not her air, her form, her face,
   Tho' matching beauty's fabled queen;
'Tis the mind that shines in ev'ry grace,
   An' chiefly in her rogueish een.

---

## THE DEAN OF FACULTY.

DIRE was the hate at old Harlaw
   That Scot to Scot did carry;
And dire the discord Langside saw
   For beauteous hapless Mary:
But Scot with Scot ne'er met so hot,
   Or were more in fury seen, Sir,
Than 'twixt Hal and Bob for the famous job—
   Who should be Faculty's Dean, Sir.

This Hal for genius, wit, and lore,
   Among the first was number'd;     10
But pious Bob, 'mid learning's store,
   Commandment the tenth remember'd.
Yet simple Bob the victory got,
   And won his heart's desire;
Which shews that heaven can boil the pot,
   Tho' the devil piss in the fire.

Squire Hal besides had, in this case,
   Pretensions rather brassy,
For talents to deserve a place
   Are qualifications saucy;     20
So their worships of the Faculty,
   Quite sick of merit's rudeness,
Chose one who should owe it all, d'ye see,
   To their gratis grace and goodness.

As once on Pisgah purg'd was the sight
　　Of a son of Circumcision,
So may be, on this Pisgah height,
　　Bob's purblind mental vision;
Nay, Bobby's mouth may be open'd yet,
　　Till for eloquence you hail him,　　　　30
And swear he has the Angel met
　　That met the Ass of Balaam.

In your heretic sins may ye live and die,
　　Ye heretic eight and thirty!
But accept, ye sublime Majority,
　　My congratulations hearty.
With your Honours and a certain King,
　　In your servants this is striking—
The more incapacity they bring,
　　The more they're to your liking.　　　40

———••———

## COULD AUGHT OF SONG.

COULD aught of song declare my pains,
　　Could artful numbers move thee,
The Muse should tell, in labour'd strains,
　　O Mary, how I love thee!

They who but feign a wounded heart
　　May teach the lyre to languish;
But what avails the pride of art,
　　When wastes the soul with anguish?

Then let the sudden bursting sigh
　　The heart-felt pang discover;　　　　10
And in the keen, yet tender eye,
　　O read th' imploring lover!

For well I know thy gentle mind
　　Disdains art's gay disguising;
Beyond what fancy e'er refin'd,
　　The voice of nature prizing.

## O LEAVE NOVELS.

O LEAVE novéls, ye Mauchline belles,
  Ye're safer at your spinning wheel;
Such witching books are baited hooks
  For rakish rooks, like Rob Mossgiel.

Your fine Tom Jones and Grandisons,
  They make your youthful fancies reel;
They heat your brains, and fire your veins,
  And then you're prey for Rob Mossgiel.

Beware a tongue that's smoothly hung;
  A heart that warmly seems to feel;          10
That feeling heart but acts a part,
  'Tis rakish art in Rob Mossgiel.

The frank address, the soft caress,
  Are worse than poison'd darts of steel;
The frank address, and politesse,
  Are all finesse in Rob Mossgiel.

## ADDRESS TO GENERAL DUMOURIER.

You're welcome to Despots, Dumourier;
You're welcome to Despots, Dumourier;
How does Dampière do?
Aye, and Bournonville too?
Why did they not come along with you, Dumourier?

I will fight France with you, Dumourier;
I will fight France with you, Dumourier;
I will fight France with you,
I will take my chance with you;
By my soul I'll dance a dance with you, Dumourier.  10

Then let us fight about, Dumourier;
Then let us fight about, Dumourier;
Then let us fight about,
Till freedom's spark is out,
Then we'll be damn'd no doubt, Dumourier.

———◆◆———

## SWEETEST MAY.

SWEETEST May, let Love incline thee;
Take a heart which he designs thee;
As thy constant slave regard it;
For its faith and truth reward it.

Proof to shot of birth or money,
Not the wealthy, but the bonnie;
Not high-born, but noble-minded,
In love's silken band can bind it!

———◆◆———

## ONE NIGHT AS I DID WANDER.

ONE night as I did wander,
　　When corn begins to shoot,
I sat me down to ponder,
　　Upon an auld tree root:

Auld Ayr ran by before me,
　　And bicker'd to the seas;
A cushat crooded o'er me
　　That echoed thro' the braes.

\*　　\*　　\*　　\*　　\*　　\*:　　\*

## THE WINTER IT IS PAST.

THE winter it is past, and the simmer comes at last,
   And the small birds sing on every tree;
Now every thing is glad, while I am very sad,
   Since my true love is parted from me.

The rose upon the brier, by the waters running clear,
   May have charms for the linnet or the bee;
Their little loves are blest, and their little hearts at rest,
   But my true love is parted from me.

## FRAGMENT.

HER flowing locks, the raven's wing,
   Adown her neck and bosom hing;
How sweet unto that breast to cling,
   And round that neck entwine her!

Her lips are roses wet wi' dew!
O, what a feast her bonnie mou!
Her cheeks a mair celestial hue,
   A crimson still diviner!

## THE CHEVALIER'S LAMENT.

THE small birds rejoice in the green leaves returning,
   The murmuring streamlet winds clear thro' the vale;
The hawthorn trees blow in the dews of the morning,
   And wild scatter'd cowslips bedeck the green dale:

But what can give pleasure, or what can seem fair,
   While the lingering moments are number'd by care?
No flowers gaily springing, nor birds sweetly singing,
   Can soothe the sad bosom of joyless despair.

The deed that I dared could it merit their malice,
  A King and a Father to place on his throne?    10
His right are these hills, and his right are these valleys,
  Where the wild beasts find shelter, but I can find none.

But 'tis not my sufferings thus wretched, forlorn,
  My brave gallant friends, 'tis your ruin I mourn:
Your deeds prov'd so loyal in hot bloody trial,
  Alas! can I make you no sweeter return?

---

## THE BELLES OF MAUCHLINE.

In Mauchline there dwells six proper young Belles,
  The pride of the place and it's neighbourhood a';
Their carriage and dress, a stranger would guess,
  In Lon'on or Paris they'd gotten it a':

Miss Miller is fine, Miss Markland's divine,
  Miss Smith she has wit, and Miss Betty is braw:
There's beauty and fortune to get wi' Miss Morton,
  But Armour's the jewel for me o' them a'.

---

## THE TARBOLTON LASSES.

If ye gae up to yon hill-tap,
  Ye'll there see bonnie Peggy;
She kens her father is a laird,
  And she forsooth's a leddy.

There Sophy tight, a lassie bright,
  Besides a handsome fortune:
Wha canna win her in a night,
  Has little art in courting.

Gae down by Faile, and taste the ale,
    And tak a look o' Mysie;        10
She's dour and din, a deil within,
    But aiblins she may please ye.

If she be shy, her sister try,
    Ye'll maybe fancy Jenny,
If ye'll dispense wi' want o' sense—
    She kens hersel she's bonnie.

As ye gae up by yon hill-side,
    Speer in for bonnie Bessy;
She'll gi'e ye a beck, and bid ye light,
    And handsomely address ye.        20

There's few sae bonnie, nane sae gude,
    In a' King George' dominion;
If ye should doubt the truth o' this—
    It's Bessy's ain opinion!

## THE TARBOLTON LASSES.

In Tarbolton, ye ken, there are proper young men,
    And proper young lasses and a', man;
But ken ye the Ronalds that live in the Bennals,
    They carry the gree frae them a', man.

Their father's a laird, and weel he can spare't,
    Braid money to tocher them a', man;
To proper young men, he'll clink in the hand
    Gowd guineas a hunder or twa, man.

There's ane they ca' Jean, I'll warrant ye've seen
    As bonnie a lass or as braw, man;        10
But for sense and guid taste she'll vie wi' the best,
    And a conduct that beautifies a', man.

The charms o' the min', the langer they shine,
　　The mair admiration they draw, man ;
While peaches and cherries, and roses and lilies,
　　They fade and they wither awa, man.


If ye be for Miss Jean, tak this frae a frien',
　　A hint o' a rival or twa, man ;
The Laird o' Blackbyre wad gang through the fire,
　　If that wad entice her awa, man.                     20


The Laird o' Braehead has been on his speed,
　　For mair than a towmond or twa, man ;
The Laird o' the Ford will straught on a board,
　　If he canna get her at a', man.


Then Anna comes in, the pride o' her kin,
　　The boast of our bachelors a', man :
Sae sonsy and sweet, sae fully complete,
　　She steals our affections awa, man.


If I should detail the pick and the wale
　　O' lasses that live here awa, man,                   30
The fault wad be mine, if they didna shine,
　　The sweetest and best o' them a', man.


I lo'e her mysel, but darena weel tell,
　　My poverty keeps me in awe, man ;
For making o' rhymes, and working at times,
　　Does little or naething at a', man.


Yet I wadna choose to let her refuse,
　　Nor ha'e 't in her power to say na, man ;
For though I be poor, unnoticed, obscure,
　　My stomach's as proud as them a', man.              40


Though I canna ride in weel-booted pride,
　　And flee o'er the hills like a craw, man,
I can haud up my head wi' the best o' the breed,
　　Though fluttering ever so braw, man.

My coat and my vest, they are Scotch o' the best,
  O' pairs o' guid breeks I ha'e twa, man,
And stockings and pumps to put on my stumps,
  And ne'er a wrang steek in them a', man.

My sarks they are few, but five o' them new,
  Twal' hundred, as white as the snaw, man,       50
A ten-shillings hat, a Holland cravat;
  There are no mony poets sae braw, man.

I never had frien's, weel stockit in means,
  To leave me a hundred or twa, man;
Nae weel tochered aunts, to wait on their drants,
  And wish them in hell for it a', man.

I never was canny for hoarding o' money,
  Or claughtin't together at a', man,
I've little to spend, and naething to lend,       60
  But deevil a shilling I awe, man.

     *      *      *      *      *

---

## HERE'S A HEALTH TO THEM THAT'S AWA.

        Here's a health to them that's awa,
        Here's a health to them that's awa;
        And wha winna wish guid luck to our cause,
        May never guid luck be their fa'!
        It's guid to be merry and wise,
        It's guid to be honest and true,
        It's guid to support Caledonia's cause,
        And bide by the buff and the blue.

        Here's a health to them that's awa,
        Here's a health to them that's awa,       10
        Here's a health to Charlie the chief o' the clan,
        Altho' that his band be but sma'.
        May liberty meet wi' success!
        May prudence protect her frae evil!
        May tyrants and tyranny tine in the mist,
        And wander their way to the devil!

Here 's a health to them that 's awa,
Here 's a health to them that 's awa ;
Here 's a health to Tammie, the Norland laddie,
That lives at the lug o' the law !     20
Here 's freedom to him that wad read,
Here 's freedom to him that wad write !
There 's nane ever fear'd that the truth should be heard,
But they wham the truth wad indite.
Here 's a health to them that 's awa,
Here 's a health to them that 's awa,
Here 's Chieftain M'Leod, a Chieftain worth gowd,
Tho' bred among mountains o' snaw !

---

## I'M OWRE YOUNG TO MARRY YET.

I AM my mammie's ae bairn,
    Wi' unco folk I weary, Sir ;
And lying in a man's bed,
    I'm fley'd wad mak me eerie, Sir.

    I'm owre young, I'm owre young,
       I'm owre young to marry yet ;
    I'm owre young, 'twad be a sin
       To tak me frae my mammie yet.

My mammie coft me a new gown,
    The kirk maun hae the gracing o't ;     10
Were I to lie wi' you, kind Sir,
    I'm fear'd ye'd spoil the lacing o't.

Hallowmas is come and gane,
    The nights are lang in winter, Sir ;
And you an' I in ae bed,
    In troth I dare na venture, Sir.

Fu' loud and shrill the frosty wind
    Blaws thro' the leafless timmer, Sir ;
But if ye come this gate again,
    I'll aulder be gin simmer, Sir.     20

## DAMON AND SYLVIA.

Yon wand'ring rill, that marks the hill,
 And glances o'er the brae, Sir,
Slides by a bower where mony a flower
 Sheds fragrance on the day, Sir.

There Damon lay, with Sylvia gay :
 To love they thought nae crime, Sir ;
The wild-birds sang, the echoes rang,
 While Damon's heart beat time, Sir.

———+·———

## MY LADY'S GOWN THERE'S GAIRS UPON'T.

My lady's gown there's gairs upon't,
 And gowden flowers sae rare upon't;
But Jenny's jimps and jirkinet,
 My lord thinks muckle mair upon't.

My lord a-hunting he is gane,
But hounds or hawks wi' him are nane,
By Colin's cottage lies his game,
If Colin's Jenny be at hame.

My lady's white, my lady's red,
And kith and kin o' Cassillis' blude,        10
But her ten-pund lands o' tocher guid
Were a' the charms his lordship lo'ed.

Out o'er yon muir, out o'er yon moss,
Where gor-cocks thro' the heather pass,
There wons auld Colin's bonnie lass,
A lily in a wilderness.

Sae sweetly move her genty limbs,
Like music notes o' lover's hymns :
The diamond dew in her een sae blue,
Where laughing love sae wanton swims.        20

My lady's dink, my lady's drest,
The flower and fancy o' the west;
But the lassie that a man lo'es best,
O that's the lass to make him blest.

## O AYE MY WIFE SHE DANG ME.

O AYE my wife she dang me,
An' aft my wife did bang me;
If ye gie a woman a' her will,
Guid faith! she'll soon o'ergang ye.

On peace and rest my mind was bent,
And fool I was I married;
But never honest man's intent
As cursedly miscarried.

Some sa'r o' comfort still at last,
When a' thir days are done, man,                    10
My pains o' hell on earth are past,
I'm sure o' bliss aboon, man.

## THE BANKS OF NITH.

To thee, lov'd Nith, thy gladsome plains,
Where late wi' careless thought I rang'd,
Though prest wi' care and sunk in woe,
To thee I bring a heart unchang'd.

I love thee, Nith, thy banks and braes,
Tho' mem'ry there my bosom tear;
For there he rov'd that brake my heart,
Yet to that heart, ah, still how dear!

## BONNIE PEG.

As I came in by our gate end,
　　When day was waxin' weary,
O wha came tripping down the street,
　　But bonnie Peg, my dearie!

Her air sae sweet, and shape complete,
　　Wi' nae proportion wanting,
The Queen of Love did never move
　　Wi' motion mair enchanting.

Wi' linkèd hands, we took the sands
　　Adown yon winding river;　　　　　10
And, oh! that hour and broomy bower,
　　Can I forget it ever?

## O LAY THY LOOF IN MINE, LASS.

O LAY thy loof in mine, lass,
　　In mine, lass, in mine, lass,
And swear in thy white hand, lass,
　　That thou wilt be my ain.

A slave to Love's unbounded sway,
He aft has wrought me meikle wae;
But now he is my deadly fae,
　　Unless thou be my ain.

There's mony a lass has broke my rest,
That for a blink I hae lo'ed best;　　　10
But thou art Queen within my breast,
　　For ever to remain.

## O WHY THE DEUCE.

O why the deuce should I repine,
  And be an ill foreboder?
I'm twenty-three, and five feet nine—
  I'll go and be a sodger.

I gat some gear wi' meikle care,
  I held it weel thegither;
But now it's gane and something mair
  I'll go and be a sodger.

## POLLY STEWART.

O lovely Polly Stewart,
  O charming Polly Stewart,
There's ne'er a flower that blooms in May,
  That's half so fair as thou art.

The flower it blaws, it fades, it fa's,
  And art can ne'er renew it;
But worth and truth eternal youth
  Will gie to Polly Stewart.

May he, whase arms shall fauld thy charms,
  Possess a leal and true heart;          10
To him be given to ken the heaven
  He grasps in Polly Stewart.

## ROBIN SHURE IN HAIRST.

Robin shure in hairst,
  I shure wi' him ;
Fient a heuk had I,
  Yet I stack by him.

I gaed up to Dunse,
  To warp a wab o' plaiden ;
At his daddie's yett,
  Wha met me but Robin?

Was na Robin bauld,
  Tho' I was a cotter,                   10
Play'd me sick a trick
  And me the eller's dochter?

Robin promis'd me
  A' my winter vittle ;
Fient haet he had but three
  Goose feathers and a whittle.

## THE DEUK'S DANG O'ER MY DADDIE.

The bairns gat out wi' an unco shout,
  The deuk's dang o'er my daddie O !
The fient ma care, quo' the feirie auld wife,
  He was but a paidlin body O !
He paidles out, and he paidles in,
  An' he paidles late and early O ;
This seven lang years I hae lien by his side,
  An' he is but a fusionless carlie O.

O haud your tongue, my feirie auld wife,
  O haud your tongue now, Nansie, O :    10
I've seen the day, and sae hae ye,
  Ye wadna been sae donsie. O ;

I've seen the day ye butter'd my brose,
　　And cuddl'd me late and earlie, O ;
But downa do 's come o'er me now,
　　And, oh, I find it sairly, O !

———◆◆———

## MY HARRY WAS A GALLANT GAY.

My Harry was a gallant gay,
　　Fu' stately strade he on the plain !
But now he 's banish'd far away,
　　I'll never see him back again.

　　O for him back again !
　　　　O for him back again !
　　I wad gie a' Knockhaspie's land,
　　　　For Highland Harry back again.

When a' the lave gae to their bed,
　　I wander dowie up the glen ;　　　　　　　10
I sit me down and greet my fill,
　　And aye I wish him back again.

O were some villains hangit high,
　　And ilka body had their ain,
Then I might see the joyfu' sight,
　　My Highland Harry back again !

———◆◆———

## TIBBIE DUNBAR.

O WILT thou go wi' me, sweet Tibbie Dunbar ?
O wilt thou go wi' me, sweet Tibbie Dunbar ?
Wilt thou ride on a horse, or be drawn in a car,
Or walk by my side, O sweet Tibbie Dunbar ?
I care na thy daddie, his lands and his money,
I care na thy kin, sae high and sae lordly :
But say thou wilt hae me for better for waur,
And come in thy coatie, sweet Tibbie Dunbar.

## WEE WILLIE.

Wee Willie Gray, and his leather wallet;
Peel a willow-wand, to be him boots and jacket:
The rose upon the briar will be him trews and doublet,
The rose upon the briar will be him trews and doublet!
Wee Willie Gray, and his leather wallet;
Twice a lily flower will be him sark and cravat;
Feathers of a flee wad feather up his bonnet,
Feathers of a flee wad feather up his bonnet.

---

## CRAIGIE-BURN-WOOD.

Beyond thee, dearie, beyond thee, dearie,
   And O to be lying beyond thee!
O sweetly, soundly, weel may he sleep,
   That's laid in the bed beyond thee.

Sweet closes the evening on Craigie-burn-wood,
   And blythely awakens the morrow;
But the pride of the spring in the Craigie-burn-wood
   Can yield to me nothing but sorrow.

I see the spreading leaves and flowers,
   I hear the wild birds singing;      10
But pleasure they hae nane for me,
   While care my heart is wringing.

I canna tell, I maun na tell,
   I dare na for your anger;
But secret love will break my heart
   If I conceal it langer.

I see thee gracefu', straight and tall,
   I see thee sweet and bonnie;
But oh, what will my torments be,
   If thou refuse thy Johnnie!      20

To see thee in anither's arms,
  In love to lie and languish,
'Twad be my dead, that will be seen,
  My heart wad burst wi' anguish.

But, Jeanie, say thou wilt be mine,
  Say thou lo'es nane before me ;
An' a' my days o' life to come,
  I'll gratefully adore thee.

---

## HERE 'S HIS HEALTH IN WATER !

ALTHO' my back be at the wa',
  And tho' he be the fautor ;
Altho' my back be at the wa',
  Yet, here 's his health in water !
O ! wae gae by his wanton sides,
  Sae brawlie he could flatter ;
Till for his sake I'm slighted sair,
  And dree the kintra clatter.
But tho' my back be at the wa',
  And tho' he be the fautor ;      10
But tho' my back be at the wa',
  Yet, here 's his health in water !

---

## AS DOWN THE BURN THEY TOOK THEIR WAY.

As down the burn they took their way,
  And thro' the flowery dale ;
His cheek to hers he aft did lay,
  And love was aye the tale.

With 'Mary, when shall we return,
  Sic pleasure to renew ?'
Quoth Mary, 'Love, I like the burn,
  And aye shall follow you.'

## LADY ONLIE.

A' THE lads o' Thornie-bank,
  When they gae to the shore o' Bucky,
They'll step in an' tak' a pint
  Wi' Lady Onlie, honest Lucky!
    Ladie Onlie, honest Lucky,
      Brews good ale at shore o' Bucky;
    I wish her sale for her gude ale,
      The best on a' the shore o' Bucky.

Her house sae bien, her curch sae clean,
  I wat she is a dainty chucky;        10
And cheery blinks the ingle-gleed
  Of Lady Onlie, honest Lucky!
    Lady Onlie, honest Lucky,
      Brews gude ale at shore o' Bucky;
    I wish her sale for her gude ale,
      The best on a' the shore o' Bucky.

## AS I WAS A WANDERING.

As I was a wand'ring ae midsummer e'enin',
  The pipers and youngsters were making their game;
Amang them I spied my faithless fause lover,
  Which bled a' the wounds o' my dolour again.

Weel, since he has left me, may pleasure gae wi' him;
  I may be distress'd, but I winna complain;
I flatter my fancy I may get anither,
  My heart it shall never be broken for ane.

I could na get sleeping till dawin' for greetin',
  The tears trickled down like the hail and the rain;  10
Had I na got greetin', my heart wad a broken,
  For, oh! love forsaken 's a tormenting pain.

Altho' he has left me for greed o' the siller,
  I dinna envy him the gains he can win ;
I rather wad bear a' the lade o' my sorrow
  Than ever hae acted sae faithless to him.

Weel, since he has left me, may pleasure gae wi' him,
  I may be distress'd, but I winna complain :
I flatter my fancy I may get anither,
  My heart it shall never be broken for ane.    20

## BANNOCKS O' BARLEY.

BANNOCKS o' bear meal,
  Bannocks o' barley ;
Here's to the Highlandman's
  Bannocks o' barley.
Wha in a brulzie
  Will first cry a parley ?
Never the lads wi'
  The bannocks o' barley.

Bannocks o' bear meal,
  Bannocks o' barley ;    10
Here's to the lads wi'
  The bannocks o' barley ;
Wha in his wae-days
  Were loyal to Charlie ?
Wha but the lads wi'
  The bannocks o' barley.

## AWA, WHIGS.

AWA, Whigs, awa !
  Awa, Whigs, awa !
Ye're but a pack o' traitor louns,
  Ye'll do nae good at a'.

Our thrissles flourish'd fresh and fair,
  And bonnie bloom'd our roses;
But Whigs cam' like a frost in June,
  And wither'd a' our posies.

Our ancient crown's fa'en in the dust—
  Deil blin' them wi' the stoure o't;    10
And write their names in his black beuk,
  Wha gae the Whigs the power o't.

Our sad decay in Church and State
  Surpasses my descriving;
The Whigs came o'er us for a curse,
  And we hae done with thriving.

Grim vengeance lang has ta'en a nap,
  But we may see him wauken;
Gude help the day when royal heads
  Are hunted like a maukin!    20

Awa, Whigs, awa!
  Awa, Whigs, awa!
Ye're but a pack o' traitor louns,
  Ye'll do nae gude at a'.

---

## PEG-A-RAMSEY.

CAULD is the e'enin' blast
  O' Boreas o'er the pool,
And dawin' it is dreary
  When birks are bare at Yuïe.

O bitter blaws the e'enin' blast
  When bitter bites the frost,
And in the mirk and dreary drift
  The hills and glens are lost.

Ne'er sae murky blew the night
  That drifted o'er the hill,
But bonnie Peg-a-Ramsey
  Gat grist to her mill.

10

———••———

## COME BOAT ME O'ER TO CHARLIE.

Come boat me o'er, come row me o'er,
  Come boat me o'er to Charlie;
I'll gie John Ross another bawbee,
  To boat me o'er to Charlie.

We'll o'er the water and o'er the sea,
  We'll o'er the water to Charlie;
Come weal, come woe, we'll gather and go,
  And live or die wi' Charlie.

I lo'e weel my Charlie's name,
  Tho' some there be abhor him:
But O, to see auld Nick gaun hame,
  And Charlie's faes before him!

10

I swear and vow by moon and stars,
  And sun that shines so clearly,
If I had twenty thousand lives,
  I'd die as aft for Charlie.

We'll o'er the water and o'er the sea,
  We'll o'er the water to Charlie;
Come weal, come woe, we'll gather and go,
  And live or die with Charlie!

20

———••———

## SAE FAIR HER HAIR.

BRAW, braw lads of Gala Water!
O braw lads of Gala Water!
I'll kilt my coats aboon my knee,
 And follow my love through the water.

Sae fair her hair, sae brent her brow,
 Sae bonnie blue her een, my dearie;
Sae white her teeth, sae sweet her mou',
 The mair I kiss she's aye my dearie.

O'er yon bank and o'er yon brae,
 O'er yon moss amang the heather;     10
I'll kilt my coats aboon my knee,
 And follow my love through the water.

Down amang the broom, the broom,
 Down amang the broom, my dearie,
The lassie lost a silken snood,
 That cost her mony a blirt and blear ee.

Braw, braw lads of Gala Water!
 O braw lads of Gala Water:
I'll kilt my coats aboon my knee,
 And follow my love through the water.    20

## COMING THROUGH THE RYE.

COMING through the rye, poor body,
 Coming through the rye,
She draiglet a' her petticoatie,
 Coming through the rye.

Gin a body meet a body
Coming through the rye ;
Gin a body kiss a body,
Need a body cry ?

Gin a body meet a body
Coming through the glen ;
Gin a body kiss a body,
Need the world ken ?                                    10

Jenny 's a' wat, poor body ;
Jenny 's seldom dry ;
She draiglet a' her petticoatie,
Coming through the rye.

## THE LASS OF ECCLEFECHAN.

GAT ye me, O gat ye me,
O gat ye me wi' naething ?
Rock and reel, and spinnin' wheel,
A mickle quarter basin.
Bye attour, my gutcher has
A heigh house and a laigh ane,
A' forbye, my bonnie sel',
The toss of Ecclefechan.

O haud your tongue now, Luckie Laing,
O haud your tongue and jauner ;                        10
I held the gate till you I met,
Syne I began to wander :
I tint my whistle and my sang,
I tint my peace and pleasure ;
But your green graff, now, Luckie Laing,
Wad airt me to my treasure.

## THE SLAVE'S LAMENT.

IT was in sweet Senegal that my foes did me enthral,
  For the lands of Virginia O ;
Torn from that lovely shore, I must never see it more,
  And alas I am weary, weary O !

All on that charming coast is no bitter snow or frost,
  Like the lands of Virginia O ;
There streams for ever flow, and there flowers for ever blow,
  And alas I am weary, weary O !

The burden I must bear, while the cruel scourge I fear,
  In the lands of Virginia O ;                                    10
And I think on friends most dear, with the bitter, bitter
      tear,
  And alas I am weary, weary O !

———◆———

## HAD I THE WYTE.

HAD I the wyte, had I the wyte,
  Had I the wyte ? she bade me !
She watch'd me by the hie-gate side,
  And up the loan she shaw'd me ;
And when I wadna venture in,
  A coward loon she ca'd me :
Had kirk and state been in the gate,
  I lighted when she bade me.

Sae craftilie she took me ben,
  And bade me make nae clatter ;                                  10
' For our ramgunshoch glum gudeman
  Is out and owre the water : '
Whae'er shall say I wanted grace,
  When I did kiss and daut her,
Let him be planted in my place,
  Syne say I was the fautor.

Could I for shame, could I for shame,
  Could I for shame refused her?
And wadna manhood been to blame,
  Had I unkindly used her?                          20
He clawed her wi' the ripplin-kame,
  And blae and bluidy bruised her;
When sic a husband was frae hame,
  What wife but had excused her?

I dighted ay her een sae blue,
  And bann'd the cruel randy;
And weel I wat her willing mou'
  Was e'en like sugar-candy.
At gloamin-shot it was I trow,
  I lighted on the Monday;                          30
But I cam through the Tysday's dew,
  To wanton Willie's brandy.

———•♦•———


### HEE BALOU.

HEE balou! my sweet wee Donald,
Picture o' the great Clanronald;
Brawlie kens our wanton chief
Wha got my young Highland thief.

Leeze me on thy bonnie craigie!
An' thou live, thou'll steal a naigie:
Travel the country thro' and thro',
And bring hame a Carlisle cow.

Thro' the Lawlands, o'er the border,
Weel, my babie, may thou furder:                    10
Herry the louns o' the laigh countree,
Syne to the Highlands hame to me.

———•♦•———

## HER DADDIE FORBAD.

HER daddie forbad, her minnie forbad;
  Forbidden she wadna be :
She wadna trow't the browst she brew'd
  Wad taste sae bitterlie.
    The lang lad they ca' Jumpin' John
      Beguiled the bonnie lassie,
    The lang lad they ca' Jumpin' John
      Beguiled the bonnie lassie.

A cow and a cauf, a yowe and a hauf,
  And thretty gude shillin's and three ;     20
A verra gude tocher, a cotter-man's dochter,
  The lass with the bonnie black ee.
    The lang lad they ca' Jumpin' John
      Beguiled the bonnie lassie,
    The lang lad they ca' Jumpin John
      Beguiled the bonnie lassie.

---

## HERE'S TO THY HEALTH, MY BONNIE LASS.

HERE's to thy health, my bonnie lass!
  Gude night, and joy be wi' thee!
I'll come nae mair to thy bower door,
  To tell thee that I lo'e thee.
O dinna think, my pretty pink,
  But I can live without thee :
I vow and swear I dinna care
  How lang ye look about ye.

Thou'rt aye sae free informing me
  Thou hast nae mind to marry ;     10
I'll be as free informing thee
  Nae time hae I to tarry.
I ken thy friends try ilka means
  Frae wedlock to delay thee,
Depending on some higher chance—
  But fortune may betray thee.

I ken they scorn my low estate,
  But that does never grieve me;
For I'm as free as any he,—
  Sma' siller will relieve me.        20
I count my health my greatest wealth,
  Sae lang as I'll enjoy it:
I'll fear nae scant, I'll bode nae want,
  As lang's I get employment.

But far-aff fowls hae feathers fair,
  And aye until ye try them:
Tho' they seem fair, still have a care,
  They may prove waur than I am.
But at twal at night, when the moon shines bright,
  My dear, I'll come and see thee;      30
For the man that lo'es his mistress weel,
  Nae travel makes him weary.

———•• ———

## HEY, THE DUSTY MILLER.

HEY, the dusty miller,
  And his dusty coat;
He will win a shilling,
  Or he spend a groat.
    Dusty was the coat,
      Dusty was the colour,
    Dusty was the kiss
      That I got frae the miller.

Hey, the dusty miller,
  And his dusty sack;      10
Leeze me on the calling
  Fills the dusty peck.
    Fills the dusty peck,
      Brings the dusty siller;
    I wad gie my coatie
      For the dusty miller.

## THE CARDIN' O'T.

I COFT a stane o' haslock woo',
   To make a coat to Johnny o't;
For Johnny is my only jo,
   I lo'e him best of ony yet.
      The cardin' o't, the spinnin' o't;
         The warpin' o't, the winnin' o't;
      When ilka ell cost me a groat,
         The tailor staw the linin' o't.

For though his locks be lyart gray,
   And though his brow be beld aboon;            10
Yet I hae seen him on a day,
   The pride of a' the parishen.
      The cardin' o't, the spinnin' o't,
         The warpin' o't, the winnin' o't;
      When ilka ell cost me a groat,
         The tailor staw the linin' o't.

## THE JOYFUL WIDOWER.

I MARRIED with a scolding wife
   The fourteenth of November;
She made me weary of my life,
   By one unruly member.
Long did I bear the heavy yoke,
   And many griefs attended;
But, to my comfort be it spoke,
   Now, now her life is ended.

We lived full one-and-twenty years
   A man and wife together;                      10
At length from me her course she steer'd,
   And gone I know not whither:
Would I could guess! I do profess,
   I speak, and do not flatter,
Of all the women in the world,
   I never would come at her.

Her body is bestowèd well,
   A handsome grave does hide her ;
But sure her soul is not in hell,
   The deil would ne'er abide her.     20
I rather think she is aloft,
   And imitating thunder ;
For why,—methinks I hear her voice
   Tearing the clouds asunder.

———◆◆———

## THENIEL MENZIES' BONNIE MARY.

In coming by the brig o' Dye,
   At Darlet we a blink did tarry ;
As day was dawin in the sky
     We drank a health to bonnie Mary.
     Theniel Menzies' bonnie Mary,
        Theniel Menzies' bonnie Mary ;
     Charlie Gregor tint his plaidie,
        Kissin' Theniel's bonnie Mary.

Her een sae bright, her brow sae white,
   Her haffet locks as brown's a berry,     10
An' aye they dimpled wi' a smile
     The rosy cheeks o' bonnie Mary.
     Theniel Menzies' bonnie Mary,
        Theniel Menzies' bonnie Mary ;
     Charlie Gregor tint his plaidie,
        Kissin' Theniel's bonnie Mary.

We lap an' danced the lee-lang day,
   Till piper lads were wae an' weary,
But Charlie gat the spring to pay
     For kissin' Theniel's bonnie Mary.     20
     Theniel Menzies' bonnie Mary,
        Theniel Menzies' bonnie Mary ;
     Charlie Gregor tint his plaidie,
        Kissin' Theniel's bonnie Mary.

## IT IS NA, JEAN, THY BONNIE FACE.

It is na, Jean, thy bonnie face,
  Nor shape that I admire,
Although thy beauty and thy grace
  Might weel awake desire.
Something, in ilka part o' thee,
  To praise, to love, I find ;
But dear as is thy form to me,
  Still dearer is thy mind.

Nae mair ungenerous wish I hae,
  Nor stronger in my breast,     10
Than if I canna mak thee sae,
  At least to see thee blest.
Content am I, if Heaven shall give
  But happiness to thee :
And as wi' thee I'd wish to live,
  For thee I'd bear to die.

——◦—

## MY HEART WAS ANCE.

My heart was ance as blythe and free
  As simmer days were lang,
But a bonnie westlin weaver lad
  Has gart me change my sang.
    To the weavers gin ye go, fair maids,
      To the weavers gin ye go ;
    I rede you right gang ne'er at night,
      To the weavers gin ye go.

My mither sent me to the town,
  To warp a plaiden wab ;     10
But the weary, weary warpin o't
  Has gart me sigh and sab.

A bonnie westlin weaver lad
    Sat working at his loom;
He took my heart as wi' a net,
    In every knot and thrum.

I sat beside my warpin-wheel,
    And aye I ca'd it roun';
But every shot and every knock,
    My heart it gae a stoun.                    20

The moon was sinking in the west
    Wi' visage pale and wan,
As my bonnie westlin weaver lad
    Convoy'd me through the glen.

But what was said, or what was done,
    Shame fa' me gin I tell;
But oh! I fear the kintra soon
    Will ken as weel's mysel.

To the weavers gin ye go, fair maids,
    To the weavers gin ye go;                   30
I rede you right gang ne'er at night,
    To the weavers gin ye go.

---

## LOVELY DAVIES.

O HOW shall I, unskilfu', try
    The poet's occupation?
The tunefu' powers, in happy hours,
    That whisper inspiration—
Even they maun dare an effort mair,
    Than aught they ever gave us,
Or they rehearse, in equal verse,
    The charms o' lovely Davies.

Each eye it cheers when she appears,
   Like Phœbus in the morning,
When past the shower, and ev'ry flower
   The garden is adorning.
As the wretch looks o'er Siberia's shore,
   When winter-bound the wave is;
Sae droops our heart when we maun part
   Frae charming lovely Davies.

Her smile's a gift frae 'boon the lift
   That maks us mair than princes;
A scepter'd hand, a King's command,
   Is in her darting glances:
The man in arms 'gainst female charms,
   Even he her willing slave is;
He hugs his chain, and owns the reign
   Of conquering lovely Davies.

My Muse, to dream of such a theme,
   Thy feeble powers surrender!
The eagle's gaze alone surveys
   The sun's meridian splendour:
I wad in vain essay the strain,
   The deed too daring brave is;
I'll drap the lyre, and mute admire
   The charms o' lovely Davies.

---

## SAE FAR AWA.

O SAD and heavy should I part,
   But for her sake, sae far awa;
Unknowing what my way may thwart,
   My native land sae far awa.
Thou that of a' things Maker art,
   That form'd this Fair sae far awa,
Gie body strength, then I'll ne'er start
   At this my way sae far awa.

How true is love to pure desert!
    Like mine for her, sae far awa:       10
And nocht can heal my bosom's smart,
    While, oh! she is sae far awa.
Nane other love, nane other dart,
    I feel but her's, sae far awa;
But fairer never touch'd a heart
    Than her's, the fair sae far awa.

<hr />

## O STEER HER UP.

O STEER her up, and haud her gaun—
    Her mother's at the mill, jo;
And gin she winna take a man,
    E'en let her take her will, jo:
First shore her wi' a kindly kiss,
    And ca' another gill, jo;
And gin she take the thing amiss,
    E'en let her flyte her fill, jo.

O steer her up, and be na blate,
    An' gin she tak it ill, jo,       10
Then lea'e the lassie till her fate,
    And time nae langer spill, jo:
Ne'er break your heart for ae rebute,
    But think upon it still, jo;
Then gin the lassie winna do't,
    Ye'll fin' anither will, jo.

<hr />

## O WHARE DID YE GET.

O WHARE did ye get that hauver-meal bannock?
  O silly blind body, O dinna ye see?
I gat it frae a brisk young sodger laddie,
  Between Saint Johnston and bonnie Dundee.

O gin I saw the laddie that gae me't!
  .Aft has he doudled me on his knee;
May Heaven protect my bonnie Scots laddie,
  And send him safe hame to his babie and me!

My blessin's upon thy sweet wee lippie,
  My blessin's upon thy bonnie e'e bree!          10
Thy smiles are sae like my blythe sodger laddie,
  Thou's aye the dearer and dearer to me!
But I'll big a bower on yon bonnie banks,
  Where Tay rins wimplin' by sae clear;
And I'll cleed thee in the tartan sae fine,
  And mak thee a man like thy daddie dear.


———•———


## SIMMER'S A PLEASANT TIME.

Simmer's a pleasant time,
  Flow'rs of ev'ry colour;
The water rins o'er the heugh,
  And I long for my true lover.
    Ay waukin O,
      Waukin still and wearie:
    Sleep I can get nane
      For thinking on my dearie.

When I sleep I dream,
  When I wauk I'm eerie;                          10
Sleep I can get nane
  For thinking on my dearie.

Lanely night comes on,
  A' the lave are sleeping;
I think on my bonnie lad
  And I bleer my een with greetin'.
    Ay waukin O,
      Waukin still and wearie;
    Sleep I can get nane
      For thinking on my dearie.                  20

# THE BLUDE RED ROSE AT YULE MAY BLAW.

THE blude red rose at Yule may blaw,
The simmer lilies bloom in snaw,
The frost may freeze the deepest sea;
But an auld man shall never daunton me.

To daunton me, and me sae young,
Wi' his fause heart and flatt'ring tongue,
That is the thing you ne'er shall see;
For an auld man shall never daunton me.

For a' his meal and a' his maut,
For a' his fresh beef and his saut,                    10
For a' his gold and white monie,
An auld man shall never daunton me.

His gear may buy him kye and yowes,
His gear may buy him glens and knowes;
But me he shall not buy nor fee,
For an auld man shall never daunton me.

He hirples twa fauld as he dow,
Wi' his teethless gab and his auld beld pow,
And the rain rains down frae his red bleer'd ee—
That auld man shall never daunton me.       20

To daunton me, and me sae young,
Wi' his fause heart and flatt'ring tongue,
That is the thing you ne'er shall see;
For an auld man shall never daunton me.

———◆◆———

# THE HIGHLAND LADDIE.

THE bonniest lad that e'er I saw,
  Bonnie laddie, Highland laddie,
Wore a plaid and was fu' braw,
  Bonnie Highland laddie.

On his head a bonnet blue,
  Bonnie laddie, Highland laddie,
His royal heart was firm and true,
  Bonnie Highland laddie.

Trumpets sound and cannons roar,
  Bonnie lassie, Lawland lassie,           10
And a' the hills wi' echoes roar,
  Bonnie Lawland lassie.
Glory, Honour, now invite,
  Bonnie lassie, Lawland lassie,
For Freedom and my King to fight,
  Bonnie Lawland lassie.

The sun a backward course shall take,
  Bonnie laddie, Highland laddie,
Ere aught thy manly courage shake,
  Bonnie Highland laddie.           20
Go, for yoursel procure renown,
  Bonnie laddie, Highland laddie,
And for your lawful King his crown,
  Bonnie Highland laddie!

———◆◆———

## THE COOPER O' CUDDIE.

THE cooper o' Cuddie cam here awa,
And ca'd the girrs out owre us a'—
And our gude-wife has gotten a ca'
  That anger'd the silly gude-man, O.

We'll hide the cooper behind the door,
Behind the door, behind the door;
We'll hide the cooper behind the door,
  And cover him under a mawn, O.

He sought them out, he sought them in,
Wi', Deil hae her! and, Deil hae him!       10
But the body he was sae doited and blin',
  He wist na where he was gaun, O.

They cooper'd at e'en, they cooper'd at morn,
Till our gude-man has gotten the scorn;
On ilka brow she's planted a horn,
  And swears that they shall stan', O.

---

# THE HIGHLAND WIDOW'S LAMENT.

Oh! I am come to the low countrie,
  Och-on, och-on, och-rie!
Without a penny in my purse,
  To buy a meal to me.

It was nae sae in the Highland hills,
  Och-on, och-on, och-rie!
Nae woman in the country wide
  Sae happy was as me.

For then I had a score o' kye,
  Och-on, och-on, och-rie!                    10
Feeding on yon hills so high,
  And giving milk to me.

And there I had three score o' yowes,
  Och-on, och-on, och-rie!
Skipping on yon bonnie knowes,
  And casting woo' to me.

I was the happiest of the clan,
  Sair, sair may I repine;
For Donald was the brawest lad,
  And Donald he was mine.                     20

Till Charlie Stewart cam at last,
  Sae far to set us free;
My Donald's arm was wanted then,
  For Scotland and for me.

Their waefu' fate what need I tell,
  Right to the wrang did yield:
My Donald and his country fell
  Upon Culloden field.

Oh! I am come to the low countrie,
  Och-on, och-on, och-rie!                           30
Nae woman in the world wide
  Sae wretched now as me.

———•———

## THE WEARY PUND O' TOW.

THE weary pund, the weary pund,
  The weary pund o' tow;
I think my wife will end her life
  Before she spin her tow.

I bought my wife a stane o' lint
  As gude as e'er did grow;
And a' that she has made o' that,
  Is ae poor pund o' tow.

There sat a bottle in a bole,
  Beyond the ingle lowe,                              10
And aye she took the tither souk
  To drouk the stowrie tow.

Quoth I, For shame, ye dirty dame,
  Gae spin your tap o' tow!
She took the rock, and wi' a knock
  She brak it o'er my pow.

At last her feet—I sang to see't—
  Gaed foremost o'er the knowe;
And or I wad anither jad,
  I'll wallop in a tow.                               20

## THE PLOUGHMAN.

THE ploughman he's a bonnie lad,
   His mind is ever true, jo,
His garters knit below his knee,
   His bonnet it is blue, jo.

Then up wi't a', my ploughman lad,
   And hey, my merry ploughman ;
Of a' the trades that I do ken,
   Commend me to the ploughman.

My ploughman he comes hame at e'en.
   He's aften wat and weary ;         10
Cast off the wat, put on the dry,
   And gae to bed, my Dearie !

I will wash my ploughman's hose,
   And I will dress his o'erlay ;
I will mak my ploughman's bed,
   And cheer him late and early.

I hae been east, I hae been west,
   I hae been at Saint Johnston ;
The bonniest sight that e'er I saw
   Was the ploughman laddie dancin'.    20

Snaw-white stockin's on his legs,
   And siller buckles glancin' ;
A gude blue bonnet on his head,
   And O, but he was handsome !

Commend me to the barn-yard,
   And the corn-mow, man ;
I never gat my coggie fou
   Till I met wi' the ploughman

## THE CARLES OF DYSART.

Up wi' the carles of Dysart,
    And the lads o' Buckhaven,
And the kimmers o' Largo,
    And the lasses o' Leven.
        Hey, ca' thro', ca' thro',
           For we hae mickle ado ;
        Hey, ca' thro', ca' thro',
           For we hae mickle ado.

We hae tales to tell,
    And we hae sangs to sing ;        10
We hae pennies to spend,
    And we hae pints to bring.

We'll live a' our days,
    And them that come behin',
Let them do the like,
    And spend the gear they win.

---

## NITHSDALE'S WELCOME HAME.

The noble Maxwells and their powers
    Are coming o'er the border,
And they'll gae bigg Terreagles' towers,
    An' set them a' in order,
And they declare Terreagles fair,
    For their abode they choose it ;
There 's no a heart in a' the land
    But 's lighter at the news o't.

Tho' stars in skies may disappear,
    And angry tempests gather ;        10
The happy hour may soon be near
    That brings us pleasant weather :

The weary night o' care and grief
May hae a joyful morrow;
So dawning day has brought relief
Fareweel our night o' sorrow!

———+·———

## THE TAILOR FELL THRO' THE BED.

The Tailor fell thro' the bed, thimbles an' a',
The Tailor fell thro' the bed, thimbles an' a';
The blankets were thin, and the sheets they were sma',
The Tailor fell thro' the bed, thimbles an' a'.

The sleepy bit lassie, she dreaded nae ill,
The sleepy bit lassie, she dreaded nae ill;
The weather was cauld, and the lassie lay still,
She thought that a tailor could do her nae ill.

Gie me the groat again, canny young man;
Gie me the groat again, canny young man;               10
The day it is short, and the night it is lang,
The dearest siller that ever I wan!

There's somebody weary wi' lying her lane;
There's somebody weary wi' lying her lane;
There's some that are dowie I trow wad be fain
To see the bit tailor come skippin' again.

———+·———

## THE TITHER MORN.

THE tither morn,
When I forlorn
Aneath an aik sat moaning,
    I did na trow
    I'd see my jo
Beside me, 'gain the gloaming.
    But he sae trig
    Lap o'er the rig,
And dawtingly did cheer me,
    When I, what reck?          10
    Did least expec'
To see my lad so near me.

    His bonnet he,
    A thought ajee,
Cock'd sprush when first he clasp'd me;
    And I, I wat,
    Wi' fainness grat,
While in his grips he press'd me.
    Deil tak' the war!
    I late and ear'          20
Hae wish'd since Jock departed;
    But now as glad
    I'm wi' my lad,
As short syne broken-hearted.

    Fu' aft at e'en
    Wi' dancing keen,
When a' were blythe and merry,
    I car'd na by,
    Sae sad was I
In absence o' my dearie.          30
    But, praise be blest!
    My mind's at rest,
I'm happy wi' my Johnny:
    At kirk and fair,
    I'se aye be there,
And be as canty's ony.

## JAMIE, COME TRY ME.

Jamie, come try me,
    Jamie, come try me ;
If thou would win my love,
    Jamie, come try me.

If thou should ask my love,
    Could I deny thee ?
If thou would win my love,
    Jamie, come try me.

If thou should kiss me, love,
    Wha could espy thee ?        10
If thou wad be my love,
    Jamie  come try me.

---

## EPPIE M'NAB.

O saw ye my dearie, my Eppie M'Nab?
O saw ye my dearie, my Eppie M'Nab?
She 's down in the yard, she 's kissin' the laird,
She winna come hame to her ain Jock Rab.
O come thy ways to me, my Eppie M'Nab!
O come thy ways to me, my Eppie M'Nab!
Whate'er thou has done, be it late, be it soon,
Thou 's welcome again to thy ain Jock Rab.

What says she, my dearie, my Eppie M'Nab?
What says she, my dearie, my Eppie M'Nab?    10
She lets thee to wot that she has thee forgot,
And for ever disowns thee, her ain Jock Rab.
O had I ne'er seen thee, my Eppie M'Nab!
O had I ne'er seen thee, my Eppie M'Nab!
As light as the air, and fause as thou 's fair,
Thou 's broken the heart o' thy ain Jock Rab.

## AN, O! MY EPPIE.

An' O! my Eppie,
My jewel, my Eppie!
Wha wadna be happy
  Wi' Eppie Adair?
By love, and by beauty,
By law, and by duty,
I swear to be true to
  My Eppie Adair!

An' O! my Eppie,
My jewel, my Eppie!          10
Wha wadna be happy
  Wi' Eppie Adair?
A' pleasure exile me,
Dishonour defile me,
If e'er I beguile thee,
  My Eppie Adair!

## YE SONS OF OLD KILLIE.

Ye sons of old Killie, assembled by Willie,
  To follow the noble vocation;
Your thrifty old mother has scarce such another
  To sit in that honourèd station.
I've little to say, but only to pray,
  As praying's the ton of your fashion;
A prayer from the Muse you well may excuse,
  'Tis seldom her favourite passion.

Ye powers who preside o'er the wind and the tide,
  Who markèd each element's border;      10
Who formèd this frame with beneficent aim,
  Whose sovereign statute is order;
Within this dear mansion may wayward contention
  Or witherèd envy ne'er enter;
May secrecy round be the mystical bound,
  And brotherly love be the centre!

## YE JACOBITES BY NAME.

Ye Jacobites by name, give an ear, give an ear;
 Ye Jacobites by name, give an ear;
  Ye Jacobites by name,
   Your fautes I will proclaim,
    Your doctrines I maun blame—
     You shall hear.

What is right and what is wrang, by the law, by the law?
 What is right and what is wrang by the law?
  What is right and what is wrang?
   A short sword and a lang,    10
    A weak arm and a strang,
     For to draw.

What makes heroic strife, fam'd afar, fam'd afar?
 What makes heroic strife fam'd afar?
  What makes heroic strife?
   To whet th' assassin's knife,
    Or hunt a parent's life
     Wi' bluidie war.

Then let your schemes alone, in the state, in the state;
 Then let your schemes alone in the state;  20
  Then let your schemes alone,
   Adore the rising sun,
    And leave a man undone
     To his fate.

---

## GOODE'EN TO YOU, KIMMER.

Goode'en to you, Kimmer,
 And how do ye do?
Hiccup, quo' Kimmer,
 The better that I'm fou.
  We're a' noddin, nid nid noddin,
  We're a' noddin at our house at hame.

Kate sits i' the neuk,
  Suppin' hen broo ;
Deil tak Kate
  An' she be noddin too!          10

How's a' wi' you, Kimmer,
  And how do ye fare?
A pint o' the best o't,
  And twa pints mair.

How's a' wi' you, Kimmer,
  And how do ye thrive ;
How mony bairns hae ye?
  Quo' Kimmer, I hae five.

Are they a' Johnny's?
  Eh! atweel na :          20
Twa o' them were gotten
  When Johnny was awa.

Cats like milk,
  And dogs like broo ;
Lads like lasses weel,
  And lasses lads too.

----&bull;----

## AH, CHLORIS.

AH, Chloris, since it may na be,
  That thou of love wilt hear ;
If from the lover thou maun flee,
  Yet let the friend be dear.

Altho' I love my Chloris mair
  Than ever tongue could tell ;
My passion I will ne'er declare,
  I'll say I wish thee well :

Tho' a' my daily care thou art,
  And a' my nightly dream,        10
I'll hide the struggle in my heart,
  And say it is esteem.

---

## WHAN I SLEEP I DREAM.

WHAN I sleep I dream,
  Whan I wauk I'm eerie,
Sleep I canna get,
  For thinkin' o' my dearie.

Lanely night comes on,
  A' the house are sleeping;
I think on the bonnie lad
  That has my heart a keeping.

Lanely night comes on,
  A' the house are sleeping,        10
I think on my bonnie lad,
  An' I bleer my een wi' greetin'!
    Aye waukin O, waukin aye and wearie,
    Sleep I canna get for thinkin' o' my dearie.

---

## KATHARINE JAFFRAY.

THERE liv'd a lass in yonder dale,
  And down in yonder glen O;
And Katherine Jaffray was her name,
  Weel known to many men O.

Out came the Lord of Lauderdale
  Out frae the south countrie O,
All for to court this pretty maid,
  Her bridegroom for to be O.

He 's tell'd her father and mother baith,
　　As I hear sindry say, O ;                              10
But he has na tell'd the lass hersel'
　　Till on her wedding day, O.

Then came the Laird o' Lochinton
　　Out frae the English border,
All for to court this pretty maid,
　　All mounted in good order.

　　　*　　*　　*　　*　　*　　*　　*

———◆◆———

# THE COLLIER LADDIE.

O WHARE live ye my bonnie lass,
　　And tell me how they ca' ye?
My name, she says, is Mistress Jean,
　　And I follow my Collier laddie.

O see ye not yon hills and dales
　　The sun shines on sae brawly :
They a' are mine, and they shall be thine,
　　If ye'll leave your Collier laddie.

And ye shall gang in rich attire,
　　Weel buskit up fu' gaudy ;                             10
And ane to wait at every hand,
　　If ye'll leave your Collier laddie.

Tho' ye had a' the sun shines on,
　　And the earth conceals sae lowly ;
I would turn my back on you and it a',
　　And embrace my Collier laddie.

I can win my five pennies in a day,
　　And spend it at night full brawlie ;
I can mak my bed in the Collier's neuk,
　　And lie down wi' my Collier laddie.                    20

Love for love is the bargain for me,
  Tho' the wee cot-house should haud me;
And the warld before me to win my bread,
  And fare fa' my Collier laddie!

------◆------

## WHEN I THINK ON THE HAPPY DAYS.

WHEN I think on the happy days
  I spent wi' you, my dearie;
And now what lands between us lie,
  How can I be but eerie!

How slow ye move, ye heavy hours,
  As ye were wae and weary!
It was na sae ye glinted by
  When I was wi' my dearie.

------◆------

## YOUNG JAMIE, PRIDE OF A' THE PLAIN.

YOUNG Jamie, pride of a' the plain,
Sae gallant and sae gay a swain;
Thro' a' our lasses he did rove,
And reign'd resistless King of Love:
But now wi' sighs and starting tears,
He strays amang the woods and briers:
Or in the glens and rocky caves
His sad complaining dowie raves:

I wha sae late did range and rove,
And changed with every moon my love,      10
I little thought the time was near,
Repentance I should buy sae dear;
The slighted maids my torment see,
And laugh at a' the pangs I dree;
While she, my cruel, scornfu' fair,
Forbids me e'er to see her mair!

## THE HEATHER WAS BLOOMING.

THE heather was blooming, the meadows were mawn,
Our lads gaed a-hunting, ae day at the dawn,
O'er moors and o'er mosses and mony a glen ;
At length they discover'd a bonnie moor-hen.

 I red you beware at the hunting, young men ;
 I red you beware at the hunting, young men ;
 Tak some on the wing, and some as they spring,
 But cannily steal on a bonnie moor-hen.

Sweet brushing the dew from the brown heather-bells,
Her colours betray'd her on yon mossy fells ;   10
Her plumage outlustred the pride o' the spring,
And O ! as she wanton'd gay on the wing.

Auld Phœbus himsel, as he peep'd o'er the hill,
In spite at her plumage he tried his skill :
He levell'd his rays where she bask'd on the brae—
His rays were outshone, and but mark'd where she lay.

They hunted the valley, they hunted the hill,
The best of our lads wi' the best o' their skill ;
But still as the fairest she sat in their sight,
Then whirr ! she was over, a mile at a flight.   20

---

## WAE IS MY HEART.

WAE is my heart, and the tear's in my ee ;
Lang, lang joy's been a stranger to me :
Forsaken and friendless my burden I bear,
And the sweet voice o' pity ne'er sounds in my ear.

Love, thou hast pleasures ; and deep hae I loved ;
Love, thou hast sorrows ; and sair hae I proved :
But this bruisèd heart that now bleeds in my breast,
I can feel its throbbings will soon be at rest.

O if I were where happy I hae been ;
Down by yon stream and yon bonnie castle green:　10
For there he is wand'ring and musing on me,
Wha wad soon dry the tear frae Phillis's ee.

———————

## O THAT I HAD NE'ER BEEN MARRIED.

O that I had ne'er been married,
　I wad never had nae care ;
Now I've gotten wife and bairns,
　An' they cry crowdie ever mair.
　　Ance crowdie, twice crowdie,
　　　Three times crowdie in a day ;
　　Gin ye crowdie ony mair,
　　　Ye'll crowdie a' my meal away.

Waefu want and hunger fley me,
　Glowrin' by the hallen en' ;　　　　　　　　10
Sair I fecht them at the door,
　But aye I'm eerie they come ben.

———————

## THERE'S NEWS, LASSES.

There's news, lasses, news,
　Gude news I've to tell !
There's a boat fu' o' lads
　Come to our town to sell.
　　The wean wants a cradle,
　　　An' the cradle wants a cod.
　　An' I'll no gang to my bed
　　　Until I get a nod.

Father, quo' she, Mither, quo' she,
　Do what ye can,　　　　　　　　　　　　10
I'll no gang to my bed
　Till I get a man.

I hae as gude a craft rig
  As made o' yird and stane ;
And waly fa' the ley-crap
  For I maun till'd again.

---

## SCROGGAM.

THERE was a wife wonn'd in Cockpen,
          Scroggam ;
She brew'd gude ale for gentlemen,
Sing auld Cowl, lay you down by me,
Scroggam, my dearie, ruffum.

The gudewife's dochter fell in a fever,
          Scroggam ;
The priest o' the parish fell in anither,
Sing auld Cowl, lay you down by me,
Scroggam, my dearie, ruffum.                          10

They laid the twa i' the bed thegither,
          Scroggam ;
That the heat o' the tane might cool the tither,
Sing auld Cowl, lay you down by me,
Scroggam, my dearie, ruffum.

---

## FRAE THE FRIENDS AND LAND I LOVE

FRAE the friends and land I love,
  Driven by Fortune's felly spite,
Frae my best belov'd I rove,
  Never mair to taste delight ;
Never mair maun hope to find
  Ease frae toil, relief frae care :
When remembrance wrecks the mind,
  Pleasures but unveil despair.

Brightest climes shall mirk appear,
  Desert ilka blooming shore,        10
Till the Fates, nae mair severe,
  Friendship, love, and peace restore ;
Till revenge, wi' laurell'd head,
  Bring our banish'd hame again ;
And ilka loyal, bonnie lad
  Cross the seas and win his ain.

---

## THE LADDIES BY THE BANKS O' NITH.

### ELECTION BALLAD, 1789.

THE laddies by the banks o' Nith
  Wad trust his Grace wi' a', Jamie,
But he'll ser' them as he ser'd the king—
  Turn tail and rin awa, Jamie.
    Up and waur them a', Jamie,
      Up and waur them a' ;
    The Johnstons hae the guidin' o't,—
      Ye turncoat Whigs, awa !

The day he stude his country's friend,
  Or gied her faes a claw, Jamie,        10
Or frae puir man a blessin' wan,
  That day the duke ne'er saw, Jamie.

But wha is he, his country's boast ?
  Like him there is na twa, Jamie ;
There 's no a callant tents the kye,
  But kens o' Westerha', Jamie.

To end the wark, here's Whistlebirt,—
  Lang may his whistle blaw, Jamie !
And Maxwell true o' sterling blue ;
  And we'll be Johnstons a', Jamie.        20

## THE BONNIE LASS OF ALBANY.

My heart is wae, and unco wae,
  To think upon the raging sea,
That roars between her gardens green
  And the bonnie Lass of Albany.

This lovely maid's of royal blood
  That rulèd Albion's kingdoms three,
But oh, alas! for her bonnie face,
  They hae wrang'd the Lass of Albany.

In the rolling tide of spreading Clyde
  There sits an isle of high degree,                        10
And a town of fame whose princely name
  Should grace the Lass of Albany.

But there's a youth, a witless youth,
  That fills the place where she should be;
We'll send him o'er to his native shore,
  And bring our ain sweet Albany.

Alas the day, and woe the day!
  A false usurper wan the gree,
Who now commands the towers and lands—
  The royal right of Albany.                                20

We'll daily pray, we'll nightly pray,
  On bended knees most fervently,
The time may come, with pipe and drum
  We'll welcome hame fair Albany.

---

## WHEN FIRST I SAW.

When first I saw fair Jeanie's face,
  I couldna tell what ailed me,
My heart went fluttering pit-a-pat,
  My een they almost failed me.

She's aye sae neat, sae trim, sae tight,
　　All grace does round her hover;
Ae look deprived me o' my heart,
　　And I became a lover.

She's aye, aye sae blythe, sae gay,
　　She's aye so blythe and cheerie:　　　10
She's aye sae bonnie, blythe, and gay,
　　O gin I were her dearie!

Had I Dundas's whole estate,
　　Or Hopetoun's wealth to shine in;
Did warlike laurels crown my brow,
　　Or humbler bays entwining—
I'd lay them a' at Jeanie's feet,
　　Could I but hope to move her,
And prouder than a belted knight,
　　I'd be my Jeanie's lover.　　　　　　20

But sair I fear some happier swain
　　Has gained sweet Jeanie's favour:
If so, may every bliss be hers,
　　Though I maun never have her:
But gang she east, or gang she west,
　　'Twixt Forth and Tweed all over,
While men have eyes, or ears, or taste,
　　She'll always find a lover.

—— ·•· ——

## THE RANTIN' DOG THE DADDIE O'T.

O WHA my babie-clouts will buy?
Wha will tent me when I cry?
Wha will kiss me whare I lie?
　　The rantin' dog the daddie o't.

Wha will own he did the faut?
Wha will buy my groanin' maut?
Wha will tell me how to ca't?
　　The rantin' dog the daddie o't.

When I mount the creepie-chair,
Wha will sit beside me there?        10
Gie me Rob, I seek nae mair,
    The rantin' dog the daddie o't.

Wha will crack to me my lane?
Wha will mak me fidgin' fain?
Wha will kiss me o'er again?
    The rantin' dog the daddie o't.

## I DO CONFESS THOU ART SAE FAIR.

I DO confess thou art sae fair,
    I wad been o'er the lugs in love;
Had I not found the slightest prayer
    That lips could speak thy heart could move.

I do confess thee sweet, but find
    Thou art sae thriftless o' thy sweets,
Thy favours are the silly wind
    That kisses ilka thing it meets.

See yonder rose-bud rich in dew,
    Amang its native briers sae coy,        10
How soon it tines its scent and hue
    When pu'd and worn a common toy!

Sic fate ere lang shall thee betide,
    Tho' thou may gaily bloom a while;
Yet soon thou shalt be thrown aside,
    Like ony common weed and vile.

## YON WILD MOSSY MOUNTAINS.

Yon wild mossy mountains sae lofty and wide,
That nurse in their bosom the youth o' the Clyde,
Where the grouse lead their coveys thro' the heather to feed.
And the shepherd tents his flock as he pipes on his reed :

Not Gowrie's rich valley, nor Forth's sunny shores,
To me hae the charms o' yon wild mossy moors ;
For there, by a lanely, sequester'd clear stream,
Resides a sweet lassie, my thought and my dream.

Amang thae wild mountains shall still be my path,
Ilk stream foaming dowr. its ain green narrow strath ;  10
For there, wi' my lassie, the day lang I rove,
While o'er us unheeded fly the swift hours o' love.

She is not the fairest, altho' she is fair ;
O' nice education but sma' is her share ;
Her parentage humble as humble can be,
But I lo'e the dear lassie because she lo'es me.

To Beauty what man but maun yield him a prize,
In her armour of glances, and blushes, and sighs?
And when wit and refinement hae polish'd her darts,
They dazzle our een, as they fly to our hearts.  20

But kindness, sweet kindness, in the fond sparkling ee,
Has lustre outshining the diamond to me ;
And the heart beating love, as I'm clasp'd in her arms,
O, these are my lassie's all-conquering charms !

———•·———

## ADOWN WINDING NITH.

Adown winding Nith I did wander,
To mark the sweet flowers as they spring ;
Adown winding Nith I did wander,
Of Phillis to muse and to sing.

Awa wi' your belles and your beauties,
They never wi' her can compare ;
Whaever has met wi' my Phillis,
Has met wi' the queen o' the fair.

The daisy amus'd my fond fancy,
So artless, so simple, so wild ;　　　　　10
Thou emblem, said I, o' my Phillis,
For she is Simplicity's child.

The rose-bud 's the blush o' my charmer,
Her sweet balmy lip when 'tis prest :
How fair and how pure is the lily,
But fairer and purer her breast.

Yon knot of gay flowers in the arbour,
They ne'er wi' my Phillis can vie :
Her breath is the breath o' the woodbine,
Its dew-drop o' diamond her eye.　　　　20

Her voice is the song of the morning
That wakes through the green-spreading grove,
When Phœbus peeps over the mountains,
On music, and pleasure, and love.

But beauty how frail and how fleeting !
The bloom of a fine summer's day !
While worth in the mind o' my Phillis
Will flourish without a decay.

———◦———

## CASTLE GORDON.

Streams that glide in orient plains,
Never bound by winter's chains !
Glowing here on golden sands,
There commix'd with foulest stains
From tyranny's empurpled hands :

These, their richly-gleaming waves,
I leave to tyrants and their slaves ;
Give me the stream that sweetly laves
    The banks by Castle Gordon.

Spicy forests, ever gay,          10
Shading from the burning ray
    Hapless wretches sold to toil,
Or the ruthless native's way,
    Bent on slaughter, blood, and spoil :
Woods that ever verdant wave,
I leave the tyrant and the slave ;
Give me the groves that lofty brave
    The storms, by Castle Gordon.

Wildly here without control,
Nature reigns and rules the whole ;     20
    In that sober pensive mood,
Dearest to the feeling soul,
    She plants the forest, pours the flood ;
Life's poor day I'll musing rave,
And find at night a sheltering cave,
Where waters flow and wild woods wave,
    By bonnie Castle Gordon.

———•———

## CHARMING MONTH OF MAY.

It was the charming month of May,
When all the flowers were fresh and gay,
One morning, by the break of day,
    The youthful, charming Chloe ;

From peaceful slumber she arose,
Girt on her mantle and her hose,
And o'er the flowery mead she goes,
    The youthful, charming Chloe.

Lovely was she by the dawn,
    Youthful Chloe, charming Chloe,                    10
Tripping o'er the pearly lawn,
    The youthful, charming Chloe.

The feather'd people you might see
Perch'd all around on every tree ;
In notes of sweetest melody
    They hail the charming Chloe ;

Till, painting gay the eastern skies,
The glorious sun began to rise,
Out-rival'd by the radiant eyes
    Of youthful, charming Chloe.                        20

---

## LET NOT WOMAN E'ER COMPLAIN.

LET not woman e'er complain
    Of inconstancy in love ;
Let not woman e'er complain,
    Fickle man is apt to rove :
Look abroad through Nature's range,
Nature's mighty law is change ;
Ladies, would it not be strange,
    Man should then a monster prove ?

Mark the winds, and mark the skies ;
    Ocean's ebb, and ocean's flow :                      10
Sun and moon but set to rise,
    Round and round the seasons go.
Why then ask of silly man,
To oppose great Nature's plan ?
We'll be constant while we can—
    You can be no more, you know.

## PHILLY AND WILLY.   A DUET.

### *He.*

O PHILLY, happy be that day
When, roving thro' the gather'd hay,
My youthfu' heart was stown away,
    And by thy charms, my Philly.

### *She.*

O Willy, aye I bless the grove
Where first I own'd my maiden love,
Whilst thou didst pledge the Powers above
    To be my ain dear Willy.

### *He.*

As songsters of the early year
Are ilka day mair sweet to hear,                    10
So ilka day to me mair dear
    And charming is my Philly.

### *She.*

As on the brier the budding rose
Still richer breathes and fairer blows,
So in my tender bosom grows
    The love I bear my Willy.

### *He.*

The milder sun and bluer sky,
That crown my harvest cares wi' joy,
Were ne'er sae welcome to my eye
    As is a sight o' Philly.                   20

### *She.*

The little swallow's wanton wing,
Tho' wafting o'er the flowery spring,
Did ne'er to me sic tidings bring
    As meeting o' my Willy.

*He.*

The bee that thro' the sunny hour
Sips nectar in the opening flower,
Compar'd wi' my delight is poor,
    Upon the lips o' Philly.

*She.*

The woodbine in the dewy weet,
When evening shades in silence meet,     30
Is nocht sae fragrant or sae sweet
    As is a kiss o' Willy.

*He.*

Let fortune's wheel at random rin,
And fools may tyne, and knaves may win;
My thoughts are a' bound up in ane,
    And that's my ain dear Philly.

*She.*

What's a' the joys that gowd can gie!
I care na wealth a single flie;
The lad I love's the lad for me,
    And that's my ain dear Willy.     40

---

## CANST THOU LEAVE ME THUS?

Canst thou leave me thus, my Katy?
Canst thou leave me thus, my Katy?
Well thou know'st my aching heart,
    And canst thou leave me thus for pity?

Is this thy plighted, fond regard,
    Thus cruelly to part, my Katy?
Is this thy faithful swain's reward—
    An aching, broken heart, my Katy?

Farewell! and ne'er such sorrows tear
  That fickle heart of thine, my Katy!     10
Thou may'st find those will love thee dear—
  But not a love like mine, my Katy.

———•◦•———

## ON CHLORIS BEING ILL.

Long, long the night,
  Heavy comes the morrow,
While my soul's delight
  Is on her bed of sorrow.

Can I cease to care,
  Can I cease to languish,
While my darling fair
  Is on the couch of anguish?

Every hope is fled,
  Every fear is terror;     10
Slumber e'en I dread,
  Every dream is horror.

Hear me, Pow'rs divine!
  Oh, in pity hear me!
Take aught else of mine,
  But my Chloris spare me!

———•◦•———

## FAREWELL TO ELIZA.

From thee, Eliza, I must go,
  And from my native shore;
The cruel fates between us throw
  A boundless ocean's roar:
But boundless oceans, roaring wide,
  Between my Love and me,
They never, never can divide
  My heart and soul from thee.

Farewell, farewell, Eliza dear,
  The maid that I adore!      10
A boding voice is in mine ear,
  We part to meet no more!
But the last throb that leaves my heart,
  While death stands victor by,
That throb, Eliza, is thy part
  And thine that latest sigh!

## CAPTAIN GROSE.

Ken ye ought o' Captain Grose?
  Igo, and ago,
If he's amang his friends or foes?
  Iram, coram, dago.

Is he South, or is he North?
  Igo, and ago,
Or drowned in the river Forth?
  Iram, coram, dago.

Is he slain by Highland bodies?
  Igo, and ago,      10
And eaten like a wether-haggis?
  Iram, coram, dago.

Is he to Abram's bosom gane?
  Igo, and ago,
Or haudin Sarah by the wame?
  Iram, coram, dago.

Where'er he be, the Lord be near him!
  Igo, and ago,
As for the deil, he daur na steer him.
  Iram, coram, dago.      20

But please transmit th' enclosèd letter,
  Igo, and ago,
Which will oblige your humble debtor.
  Iram, coram, dago.

So may ye hae auld stanes in store,
  Igo, and ago,
The very stanes that Adam bore.
  Iram, coram, dago.

So may ye get in glad possession
  Igo, and ago,           30
The coins o' Satan's coronation!
  Iram, coram, dago.

## A ROSE-BUD BY MY EARLY WALK.

A ROSE-BUD by my early walk,
Adown a corn-enclosèd bawk,
Sae gently bent its thorny stalk,
  All on a dewy morning.

Ere twice the shades o' dawn are fled,
In a' its crimson glory spread,
And drooping rich the dewy head,
  It scents the early morning.

Within the bush, her covert nest
A little linnet fondly prest,
The dew sat chilly on her breast       10
  Sae early in the morning.

She soon shall see her tender brood,
The pride, the pleasure o' the wood,
Amang the fresh green leaves bedew'd,
  Awake the early morning.

So thou, dear bird, young Jeany fair,
On trembling string or vocal air,
Shalt sweetly pay the tender care
  That tents thy early morning.      20

So thou, sweet rose-bud, young and gay,
Shalt beauteous blaze upon the day,
And bless the parent's evening ray
    That watch'd thy early morning.

## O, WERE I ON PARNASSUS' HILL!

O, WERE I on Parnassus' hill,
Or had of Helicon my fill!
That I might catch poetic skill,
    To sing how dear I love thee.
But Nith maun be my Muse's well,
My Muse maun be thy bonnie sel;
On Corsincon I'll glowr and spell,
    And write how dear I love thee.

Then come, sweet Muse, inspire my lay!
For a' the lee-lang simmer's day,       10
I could na sing, I could na say,
    How much, how dear, I love thee.
I see thee dancing o'er the green,
Thy waist sae jimp, thy limbs sae clean,
Thy tempting looks, thy roguish een—
    By Heaven and earth I love thee!

By night, by day, a-field, at hame,
The thoughts o' thee my breast inflame
And aye I muse and sing thy name—
    I only live to love thee.       20
Tho' I were doom'd to wander on,
Beyond the sea, beyond the sun,
Till my last weary sand was run;
    Till then—and then I'd love thee.

## SLEEP'ST THOU, OR WAK'ST THOU.

SLEEP'ST thou, or wak'st thou, fairest creature?
  Rosy morn now lifts his eye,
Numbering ilka bud which Nature
    Waters wi' the tears o' joy:
    Now thro' the leafy woods,
    And by the reeking floods,
Wild Nature's tenants freely, gladly stray;
    The lintwhite in his bower
    Chants o'er the breathing flower;
    The lav'rock to the sky           10
    Ascends wi' sangs o' joy,
While the sun and thou arise to bless the day.

Phœbus, gilding the brow o' morning,
  Banishes ilk darksome shade,
Nature gladdening and adorning;
    Such to me my lovely maid.
    When absent frae my fair,
    The murky shades o' care
With starless gloom o'ercast my sullen sky:
    But when, in beauty's light,          20
    She meets my ravish'd sight,
    When thro' my very heart
    Her beaming glories dart—
'Tis then I wake to life, to light, and joy.

————•————

## THE POSIE.

O LUVE will venture in, where it daur na weel be seen,
O luve will venture in, where wisdom ance has been;
But I will down yon river rove, amang the wood sae green,
  And a' to pu' a Posie to my ain dear May.

The primrose I will pu', the firstling o' the year,
And I will pu' the pink, the emblem o' my dear,
For she 's the pink o' womankind, and blooms without a peer :
   And a' to be a Posie to my ain dear May.

I'll pu' the budding rose, when Phoebus peeps in view,
For it 's like a baumy kiss o' her sweet bonnie mou ;  10
The hyacinth 's for constancy, wi' its unchanging blue,
   And a' to be a Posie to my ain dear May.

The lily it is pure, and the lily it is fair,
And in her lovely bosom I'll place the lily there ;
The daisy 's for simplicity and unaffected air,
   And a' to be a Posie to my ain dear May.

The hawthorn I will pu', wi' its locks o' siller grey,
Where, like an aged man, it stands at break o' day,
But the songster's nest within the bush I winna tak away ;
   And a' to be a Posie to my ain dear May.  20

The woodbine I will pu' when the e'ening star is near,
And the diamond drops o' dew shall be her een sae clear :
The violet 's for modesty which weel she fa's to wear,
   And a' to be a Posie to my ain dear May.

I'll tie the Posie round wi' the silken band o' luve,
And I'll place it in her breast, and I'll swear by a' above,
That to my latest draught o' life the band shall ne'er remove,
   And this will be a Posie to my ain dear May.

———•———

## WILLIE'S WIFE.

WILLIE WASTLE dwalt on Tweed,
   The spot they ca'd it Linkumdoddie;
Willie was a wabster guid,
   Cou'd stown a clue wi' ony body.
He had a wife was dour and din,
   O Tinkler Madgie was her mither ;
Sic a wife as Willie had,
   I wad na gie a button for her !

She has an ee, she has but ane,
 The cat has twa the very colour:   10
Five rusty teeth, forbye a stump,
 A clapper tongue wad deave a miller;
A whiskin beard about her mou,
 Her nose and chin they threaten ither;
Sic a wife, &c.

She's bow-hough'd, she's hein shinn'd,
 Ae limpin leg a hand-breed shorter;
She's twisted right, she's twisted left,
 To balance fair in ilka quarter:
She has a hump upon her breast,
 The twin o' that upon her shouther;  20
Sic a wife, &c.

Auld baudrons by the ingle sits,
 An' wi' her loof her face a-washin;
But Willie's wife is nae sae trig,
 She dights her grunzie wi' a hushion;
Her walie nieves like midden-creels,
 Her face wad fyle the Logan-water;
Sic a wife as Willie had,
 I wad na gie a button for her!

---

## LOUIS, WHAT RECK I BY THEE?

Louis, what reck I by thee,
 Or Geordie on his ocean?
Dyvour, beggar loons to me,—
 I reign in Jeanie's bosom!

Let her crown my love her law,
 And in her breast enthrone me:
Kings and nations, swith awa!
 Reif randies, I disown ye!

## BONNIE BELL.

THE smiling spring comes in rejoicing,
    And surly winter grimly flies :
Now crystal clear are the falling waters,
    And bonnie blue are the sunny skies ;
Fresh o'er the mountains breaks forth the morning,
    The ev'ning gilds the ocean's swell ;
All creatures joy in the sun's returning,
    And I rejoice in my bonnie Bell.

The flowery spring leads sunny summer,
    And yellow autumn presses near ;                    10
Then in his turn comes gloomy winter,
    Till smiling spring again appear.
Thus seasons dancing, life advancing,
    Old Time and Nature their changes tell ;
But never ranging, still unchanging,
    I adore my bonnie Bell.

------◆------

## THE LOVELY LASS OF INVERNESS.

THE lovely lass o' Inverness,
    Nae joy nor pleasure can she see ;
For e'en and morn she cries, alas !
    And aye the saut tear blins her ee :
Drumossie moor, Drumossie day,
    A waefu' day it was to me ;
For there I lost my father dear,
    My father dear, and brethren three.

Their winding-sheet the bluidy clay,
    Their graves are growing green to see ;            10
And by them lies the dearest lad
    That ever blest a woman's ee !
Now wae to thee, thou cruel lord,
    A bluidy man I trow thou be ;
For mony a heart thou hast made sair,
    That ne'er did wrang to thine or thee.

## THERE'S A YOUTH IN THIS CITY.

THERE's a youth in this city, it were a great pity
   That he from our lasses should wander awa;
For he's bonnie and braw, weel favour'd witha',
   And his hair has a natural buckle and a'.
His coat is the hue of his bonnet sae blue;
   His fecket is white as the new-driven snaw;
His hose they are blae, and his shoon like the slae,
   And his clear siller buckles they dazzle us a'.

For beauty and fortune the laddie's been courtin;   9
   Weel-featur'd, weel-tocher'd, weel-mounted and braw;
But chiefly the siller, that gars him gang till her,
   The penny's the jewel that beautifies a'.
There's Meg wi' the mailin, that fain wad a haen him,
   And Susy whase daddy was Laird o' the ha';
There's lang-tocher'd Nancy maist fetters his fancy,
   —But the laddie's dear sel he lo'es dearest of a'.

---·•·---

## SAE FLAXEN WERE.

SAE flaxen were her ringlets,
   Her eyebrows of a darker hue,
Bewitchingly o'erarching
   Twa laughing een o' bonnie blue.
Her smiling, sae wyling,
   Wad make a wretch forget his woe;
What pleasure, what treasure,
   Unto these rosy lips to grow!
Such was my Chloris' bonnie face,
   When first her bonnie face I saw,   10
And aye my Chloris' dearest charm,
   She says she lo'es me best of a'.

Like harmony her motion;
   Her pretty ancle is a spy
Betraying fair proportion,
   Wad make a saint forget the sky;

Sae warming, sae charming,
   Her faultless form and gracefu' air;
Ilk feature—auld Nature
   Declar'd that she could do nae mair: 20
Hers are the willing chains o' love,
   By conquering beauty's sovereign law;
And aye my Chloris' dearest charm,
   She says she lo'es me best of a'.


Let others love the city,
   And gaudy show at sunny noon;
Gie me the lonely valley,
   The dewy eve, and rising moon
Fair beaming, and streaming
   Her silver light the boughs amang; 30
While falling, recalling,
   The amorous thrush concludes his sang:
There, dearest Chloris, wilt thou rove
   By wimpling burn and leafy shaw,
And hear my vows o' truth and love,
   And say thou lo'es me best of a'?

—◆—

## WEARY FA' YOU, DUNCAN GRAY.

Weary fa' you, Duncan Gray—
   Ha, ha, the girdin o't!
Wae gae by you, Duncan Gray—
   Ha, ha, the girdin o't!
When a' the lave gae to their play,
Then I maun sit the lee-lang day,
And jog the cradle wi' my tae,
   And a' for the girdin o't.


Bonnie was the Lammas moon—
   Ha, ha, the girdin o't! 10
Glowrin' a' the hills aboon—
   Ha, ha, the girdin o't!

The girdin brak, the beast cam down,
I tint my curch, an baith my shoon;
Ah! Duncan, ye're an unco loon—
  Wae on the bad girdin o't!

But, Duncan, gin ye'll keep your aith—
  Ha, há, the girdin o't!
I'se bless you wi' my hindmost breath—
  Ha, ha, the girdin o't!                    20
Duncan, gin ye'll keep your aith,
The beast again can bear us baith,
And auld Mess John will mend the skaith,
  And clout the bad girdin o't.

## MY HOGGIE.

WHAT will I do gin my Hoggie die?
  My joy, my pride, my Hoggie!
My only beast, I had na mae,
  And vow but I was vogie!

The lee-lang night we watch'd the fauld,
  Me and my faithfu' doggie;
We heard nought but the roaring linn,
  Amang the braes sae scroggie;

But the howlet cried frae the castle wa',
  The blitter frae the boggie,
The tod replied upon the hill,            10
  I trembled for my Hoggie.

When day did daw, and cocks did craw,
  The morning it was foggie;
An' unco tyke lap o'er the dyke,
  And maist has kill'd my Hoggie.

## WHERE HAE YE BEEN?

WHARE hae ye been sae braw, lad?
  Where hae ye been sae brankie, O?
O, whare hae ye been sae braw, lad?
  Cam ye by Killiecrankie, O?
An' ye had been whare I hae been,
  Ye wad na been so cantie, O;
An' ye had seen what I hae seen,
  On the braes o' Killiecrankie, O.

I fought at land, I fought at sea;
  At hame I fought my auntie, O;                    10
But I met the Devil an' Dundee,
  On the braes o' Killiecrankie, O.
The bauld Pitcur fell in a furr,
  An' Clavers got a clankie, O;
Or I had fed an Athole gled,
  On the braes o' Killiecrankie, O.

## COCK UP YOUR BEAVER.

WHEN first my brave Johnnie lad
  Came to this town,
He had a blue bonnet
  That wanted the crown;
But now he has gotten
  A hat and a feather,—
Hey, brave Johnnie lad,
  Cock up your beaver!

Cock up your beaver,
  And cock it fu' sprush,                    10
We'll over the border
  And gie them a brush;
There's somebody there
  We'll teach better behaviour—
Hey, brave Johnnie lad,
  Cock up your beaver!

## O, ONCE I LOV'D A BONNIE LASS.

O, ONCE I lov'd a bonnie lass,
    Aye, and I love her still,
And whilst that virtue warms my breast
    I love my handsome Nell.
                Fal lal de ral, &c.


As bonnie lasses I hae seen,
    And mony full as braw,
But for a modest gracefu' mien
    The like I never saw.


A bonnie lass, I will confess,          10
    Is pleasant to the ee,
But without some better qualities
    She 's no a lass for me.


But Nelly's looks are blithe and sweet,
    And what is best of a',
Her reputation is complete,
    And fair without a flaw.


She dresses aye sae clean and neat,
    Both decent and genteel ;
And then there 's something in her gait     20
    Gars ony dress look weel.


A gaudy dress and gentle air
    May slightly touch the heart,
But it 's innocence and modesty
    That polishes the dart.


'Tis this in Nelly pleases me,
    'Tis this enchants my soul !
For absolutely in my breast
    She reigns without control.

## FRAGMENTARY VERSES.

I MET a lass, a bonnie lass,
 Coming o'er the braes o' Couper,
Bare her leg and bright her een,
 And handsome ilka bit about her.
Weel I wat she was a quean
 Wad made a body's mouth to water;
Our Mess John, wi' his lyart pow,
 His haly lips wad lickit at her.

O WAT ye what my minnie did,
 My minnie did, my minnie did,
O wat ye what my minnie did
 On Tysday 't een to me, jo?
She laid me in a saft bed,
 A saft bed, a saft bed,
She laid me in a saft bed,
 And bade gudeen to me, jo.

An' wat ye what the parson did,
 The parson did, the parson did,  10
An' wat ye what the parson did,
 A' for a penny fee, jo?
He loosed on me a lang man,
 A mickle man, a strang man,
He loosed on me a lang man,
 That might hae worried me, jo.

An' I was but a young thing,
 A young thing, a young thing,
An' I was but a young thing,
 Wi' nane to pity me, jo.  20
I wat the kirk was in the wyte,
 In the wyte, in the wyte,
To pit a young thing in a fright
 An' loose a man on me, jo.

Lass, when your mither is frae hame,
  Might I but be sae bauld
As come to your bower-window,
  And creep in frae the cauld,
As come to your bower-window,
  And when it 's cauld and wat,
Warm me in thy sweet bosom ;
  Fair lass, wilt thou do that?

Young man, gif ye should be sae kind,
  When our gudewife's frae hame,                    10
As come to my bower-window,
  Whare I am laid my lane,
And warm thee in my bosom—
  But I will tell thee what,
The way to me lies through the kirk ;
  Young man, do ye hear that?

———◆———


O can ye labour lea, young man,
  An' can ye labour lea ;
Gae back the gate ye cam' again,
  Ye'se never scorn me.

I fee'd a man at Martinmas,
  Wi' arle pennies three ;
An' a' the faut I fan' wi' him,
  He couldna labour lea.

The stibble rig is easy plough'd,
  The fallow land is free ;                          10
But wha wad keep the handless coof,
  That couldna labour lea?

———◆◆———

Ye hae lien a' wrang, lassie,
  Ye've lien a' wrang;
Ye've lien in an unco bed,
  And wi' a fremit man.
O ance ye danced upon the knowes,
  And ance ye lightly sang—
But in herrying o' a bee byke,
  I'm rad ye've got a stang.

---

O GIE my love brose, brose,
  Gie my love brose and butter;
For nane in Carrick or Kyle
   Can please a lassie better.
The lav'rock lo'es the grass,
  The muirhen lo'es the heather;
But gie me a braw moonlight,
  And me and my love together.

---

Jenny M'Craw, she has ta'en to the heather,
Say, was it the covenant carried her thither;
Jenny M'Craw to the mountains is gane,
Their leagues and their covenants a' she has ta'en
My head and my heart, now, quo' she, are at rest,
And as for the lave, let the Deil do his best.

---

The last braw bridal that I was at,
  'Twas on a Hallowmass day,
And there was routh o' drink and fun,
  And mickle mirth and play.
The bells they rang, and the carlins sang,
  And the dames danced in the ha';
The bride went to bed wi' the silly bridegroom,
  In the midst o' her kimmers a'.

---

THERE came a piper out o' Fife,
　I watna what they ca'd him;
He play'd our cousin Kate a spring
　When fient a body bade him;
And aye the mair he hotch'd an' blew,
　The mair that she forbade him.

# ADDENDA

---

## ODE ON THE DEPARTED REGENCY BILL

### (MARCH, 1789).

DAUGHTER of chaos' doting years,
Nurse of ten thousand hopes and fears,
Whether thy airy insubstantial shade
(The rites of sepulture now duly paid)
Spread abroad its hideous form
On the roaring civil storm,
Deafening din and warring rage
Factions wild with factions wage ;
      Or underground
      Deep-sunk profound          10
Among the demons of the earth,
      With groans that make
      The mountains shake,
Thou mourn thy ill-starr'd blighted birth ;
Or in the uncreated void
      Where seeds of future being fight,
With lessened step thou wander wide
      To greet thy mother, Ancient Night,
And, as each jarring monster-mass is past,
Fond recollect what once thou wast :       20
In manner due, beneath this sacred oak,
Hear, spirit, hear ! thy presence I invoke !
    By a Monarch's heaven-struck fate,
    By a disunited State,

By a generous Prince's wrongs,
By a Senate's strife of tongues,
By a Premier's sullen pride,
Louring on the changing tide ;
By dread Thurlow's powers to awe—
Rhetoric, blasphemy and law ;                         30
By the turbulent ocean—
A Nation's commotion,
By the harlot-caresses
Of borough addresses,
By days few and evil,
(Thy portion, poor devil!)
By Power, Wealth and Show,
    (The gods by men adored,)
By nameless Poverty,
    (Their hell abhorred,)                           40
By all they hope, by all they fear,
Hear ! and appear !


Stare not on me, thou ghastly Power!
Nor grim with chained defiance lour ;
No Babel-structure would *I* build
    Where, order exiled from his native sway,
Confusion may the Regent-sceptre wield,
    While all would rule and none obey :


Go, to the world of Man relate
The story of thy sad eventful fate ;                 50
And call presumptuous Hope to hear,
And bid him check his blind career ;
And tell the sore-prest sons of Care,
    Never, never to despair !


Paint Charles's speed on wings of fire,
The object of his fond desire,
Beyond his boldest hopes, at hand :
Paint all the triumph of the Portland Band ;
Hark how they lift the joy-elated voice !
And who are these that equally rejoice ?             60
Jews, Gentiles, what a motley crew !
The iron tears their flinty cheeks bedew ;

See how unfurled the parchment ensigns fly,
And Principal and Interest all the cry !
But just as hopes to warm enjoyment rise,
Cry Convalescence ! and the vision flies.

Then next pourtray a dark'ning twilight gloom,
  Eclipsing sad a gay, rejoicing morn,
While proud Ambition to th' untimely tomb
  By gnashing, grim, despairing fiends is borne :  70
Paint ruin, in the shape of high D(undas)
  Gaping with giddy terror o'er the brow ;
In vain he struggles, the fates behind him press,
  And clam'rous hell yawns for her prey below :
How fallen *That*, whose pride late scaled the skies !
And *This*, like Lucifer, no more to rise !
  Again pronounce the powerful word ;
See Day, triumphant from the night, restored.

    Then know this truth, ye Sons of Men !
      (Thus ends thy moral tale,)        80
    Your darkest terrors may be vain,
      Your brightest hopes may fail.

—••—

# A NEW PSALM FOR THE CHAPEL OF KILMARNOCK.

(ON THE THANKSGIVING-DAY FOR HIS MAJESTY'S RECOVERY.)

  O SING a new Song to the Lord ;
    Make, all and every one,
  A joyful noise, even for the King
    His restoration.

  The sons of Belial in the land
    Did set their heads together ;
  Come, let us sweep them off, said they,
    Like an o'erflowing river.

They set their heads together, I say,
　They set their heads together ;　　　　　　　　10
On right, on left, and every hand,
　We saw none to deliver.

Thou madest strong two chosen ones,
　To quell the wicked's pride :
That young man, great in Issachar,
　The burden-bearing tribe ;

And him, among the princes chief
　In our Jerusalem,
The Judge that's mighty in thy law,
　The man that fears thy name.　　　　　　　　20

Yet they, even they, with all their strength
　Began to faint and fail,
Even as two howling ravenous wolves
　To dogs do turn their tail.

The ungodly o'er the just prevailed,
　For so thou hadst appointed,
That thou might'st greater glory give
　Unto thine own anointed.

And now thou hast restored our State,
　Pity our Kirk also ;　　　　　　　　　　　　30
For she by tribulations
　Is now brought very low.

Consume that high place Patronage
　From off thy holy hill,
And in thy fury burn the book
　Even of the man M'Gill.

Now hear our prayer, accept our song,
　And fight thy chosen's battle :
We seek but little, Lord, from thee —
　Thou kens we get as little !　　　　　　　　40

## EPIGRAM ON THE ROADS

### BETWEEN KILMARNOCK AND STEWARTON.

I'M now arrived, thanks to the gods!
  Thro' pathways rough and muddy,—
A certain sign that making roads
  Is not this people's study.
And tho' I'm not with scripture crammed,
  I'm sure the bible says
That heedless sinners shall be damned
  Unless they mend their ways.

---

## SYLVANDER TO CLARINDA.

### EXTEMPORE REPLY TO HER VERSES ENTITLED

*On Burns saying he 'had nothing else to do.'*

WHEN dear Clarinda, matchless fair,
  First struck Sylvander's raptured view,
He gazed, he listened to despair—
  Alas! 'twas all he dared to do.

Love from Clarinda's heavenly eyes
  Transfixed his bosom thro' and thro',
But still in Friendship's guarded guise—
  For more the demon feared to do.

That heart, already more than lost,
  The imp beleaguered all perdu,
For frowning Honour kept his post:
  To meet that frown, he shrunk to do.

His pangs the bard refused to own,
  Tho' half he wished Clarinda knew;
But anguish wrung the unweeting groan—
  *Who* blames what frantic pain must do?

That heart, where motley follies blend,
  Was sternly still to honour true ;
To prove Clarinda's fondest friend
  Was what a lover sure might do.          20

The muse his ready quill employed,
  No nearer bliss he could pursue ;
That bliss Clarinda cold denied—
  'Send word by Charles how you do.'

The chill behest disarmed his muse,
  Till passion all impatient grew :
He wrote, and hinted for excuse
  'Twas 'cause *he'd nothing else to do.*

But by those hopes I have above,
  And by those faults I dearly rue,          30
The deed—the boldest mark of love—
  For thee that deed I dare to do !

O could the fates but name the price
  Would bless me with your charms and you !
With frantic joy I'd pay it thrice,
  If human art and power could do.

Then take, Clarinda ! friendship's hand
  (Friendship at least I may avow) ;
And lay no more your chill command,—
  I'll write whatever I've to do !          40
                        SYLVANDER.

——◆◆——


## ADDITIONAL STANZAS

TO A SONG WRITTEN BY CLARINDA.

YOUR friendship much can make me blest ;
  O why that bliss destroy ?
Why urge the only one request
  You know I must deny ?

Your thought—if love must harbour there,
　　Conceal it in that thought ;
Nor cause me from my bosom tear
　　The very friend I sought.

---

## STANZA

ADDED BY BURNS TO CLARINDA'S SONG

*Go on, Sweet Bird.*

FOR thee is laughing nature gay,
For thee she pours the vernal day ;
For *me* in vain is nature drest
While joy's a stranger to my breast.

---

## THE FIRST KISS AT PARTING.

HUMID seal of soft affections,
　　Tenderest pledge of future bliss,
Dearest tie of young connections,
　　Love's first snowdrop, virgin kiss !
Speaking silence, dumb confession,
　　Passion's birth, and infants' play,
Dove-like fondness, chaste concession,
　　Glowing dawn of future day !
Sorrowing joy, adieu's last action,
　　(Lingering lips must now disjoin) ;　　10
What words can ever speak affection
　　So thrilling and sincere as thine?

---

## ON GLENRIDDELL'S FOX BREAKING HIS CHAIN.

THOU, Liberty, thou art my theme;
Not such as idle poets dream,
Who trick thee up a heathen goddess
That a fantastic cap and rod has:
Such stale conceits are poor and silly:
I paint thee out a highland filly,
A sturdy, stubborn, handsome dapple,
As sleek's a mouse, as round's an apple;
Who when thou pleasest can do wonders;
But, when thy luckless rider blunders,　　　　　10
Or if thy fancy should demur there,
Wilt break thy neck ere thou go further.

These things premised, I sing a Fox,
Was caught among his native rocks,
And to a dirty kennel chained,—
How he his liberty regained.

Glenriddell, whig without a stain,
A whig in principle and grain,
Couldst thou enslave a free-born creature,
A native denizen of Nature?　　　　　　　20
How couldst thou with a heart so good
(A better ne'er was sluiced with blood!)
Nail a poor devil to a tree
That ne'er did harm to thine or thee?

The staunchest whig, Glenriddell was
Quite frantic in his country's cause;
And oft was Reynard's prison passing,
And with his brother-whigs canvássing
The rights of men, the powers of women,
With all the dignity of freemen.　　　　　　30

Sir Reynard daily heard debates
Of princes', kings', and Nations' fates,
With many rueful bloody stories
Of tyrants, Jacobites, and tories:

From liberty how angels fell,
And now are galley-slaves in hell ;
How Nimrod first the trade began
Of binding slavery's chain on man ;
How fell Semiramis (God damn her !)
Did first with sacrilegious hammer                       40
(All ills till then were trivial matters)
For man dethroned forge ' hen-peck ' fetters ;
How Xerxes, that abandoned tory,
Thought cutting throats was reaping glory,
Until the stubborn whigs of Sparta
Taught him great Nature's *Magna Charta;*
How mighty Rome her fiat hurled
Resistless o'er a bowing world,
And, kinder than they did desire,
Polished mankind with sword and fire ;                   50
With much, too tedious to relate,
Of ancient and of modern date,
But ending still how Billy Pitt,
Unlucky boy ! with wicked wit,
Has gagged old Britain, drained her coffer,
As butchers bind and bleed a heifer.

Thus wily Reynard by degrees,
In kennel listening at his ease,
Sucked in a mighty stock of knowledge,
As much as some folk at a College ;                      60
Knew Britain's rights and constitution,
Her aggrandisement, diminution ;
How fortune wrought us good from evil :
Let no man then despise the Devil,
As who should say ' I ne'er can need him,'-
Since we to scoundrels owe our freedom.

\*        \*        \*        \*        \*        \*        \*        \*

# POEMS, GENERALLY DENIED TO BURNS, BUT PROBABLY HIS COMPOSITION.

## ELEGY

WRITTEN IN A CHURCH-YARD IN GREENOCK AT THE GRAVE OF MARY CAMPBELL—BURNS'S HIGHLAND MARY.

STRAIT is the spot and green the sod,
    From whence my sorrows flow;
And soundly sleeps the ever dear
    Inhabitant below.

Pardon my transport, gentle shade,
    While o'er the turf I bow!
Thy earthly house is circumscrib'd,
    And solitary now.

Not one poor stone to tell thy name,
    Or make thy virtues known:      10
But what avails to me, to thee,
    The sculpture of a stone?

I'll sit me down upon this turf,
    And wipe away this tear:
The chill blast passes swiftly by,
    And flits around thy bier.

Dark is the dwelling of the Dead,
    And sad their house of rest:
Low lies the head by Death's cold arm
    In awful fold embrac'd.      20

I saw the grim Avenger stand
    Incessant by thy side;
Unseen by thee, his deadly breath
    Thy lingering frame destroy'd.

Pale grew the roses on thy cheek,
　And wither'd was thy bloom,
Till the slow poison brought thy youth
　Untimely to the tomb.

Thus wasted are the ranks of men,
　Youth, Health, and Beauty fall:　　　　30
The ruthless ruin spreads around,
　And overwhelms us all.

Behold where round thy narrow house
　The graves unnumber'd lie!
The multitudes that sleep below
　Existed but to die.

Some, with the tottering steps of Age,
　Trod down the darksome way:
And some, in youth's lamented prime,
　Like thee, were torn away.　　　　40

Yet these, however hard their fate,
　Their native earth receives:
Amid their weeping friends they died,
　And fill their fathers' graves.

From thy lov'd friends when first thy heart
　Was taught by Heaven to flow,
Far, far remov'd, the ruthless stroke
　Surpris'd and laid thee low.

At the last limits of our isle,
　Wash'd by the western wave,　　　　50
Touch'd by thy fate, a thoughtful bard
　Sits lonely on thy grave.

Pensive he eyes before him spread
　The deep, outstretch'd and vast;
His mourning notes are borne away
　Along the rapid blast.

And while, amid the silent Dead
    Thy hapless fate he mourns,
His own long sorrows freshly bleed,
    And all his grief returns.                    60

Like thee, cut off in early youth
    And flower of beauty's pride,
His friend, his first and only joy,
    His much loved Stella, died.

Him, too, the stern impulse of Fate
    Resistless bears along;
And the same rapid tide shall whelm
    The Poet and the Song.

The tear of pity which he shed,
    He asks not to receive;                    70
Let but his poor remains be laid
    Obscurely in the grave.

His grief-worn heart, with truest joy,
    Shall meet the welcome shock;
His airy harp shall lie unstrung
    And silent on the rock.

O, my dear maid, my Stella, when
    Shall this sick period close,
And leave the solitary bard
    To his beloved repose?                    80

—•—

## NAETHING.

(PROBABLY ADDRESSED TO GAVIN HAMILTON, 1786.)

To you, Sir, this summons I've sent,
    Pray whip till the pownie is fraething,
But if you demand what I want,
    I honestly answer you—naething.

Ne'er scorn a poor Poet like me,
  For idly just living and breathing,
While people of every degree
  Are busy employed about—naething.

Poor Centum-per-centum may fast,
  And grumble his hurdies their claithing ;    10
He'll find, when the balance is cast,
  He's gane to the devil for—naething.

The courtier cringes and bows,
  Ambition has likewise its plaything ;
A coronet beams on his brows :
  And what is a coronet?—naething.

Some quarrel the Presbyter gown,
  Some quarrel Episcopal graithing,
But every good fellow will own
  Their quarrel is all about—naething.    20

The lover may sparkle and glow,
  Approaching his bonnie bit gay thing :
But marriage will soon let him know
  He's gotten a buskit up naething.

The Poet may jingle and rhyme
  In hopes of a laureate wreathing,
And when he has wasted his time
  He's kindly rewarded with naething.

The thundering bully may rage,
  And swagger and swear like a heathen ;    30
But collar him fast, I'll engage,
  You'll find that his courage is naething.

Last night with a feminine whig,
  A Poet she couldna put faith in,
But soon we grew lovingly big,
  I taught her her terrors were naething.

Her whigship was wonderful pleased,
  But charmingly tickled with ae thing;
Her fingers I lovingly squeezed,
  And kissed her and promised her—naething.    40

The priest anathémas may threat,—
  Predicament, Sir, that we're baith in;
But when honour's reveillé is beat,
  The holy artillery's naething.

And now, I must mount on the wave,
  My voyage perhaps there is death in:
But what of a watery grave?
  The drowning a Poet is naething.

And now, as grim death's in my thought,
  To you, Sir, I make this bequeathing:    50
My service as long as ye've aught,
  And my friendship, by God! when ye've naething.

———••———

## FRAGMENTARY VERSES.

His face with smile eternal drest—
Just like the Landlord's to his Guest,
High where they hang, with creaking din,
To index out a country inn.

———••———

A head pure, sinless quite, of brain or soul:
The very image of a barber's poll—
It shows a human face, and wears a wig,
And looks, when well preserved, amazing big.

———••———

He looks as sign-board Lions do,
As fierce, and just as harmless too.

# NOTES

---

Page 1. **Tam o' Shanter.** Burns thought this poem his best ; and Sir Walter Scott, no bad judge of a tale of diablerie, approved his judgement. It was written late in the autumn of 1790, when the poet was near the close of his thirty-second year. He was then resident on his farm at Ellisland, a few miles up the Nith from Dumfries ; but, though still a farmer, he had already commenced the active duties of a gauger, or excise-officer. The occasion of the poem was an arrangement with Grose, the antiquary, who promised to include, in his collection of the pictured Antiquities of Scotland, the primitive Kirk of Alloway, near Ayr, if Burns on his part furnished a witch story to accompany the engraving. Burns not only gave him the metrical Tale of *Tam o' Shanter*, but sketched in prose three legends of Kirk Alloway besides —one of which is of interest as the groundwork of the poem : here it is in Burns's own words :

On a market day, in the town of Ayr, a farmer from Carrick, and consequently whose way lay by the very gate of Alloway Kirk-yard, in order to cross the river Doon at the old bridge, which is about two or three hundred yards farther on than the said gate, had been detained by his business, till by the time he reached Alloway it was the wizard hour, between night and morning.

Though he was terrified with a blaze streaming from the Kirk, yet as it is a well known fact, that to turn back on these occasions is running by far the greatest risk of mischief, he prudently advanced on his road. When he had reached the gate of the Kirk-yard, he was surprised and entertained, through the ribs and arches of an old Gothic window, which still faces the highway, to see a dance of witches merrily footing it round their old sooty blackguard master, who was keeping all alive with the power of his bagpipe. The farmer, stopping his horse to observe them a little, could plainly descry the faces of many old women of his acquaintance and neighbourhood. How the gentleman was dressed, tradition does not say, but that the ladies were all in their smocks ; and one of them happening unluckily to have a smock which was considerably too short to answer all the purposes of that piece of dress, our farmer was so tickled that he involuntarily burst out, with a loud laugh, 'Weel looppen Maggy wi' the short sark!' and, recollecting himself, instantly spurred his horse to the top of his speed. I need not mention the universally known fact, that no diabolical power can pursue you beyond the middle of a running stream. Lucky it was for the poor farmer that the river Doon was so near, for notwithstanding the speed of his horse, which was a good one, against he reached the middle of the arch of the bridge, and consequently the middle of the stream, the pursuing, vengeful hags were so close at his heels, that one of them actually sprang to seize him; but it was too late; nothing was on her side of the stream but the horse's tail, which immediately gave way at her infernal grip, as if blasted by a stroke of lightning; but the farmer was beyond her reach. However, the unsightly, tailless condition of the vigorous steed was, to the last hours of the noble creature's life, an awful warning to the Carrick farmers not to stay too late in Ayr markets.

Shanter is a farm near Kirkoswald, in the Carrick, or southern, division of Ayrshire, and its tenant, Douglas Graham, may have been the prototype of Tam. Burns, who took lessons in land-surveying at Kirkoswald in his seventeenth year, was well acquainted with the neighbourhood.

Line 19. skellum. In German, *schelm*, a rascal.

ll. 45, 46. Cp. Dunbar:

> Thay sportit thame, and makis mirry cheir
> *With sangis lowd*, baith Symone and the Freir;
> And on thiss wyiss *the lang nicht thay ourdraif.*
> > *The Freiris of Berwick*, ll. 415-417.

> Bot thay wer blyth annwche, God watt, *and sang*,
> For ay the wyne was rakand thame amang.—Id., ll. 439, 440.

ll. 51, 52. Cp. Thomson:

> Much he talks,
> And much he laughs, nor recks the storm that blows
> Without, and rattles on his humble roof.
> > *The Seasons* ('Spring,' ll. 89-91).

l. 61. Supply the relative pronoun 'that' between 'snow' and 'falls.' For its omission when in the nominative case, cp. Scott:

> There is a nun in Dryburgh bower
> Ne'er looks upon the sun.
> > *Eve of St. John.*

l. 63. For 'race' it has been suggested that Burns meant 'rays.' But see his poem *The Vision*, pp. 53, 56, &c., *infra*, for his use of this word.

l. 105. Whisky.

ll. 131-140. Cp. the incantation of the witches in *Macbeth*. Burns struck out the following four lines :

> Three lawyers' tongues turn'd inside out,
> Wi' lies seam'd like a beggar's clout;
> And priests' hearts rotten, black as muck,
> Lay stinking vile in every neuk.

l. 164. This line is taken from Allan Ramsay :

> She was a winsome wench and wally,
> And cou'd put on her claes fu' brawly, &c.
>                                            *The Three Bonnets*, canto i, ll. 83, 84.

l. 177. A pund Scots was equal to twenty *pence*, sterling.

l. 208. 'It is a well-known fact that witches, or any evil spirits, have no power to follow a poor wight any farther than the middle of the next running stream. It may be proper likewise to mention to the benighted traveller that when he falls in with *bogles* [goblins], whatever danger may be in going forward, there is much more hazard in turning back.' *Note by Burns.*

**Page 7. The Jolly Beggars.** This cantata was written in the autumn of 1785, when Burns was nearing the close of his twenty-sixth year. He was then tenant, conjointly with his brother Gilbert, of Mossgiel farm near Mauchline. His father had died about a year and a half before. The immediate occasion of the poem was a night visit to a low alehouse in the village of Mauchline, kept by 'Poosie Nansie' (Nancy Gibson), and much frequented by vagrants and vagabonds. Burns was accompanied on the occasion by two of his friends, young men of about his own age, James Smith and John Richmond. But the idea of a poem on such a subject was probably suggested to Burns by *The Happy Beggars* and *The Merry Beggars* in Allan Ramsay's *Tea-Table Miscellany*. In the former of those 'choice' old songs there are six female characters who successively despise wealth, dress, cosmetics, and continence, and defy scandal, care, and 'the vapours': they join in chorus in praise of drink. In the latter there are also six characters —a poet, a lawyer, a soldier, a courtier, a gut-scraper (or fiddler), and a 'fanatical' preacher; all of them, of course, in reduced circumstances : the poet provides them with a chorus—

> Whoe'er would be merry and free,
>    Let him list, and from us he may learn ;
> In palaces who shall we see
>    Half so happy as we in a barn?
> Tol de rol, &c.

*The Jolly Beggars* seems to have been thought poorly of by its author, though Carlyle and Matthew Arnold regard it as his most original

effort, superior to *Tam o' Shanter*.  It was never printed in his lifetime ;
and eight years after writing it he had nearly forgotten all about it ;
'however,' he wrote (1793), 'I remember that none of the songs pleased
myself except the last, something about

> Courts for cowards were erected,
> Churches built to please the priest.'

Burns's friend Richmond recollected songs by a sweep and a sailor,
which do not now appear in the cantata.  The sweep's song seems to
be lost with the sweep.  The sailor's song is probably the one beginning
'Though women's minds' (which I give on p. 17), part of which is in-
corporated with the bard's song on p. 15.  The song on p. 18 is also
probably a part of the cantata : it suits the caird, and may be regarded
as his second effort to maintain the general jollity at Pussie Nancy's.

*The Jolly Beggars* was first published, but in an incomplete form, in
Stewart and Meikle's Tracts in 1799 : the character and song of Merry
Andrew (pp. 9, 10) were added in 1802 from a manuscript of the poet's
own in the possession of Richmond.

**ll. 1–14.** These lines comprise a stanza of singular construction,
the difficulties of which Burns seems to have overcome at once.  It
was a favourite measure with the older ' makers '—Allan Ramsay (*The
Vision*, pub. 1724), Alexander Montgomery (*The Cherrie and the Slae*, pub.
1597), &c.  For an earlier use of the measure see Maitland's *Creation
and Paradyse Lost* in Ramsay's *Evergreen* ; or, better, in the Bannatyne
MS., compiled in 1568, and printed for the Hunterian Club in 1873.
It is there entitled ' Ane Ballat of the Creatioun of the World, Man
his Fall and Redemption, maid to the tone of *The Banks of Hellicone*.'
The old song of *The Banks of Helicon* will be found in Pinkerton (*Anc.
Scot. Poems*, ii. 237).  Dr. Guest (*Hist. of English Rhythms*) thinks it as
old as 1550, and the oldest specimen of this singular stanza.

**l. 2. The baukie bird.**  'The old Scotch name for the bat.'  *Note by
Burns.*

**l. 5. Infant frosts.**  In *The Brigs of Ayr*, l. 175, Burns has ' infant ice.'

**l. 35.** At the capture of Quebec by Wolfe in 1759.

**l. 37. El Morro**, the fortress which commanded the entrance to the
harbour of Santiago, on the south shore of Cuba, West Indies.  It was
reduced ('laid low ') by the British in 1762, and thereafter Havanna
surrendered.

**l. 38.** At the siege of Gibraltar, in 1762.

**l. 40. Elliot**, who defended Gibraltar for three years, and was raised
to the peerage with the title of Lord Heathfield.

**l. 46.** Cp. *The Matron's Wish* (Ramsay's *Tea-Table Miscellany*): 'When my
locks are grown hoary.'

**l. 58.** Cp. *Merry Beggars* : ' I once was a poet at London,' &c.

l. 189. Cp. *Merry Beggars* : ' I still am a merry gut-scraper.'

l. 216. Kilbaigie, a whisky distillery in Clackmannan. Burns notes that 'Kilbaigie was a peculiar sort of whisky, a great favourite with Poosie Nansie's clubs.'

ll. 241–244. Cp. Goldsmith's *Mistress Mary Blaize*, who ' never followed wicked ways unless when she was sinning !'

ll. 254–257. Cp Fergusson :

> O Muse ! be kind, an' dinna fash us
> To flee awa' beyond Parnassus,
> Nor seek for Helicon to wash us,
>     That heathenish spring ;
> Wi' highland whisky scour our hawses,
>     An' gar us sing.            *The King's Birthday.*

l. 258. Cp. ' Great love they bare to Fairly fair ' (*Hardyknute*).

l. 282. Cp. Ramsay :

> Thy last oration orthodox,
> Thy innocent auld-farren jokes,
> Thy sonsy saw of three provokes
>     Me anes again,
> Tod-lowrie-like, to loose my pocks
>     And pump my brain.
>         *Third Epistle to Hamilton of Gilbertfield*, 1719.

ll. 292, 293. Cp. Ramsay's *Tea-Table Miscellany* :

> A fig for gaudy fashions, &c.

and

> We all agree in liberty, &c.—*The Happy Beggars.*

ll. 296–299. Cp. *Tea-Table Miscellany* :

> How blest are beggar-lasses
>     Who never toil for treasure !
> Who know no care but how to share
>     Each day's successive pleasure !
> \*     \*     \*     \*     \*
> We know no shame or scandal, &c.
>         *The Happy Beggars.*

l. 303. Doxy, literally, little doll ; introduced from the Netherlands, *dokke*, a duck, a doll. The word is rare in Scotland ; Burns probably found it in Shakespeare :

> When daffodils begin to peer—
>     With heigh ! the doxy over the dale, &c.
>         Autolycus's song in *The Winter's Tale*, Act iv, sc. 2.

l. 338. Burns may have caught the words of this toast from his seaman friend at Irvine, Richard Brown. See his letter to Dr. Moore for Brown's influence upon him.

**Page 18. Halloween.** This poem, like the preceding, belongs also to the late autumn of 1785, and to the Mossgiel period of the poet's life. It contains a larger proportion of old Scottish words than any other composition of the author's; and he accompanied its publication in the first (or Kilmarnock) edition of his poems with copious explanatory notes : these are reproduced here over his initials. The measure is that of *Christ's Kirk on the Green.*

Halloween is the eve of All Hallows (All Saints), October 31. It is still celebrated in Scotland ; but the element of superstitious terror is now, even among rustics, entirely eliminated from the ceremonies proper to the festival.

Burns begins his annotation of *Halloween* with the following preface:—

'This poem will, by many readers, be well enough understood ; but for the sake of those who are unacquainted with the manners and traditions of the country where the scene is cast, notes are added, to give some account of the principal charms and spells of that night, so big with prophecy to the peasantry in the west of Scotland. The passion of prying into futurity makes a striking part of the history of human nature, in its rude state, in all ages and nations ; and it may be some entertainment to a philosophic mind, if any such should honour the Author with a perusal, to see the remains of it, among the more unenlightened in our own.'

*Note to Title.* 'Halloween is thought to be a night when witches, devils, and other mischief-making beings are all abroad on their baneful, midnight errands ; particularly those aërial people, the fairies, are said, on that night, to hold a grand anniversary.' R. B.

l. 2. 'Certain little, romantic, rocky, green hills, in the neighbourhood of the ancient seat of the Earls of Cassilis.' R. B.

l. 7. 'A noted cavern near Colean house, called the Cove of Colean : which, as well as Cassilis Downans, is famed in country story for being a favourite haunt of fairies.' R. B.

l. 12. 'The famous family of that name, the ancestors of Robert, the great deliverer of his country, were Earls of Carrick.' R. B.

ll. 19–27. Cp. the first two stanzas of *Christ's Kirk on the Green*, a humorous Scottish poem of the fifteenth century, probably written by King James I. Burns would see this famous old poem in Ramsay's *Evergreen.*

l. 29. 'The first ceremony of Halloween is, pulling each a *stock*, or plant of kail. They must go out, hand in hand, with eyes shut, and pull the first they meet with. Its being big or little, straight or crooked, is prophetic of the size and shape of the grand object of all their spells—the husband or wife. If any *yird*, or earth, stick to the root, that is tocher, or fortune ; and the taste of the *custock*, that is, the heart of the stem, is indicative of the natural temper and disposition.

Lastly, the stems, or, to give them their ordinary appellation, the *runts*, are placed somewhere above the head of the door; and the Christian names of the people whom chance brings into the house, are, according to the priority of placing the *runts*, the names in question.' R. B.

l. 39. See l. 21 of *The Cotter's Saturday Night*.

l. 47. 'They go to the barn-yard, and pull each, at three several times, a stalk of oats. If the third stalk wants the *tap-pickle*, that is, the grain at the top of the stalk, the party in question will come to the marriage-bed anything but a maid.' R. B.

l. 53. 'When the corn is in a doubtful state, by being too green, or wet, the stack-builder, by means of old timber, &c., makes a large apartment in his stack, with an opening in the side which is fairest exposed to the wind: this he calls a *Fause-house*.' R. B.

l. 55. 'Burning the nuts is a famous charm. They name the lad and the lass to each particular nut, as they lay them in the fire; and accordingly as they burn quietly together, or start from beside one another, the course and issue of the courtship will be.' R. B.

l. 98. 'Whoever would, with success, try this spell, must strictly observe these directions: Steal out, all alone, to the *kiln*, and, darkling, throw into the *pot* a clue of blue yarn: wind it in a new clue off the old one; and towards the latter end, something will hold the thread; demand, *Wha hauds?* i. e. who holds? an answer will be returned from the kiln-pot, by naming the Christian and surname of your future spouse.' R. B.

l. 111. 'Take a candle, and go alone to a looking-glass: eat an apple before it, and some traditions say you should comb your hair all the time; the face of your conjugal companion, *to be*, will be seen in the glass, as if peeping over your shoulder.' R. B.

l. 118. Minx. Burns explains it as a 'technical term in female scolding.'

l. 127. The battle of Sheriffmuir was in 1715.

l. 136. Our leader. Interesting to notice the name—not a common one—on a tombstone at Kirkoswald.

l. 140. 'Steal out unperceived, and sow a handful of hemp-seed; harrowing it with anything you can conveniently draw after you. Repeat now and then, 'Hemp-seed, I saw thee; hemp-seed, I saw thee; and him (or her) that is to be my true-love, come after me and pou thee.' Look over your left shoulder, and you will see the appearance of the person invoked, in the attitude of pulling hemp. Some traditions say, 'come after me, and shaw thee,' that is show thyself: in which case it simply appears. Others omit the harrowing, and say, "come after me, and harrow thee."' R. B. But the custom was also observed in England. Gay's version of the ceremony has some interesting points of difference:

At eve last midsummer, &c.—*The Shepherd's Week* (Thursday).

l. 182. 'This charm must likewise be performed unperceived, and alone. You go to the *barn*, and open both doors, taking them off the hinges, if possible : for there is danger, that the *being*, about to appear, may shut the doors, and do you some mischief. Then take that instrument used in winnowing the corn, which, in our country dialect, we call a *wecht* ; and go through all the attitudes of letting down corn against the wind. Repeat it three times ; and the third time an apparition will pass through the barn, in at the windy door, and out at the other, having both the figure in question, and the appearance or retinue, marking the employment or station in life.' R. B.

l. 201. 'Take an opportunity of going, unnoticed, to a *Bear-stack*, and fathom it three times round. The last fathom of the last time, you will catch in your arms the appearance of your future conjugal yoke-fellow.' R. B.

l. 214. 'You go out, one or more (for this is a social spell), to a south running spring or rivulet, where "three lairds' lands meet," and dip your left shirt sleeve. Go to bed in sight of a fire, and hang your wet sleeve before it to dry. Lie awake ; and some time near midnight, an apparition, having the exact figure of the grand object in question will come and turn the sleeve, as if to dry the other side of it.' R. B.

l. 220. Alexander Hume, minister of Logie (died 1609), notes, in his fine poem *The Day Estival*,

> The bells and circles on the weills
> Thro' leaping of the trouts.

l. 223. Cookit. This word is almost always misinterpreted. It does not mean 'crept,' or 'disappeared,' but 'peeped slily, quietly, and quickly.' It used to be a common cry *to cook oot*, at the Scottish schoolboys' game of *I spy*. 'Cookit' should be taken along with the tag, or bob, 'Unseen that night' ; and the expression signifies the faintest glimmer or sparkle of water in the shadow of the hazel-bank, as of an eye peeping out shyly and immediately disappearing. The word is chosen with fine artistic feeling. 'Keekit' is another form.

l. 236. 'Take three dishes ; put clean water in one, foul water in another, leave the third empty : blindfold a person, and lead him to the hearth where the dishes are ranged ; he (or she) dips the left hand : if by chance in the clean water, the future husband or wife will come to the bar of matrimony, a maid : if in the foul, a widow : if in the empty dish, it foretells, with equal certainty, no marriage at all. It is repeated three times ; and every time the arrangement of the dishes is altered.' R. B.

l. 240. Mar's year was the year 1715, which witnessed the supression of the Jacobite rebellion raised by the Earl of Mar.

l. 248. 'Sowens, with butter instead of milk to them, is always the *Halloween Supper*.' R. B.

**Page 26. The Cotter's Saturday Night.** This poem was written at Mossgiel in the early winter of 1785. It is on the model of *The Schoolmistress* of Shenstone, and (more especially) of *The Farmer's Ingle* of Robert Fergusson. Unlike the latter, however, it maintains the perfect form of the Spenserian stanza. Burns inscribed it to Robert Aiken, a writer or solicitor in the town of Ayr, one of his early patrons, and whom the poet described as having 'read him into fame.' A stanza from Gray's *Elegy* ('Let not ambition mock,' &c.) was prefixed by way of motto to the poem on its first appearance in print, in the Kilmarnock edition of Burns's Poems, in 1786. The historical value of the poem is at least equal to its poetical merit ; it faithfully describes a phase of peasant life in Scotland which is fast disappearing.

Line 1. **Much respected friend.** Robert Aiken, writer, Ayr. See preceding note.

l. 6. **Life's sequester'd scene.** Cf. Gray's 'cool sequestered vale of life.'

ll. 10–18. Cf. the opening stanza of Gray's *Elegy*.

ll. 21, 22. Cf. Gray's line, 'No children run to lisp their sire's return.'

l. 26. **Kiaugh and care.** Altered to 'carking cares' in ed. 1793.

l. 31. **A neibor town.** A farm-town in the neighbourhood.

ll. 82–90. Cf. the passage in Burns's own later poem, *A Winter Night*, beginning 'Is there, beneath Love's noble name': see pp. 96, 97, ll. 62–72. Cf. also the passage in Goldsmith's *Deserted Village*, beginning 'Ah ! turn thine eyes,' l. 325.

l. 99. A year old since the flax was in bloom.

ll. 111–113. **Dundee . . . Elgin . . . Martyrs.** Names of psalm-tunes, once common in Scottish churches.

l. 138. The true quotation is 'And mounts exulting on triumphant wings'—said of the pheasant, in Pope's *Windsor Forest*.

l. 140. A recollection of Milton's address to Light :

> Bright effluence of bright essence increate. (*Par. Lost*, bk. iii.)

l. 163. Cf. Thomson's *Seasons* ('Summer,' ll. 423, 424) :

> A simple scene ! yet hence
> Britannia sees her solid grandeur rise, &c.

l. 165. Cf. Goldsmith's line, 'A breath can make them, as a breath has made.' (*Deserted Village*.)

l. 166. Quoted from Pope's *Essay on Man*.

ll. 167, 168. Cf. Milton's *Comus* :

> Which oft is sooner found in lowly sheds,
> With smoky rafters, than in tapestry halls
> And courts of princes. (ll. 323-325).

ll. 169–171. Cf. Goldsmith's *Deserted Village*, ll. 275–282 ; also Burns's own poem, *A Winter Night*, p. 96, ll. 50–64.

ll. 172–180. Thomson has the same patriotic prayer, expressed in similar words :

> O Thou by whose almighty nod the scale
> Of empire rises or alternate falls,
> Send forth the saving virtues round the land
> In bright patrol ! &c.  *The Seasons* ('Summer,' ll. 1602–1619).

**P. 31. The Holy Fair.** A 'Holy Fair' was a summer gathering of Christians convoked at some central rural spot for the purpose of religious exercises, preparatory to a celebration of the Lord's Supper. The religious exercises took place in the open air, and were continued without intermission throughout the day, while the more sacred ordinance of the Sacrament was dispensed to communicants, coming and retiring in relays, under the roof of the little adjoining church.' *In Scottish Fields*, Hugh Haliburton.

The 'Holy Fair' described by Burns was held in the village of Mauchline. The poem was written in 1786. It was suggested by, and composed on the lines of, Fergusson's *Leith Races*. In respect of theme, of plan, of treatment, and of measure, it strongly resembles *Leith Races*. Burns's Letters show that in the Spring of 1786 he was an enthusiastic student of Fergusson's Scottish poems.

Lines 1–4. Cf. the opening stanza of *Leith Races* :

> In July month ae bonny morn
> When Nature's rokelay green
> Was spread owre ilka rig o' corn
> To charm our rovin' een.

l. 5. Galston is a parish bordering on that of Mauchline.

l. 10. Cf. Fergusson (*Leith Races*) :

> Glow'rin about I saw a quean
> The fairest 'neath the lift, &c.

ll. 28–37. Cf. Fergusson :

> 'And wha are ye, my winsome dear,
> That taks the gate sae early?
> Where do you win ? if ane may speer ;
> For I right meikle ferly
> That sic braw-buskit laughin' lass
> Thir bonny blinks should gie,
> And loup, like Hebe, owre the grass
> As wanton, and as free
> Frae dool this day.'

> ' I dwall amang the cauler springs
>  That weet the Land o' Cakes,
> And aften tune my canty strings
>  At bridals and late-wakes.
> They ca' me Mirth '

l. 75. Racer Jess was Jess Gibson, a daughter of ' Poussie Nansie.'

l. 91. This is a line of a Psalm (Ps. cxlvi. 5).

l. 102. Moodie was one of the local clergymen who had come to assist the parish minister at the celebration of the Sacrament. Others were Smith, Peebles, Miller, and Russel. The ' holy door' means the 'tent' (l. 118) or open-air pulpit.

l. 103. Originally ' tidings o' salvation '—altered at the suggestion of the Rev. Hugh Blair, an Edinburgh minister, at one time Professor of Rhetoric in Edinburgh University.

l. 104. See the Book of Job, chap. i.

l. 143. The Cowgate was a street in Mauchline, near the church.

l. 188. Quoted from Shakespeare's *Hamlet*, i. 5.

**P. 38. The Twa Dogs.** Written in 1786.

l. 2. Coil or Kyle is one of the three divisions of Ayrshire ; it lies between the Ayr and the Doon. Carrick is on the south of it, Cunningham on the north. King Coil is one of the traditional chieftains of the ancient kingdom of Strathclyde.

l. 12. Newfoundland.

l. 24. Cf. ' Rantin', rovin' Robin' in Burns's song *There was a lad*.

l. 26. Luath was the name, as Burns himself tells us, of ' Cuchullin's dog in Ossian's *Fingal*.'

l. 65. Blastit wonner. The same expression occurs in *To a Louse*, l. 7.

l. 115. A quart of ale, value one penny sterling, twelve pennies Scots.

l. 119. Patrons and ministers. 'Patronage was abolished in the Kirk of Scotland in 1874. The appointment now rests with the congregation.

l. 144. The ' rascal' is the factor of l. 96.

l. 146. ' Gentle' in the sense of well born,—as in the title of Ramsay's rustic drama, *The Gentle Shepherd*.

ll. 155–168. See the scene in *The Way to Win Him*, where the ladies of Spain, Italy, Holland, &c. are discussed.

l. 162. Bull-baiting.

l. 181. Felling the trees on their estate. The expression occurs in Farquhar's *The Recruiting Officer*.

l. 196. Cf. Burns's own line (*First Epistle to Lapraik*), 'They gang in stirks an' come oot asses.'

l. 204. So many dozens (of hanks of thread) spun by her.

ll. 213, 214. Cf. Goldsmith (*The Deserted Village*) :

> To me more dear, congenial to my heart,
> One native charm than all the gloss of art.
> \*       \*       \*       \*       \*       \*
> But the long pomp, the midnight masquerade,
> With all the freaks of wanton wealth array'd,
> In these, ere triflers half their wish obtain,
> The toiling pleasure sickens into pain,
> And, even while fashion's brightest arts decoy,
> The heart distrusting asks if this be joy.

l. 226. Playing-cards.

l. 227. The whole year's crop on a farm.

l. 233. Cf. Gray's line, 'Save where the beetle wheels his droning flight' (*The Elegy*).

**P. 45. The Brigs of Ayr.** Written in 1786, and inscribed to the Provost of Ayr, John Ballantine, banker, under whose municipal rule the erection of a new bridge over the river Ayr was then proceeding. The poem was composed on the plan and in the style of Robert Fergusson's *Mutual Complaint of Plainstanes and Causeway*, or, perhaps preferably, his *Twa Ghaists*, and the *Drink Eclogue*.

Lines 2–6. 'I never hear . . . the wild mixing cadence of a troop of gray plovers in an autumnal morning without feeling an elevation of soul like the enthusiasm of devotion or poetry.' Burns's *Letters—To Mrs. Dunlop*, January, 1789.

ll. 29–33. Cf. Thomson's *Seasons* ('Autumn,' ll. 1172–1192).

l. 50. **Prest wi' care.** The expression occurs in *Man was made to Mourn*, and in *The Gloomy Night*.

l. 52. 'A noted tavern at the Auld Brig end.' *Note by Burns.*

l. 56. This line occurs in *The Epistle to Davie*, stanza iv.

ll. 57, 58. 'The two steeples.' *Note by Burns.* They are now removed.

l. 62. Cf. Low's song, *Mary's Dream* ('The Moon had climbed, &c.')

l. 68. 'The Gos-hawk, or Falcon.' R. B.

l. 80. Cf. Fergusson (*The Election*) :

> The dinner done, for brandy strang
>     They cry, to weet their thrapple,
> To gar the stamack *bide the bang*,
>     An' wi' its lading grapple.

l. 103. 'A noted ford just above the Auld Brig.' R. B.

l. 110. A prophecy partly fulfilled in 1877.

ll. 113–124. This is after Thomson (*The Seasons*, 'Winter,' ll. 94–105).

l. 118. 'The banks of Garpal Water is one of the few places in the West of Scotland where those fancy-scaring beings, known by the name of Ghaists, still continue pertinaciously to inhabit.' R. B.

l. 123. **Glenbuck.** 'The source of the river Ayr.' R. B. The Ratton-key—'a small landing-place above the large quay.' R. B.

l. 124. Cf. Thomson's line, 'A shoreless ocean tumbled round the globe.'

l. 145. Cf. Shakespeare (*Midsummer Night's Dream*) :

> In shady cloister mew'd
> To live a barren sister all your life
> Chanting faint hymns to the cold fruitless moon.

ll. 184, 185. For these two lines the first draught of the poem gave :

> Nae mair down street the council quorum waddles
> With wigs like mainsails on their logger-noddles,
> Nae difference but bulkiest or tallest,
> With comfortable dulness in for ballast ;
> Nor shoals nor currents need a pilot's caution,
> For, regularly slow, they only witness motion.

l. 202. **M'Lauchlan.** 'A well-known performer of Scottish music on the violin.' R. B.

ll. 213–216. Cf. Milton's *Lycidas* : 'Next Camus, reverend sire,' &c.

l. 226. The Faile water is a tributary of the Ayr.

l. 228. A compliment to Mrs. Stewart of Stair.

l. 229. Professor Dugald Stewart, of Catrine, the well-known philosopher.

**P. 51. The Vision.** This poem, mostly written in 1786, is divided into *Duans*. A *Duan*, as Burns informs us, is ' a term of Ossian's for the different divisions of a digressive poem. See his Cath-Loda, vol. 2 of M'Pherson's translation.' It was from Pope's *Rape of the Lock*, rather than from Milton's *Comus*, that Burns got the idea of guardian spirits for *The Vision*. Burns had the good taste to keep some of the stanzas of this poem in MS.

Lines 3–6. Cf. Thomson *The Seasons* ('Winter') :

> The foodless wilds
> Pour forth their brown inhabitants. The hare
> \*     \*     \*     \*     \*     \*     \*
> The garden seeks.

ll. 19–38. Their devotion to poetry as an art is announced by both Goldsmith and Burns with the same fervour and in very similar language. Both debate the worldly wisdom of this devotion, with the same ultimate open-eyed choice of poetry and poverty, preferably to plenty and prose. It was in the following frank, devoted style that Goldsmith wooed the muse :

> Sweet Poesy, thou loveliest maid !
> Dear charming Nymph !    .    .    .    .
> My shame in crowds, my solitary pride,
> Thou source of all my bliss and all my woe,
> That found'st me poor at first, and keep'st me so, &c.

Burns admits us to a dramatic view of the manner of his decision in *The Vision.*

l. 98. 'The Wallaces.' R. B.

l. 103. 'William Wallace.' R. B.

l. 104. 'Adam Wallace of Richardton, cousin to the immortal preserver of Scottish independence.' R. B.

l. 105. 'Wallace, laird of Craigie, who was second in command, under Douglas, Earl of Ormond, at the famous battle on the banks of Sark, fought in 1448. The glorious victory was principally owing to the judicious conduct and intrepid valour of the gallant laird of Craigie, who died of his wounds after the action.' R. B.

ll. 109, 110. 'Coilus, King of the Picts, from whom the district of Kyle is said to take its name, lies buried, as tradition says, near the family seat of the Montgomeries of Coilsfield, where his burial-place is still shown.' R. B.

l. 119. 'Barskimming, the seat of the Lord Justice-Clerk.' R. B.

l. 122. 'Catrine, the seat of the late Doctor, and of the present Professor Stewart.' R. B. The father was a mathematician, the son a moral philosopher.

l. 127. 'Col. Fullerton.' R. B. He was the ward, during his minority, of Patrick Brydone, author of *A Tour through Sicily.*

ll. 145–199. Suggested by Pope's *Rape of the Lock,* ll. 41–67 :

> Know that unnumbered spirits round thee fly, &c.

ll. 199, 200. Cf. Pope (*Rape of the Lock*) :

> Of these am I, who thy protection claim,
> A watchful sprite, and Ariel is my name.

ll. 235–240. Cf. Young's *Night Thoughts* (Night the Seventh) :

> What tho' our passions are run mad, and stoop
> With low terrestrial appetite to graze
> On trash, on toys, dethroned from high desire?
> Yet still, thro' their disgrace, no feeble ray
> Of greatness shines, and tells us whence they fell.

See also Burns's *Prayer on the Prospect of Death,* Stanza 3.

ll. 249–252. Cf. the following lines from Beattie's satire on Bufo (Churchill), *On the Report of a Monument to be erected in Westminster Abbey to the Memory of a late Author* :

> Is this the land where Gray's unlaboured art
> Soothes, melts, alarms, and ravishes the heart;

> While the lone wanderer's sweet complainings flow
> In simple majesty of manly woe? . . .
> Is this the land, o'er Shenstone's recent urn
> Where all the Loves and gentler Graces mourn?

l. 271. Cf., for this conclusion, Congreve's Ovid's *Art of Love*, bk. iii.

**P. 59. The Death and Dying Words of Poor Mailie.** This poem was composed in the field, where the author was ploughing, one afternoon in the spring of 1782. The subject was apparently suggested, as adapted for humorous treatment, by Hamilton of Gilbertfield's *Dying Words of Bonny Heck, a famous greyhound.* 'Mailie' is the childish or pet name for 'Mary,'—otherwise Mally or Molly.

Line 6. **Hughoc**, little Hugh Wilson, 'a neibor herd-callant, about three-fourths as wise as other folk'—said Burns, about him.

**P. 61. Poor Mailie's Elegy.** This poem is closely on the model of Robert Sempill of Beltrees' *Epitaph of Habbie Simpson, Piper of Kilbarchan* —a poem long looked upon as the standard specimen of its kind ('standart Habbie'). The stanza-form of this *Elegy* has been appropriated, in a peculiar sense, by the genius of Burns : it has come to be regarded as his favourite measure. Ramsay and Fergusson had, however, popularized it in Scotland before Burns began to write. One of the earliest—if not indeed the first—to use it in Scotland was the old *makar* Alexander Scott : see his *Cupid Quarrelled* in Ramsay's *Evergreen.* (See Guest for the origin and history of the measure.)

Line 37. Cf. Francis Sempill's use of the expression ; writing of *Povertie* he says : ' Wae worth the time that I him saw.'

**P. 62. Death and Dr. Hornbook.** Composed at Mossgiel in the spring of 1785. Dr. Hornbook was John Wilson, schoolmaster of Tarbolton, the next village to Mauchline. Burns met him at a masonic meeting, and was both amused and offended at his boastful parade of medical knowledge, and his success as a vendor of drugs and quack medicines in the village. The satire had the effect of driving Wilson from Tarbolton. He removed to Glasgow, where he prospered, not as an apothecary, but as session-clerk in the Gorbals, a suburb of the city. He was younger than Burns by a year or two, and survived till 1839. It is interesting to observe that William Dunbar, Scotland's earlier Burns, had exposed in *The Frier of Tungland* an earlier Hornbook, equally thoroughgoing in his profession and far more sanguinary in his practice. It is scarcely possible that Burns knew of Dunbar's satire. (See *In Scottish Fields*, Hugh Haliburton.)

Line 26. The mill of William Muir was on the road between Tarbolton and the farm of Mossgiel. Burns wrote ' Willie's ' epitaph about ten years before his own father's death : he calls him 'my own and my father's friend.'

l. 37. An ell Scots is a yard English *plus* one inch.

l. 43. The scythe suggested mowing. But, as Burns informs us, 'the rencontre happened in seedtime.'

ll. 57, 58. I wad be kittle to be mislear'd. Either 'I should be likely to do you a mischief,' or, more probably, 'I should be loth to be rude.' The difficulty is with 'kittle,' which signifies, generally, 'difficult' or 'far from easy,' and, more particularly, 'apt' or 'likely.' (Cf. the second stanza of the *Epistle to Graham of Fintry*, p. 202, 'I wad na be uncivil.')

l. 77. The hornbook, or child's first school-book, is described by Cowper in *Tirocinium* as being :

> Neatly secured from being soiled or torn
> Beneath a pane of thin translucent horn.

It was called a book, 'though but a single page.' Shenstone (a poet whom Burns much admired) also describes it in *The Schoolmistress.*

l. 81. Buchan's *Domestic Medicine* is even yet in remote rural districts of Scotland the peasant's medical manual.

l. 133. The graveyard. Johnny Ged was the grave-digger ; his 'Hole,' an open grave.

l. 135. Calf-ward. The graveyard. A calf-ward, near a Scottish farm-town, is a small field for rearing calves in.

l. 145. A strae-death is a death in bed. ' Our simple forefathers,' says Dr. Jamieson, ' slept on straw.'

P. 67. A Dream. 'On reading in the public papers the Laureate's Ode, with the other parade of June 4, 1786, the Author was no sooner dropt asleep than he imagined himself transported to the Birthday Levee, and in his dreaming fancy, made the following address.' *Burns's Preface to this Poem.* The idea of plain-speaking on forbidden or delicate subjects may have been suggested to Burns by the practice of his rhyming friend Rankine. The measure, and much of the manner, of this poem are those of Allan Ramsay's *Edinburgh's Salutation to the Marquis of Carnarvon.* The Poet Laureate in 1786 was William Whitehead. The King was George III, then in the middle of his long reign.

Lines 12, 13. Cf. Young's *Night Thoughts* (Book iii), 'The cuckoo seasons sing the same dull note.'

l. 33. The American colonies had been lost about three years before.

ll. 61, 62. The reference is to a debate in parliament, in the early part of 1786, on a proposal to reduce the strength of the navy.

l. 89. Fox.

l. 97. Falstaff, in Shakespeare's *King Henry IV.*

l. 100. Prince Frederick, first a bishop, afterwards Duke of York.

ll. 109, 110. Prince William's *amour* ; Mrs. Jordan, the actress.

ll. 131–135. Cf. Ramsay's *Gentle Shepherd* (Act. i, Sc. 2) :

> Like dautit wean, that tarrows at its meat,
> That for some feckless whim will orp an' greet;
> The lave laugh at it till the dinner 's past,
> An' syne the fool thing is obliged to fast,
> Or scart anither's leavings at the last.

**P. 71. Address to the Deil.** Composed at Mossgiel in the end of 1785.

Lines 1, 2. Imitated from Pope's *Dunciad* (Book i, ll. 19, 20) :

> O thou, whatever title please thine ear,
> Dean, Drapier, Bickerstaff, or Gullivér !

'Auld Nick,' for the Devil, is as old in Scottish poetry as 1724 at least ; it occurs in Ramsay's *Evergreen*, in his interpretations of a poem of Dunbar, *The Devil's Advice to his Best Friends.* The word 'Nick' is cognate with 'nixey,' and both are derived from 'nicor,' the water-sprite of our Anglo-Saxon forefathers.

l. 59. A pint Scots is an imperial quart.

l. 111. See *Paradise Lost,* Book vi, ll. 323–327.

**P. 75. The Ordination.** This poem was composed in anticipation of the event it celebrates. That event was the ordination of the Rev. James Mackinlay to the Laigh (Low) Kirk, Kilmarnock. The verses were composed so early as February, the ordination was in April, 1786.

Line 7. Begbie's inn was near the Laigh Kirk.

l. 10. Common-sense, otherwise 'the New Light,' represents—to use Burns's own language—'those religious opinions which Dr. Taylor of Norwich defended so strenuously.'

l. 11. 'Maggie Lauder' was the wife of the Rev. William Lindsay, appointed minister of the Laigh Kirk twenty-two years before the ordination of the Old Light (or Evangelical) minister, Mackinlay, the subject of this poem. It was said that the patron, the Earl of Glencairn, had appointed Lindsay in deference to the wishes of 'Maggie Lauder.' Burns spoke of Lindsay as a 'worthy man' ; but his appointment had been made the theme of 'a scoffing ballad' when Burns was a child of five years old.

ll. 12, 13. Oliphant was an Old Light minister of a chapel-of-ease in Kilmarnock, when Lindsay (Common-sense) was minister of the Laigh Kirk. Russel was Oliphant's successor.

l. 22. Bangor, a psalm-tune.

ll. 30–35. Burns refers to the texts of Scripture, Genesis ix. 22 ; Numbers xxv. 8 ; Exodus iv. 25.

l. 66. The minister of Fenwick was the Rev. William Boyd, ordained in 1782.

l. 73. The Rev. John Robertson was one of the New Light ministers.

l. 79. The Netherton of Kilmarnock, where the weaving of carpets was the chief industry.

l. 82. The Rev. John Multrie, also a New Light (or 'Moderate'), was Mackinlay's predecessor.

l. 98. James Beattie, author of *The Minstrel* ; author also of an *Essay on Truth.* The *Essay*—'a blast impotently intended to sweep David Hume's philosophy behind the horizon, revealed him as one of the "Moderate" party in the clerical dissensions of the time. Sir Joshua had painted Beattie as a champion aiding an angel in strife with Scepticism, Folly, and Prejudice. His *Essay on Truth* brought him the compliment from Reynolds. But nowadays one only remembers the Essay because it explains the picture and illustrates the reference in Burns.' (*Furth in Field* : Hugh Haliburton.)

l. 118. A mutchkin is equal to a pint English. Whisky is meant.

**P. 79. The Author's Earnest Cry and Prayer, &c.** The rigorous enforcement of the Excise laws, early in 1786, alarmed the Scottish distillers, and was the occasion of a great national outcry—to which Burns gave expression in this poem.

Lines 1, 2. By an article in the Union (1707), the eldest sons of *Scottish* peers were ineligible.

l. 19. Pitt, born in the same year as Burns (1759).

l. 58. James Boswell, advocate, author of *The Life of Samuel Johnson.*

l. 92. The Scotch Militia Bill had been opposed and thrown out.

l. 115. Pitt. Boconnock, in Cornwall, was the property of the premier's grandfather.

l. 116. Nance Tinnock was hostess of an inn in Mauchline, where Burns used to discuss politics over his whisky.

l. 119. Referring to the window-tax.

l. 133. The number of representatives in the Imperial Parliament allotted to Scotland at the Union.

**P. 84. Address to the Unco Guid.**
ll. 59–62. Cf. Gray (*Elegy*) :

> No farther seek . . .
> To draw his frailties from their dread abode,
>      *    *    *    *    *    *
> The bosom of his Father and his God.

**P. 86. Holy Willie's Prayer.** Burns's own 'Argument' to this daring poem is as follows :—' Holy Willie was a rather oldish bachelor elder in the parish of Mauchline, and much and justly famed for that polemical chattering which ends in tippling orthodoxy, and for that spiritualized bawdry which refines to liquorish devotion. In a sessional process [begun August, 1784] with a gentleman in Mauchline— a Mr. Gavin Hamilton [writer]—Holy Willie [William Fisher] and his priest, Father Auld, after full hearing in the presbytery of Ayr, came off but second best; owing partly to the oratorical powers of Mr. Robert Aiken, Mr. Hamilton's counsel, but chiefly to Mr. Hamilton's being one of the most irreproachable and truly respectable characters in the county. On losing his process, the Muse overheard him at his devotions.' Mr. Hamilton was accused of 'habitual neglect of church ordinances,' and was threatened with excommunication ; he appealed for protection to the presbytery of Ayr, and (Jan. 1785) was successful in his appeal.

[An extraordinary attempt to whitewash Holy Willie was the subject of two leading articles in *The Scotsman* newspaper a few years ago (Dec. 30, 1889, and Jan. 13, 1890) : the correspondence that ensued left Holy Willie even blacker than he was before.]

**P. 89. Epistle to a Young Friend.** His name was Andrew Aiken, and he was son of Mr. Robert Aiken, writer in Ayr—the gentleman to whom Burns inscribed *The Cotter's Saturday Night*. A dropped stanza might well have been allowed to stand : it came after the sixth, and was as follows—

> If ye hae made a step aside—
> Some hap mistak' o'ertaen ye,
> Yet still keep up a decent pride
> And ne'er owre far demean ye ;
> Time comes wi' kind oblivious shade
> And daily darker sets it,
> And if nae mair mistaks are made
> The warld soon forgets it.

**P. 92. Tam Samson's Elegy.** Samson was a seedsman in Kilmarnock. 'When this worthy old sportsman,' says Burns, 'went out last muir-fowl season, he supposed it was to be—in Ossian's phrase— the last of his fields, and expressed an ardent wish to die and be buried in the muirs. On this hint [the poet composed the Elegy].' The Elegy is composed on the lines of 'standart Habbie '—Habbie Simson, the piper of Kilbarchan (by Sempill).

Line 2. Mackinlay, the hero of *The Ordination*, q.v.

l. 7. Cf. Fergusson's 'Ilk carlin noo may grunt an' grane' (*On the Death of Scots Music*).

ll. 31–33. Cf Fergusson's *Cauler Oysters* :

> In her the skate an' codlin' sail,
> The eel fu' souple wags her tail, &c.

**P. 95. A Winter's Night.** This poem belongs to the year 1786. Burns prefixed to it, by way of motto, the five lines from Shakespeare's *King Lear* beginning—

> Poor naked wretches, wheresoe'er ye are
> That bide the pelting of this pitiless storm.

Lines 19-24. Cf. Cowper (*The Task*) :

> How find the myriads that in summer cheer
> The hills and valleys with their ceaseless songs,
> Due sustenance, or where subsist they now?

ll. 37, 38. Cf. the song in *As You Like It :*

> Blow, blow, thou winter wind!
> Thou art not so unkind
> As man's ingratitude, &c.

ll. 53-55. Cf. Goldsmith (*The Deserted Village*, ll. 275-283 ; and *The Traveller*, ll. 401-404).

**P. 98. Scotch Drink.** Composed early in 1786. A set-off to Fergusson's *Cauler Water*.

Lines 1-4. Cf. Fergusson (*Cauler Water*) :

> The fuddling bardies now-a-days
> Run maukin-mad in Bacchus' praise,
> And limp and stoiter thro' their lays
> Anacreontic,
> While each his sea of wine displays
> As big's the Pontic.

ll. 8. 9. Whether whisky or ale.

l. 20. Bannocks of barley-meal.

ll. 21, 22. Scotch broth, in which barley grains are an essential ingredient, along with 'beef and greens.'

ll. 31-36. See Horace, Bk. III, Ode xxi. 'Tu spem reducis,' &c.

ll. 45-48. The reference is to Holy Fairs. The 'tents' are the open-air pulpits.

ll. 53, 54. Mulled ale, sweetened with sugar, and sharpened with whisky, is still a common drink in rural Scotland.

ll. 79-90. See Fergusson's *Drink Eclogue—Brandy and Whisky :*

> Our gentles' gabs are grown sae nice
> At thee they tout an' *never spier my price*, &c.

ll. 105-108. Cf. Fergusson (*Answer to Mr. J. S.'s Epistle*) :

> She can find a knack
> To gar auld-world wordies clack
> In hamespun rhyme,
> While ilk ane at his billy's back
> Keeps guid Scots time.

l. 109. Ferintosh whisky, from a privileged distillery, belonging to Forbes of Culloden, in Cromarty : the privilege was taken away by Act of Parliament in 1785. Compensation for the loss was given— over £20,000.

**P. 102. Elegy on Capt. Matthew Henderson.** This gentleman, the laird of Tunnochside, had held a captain's commission in the army, owned some property in Edinburgh, and was living there before his death in November, 1788. It is possible that Fergusson's *Elegy on the Death of Scots Music* contains in its third stanza the nucleus of this lament : 'Mourn, ilka nymph,' &c.

Lines 13-82. Cf. Wordsworth's *Excursion* (The Wanderer) ·

> The poets in their elegies, and songs
> Lamenting the departed, call the groves.
> They call upon the hills and streams to mourn,
> And senseless rocks ; nor idly ; for they speak, &c.

**P. 106. The Auld Farmer's Salutation, &c.**

Line 35. Kyle-Stewart is one of the divisions of Kyle (or central Ayrshire) lying between the river Ayr and Irvine water.

ll. 98-100. Cf. Smollett's *Humphry Clinker* : 'Take particular care of that trusty old veteran, who has faithfully earned his present ease by his past services' (Matthew Bramble).

ll. 101, 102. That is, 'Because I will reserve for you a good half-peck of my last bushel of corn.'

**P. 109. To a Mouse, &c.** The occasion of this poem was common-place enough. The poet was ploughing, in Nov. 1785, and the plough-share happened to turn up the nest of a field-mouse. The small creature **was** in haste to escape, when one of the farm-servants, John Blane, made after it with the plough-spade, or pattle. Burns called to him to stop, and fell into a pensive mood, in which he composed the piece just as it stands.

**P. 110. Man was made to mourn.** Burns wrote this *dirge*—for so he calls it—in his 27th year (1784). 'I had an old grand-uncle with whom my mother lived a while in her girlish years. The good old man (for such he was) was long blind ere he died, during which time his enjoyment was to sit down and cry, while my mother would sing the simple old song, *The Life and Age of Man.* It is this way of thinking, it is these melancholy truths, that make religion so precious to the poor miserable children of men.' (Burns's Letter to Mrs. Dunlop, Aug. 16, 1788.) Much of the situation and sentiment of this poem was suggested by Shenstone's *Seventh Elegy.*

Lines 9–12. Cf. Shenstone (*Seventh Elegy*) :

> Stranger, amidst this pealing rain,
> Benighted, lonesome, whither wouldst thou stray?
> *Does wealth or power thy weary step constrain?* &c.

l. 34. Cf. Shenstone (*Eleventh Elegy*) :

> Not all the force of *manhood's active might*, &c.

l. 39. Cf. Shakespeare (*As You Like It*, ii. 7.) :

> Oppressed with two weak evils, Age and Hunger.

Cf. also Gray (*Ode on Eton College*) :

> Poverty . . . and slow consuming Age.

l. 50. From Young : ' By skill divine *inwoven in our frame* ' (*Night Thoughts*, Bk. vii).

ll. 55, 56. The idea was caught from Young (*Night Thoughts*, iii) :

> Man hard of heart to man—
> Man is to man the sorest, surest ill.

See also *Night Thoughts*, Bk. v :

> Inhumanity is caught from man ;

and again, Bk. ix :

> Turn the world's history—what find we there?
> Man's revenge . . . .
> And inhumanities on man.

ll. 77–82. Cf. Young (*Night Thoughts*, Bk. v) :

> Death is the crown of life ;
> Were death denied poor man would live in vain.

**P. 113. To a Mountain Daisy.** This poem was composed in April 1786. It probably suggested to Wordsworth his image of Burns walking

> In glory and in joy
> Behind the plough upon the mountain side.
> 　　　　　　(*Resolution and Independence*.)

Lines 31–36. Cf. Goldsmith (*The Deserted Village*, ll. 329–336) :

> Her modest looks the cottage might adorn,
> Sweet as the primrose peeps beneath the thorn ;
> Now lost to all, her friends, her virtue fled,
> Near her betrayer's door she lays her head, &c.

ll. 49, 50. Cf. Gray (*The Elegy*) :

> For thee, who mindful of the unhonoured dead, &c.

ll. 51, 52. Cf. Young (*Night Thoughts*, Bk. ix) :

> Final Ruin fiercely drives
> Her ploughshare o'er creation.

P. 118. **Address to Edinburgh.** Written in Edinburgh, Dec. 1786.
l. 4. The Scots Parliament was abolished in 1707.
ll. 9–12. Cf. Goldsmith :

> Proud swells the tide with loads of freighted ore, &c.
> > (*Deserted Village.*)

l. 29. Miss Burnet, daughter of Lord Monboddo.
ll. 34–44. Edinburgh Castle and Holyrood Palace.
l. 52. A red lion rampant in a yellow field is the Scots blazon.


P. 120. **Lament for James, Earl of Glencairn.** The Lament was written in the autumn of the year 1791. The Earl had died at Falmouth in January of that year, shortly after his return from the South of Europe, whither he had gone in the hope of recruiting his health. He was the fourteenth Earl of Glencairn, and was nearly ten years the senior of Burns.
l. 36. This line will be found in Paraphrase xv. of the Scottish Bible.
l. 46. Cf. Goldsmith (*The Deserted Village*) :

> For all the bloomy flush of life is fled.

l. 77. See Isa. xlix. 15.


P. 122. **Lament of Mary Queen of Scots.**
ll. 1–6. Cf. *Leader Haughs and Yarrow,* by 'Minstrel Burn,'—familiar to Burns in Ramsay's *Tea-Table Miscellany* :

> When Phœbus bright the azure skies
> With golden rays enlight'neth, &c.

and

> Then Flora queen, with mantle green, &c.

l. 33. The 'false woman' is Queen Elizabeth.


P. 124. **The Twa Herds.** The sub-title of this poem is *The Holy Tulzie.* It belongs to the year 1786. Burns described it as 'a burlesque lamentation on a quarrel between two reverend Calvinists.' The two 'shepherds' were the Rev. John Russel, Kilmarnock, and the Rev. Alexander Moodie, Riccarton.


P. 127. **On the late Captain Grose's Peregrinations.** Burns first met Grose, the antiquary, at the table of his friend and Nithsdale neighbour, Robert Riddell, of Friars Carse, in the Summer of 1789. In his youth Grose had been a captain in the Surrey militia.
l. 1. Oatmeal cakes are meant. Johnson's description of oats is

well known. The expression 'Land o' Cakes' was first applied to
Scotland by Fergusson (*The King's Birthday in Edinburgh*) :

> Oh soldiers! for your ain dear sakes,
> For Scotland's, *alias* Land o' Cakes, &c.

l. 3. Cf. Shakespeare (*King Henry V*, iii. 6) : 'If I [Fluellen] find
a hole in his coat, I will tell him my mind.'

l. 47. Named from the maker, Jacques de Liège.

**P. 129. On Pastoral Poetry.** If Burns did not write this poem, it
is Fergusson's ; but Fergusson could scarcely have known of Barbauld
—a very indifferent Sappho *rediviva*.

ll. 1-6. Cf. Goldsmith's *Deserted Village*, ll. 407-414 : 'Sweet Poesy,
thou loveliest maid ! . . . dear, charming Nymph ! . . . thou source of
all my bliss and all my woe,' &c.

l. 19. The answer is Nobody.

l. 20. That is, they are artificial pastorals.

l. 32. Allan Ramsay, periwig-maker and poet, author of *The Gentle
Shepherd*. Ramsay died a few months before the birth of Burns.

l. 35. Tantallon Castle, now a mere ruin, an ancient stronghold of
the Earls of Angus, on the coast of East Lothian.

**P. 131. The Humble Petition of Bruar Water.** Composed by
Burns in the course of his tour in the Highlands in the autumn of
1787. The Bruar, in Blair Atholl, is an affluent of the Garry, the chief
tributary of Tay. The poem is constructed on the lines of Ramsay's
*Edinburgh's Salutation to Lord Carnarvon*, in regard both to manner and
measure.

l. 70. Cf. Blair's *Grave* : 'Moonshine chequering thro' the trees.'

ll. 87, 88. These lines contain Burns's toast at the table of the
Duke of Atholl, at Blair Atholl, where the poet spent the first two
days of September, 1787,—'the happiest days of his life,' as he said.
The toast gave great delight to the ducal family.

**P. 133. To a Haggis.**

ll. 45-48. The contrast here drawn is between their liquid fare, such
as is favoured by foreigners, and the solid and substantial home haggis.
*Skink* is not 'skinking ware' : it is a species of soup, or rather broth,
of unusual strength, made from the *shank*, or shin, of an ox. The
name is still in common use in Buchan. Shakespeare refers to the
waiters and potboys of the Boar's Head, Eastcheap, as 'skinkers'—
that is, drawers of ale or wine ; so called from drawing the liquor
through a pipe resembling a hollow *shank*-bone.

**P. 136. On Creech the Bookseller.** William Creech was the publisher of Burns's Poems (Edinburgh Edition). These lines were addressed to him in 1787; next year he became one of the city magistrates, and was elected Lord Provost in 1811. He resented the poet's familiarity, and was subsequently satirized in the *Sketch*, printed on p. 276 of this edition.

ll. 37–39. The literati of Edinburgh. Mackenzie, sometimes known as the Scottish Addison, wrote *The Man of Feeling*; Stewart (Professor Dugald Stewart) filled the chair of Moral Philosophy in the University.

**P. 138. To a Louse.**

l. 17. A 'bane' is a bone-comb.

l. 35. Lunardi means bonnet. It appears that Vincent Lunardi, the aeronaut, had been performing in Edinburgh in 1785; he was a subject of general talk.

**P. 140. The Whistle.**

'As the authentic prose history of the Whistle is curious,' writes Burns, 'I shall here give it :—In the train of Anne of Denmark, when she came to Scotland with our James the Sixth, there came over also a Danish gentleman of gigantic stature and great prowess, and a matchless champion of Bacchus. He had a little ebony whistle, which at the commencement of the orgies he laid on the table ; and whoever was last able to blow it, everybody else being disabled by the potency of the bottle, was to carry off the whistle as a trophy of victory. The Dane produced credentials of his victories, without a single defeat, at the courts of Copenhagen, Stockholm, Moscow, Warsaw, and several of the petty courts in Germany ; and challenged the Scots' Bacchanalians to the alternative of trying his prowess, or else acknowledging their inferiority. After many overthrows on the part of the Scots, the Dane was encountered by Sir Robert Lawrie of Maxwelton, ancestor of the present worthy baronet of that name, who after three days' and three nights' hard contest, left the Scandinavian under the table,

And blew on the whistle his requiem shrill.

'Sir Walter, son to Sir Robert before mentioned, afterwards lost the whistle to Walter Riddel of Glenriddel, who had married a sister of Sir Walter's. On Friday, the 16th October, 1690, at Friars Carse, the whistle was once more contended for, as related in the ballad, by the present Sir Robert Lawrie of Maxwelton ; Robert Riddel, Esq., of Glenriddel, lineal descendant and representative of Walter Riddel, who won the whistle, and in whose family it had continued ; and Alexander Ferguson, Esq., of Craigdarroch, likewise descended of the

great Sir Robert ; which last gentleman carried off the hard-won
honours of the field.' R. B.

The poem belongs to the year 1789.

**P. 142. The Kirk's Alarm.** Written in 1789 ; and annotated by
Burns himself, as under :—

l. 5. Dr. M'Gill, Ayr. (He was author of an Essay on the Death
of Christ, believed to contain heretical opinions ; and was proceeded
against accordingly. The ministers and elders satirized in the poem
were all against M'Gill.)

l. 11. John Ballantine.

l. 12. Robert Aiken.

l. 13. Dr. Dalrymple, Ayr.

l. 17. John Russel, Kilmarnock.

l. 21. James Mackinlay, Kilmarnock.

l. 25. Alexander Moodie, of Riccarton.

l. 29. William Auld, Mauchline ; for the clerk, see *Holy Willie's
Prayer*.

l. 33. David Grant, Ochiltree.

l. 37. James Young, in New Cumnock, who had lately been foiled
in an ecclesiastical prosecution against a Lieutenant Mitchell.

l. 41. William Peebles, in Newtown-upon-Ayr, a poetaster, who,
among many other things, published an ode on the centenary of the
Revolution, in which was the line—

> And bound in Liberty's endearing chain.

l. 45. Dr. Andrew Mitchel, Monkton.

l. 49. Stephen Young, of Barr.

l. 53. (In one version of this poem we find 'Cessnock-side' for
'Irvine Side,' and Burns notes that the minister of Galston, George
Smith, is meant.)

l. 57. John Shepherd, Muirkirk.

l. 61. Holy Will was William Fisher, elder, Mauchline. *Vide* the
'Prayer' of this saint.

**P. 149. Despondency.**

ll. 57-70. Cf. Gray's *Ode on Eton College*:

> To each his sufferings. All are men, &c.

**P. 156. Epistle to Davie.** Written in the early part of 1785, at
Mossgiel. The poet's correspondent was David Sillar, the son of
a crofter, in Burns's own parish of Tarbolton, Ayrshire. The stanza
of this poem was a favourite measure with Allan Ramsay (*The Vision*,
1724) and of Alexander Montgomery (*The Cherry and the Slae*, 1597).

But the earliest Scots specimen of this singular stanza, according to Dr. Guest, is to be found in a poem, belonging to the middle of the sixteenth century, say 1550, entitled *The Banks of Hellicone*. In the Bannatyne MS., compiled in 1568 and printed for the Hunterian club in 1873, occurs a poem 'maid to the tone of *The Banks of Hellicone*,' and entitled 'Ane Ballat of the Creation of the World, Man, his Fall and Redemption'—an earlier *Paradise Lost* and *Regained*. It is easily accessible in Ramsay's *Evergreen*. *The Banks of Hellicone* will be found in Pinkerton's *Ancient Scot. Poems*, ii, 237.

l. 24. 'Haill' or 'hale and fier' is an old Scots expression, found in Dunbar's *Dream*, and in Lichtoun's *Quha Douttis Dremis* (in the Bannatyne MS.).

l. 25. Burns gives this line to Ramsay, but I cannot find it. It seems to be an incorrect recollection from Ramsay's *Vision*:

> Rest but a while content,
> Not fearful, but cheerful,
> And wait the will of Fate,
> Which minds to, designs to,
> Renew your ancient state.

ll. 46-48. Cf. Goldsmith (*The Traveller*):

> Creation's heir, the world, the world is mine!

ll. 63-66. Cf. *The Traveller*:

> Vain, very vain, my weary search to find
> That bliss which only centres in the mind.

l. 116. Cf. Gray (*The Bard*):

> Dear as the ruddy drops that warm my heart.

ll. 119-122. The original version (with recollections of Goldsmith:

> In all my griefs, and God has given my share),

was as follows:

> In all my share of care and grief,
> Which fate has largely given,
> My hope and comfort and relief
> Are thoughts of her and heaven.

l. 138. Tenebrific was got from Young's mint. Burns was a close student of *The Night Thoughts*. Young's coinage is commonly pedantic, e.g. 'ichor of Bacchus' (for wine), 'a brow solute,' 'antemundane father,' 'extramundane head,' 'terræ-filial,' 'conglobe,' 'irrefragable smile,' 'grand climacterical absurdities,' &c.

P. 161. **Epistle to John Lapraik.** Dated April 1, 1785. Lapraik's farm was about fourteen miles to the east of Burns's. The song referred to at l. 13 begins:

> When I upon thy bosom lean,
>   And fondly clasp thee a' my ain,
> I glory in the sacred ties
>   That made us ane wha ance were twain.

l. 45. Crambo is a game in which one gives a word to which another finds a rhyme. In Congreve's *Love for Love* (the opening scene) we read :

*Valentine.* You are witty, you rogue. I shall want your help ; I'll have you learn to make couplets, to tag the ends of Acts ; d'ye hear? get the maids to crambo in an evening, and learn the knack of rhyming.

ll. 79, 80. Allan Ramsay (1686–1758), author of *The Gentle Shepherd*, &c. ; Robert Fergusson (1750–1774), author of *The Farmer's Ingle*, &c.

**P. 165. To the Same** (Lapraik). This reply bears date April 21, 1785.

l. 20. The poet's remonstrance with his muse recalls Lancelot's debate with his conscience before he ran away from the service of Shylock. (See *The Merchant of Venice*.)

l. 92. *Not* 'the ragged followers of the Nine,' as some editors give it. Cf. Congreve's *Love for Love*—concluding lines of Scene 1, Act i. : 'As ragged as one of the Muses.'

ll. 104–106. Cf. Milton's *Comus* :

> Where bright aërial spirits live ensphered
> In regions mild.

**P. 168. To William Simson.** This epistle was written in May, 1785. Simson was schoolmaster of Ochiltree, a village on the Lugar, some eight miles south of the farm of Mossgiel.

l. 15. Allan Ramsay and his rhyming correspondent, Lieut. William Hamilton of Gilbertfield. (See Note on *Death and Dying Words of Poor Mailie*, p. 569.)

l. 17. Robert Fergusson, author of *The Farmer's Ingle*, &c., had been an engrossing clerk in a lawyer's office in Edinburgh. To such drudgery he was compelled through domestic poverty, for he had been well educated at St. Andrews. He died in a madhouse in his 24th year.

ll. 31, 32. Coila, the protective goddess of Kyle, the middle division of Ayrshire, in which Burns was born. 'There was a lad was born in Kyle.' Coila's poets were such as Davie Sillar, William Simson, John Lapraik, &c

l. 58. Ayr, Turnberry, Irvine, Leglen Wood, &c., are all associated with the patriotic efforts of Sir William Wallace. (See the rude epic on Wallace by Harry the Minstrel.)

l. 65. For 'red-wat-shod,' cf. *Arthur* (E. E. T. Society's publications for 1864) :

> There men were wet-schoede
> All of brayn and of blode.

ll. 85–87. So Milton (*Il Penseroso*) :

> Youthful poets dream
> On summer eves by haunted stream.

l. 88. And not weary. The idiom is not uncommon, not only in Scottish verse, but in current speech. Burns uses it several times.

l. 108. Previously the poet had signed his name *Burness*. His father's signature was *Burnes*. Pronounce *Bur'nes*.

ll. 111–114. The reference is to *The Holy Tulzie*, q.v. (p. 124). 'New Light,' says Burns, in a note, ' is a cant phrase in the West of Scotland for those religious opinions which Dr. Taylor of Norwich has defended so strenuously.'

l. 140. The ministers and their congregations. ' Hissel ' is a local form of ' hirsel,' a herd or a flock.

**P. 174. Letter to John Goudie.** Written August, 1785. Goldie (or Goudie) was a self-taught genius, successful in trade, and widely known for his scientific knowledge and philosophical ability. At first he was a cabinet-maker, and afterwards he became a wine and spirit merchant, in Kilmarnock. His essays, in three volumes, bore the popular name of ' Goudie's Bible.' Burns describes him as ' Author of the Gospel recovered.'

l. 9. Rev. John Russel, Kilmarnock.

ll. 13–18. Another version of this stanza is given :—

> Auld Orthodoxy lang did grapple
> For every hole to get a stapple ;
> But noo she fetches at the thrapple
> An' fechts for breath ;
> Haste ! gie her name up i' the chapel [1]—
> *Near unto death* !

l. 25. Dr. Taylor of Norwich.

**P. 175. Third Epistle to Lapraik.** Bears date Sept. 13, 1785.

ll. 3, 4. Shearing your corn.

l. 37. Horse and bridle.

l. 38. The ' herd ' (or herdboy')'s duty was to keep the cows from the growing or ripening corn. When the corn was shorn, and ' led,' or carted, to the cornyard, where it was built into stacks, the cows were allowed to graze freely on the stubble fields, and the herd-laddie was

---

[1] Mr. Russel's Church. R. B.

dispensed with. The use of fences on modern farms has abolished the office of herdboy.

l. 51. Along with the shearers to raise the overturned sheaves.

l. 52. Leave my bagpipe.

l. 54. See the old Scottish song ' Maggy Lauder.'

**P. 177. To Rev. John M'Math.** Written Sept. 17, 1785. M'Math was assistant to the minister of Tarbolton.

l. 25. Gavin Hamilton.

**P. 180. To James Smith.** Shopkeeper in Mauchline. He afterwards went to the West Indies, where he died before Burns. This Epistle belongs to 1786, and was written about the time Burns contemplated publishing (see ll. 37, 38).

l. 133. George Dempster, M.P., a patriotic Scotsman.

**P. 185. To Gavin Hamilton.** Dated 'Mossgaville, May 3, 1786.' ' Master Tootie, *alias* Laird M'Gaun ' seems to have been a dishonest dealer in cattle. One of his evil practices was to scrape off the natural rings from the horns of cattle, in order that he might disguise their age (ll. 9, 10, and l. 35).

l. 30. John Dow's Tavern.

l. 31. To meet the worldly or greedy reptile—Master Tootie.

**P. 186. Epistle to Mr. M'Adam.** Craigen-Gillan is in Carrick.

**P. 187. Epistle to Major Logan.** Major William Logan, a retired military officer, a musician and wit of some repute, lived in Park Villa, Ayr, with his mother, and ' sentimental sister, Susie ' (ll. 74, 75). This epistle bears date, ' Mossgiel, October 30, 1786.'

l. 51. The ministers blame Eve and her daughters, &c.

l. 55. Alas for poor poets !

**P. 190. To a Tailor.** This is Burns's reply to a ' trimming epistle ' from Tammy Walker, a country tailor, who stitched and wrote doggerel in or near the village of Ochiltree.

**P. 192. To the Guidwife of Wauchope-House.** Written in answer to a rhyming letter sent to Burns by Mrs. Elizabeth Scott, wife of the laird of Wauchope, Roxburghshire. The answer is dated March, 1787.

l. 65. Than ever was any person robed in ermine.

**P. 195. Epistle to Robert Graham of Fintry.** The ' boon ' requested in this letter (written at Ellisland, 1788) was an appointment in the excise in the neighbourhood of his farm. It was granted about a year later. The opening lines of this poem may have been suggested by Garrick's lines on Goldsmith.

**P. 198. To the Rev. Dr. Blacklock.** Written at Ellisland, Oct. 21, 1789. The Rev. Thomas Blacklock, D.D., a retired clergyman of the Kirk of Scotland, blind from his birth, and a poet in a small way, was one of the literati of Edinburgh, and one of the first to discover the merits of Burns.

l. 43. Cf. Young (*Night Thoughts*, Bk. I) :

> On reason build resolve,
> That pillar of true majesty in man.

**P. 200. Letter to James Tennant, Glenconner.** Glenconner is in the parish of Ochiltree.

ll. 9, 10. Adam Smith, author of *The Wealth of Nations*, and *A Theory of Moral Sentiments* (1759)—in which he bases virtue on sympathy ; Thomas Reid, Professor of Moral Philosophy in Glasgow, commonly regarded as the father of Scottish or common-sense philosophy : he accepted Shaftesbury's theory of ' a moral sense.'

l. 22. 'Brown' is probably the English philosopher and theologian Dr. John Brown (1715-1766), author of *Essays on ' the Characteristics ' of the Earl of Shaftesbury* ; 'Boston' is Thomas Boston (1676-1732), minister of Ettrick, author of *Sermons* and *Fourfold State*.

l. 31. 'Auld Glen' is the father of the poet's correspondent.

**P. 202. Epistle to Robert Graham.**

l. 31. William, Duke of Queensberry.

l. 52. The Whig colours.

l. 53. 'Westerha'' is Sir James Johnstone, the Tory candidate.

l. 61. A huge piece of ancient artillery in Edinburgh Castle.

l. 67. M'Murdo was the Duke's chamberlain.

l. 85. 'Miller' is the father of Captain Miller, the Whig candidate ; he had been a banker. Captain Miller was returned.

l. 157. Borrowed from Ps. cxxii, metrical version.

**P. 206. Epistle to Robert Graham.** The date is Oct. 5, 1791. Part of this poem sometimes bears title 'The Poet's Progress.' There are several unimportant variations.

l. 1. The poet broke his arm by a fall from (or rather along with) his horse in March, and in the following September a similar misfortune befell him by which he severely injured his leg.

l. 7. Job's curse.

l. 22. Variation—' Her tongue, her eyes and other nameless parts.'

l. 27. A figure of the chase. Cf. Scott (*Lady of the Lake*) :

> Yelled, on the view, the *opening* pack.

l. 39. The Monroes were noted anatomists in Edinburgh University.

**P. 209. To Terraughty.** John Maxwell, of Terraughty and Munches, Dumfries. He was turned seventy when thus saluted by Burns, and he survived to the age of ninety-four. He was a descendant of Lord Herries.

**P. 210. Esopus to Maria.** Cf. *Eloise to Abelard.* Esopus, in this case, was a strolling actor, James Williamson, who occasionally performed in Dumfries, and whom, at Whitehaven, in Cumberland, the unpopular Lord Lonsdale had shut up in prison as a vagabond and vagrant. 'Maria' is the poet's once intimate friend Maria (Mrs Walter) Riddell of Woodley Park—with whom he had a bitter and lasting quarrel. It was through this quarrel the poet unfortunately lost the friendship of her relatives of Friars Carse. Williamson, like Burns, had been an occasional visitor and guest at Woodley Park. What can be said in excuse for Burns ? 'The poet in a golden clime was born,' &c.

l. 13. Quin's prologue-acknowledgement (in the words of Lord Lyttelton) on the production of Thomson's *Coriolanus.* That drama came out a year after Thomson's death. The premature death of a poet has seldom been so sincerely lamented as was that of James Thomson. (Quin was called 'th' Esopus of his age' by Thomson).

l. 31. Gillespie, an Irish officer, often entertained at Woodley Park.

l. 33. A Colonel M'Dowell, a noted lady-killer and Lothario.

l. 35. Son of Burns's friend John Bushby. The young man was an advocate (*sc.* barrister).

l. 78. Cf. *Macbeth* (Witches' prophecy).

**P. 212. To Colonel De Peyster.** He commanded the Dumfriesshire volunteers. Though of French extraction he served as a British officer during the American War ; and on retiring from active duty he settled in Dumfries. His wife was a daughter of the Provost of Dumfries.

**P. 213. Winter.** The sub-title is *A Dirge.* This is one of Burns's earliest pieces, and belongs to the winter of 1781-2.

l. 9. Burns gives this line to 'Dr. Young.' It is not however, a quotation, but a recollection from Young. The author of *Night Thoughts* was also author of *Ocean, An Ode,* part of which goes thus :

The northern blast,
The shatter'd mast,
   The syrt, the whirlpool, and the rock,
The breaking spout,
The stars gone out,
   The boiling strait, the monster's shock,
Let others fear!
To Britain dear
   Whate'er promotes her daring claim, &c.

**P. 219. Elegy on Robert Ruisseaux.** Sc. Robert Burns—a burn being Scots for a stream or rivulet.

**P. 224. The Inventory.** The surveyor of taxes was Burns's friend Mr. Aiken, of Ayr. The lines are dated from Mossgiel, Feb. 22, 1786. In 1785 Pitt ordered a tax on female-servants. Burns himself has a few notes on this poem : they are here given.

l. 8. 'Fore horse on the left hand in the plough.' R. B.

l. 10. 'Hindmost on the left hand in the plough.' R. B.

l. 11. Kilmarnock. R. B.

ll. 14, 15. [This is called 'riding the broose.']

l. 20. 'Hindmost horse on the right hand in the plough.' R. B.

l. 44. See the Westminster Assembly's *Shorter Catechism*.

l. 47. Cf. Fergusson (*Answer to J. S.'s Epistle*):

The Lord deliver frae temptation
A' honest folk !

**P. 226. Address of Beelzebub.** Prefaced with the following Note :—
'To the Right Honourable the Earl of Breadalbane, President of the Right Honourable and Honourable the Highland Society, which met on the 23rd of May last (1786) at the Shakespeare, Covent Garden, to concert ways and means to frustrate the designs of five hundred highlanders, who, as the Society was informed by Mr. M'Kenzie of Applecross, were so audacious as to attempt an escape from their lawful lords and masters whose property they are, by emigrating from the lands of Mr. Macdonald of Glengarry to the wilds of Canada, in search of that fantastic thing —Liberty !'

**P. 227. Nature's Law.**

l. 36. The poet's son and namesake, born Sept. 3, 1786.

**P. 231. On an Interview with Lord Daer.** Oct. 23, 1786. Lord Daer was the son and heir of the Earl of Selkirk.

l. 13. Cf. Ramsay—

Turn oot the brent side o' your shin
For pride iu poets is nae sin.

**P. 232. At a Rev. Friend's House.** The Manse of Loudoun (New-milns) ; the minister, Rev. George Lawrie.

**P. 235. On Scaring some Water Fowl.** Loch Turit, or Turrit, is in a lonely hollow among hills behind Ochtertyre House, some two miles from Crieff, Perthshire. Date, Oct. 1787.

**P. 239. Sir James Hunter Blair.** He was Lord Provost of Edin-burgh from 1784 to 1786. He died in 1787. Burns was then living in Edinburgh.

l. 8. St. Anthony's Chapel, on Arthur's Seat.

l. 32. ' Grateful Science ' is from Gray's *Ode on Eton College.*

l. 34. 'Fair Freedom's blossoms' may be from Goldsmith :

> And thou, fair Freedom
> Thou transitory flower !
> Still may thy blooms the changeful clime endure !

**P. 241. Prologue.** Woods had been the intimate friend of Robert Fergusson (Burns's senior by scarcely eight years).

ll. 17, 18. Reference to Scottish philosophy, as cultivated by Reid, and his disciple Dugald Stewart.

l. 19. The compliment is to Robertson the historian.

ll. 21, 22. The drama of *Douglas* (1756), by the Rev. John Home, was immensely popular in Scotland in the latter half of the eighteenth century. ' Where's your Willy Shakespeare now ? ' cried a voice from the pit of an Edinburgh theatre when *Douglas* was first presented. Harley is the lachrymose hero of the *Man of Feeling,* a sentimental novel by Henry Mackenzie—sometimes dubbed the Scotch Addison, and at least as worthy of the compliment as Home was deserving to be named in the same breath with Shakespeare !

**P. 247. Ode to the Memory of Mrs. Oswald.** She was the widow of Richard Oswald, Esq. of Auchincruive, and died Dec. 6, 1788. Burns himself narrates the occasion of its composition. ' In January last, on my road to Ayrshire, I had to put up at Bailie Whigham's in Sanquhar, the only tolerable inn in the place. The frost was keen, and the grim evening and howling wind were ushering in a night of snow and drift. My horse and I were both much fatigued by the labours of the day ; and just as my friend the Bailie and I were bidding defiance to the storm, over a smoking bowl, in wheels the funereal pageantry of the late Mrs. Oswald, and poor I am forced to brave all the terrors of the tempestuous night, and jade my horse—my young favourite horse, whom I had just christened Pegasus—farther on through the wildest hills and moors of Ayrshire to the next inn. The powers of poetry and prose sink under me when I would describe what I felt. Suffice it to say, that when a good fire at New Cumnock had so far recovered my frozen sinews, I sat down and wrote the enclosed ode.'

l. 17. The reference is to her husband, who had been a merchant in London. An army-contract seems to be hinted at.

**P. 248. Elegy on the Year 1788.**

l. 28. 'Daviely' in this line seems to be a printer's blunder for 'dowiely.' See 'dowf an' dowie' in Skinner's *Tullochgorum*.

**P. 250. Sketch.** This poem is in the manner, and in the measure, of Goldsmith's *Retaliation*.

**P. 253. Poetical Address to Mr. William Tytler.** This gentleman, the laird of Woodhouslee, was author of a 'Vindication of Mary Queen of Scots,' published 1759.

**P. 258. On a certain Commemoration.** This satire was probably at the expense of the Earl of Selkirk, who was believed to be parsimonious to the living and patronizing to the dead. It was he who crowned Thomson's bust (or rather Thomson's books) with bays at Ednam—as recorded in the preceding poem. Burns had been invited, but did not go, though he sent the Address (p. 257)—and relieved his mind by writing the satire.

**P. 259. Libertie—A Vision.** The scene is at Lincluden Abbey. An American editor (Mr. Gebbie) was the first to suggest that the first part (ll. 1–32) was intended to serve as a kind of prologue to the *Ode on Washington's Birthday* (l. 33 to the end).

**P. 262. Fragment of Ode to Prince Charles Edward.** The Ode was written for a Jacobite club at Dumfries, and in commemoration of Prince Charlie's birth. The opening lines were these :

> Afar th' illustrious exile roams
>   Whom kingdoms on this day should hail ;
> An inmate in the casual shed,
> On transient pity's bounty fed,
>   Haunted by busy memory's bitter tale !
> Beasts of the forest have their savage homes ;
>   But he, who should imperial purple wear,
> Owns not the lap of earth where rests his royal head !
>   His wretched refuge dark despair,
> While ravening wrongs and woes pursue,
> And distant far the faithful few
>   Who would his sorrow share.

Then followed the main body of the Ode, given in our text. And the poem concluded with the following epode :

Perdition ! baleful child of night !
Rise and revenge the injured right
   Of Stuart's royal race !
Lead on the unmuzzled hounds of hell
Till all the frighted echoes tell
   The blood-notes of the chase !
Full on the quarry point their view,
Full on the base usurping crew,
   The tools of faction and the Nation's curse !
Hark, how the cry grows on the wind !
They leave the lagging gale behind ;
Their savage fury pitiless they pour—
With murdering eyes already they devour !
See Brunswick spent, a wretched prey !
His life one poor despairing day
   Where each avenging hour still ushers in a worse !
Such havock, howling all abroad,
   Their utter ruin bring
The base apostates to their God,
   And rebels to their king !

**P. 318. Afton Water.**   Afton Water flows into upper Nith through the inland parish of Cumnock, Ayrshire.

**P. 319. Go fetch to me a Pint o' Wine.**
l. 6. The Ferry is Queensferry, up the Firth of Forth from Leith. The wind was therefore westerly.

**P. 320. Highland Mary.**   Burns first became acquainted with Mary Campbell in the Spring of 1786 : she was then a domestic servant in some household not far from his farm of Mossgiel. He became her accepted lover ; and they pledged mutual fidelity at parting, on the second Sunday of May, in a manner peculiarly solemn and romantic. Burns forgot his vows ; and Mary, dying in the autumn of the same year, was buried in Greenock.
l. 2. Coilsfield House is meant, occupied in 1786 by a family of the name of Montgomery.
ll. 5, 6. Cf. David's lament for Jonathan, beginning 'Ye mountains of Gilboa' (2 Sam. i. 21).

**P. 321. To Mary in Heaven.**   Much of the imagery and sentiment of this song will be found in Blair's *Grave*,—a poem well known to Burns.   For example :

'O then the longest summer's day
Seemed too too much in haste : still the full heart
Had not imparted half,' &c.

But there seems also to be a recollection of a little-known Ode by Thomson—'Tell me, thou soul of her I love !'

**P. 322. My Nannie O.** The Lugar joins the river Ayr about two miles south of Mauchline. Burns wrote Stinchar, and in all editions in his lifetime Stinchar appears where we now read the more euphonious Lugar ; but it was the poet himself that first suggested Lugar. Burns perhaps never wrote more spontaneously and happily than when he wrote lines 25–28.

**P. 323. Ae fond Kiss.** The lady was 'Clarinda '—Agnes Craig (Mrs. M'Lehose). See Burns's correspondence for the years 1787–1788.

**P. 323. My Nannie's Awa.** The reference is to 'Clarinda.'

**P. 325. Of a' the Airts.** ' This song I composed out of compliment to Mrs. Burns. N.B. It was during the honeymoon.—R. B.' It was written at Ellisland, in June 1788.

**P. 326. There was a Lad.** Kyle is the central division of Ayrshire. 'Jan. 25, 1759, the date of my bardship's vital existence.—R. B.'
l. 13. To tell his fortune by palmistry.

**P. 328. For a' that and a' that.** Produced Jan. 1, 1795. 'The piece,' wrote Burns, ' is not really poetry.' Much of the sentiment of this poem will be found in Young (*Night Thoughts*—' Night Sixth ').
l. 25. Cf. Goldsmith :

> Princes and lords may flourish or may fade;
> A breath can make them. *Deserted Village.*

l. 28. He cannot cause that to happen ; Fate has not given a King such power. See Ritson's *Scot. Songs*, vol. ii. p. 104—' Faith ! they ma' na fa' that.' See also Scott's Note xlix, *Lady of the Lake*.

**P. 329. Auld Lang Syne.** This is a reunion song—but almost always sung at *parting*. Allan Ramsay's song with this title suggested nothing to Burns but the opening line—*and* the title. For the original version, see F. Sempill's *Auld Lang Syne*.

**P. 330. Scots wha hae.**
ll. 22, 23. 'I have borrowed the last stanza from the common stall edition of *Wallace* [Hamilton of Gilbertfield's—a mere travesty of Minstrel Harry's]:

> A false usurper sinks in every foe,
> And liberty returns with every blow :

—a couplet worthy of Homer.'—BURNS.

**P. 332. Macpherson's Farewell.** This notorious freebooter was executed at Banff in 1700. Except the chorus and one stanza this wild stormful song is wholly Burns's.

**P. 333. Braw Lads.** Gala is a tributary of Tweed.

**P. 334. Ca' the Yowes.** The choral stanza is Tibbie Pagan's (1740–1821).

l. 13. Cluden or Clouden is Lincluden Abbey, at the confluence of Clouden and Nith, near Dumfries.

**P. 338. Duncan Gray.** See the 'Wowing of Jok and Jenny' in *The Evergreen*. Ailsa Craig is an island rock in the Firth of Clyde, opposite Girvan.

l. 15. Committing suicide by drowning. Cf. 'The lover's lowp' in Ramsay's *The Gentle Shepherd*.

**P. 342. The Gloomy Night.** When Burns wrote this song, in the autumn of 1786, he expected to sail to the West Indies in a few days.

ll. 5, 6. Cf. Otway's *Orphan*, v. ii. :

> So in the fields
> When the destroyer has been out for prey
> The scattered lovers of the feathered kind, &c.

**P. 344. And maun I still on Menie doat?**

ll. 21–28. Cf. Gray's *Elegy*—beginning 'Haply some hoary-headed swain may say.'

**P. 351. My ain kind Dearie O.** Otherwise entitled *The Lea-rig*. This lovely pastoral was suggested by a song in Johnson's *Scots Musical Museum*, 'mostly composed' (says Burns) 'by poor Fergusson in one of his merry humours.' With this remark David Laing agrees.

**P. 354. Clarinda.**

ll. 3, 4. Cf. Ford's *The Lady's Trial*; also Thomson's *Winter* :

> Miserable they . . . . .
> Take their last look of the descending sun.

**P. 355. Song of Death.**

ll. 11, 12. Cf. Young (*Night Thoughts*, v.) :

> Death loves a shining mark—a signal blow!

**P. 363. Willie brew'd.** Willie was William Nicol, one of the masters of the Edinburgh High School; Allan and Rab were Allan

Masterton, also of the High School, and Burns. The meeting was at Nicol's lodging (in the summer vacation) near Moffat.

**P. 364. No Churchman am I.**
ll. 21, 22. Young (*Night Thoughts*, ii.) :

> Life's cares are comforts ; such by Heaven design'd ;
> He that has none must make them or be wretched.

**P. 368. Does Haughty Gaul.** Burns joined a company of Volunteers enrolled at Dumfries in 1795, and on the occasion wrote this song.

**P. 418. The Fête Champêtre.**
ll. 8, 9. James Boswell, who accompanied Dr. Johnson (' Ursa-Major ') on his tour through the Highlands and Islands of Scotland.

**P. 461. The Dean of Faculty.**
l. 7. Henry Erskine, and Robert Dundas (of Arniston). Dundas was elected (1796).

**P. 515. Bonnie Lass of Albany.** The marriage of Prince Charles Edward Stuart (the Young Pretender) with Clementina Walkinshaw was announced, and their daughter, the Duchess of Albany, was legitimated, by the Parliament of Paris, 1787.

**P. 529. Willie's Wife.** Linkumdoddie is no imaginary place, as is commonly supposed. The son of the minister of Broughton, Mr. J. R. Cosens, Advocate, writing to *The Scotsman*, Oct. 4, 1889, thus identifies it :—' Five and a half miles above Broughton, on the road to Tweedsmuir and Moffat, there is a hill burn, which joins the Tweed, called the Logan Water, and on the bank of the Tweed, nearly opposite to the spot where the waters meet, stood a thatched cottage known as Linkumdoddie. The place is still marked by three trees, but the cottage disappeared forty years ago. An old inhabitant of this district told me that he minds his grandfather speaking to him about a Gideon Thomson, a weaver, who at the end of last century lived at Linkumdoddie. This man was what in those days was called a customer weaver, and seems to have been a character. My informant says he himself remembers the cottage, and is sure that his grandfather always spoke of the place by the name of Linkumdoddie.'

# GLOSSARY

A', *all.*
Aback, *behind, at the back.*
Abeigh, *at bay, aloof.*
Aboon, *above.*
Abread, *abroad.*
Abreed, *in breadth.*
Acquent, *acquainted.*
A'-day, *all day.*
Adle, *putrid water.*
Ae, *one; only.*
Aff, *off.*
Aff-hand, *at once, offhand.*
Aff-loof, *off-hand.*
Afore, *before.*
Aften, *often.*
A-gley, *off the right line; asquint.*
Aiblins, *perhaps.*
Aik, *an oak.*
Aiken, *oaken.*
Ain, *own.*
Air or ear', *early.*
Airl-penny, *earnest-money.*
Airles, *earnest-money.*
Airn, *iron.*
Airns, *irons.*
Airt, *point or quarter of the earth or sky; to direct.*
Airted, *directed.*
Aith, *an oath.*
Aiths, *oaths.*
Aits, *oats.*
Aiver, *horse no longer young.*
Aizle, *a hot cinder.*
Ajee, *to the one side.*
Alake! *alas!*
Alang, *along.*
Amaist, *almost.*
Amang, *among.*

An', *and.*
An's, *and is.*
Ance, *once.*
Ane, *one.*
Anes, *ones.*
Anither, *another.*
Arles, *earnest-money.*
Ase, *ashes.*
Asklent, *obliquely.*
Asteer, *astir.*
A'thegither, *altogether.*
Athort, *athwart.*
Atween, *between.*
Aught, *eight.*
Aughteen, *eighteen.*
Aughtlins, *anything, in the least.*
Auld, *old.*
Auldfarran, *sagacious, old-fashioned.*
Aumous, *alms.*
Ava, *at all.*
Awa, *away.*
Awe, *to owe.*
Awee, *a little time.*
Awfu', *awful.*
Awnie, *bearded* (said of barley).
Aye, *always.*
Ayont, *beyond.*

Ba', *a ball.*
Babie-clouts, *baby-clothes.*
Backets, *buckets.*
Bade, *endured, desired.*
Baggie (dim. of *bag*), *the stomach.*
Bainie, *bony, muscular.*
Bairns, *children.*
Bairntime, *all the children of one mother.*
Baith, *both.*

Bakes, *biscuits.*
Ballats, *ballads.*
Ban', *band.*
Banes, *bones.*
Bang, *a stroke.*
Bannet, *a bonnet.*
Bannock, *a cake of oatmeal bread, or a barley scon.*
Bardie, *dim of bard.*
Barefit, *barefooted.*
Barkit, *barked.*
Barin' (of a stone-pit), *laying bare the stones by removing the turf.*
Barley-bree, *ale or whisky.*
Barm, *yeast.*
Barmie, *frothing or fermenting.*
Batch, *a party or quantity.*
Batts, *the botts or colic.*
Bauckie-bird, *the bat.*
Baudrons, *a cat.*
Bauks, *cross-beams.*
Bauk-en', *end of a bank or cross-beam.*
Bauld, *bold.*
Baumy, *balmy.*
Bawk, *a ridge left untilled.*
Baws'nt, *having a white stripe down the face.*
Bawtie, *a familiar name for a dog.*
Be't, *be it.*
Bear, *barley.*
Beets, *adds fuel to fire, incites.*
Befa', *befall.*
Behint, *behind.*
Belang, *belong to.*
Beld, *bald.*
Bellyfu', *bellyfull.*
Belyve, *by-and-by.*
Ben, *the inner or best room of a cottage.*
Benmost bore, *the innermost recess, or hole.*
Bethankit, *the grace after meat.*
Beuk, *a book.* Devil's pictur'd beuks, *cards.*
Bicker, *a wooden bowl,* or *a short race.*
Bid, *to wish, or ask.*
Bide, *to stand, to endure.*
Biel, *a habitation.*
Bield, *shelter.*
Bien (of a person) *well-to-do ;* (of a place) *comfortable.*

Big, *to build.*
Biggin, *building.*
Bill, *a bull.*
Billie, *a comrade, fellow, young man.*
Bings, *heaps.*
Birk, *the birch.*
Birken-shaw, *a small birch-wood.*
Birkie, *a lively, young, forward fellow.*
Birring, *whirring.*
Birses, *bristles.*
Bit, *crisis ;* also, *little.*
Bizzard gled, *a kite.*
Bizz, *a bustling haste.*
Bizzy, *busy.*
Bizzies, *buzzes.*
Black Bonnet, *the elder.*
Blae, *blue, sharp, keen.*
Blastie, *a term of contempt.*
Blastit, *blasted, withered.*
Blate, *shamefaced, sheepish.*
Blather, *bladder.*
Blaud, *to slap ; a quantity of anything.*
Blaudin', *pelting or beating.*
Blaw, *to blow, to brag.*
Blawn, *blown.*
Bleerit, *bleared.*
Bleeze, *a blaze.*
Bleezin, *blazing.*
Blellum, *an idle talking fellow.*
Blether, *the bladder, nonsense.*
Blethers, *nonsense.*
Bleth'rin, *talking idly.*
Blin', *blind.*
Blink, *a short time, a look.*
Blinks, *looks smilingly.*
Blinkers, *a term of contempt, pretty girls.*
Blinkin, *smirking.*
Blitter, *the mire snipe.*
Blue-gown, *one of those beggars who get annually on the king's birthday a blue cloak or gown with a badge, a beggar, a bedesman.*
Blude, *blood.*
Bluid, *blood.*
Blume, *bloom.*
Bluntie, *a stupid person.*
Blypes, *peelings.*
Bocked, *vomited.*
Boddle, *a small coin, a halfpenny.*
Bogles, *hobgoblins.*
Bonnie, *beautiful.*

Bonnocks, *thick cakes of oatmeal bread.*

Boord, *board.*

Boortrees, *elder bushes.*

Boost, *must needs.*

Bore, *a hole or rent.*

Bouk, *a corpse.*

Bouses, *drinks.*

Bow-hough'd, *crook-thighed.*

Bow-kail, *cabbage.*

Bow't, *crooked.*

Brae, *the slope of a hill.*

Braid, *broad.*

Braid-claith, *broad-cloth.*

Braid Scots, *broad Scotch.*

Braik, *a harrow to break the clods.*

Braing't, *rushed forward.*

Brak, *did break.*

Brak's, *broke his.*

Brankie, *well attired.*

Branks, *a kind of wooden curb for horses.*

Brany, *brandy.*

Brash, *a sudden short illness.*

Brats, *clothes, aprons.*

Brattle, *a shore race.*

Braw, *handsome, gaily dressed.*

Brawly, *perfectly.*

Braxies, *sheep which have died of a disease called 'braxy.'*

Breastie, dim. of *breast.*

Breastit, *did spring up or forward.*

Brechan, *a horse-collar.*

Breckan, *fern.*

Bree, *juice, liquid.*

Breeks, *breeches.*

Brent, *high, smooth, unwrinkled.*

Brief, *a writing.*

Brig, *bridge.*

Brither, *brother.*

Brithers, *brothers.*

Brock, *a badger.*

Brogue, *a trick.*

Broo, *water, broth.*

Brooses, *races at country weddings who shall first reach the bridegroom's house on returning from church.*

Browst, *as much malt liquor as is brewed at a time.*

Browster-wives, *ale-house wives.*

Brugh, *burgh.*

Brulzie, *a broil.*

Brunstane, *brimstone.*

Brunt, *burned.*

Brust, *burst.*

Buckie, dim. of *buck.*

Buckskin, *an inhabitant of Virginia.*

Buff, *to beat.*

Bughtin-time, *the time of collecting the ewes in the pens to be milked.*

Buirdly, *strong, well-knit.*

Buke, *book.*

Bum, *to hum.*

Bum-clock, *a beetle.*

Bumming, *humming.*

Bummle, *a blunderer.*

Bunker, *a seat in a window.*

Burdies, *damsels.*

Bure, *bore, did bear.*

Burns, *streams.*

Burnie, *streamlet.*

Burnewin, i.e. *burn the wind, a blacksmith.*

Bur-thistle, *the spear-thistle.*

Busking, *dressing, decorating.*

Buskit, *dressed.*

Busks, *adorns.*

Buss, *a bush.*

Bussle, *a bustle.*

But, *without, or wanting.*

But an' ben, *kitchen and parlour.*

By, *past, apart.*

By attour, *in the neighbourhood, outside.*

Byke, *a bee-hive.*

Byre, *cowshed.*


Ca', *to drive ; a call.*

Ca'd, *named, driven ; calved.*

Ca't, *called.*

Ca' throu', *to push forward.*

Cadger, *a carrier or travelling dealer.*

Cadie, *a fellow.*

Caff, *chaff.*

Cairds, *tinkers.*

Calf-ward, *a small inclosure for calves.*

Callans, *boys.*

Caller, *fresh.*

Callet, *a trull.*

Cam, *came.*

Cankert, *cankered.*

Cankrie, *cankered.*

Canna, *cannot.*

Cannie, *carefully, softly.*

Cantie, *cheerful, lively.*
Cantrip, *a charm, a spell.*
Cape-stane, *cope-stone.*
Carl, *a carle, a man.*
Carlin, *an old woman.*
Cartes, *cards for playing.*
Cartie, dim. of *cart.*
Caudrons, *cauldrons.*
Cauf, *a calf.*
Cauk and keel, *chalk and ruddle.*
Cauld, *cold.*
Caups, *wooden bowl.*
Causey, *causeway.*
Cavie, *a hen-coop.*
Chamer, *chamber.*
Change-house, *a tavern.*
Chap, *a fellow.*
Chapman, *a pedlar.*
Chaup, *a blow.*
Cheek for chow, *cheek for jowl.*
Cheep, *chirp.*
Chiels, *young fellows.*
Chimla, *chimney.*
Chittering, *shivering with cold.*
Chows, *chews.*
Chuckie, dim. of *chuck.*
Christendie, *Christendom.*
Chuffie, *fat-faced.*
Clachan, *a hamlet.*
Claise, *clothes.*
Claith, *cloth.*
Claithing, *clothing.*
Claiver, *to talk idly or foolishly.*
Clamb, *clomb.*
Clankie, *a sharp stroke.*
Clap, *a clapper.*
Clark, *clerky, scholarly.*
Clarkit, *wrote.*
Clarty, *dirty.*
Clash, *gossip ; to talk.*
Clatter, *to talk idly.*
Claught, *clutched.*
Claughtin, *catching at anything greedily.*
Claut, *to snatch at, to lay hold of a quantity scraped together.*
Claver, *clover.*
Clavers, *idle stories.*
Claw, *scratch.*
Cleckin, *a brood.*
Cleed, *to clothe.*
Cleeding, *clothing.*

Cleek, *to seize.*
Cleekit, *linked themselves.*
Clegs, *gad-flies.*
Clink, *to rhyme; money.*
Clinkin, *sitting down neatly.*
Clinkumbell, *the church bell-ringer.*
Clips, *shears.*
Clishmaclaver, *idle talk.*
Clockin-time, *hatching-time.*
Cloot, *the hoof.*
Clootie, *Satan.*
Clours, *bumps or swellings after a blow.*
Clouts, *clothes.*
Clout, *patch.*
Clud, *a cloud.*
Coble, *a fishing-boat.*
Cock, *to erect.*
Cocks, *good fellows.*
Cod, *a pillow.*
Co'er, *to cover.*
Coft, *bought.*
Cog, *a wooden dish.*
Coggie, dim. of *cog.*
Coila, *from Kyle, a district of Ayrshire.*
Collie, *a sheep dog.*
Collieshangie, *an uproar, a quarrel.*
Commans, *commandments.*
Compleenin, *complaining.*
Cood, *the cud.*
Coofs, *fools, ninnies.*
Cookit, *appeared and disappeared,* or *peeped.*
Coost, *did cast.*
Cootie, *a kind of large spoon, or spade;* also, *feathered at the ancles.*
Corbies, *crows.*
Corn't, *fed with oats.*
Corss, *the market-cross.*
Couldna, *could not.*
Countra, *country.*
Couthie, *kindly, loving, comfortable.*
Cowp, *to tumble over.*
Cowpit, *tumbled.*
Cow'rin, *cowering.*
Cowr, *to cower.*
Cour, *to cower.*
Cowte, *a colt.*
Crack, *a story or harangue, talk.*
Crackin, *conversing, gossiping.*
Craft, *a croft.*
Craig, *the throat.*

Craigs, *crags.*

Craigy, *craggy.*

Craiks, *landrails.*

Crambo-clink, *rhymes, or doggerel verses crammed together.*

Crambo-jingle, *rhymes.*

Crankous, *fretful.*

Cranreuch, *hoar frost.*

Crap, *crop.*

Craw, *to crow.*

Creel, *a basket.*

Creepie-chair, *the chair or stool of repentance.*

Creeshie, *greasy.*

Crocks, *old sheep.*

Croods, *coos.*

Crooded, *cooed.*

Cronie, *an intimate comrade.*

Croon, *a groaning or murmuring sound.*

Crouchie, *crook-backed.*

Crouse, *brisk and bold.*

Crowdie, *porridge.*

Crowdie-time, *breakfast-time.*

Crummock, *a staff with a crooked head.*

Crump, *crisp or crumbly.*

Crunt, *a blow on the head with a cudgel.*

Cuddle, *to fondle.*

Cuifs, *blockheads, ninnies.*

Cummock, *a staff with a crooked head.*

Curch, *a female head-dress.*

Curchie, *a curtsy.*

Curmurring, *rumbling.*

Curpin, *the crupper.*

Curple, *the crupper.*

Cushats, *wood-pigeons.*

Custock, *the heart of a stalk of cabbage.*

Cutty, *short.*

Daddie, *father.*

Daes't, *stupefied, dazed.*

Daffin, *merriment.*

Daft, *foolish, sportive.*

Dails, *deals of wood.*

Daimen-icker, *an occasional ear of corn.*

Damies, *dim. of dames.*

Dam, *water.*

Dang, *knocked, pushed.*

Danton, *to subdue.*

Darklins, *darkling.*

Daud, *a lump ; to knock.*

Daudin', *pelting.*

Dauntingly, *dauntlessly.*

Daur, *to dare.*

Daurna, *dare not.*

Daut, *to fondle, to doat on.*

Daw, *to dawn.*

Dawtit, *fondled, caressed.*

Daurg, *a day's work.*

Daviely, *spiritless.* [Dowiely.]

Davie's, *King David's.*

Dead-sweer, *extremely reluctant.*

Deave, *to deafen.*

Deils, *devils.*

Deil ma care, *devil may care, no matter for all that.*

Deil haet, *devil a thing ; devil have it !*

Deleerit, *delirious.*

Delvin, *delving.*

Descrive, *to describe.*

Deservin't, *deserving of it.*

Deuk, *a duck.*

Devel, *a stunning blow.*

Diddle, *to jog, or fiddle.*

Differ, *difference.*

Dight, *cleaned from chaff, to wipe away.*

Din, *dun in colour.*

Ding, *to surpass, to beat.*

Dink, *neat, trim.*

Dinna, *do not.*

Dirl, *a thrilling blow.*

Dizzen, *a dozen.*

Dochter, *daughter.*

Doited, *stupefied.*

Donsie, *stupid, unmanageable.*

Dooked, *ducked.*

Dool, *sorrow.*

Doolfu', *sorrowful.*

Doos, *pigeons.*

Dorty, *saucy, sullen.*

Douce, *grave, sober, modest, gentle.*

Doucely, *soberly.*

Doudled, *dandled.*

Dought, *could, might.*

Dought na, *did not, or did not choose to.*

Doup, *the backside, the bottom.*

Dour, *stubborn.*

Dow, *do, can.*

Dowff, *pithless, dull.*

Dowie, *faded or worn with sorrow, sad.*

Downa bide, *cannot stand.*

Downa do, *impotence.*

Doylt, *stupid.*

Doytin, *walking stupidly.*

Dozen'd, *impotent, torpid or benumbed.*

Draiglit, *draggled.*

Drants, *sullen fits.*

Drap, *drop, a small quantity.*

Drappie, dim. of *drap.*

Drapping, *dropping.*

Draunting, *drawling, of a slow enunciation.*

Dree, *to endure.*

Dreeping, *dripping.*

Dreigh, *tedious and slow.*

Driddle, *to play on the fiddle without skill.*

Drift, *a drove.* Fell aff the drift, *wandered from his companions.*

Droddum, *the breech.*

Drone, *the bagpipe.*

Droop-rumpl't, *that droops at the crupper.*

Drouk, *to drench.*

Droukit, *wet, drenched.*

Drouth, *thirst.*

Drouthy, *thirsty.*

Druken, *drunken.*

Drumly, *muddy.*

Drummock, *meal and water mixed raw.*

Drunt, *pet, sullen humour.*

Dry, *thirsty.*

Dubs, *puddles.*

Duds, *garments.*

Duddie, *ragged.*

Duddies, *garments.*

Dung, *knocked, exhausted.*

Dunted, *beat, thumped.*

Dunts, *blows, knocks.*

Durk, *a dirk.*

Dusht, *pushed.*

Dwalling, *dwelling.*

Dwalt, *dwelt.*

Dyvors, *bankrupts, disreputable fellows.*

Earns, *eagles.*

Eastlin, *eastern.*

Ee, *eye; to watch.*

Een, *eyen.*

E'e brie, *the eyebrow.*

E'en, *evening.*

E'enins, *evenings.*

Eerie, *having or producing a superstitious feeling of dread; dismal.*

Eild, *age.*

Eke, *also.*

Elbucks, *elbows.*

Eldritch, *elvish; strange, wild, hideous.*

Eleckit, *elected.*

Eller, *an elder.*

En', *end.*

Enbrugh, *Edinburgh.*

Em'brugh, *Edinburgh.*

Enow, *enough.*

Erse, *Gaelic.*

Ether-stane, *adder-stone.*

Ettle, *design.*

Expeckit, *expected.*

Eydent, *diligent.*

Fa', *lot; also, have as one's lot, obtain.*

Faddom't, *fathomed.*

Fae, *foe.*

Faem, *foam.*

Faikit, *bated, forgiven, excused.*

Failins, *failings.*

Fair-fa', *may good befall!*

Fairin, *a present, a reward.*

Fairly, *entirely, completely.*

Fallow, *a fellow.*

Fa'n or fa'en, *have fallen.*

Fan, *found.*

Fand, *found.*

Farls, *cakes of oat-bread.*

Fash, *trouble myself.*

Fash your thumb, *trouble yourself in the least.*

Fashous, *troublesome.*

Fasten-een, *Fasten's-even (before Lent).*

Fatt'rels, *ribbon-ends.*

Faught, *a fight.*

Fauld, *a fold.*

Faulding, *folding.*

Faulding slap, *the gate of the fold.*

Fause, *false.*

Faut, *fault.*

Fautor, *a transgressor.*

Fawsont, *seemly, respectably.*

Fearfu', *fearful.*

Feat, *spruce.*

Fecht, *to fight.*

Feck, *the greater portion.*

Feckly, *mostly.*

Fecket, *an under waistcoat with sleeves.*

Feckless, *powerless, without effect.*

Feg, *a fig.*

Feide, *feud.*

Fell, *the flesh immediately under the skin; keen, biting; tasty.*

Fen, *a shift, provision.*

Fend, *to keep off, to live comfortably.*

Ferlie, *wonder.*

Fetch't, *pulled by fits and starts.*

Fey, *fated.*

Fidge, *to fidget.*

Fidgin-fain, *fidgetting with eagerness.*

Fiel, *soft, smooth.*

Fient, *fiend.* The fient a, *the devil a.*

Fier, *healthy, sound; brother, friend.*

Fiere, *companion.*

Fillie, *a filly.*

Fin', *find.*

Fissle, *bustle or rustle.*

Fit, *foot.*

Fittie-lan, *the near horse of the hindermost pair in the plough.*

Fizz, *to make a hissing noise like fermentation.*

Flaffin, *flapping, fluttering.*

Flae, *a flea.*

Flang, *did fling or caper.*

Flannen, *flannel.*

Fleech'd, *supplicated, flattered.*

Flee, *a fly.*

Fleesh, *a fleece.*

Fleg, *a fright, a random stroke.*

Fleth'rin, *flattering.*

Flewit, *a sharp blow.*

Fley'd, *scared.*

Flichterin', *fluttering.*

Flinders, *shreds.*

Flinging, *dancing wildly.*

Flingin-tree, *a flail.*

Fliskit, *fretted and capered.*

Flittering, *fluttering.*

Flyte, *to scold*

Fodgel, *squat, plump.*

Foor, *fared, went.*

Foord, *a ford.*

Foorsday, *Thursday.*

Forbears, *forefathers.*

Forbye, *besides.*

Forfairn, *worn out, jaded.*

Forfoughten, *fatigued.*

Forgather, *meet, fall in with.*

Forgie, *forgive.*

Forjesket, *jaded with fatigue.*

Forrit, *forward.*

Fother, *fodder.*

Fou, *full, tipsy.*

Foughten, *troubled.*

Fouth, *abundance.*

Fow, *full measure of corn, bushel.*

Frae, *from.*

Freath, *to froth.*

Fremit, *strange, foreign.*

Frien', *friend.*

Fu', *full.*

Fud, *hare's tail.*

Fufft, *puffed, blew.*

Furder, *furtherance, success.*

Furms, *wooden forms or seats.*

Furr-ahin, *the hindmost horse on the right hand of the plough.*

Furrs, *furrows.*

Fushionless, *pithless.*

Fy, *an exclamation of haste.*

Fyke, *trouble, fuss.*

Fyle, *to soil or dirty.*

Gab, *the mouth; to prate.*

Gae, *go, gave.*

Gaed, *went.*

Gaets, *manners, or ways.*

Gairs, *'purple patches.'*

Gane, *gone.*

Gang, *to go.*

Gangrel, *vagrant.*

Gar, *to make.*

Garten, *garter.*

Gash, *sagacious.*

Gashin, *conversing.*

Gat, *got.*

Gate, *manner, way or road.*

Gatty, *swelled.*

Gaucie, *large, bushy, full, stately.*

Gaud, *the plough shaft.*

Gaudsman, *a ploughboy, the boy who drives the horses in the plough.*

Gaun, *going.*

Gaunted, *yawned.*

Gawcie, *jolly, large, flourishing.*
Gawkies, *foolish persons.*
Gawn, *Gavin.*
Gaylies, *pretty well.*
Gear, *wealth, goods.*
Geck, *to toss the head in scorn.*
Geds, *pike.*
Genty, *slender.*
Geordie, *George.* The yellow letter'd Geordie, *a guinea.*
Get, *child.*
Ghaists, *ghosts.*
Gie, *give.*
Gied, *gave.*
Gien, *given.*
Gi'en, *given.*
Gies, *give us.*
Gif', *if.*
Giftie, dim. of *gift.*
Giglets, *laughing children.*
Gillie, dim. of *gill.*
Gilpey, *a young person.*
Gimmer, *a ewe two years old.*
Gin, *if.*
Girdle, *a circular plate of iron for toasting cakes on the fire.*
Girn, *to grin.*
Girrs, *hoops.*
Gizz, *a wig.*
Glaikit, *thoughtless, giddy.*
Glaizie, *smooth, glossy.*
Glamour, *effect of a charm.*
Glaum'd, *grasped.*
Gled, *a kite.*
Gleed, *a live coal.*
Gleg, *sharp; cleverly, swiftly.*
Gleib, *a gleb or portion.*
Glib-gabbet, *that speaks smoothly and readily.*
Glinted, *glanced.*
Gloamin, *twilight.*
Gloamin-shot, *a twilight interview.*
Glowrin, *staring.*
Glowr'd, *looked earnestly, stared.*
Glunch, *a frown.*
Goavan, *moving and looking vacantly.*
Gotten, *got.*
Gowan, *the daisy.*
Gowd, *gold.*
Gowden, *golden.*
Gowff'd, *golfed.*
Gowk, *a fool.*

Gowling, *howling.*
Graff, *a grave.*
Grained, *groaned.*
Graip, *a pronged instrument.*
Graith, *harness accoutrements.*
Granes, *groans.*
Grannie, *grandmother.*
Grape, *to grope.*
Grapit, *groped.*
Grat, *wept.*
Gree, *a prize; to agree.*
Gree't, *agreed.*
Greet, *to weep.*
Griens, *longs for.*
Grippet, *gripped, caught hold of.*
Grissle, *gristle.*
Grit, *great.*
Grozet, *a gooseberry.*
Grumphie, *the sow.*
Grun', *the ground.*
Grunstane, *a grindstone.*
Gruntle, *the countenance, a grunting noise.*
Grunzie, *the mouth.*
Grushie, *thick, of thriving growth.*
Grusome, *ill favoured.*
Grutten, *wept.*
Gudeen, *good even.*
Gudeman, *goodman.*
Gudes, *goods.*
Guid, *good.*
Guid-e'en, *good even.*
Guidfather, *father-in-law.*
Guidwife, *the mistress of the house, the landlady.*
Guid-willie, *hearty.*
Gully, *a large knife.*
Gulravage, *riotous and hasty.*
Gumlie, *muddy, discoloured.*
Gumption, *understanding.*
Gusty, *tasteful.*
Gutcher, *grandfather, goodsire.*

Ha', *hall.*
Haddin, *holding, inheritance.*
Hae, *have.*
Haffets, *the temples.*
Hafflins, *partly; also, growing lads.*
Hafflins-wise, *almost half.*
Hag, *a pit in mosses and moors.*
Haggis, *a kind of pudding boiled in the stomach of an ox or a sheep.*

Hain, *to spare, to save.*
Hain'd, *spared.*
Hairst, *harvest.*
Haith, *faith!*
Haivers, *idle talk.*
Hald, *an abiding-place.*
Hale, *whole, entire.*
Haly, *holy.*
Hallan, *a partition-wall in a cottage, hall-end.*
Hallions, *clowns, roysterers.*
Hallowmas, *the 31st of October.*
Hame, *home.*
Han', *hand.*
Han' afore, *the foremost horse on the left hand in the plough.*
Han' ahin, *the hindmost horse on the left hand in the plough.*
Hand-breed, *a hand-breadth.*
Hand-waled, *carefully selected by hand.*
Handless, *without hands, useless, awkward.*
Hangit, *hanged.*
Hansel, *a gift for a particular season, or the first money on any particular occasion.*
Hap, *to wrap.* Winter hap, *winter clothing.*
Hap, *hop.*
Happer, *a hopper.*
Happing, *hopping.*
Hap-step-an'-lowp, *hop, step, and jump.*
Harkit, *hearkened.*
Harn, *coarse linen.*
Har'sts, *harvests.*
Hash, *a soft, useless fellow.*
Hash'd, *cut.*
Haslock, *the finest wool, being the lock that grows on the* hals *or throat.*
Hastit, *hasted.*
Haud, *to hold.*
Hauf, *the half.*
Haughs, *low-lying lands on the border of a river.*
Hauns, *hands.*
Haurl, *to drag.*
Haurlin, *peeling, dragging off.*
Hauver, *coarsely ground.*
Havins, *good manners.*
Hav'rel, *half-witted.*

Hawkie, *a cow, properly one with a white face.*
Healsome, *wholesome.*
Heapit, *heaped.*
Hearin', *hearing.*
Hearse, *hoarse.*
Hech, *an exclamation of surprise and grief.*
Hecht, *foretold, offered.*
Hechtin', *making to pant.*
Heckle, *a comb used in dressing hemp, flax, &c.*
Heels-o'er-gowdy, *head-over-heels.*
Heeze, *to elevate, to hoist.*
Heft, *haft.*
Hellim, *the helm.*
Hen-broo, *hen-broth.*
Herriet, *harried.*
Herryment, *plundering, devastation.*
Hersel, *herself.*
Het, *hot.*
Heugh, *a pit or ravine.*
Heuk, *a reaping-hook.*
Hich, *high.*
Hidin', *hiding.*
Hie, *high.*
Hilch, *to hobble.*
Hilchin, *halting.*
Hill-tap, *hill-top.*
Hiltie-skiltie, *helter-skelter.*
Himsel, *himself.*
Hiney, *honey.*
Hing, *to hang.*
Hirploe, *walks as if crippled.*
Hissel, hirsel, *as many cattle or sheep as one person can attend.*
Histie, *dry, barren.*
Hitch, *a loop or knot.*
Hizzies, *young women.*
Hoast, *a cough.*
Hoddin, *jogging, plodding.*
Hoggie, *a young sheep one year old.*
Hog-score, *a line drawn across the rink in the game of curling.*
Hog-shouther, *a kind of horse-play by justling with the shoulder.*
Hol't, *holed, perforated.*
Hoodie-craw, *the hooded crow.*
Hool, *the outer skin or case.*
Hoolie! *stop! cautiously! softly!*
Hoord, *hoard.*
Hoordet, *hoarded.*

Horn, *a spoon or a comb made of horn.*
Hornie, *Satan.*
Host *or* hoast, *a cough.*
Hostin, *coughing.*
Hotch'd, *fidgetted.*
Houghmagandie, *fornication.*
Houlets, *owls.*
Hov'd, *swelled.*
Howdie, *a midwife.*
Howe, *hollow.*
Howe-backit, *sunk in the back.*
Howes, *hollows.*
Howkit, *digged, dug up.*
Hoyse, *hoist.*
Hoy't, *urged.*
Hoyte, *to move clumsily.*
Hughoc, *Hugh.*
Hunder, *a hundred.*
Hunkers, *the hams.*
Huntit, *hunted.*
Hurcheon, *a hedgehog.*
Hurchin, *an urchin.*
Hurdies, *hips.*
Hurl, *to wheel or whirl.*
Hushion, *stocking-leg, worn on the arm.*
Hyte, *mad.*

Icker, *an ear of corn.*
Ier'oe, *a great-grandchild.*
Ilk, *each.*
Ilka, *every.*
Ill o't, *bad at it.*
Ill-willie, *ill-natured.*
Indentin, *indenturing.*
Ingine, *genius, ingenuity.*
Ingle-cheek, *the fireside.*
Ingle-lowe, *the household fire.*
I'se, *I shall or will.*
Isna, *is not.*
Ither, *other.*
Itsel, *itself.*

Jad, *a jade, a wild young woman.*
Janwar, *January.*
Jauk, *to dally, to trifle.*
Jaukin, *trifling, dallying.*
Jauner, *foolish talk.*
Jaups, *splashes.*
Jillet, *a jilt.*
Jimp, *slender.*

Jimply, *neatly.*
Jink, *to dodge.*
Jinker, *that turns quickly.*
Jinkers, *gay, sprightly girls.*
Jinkin, *dodging.*
Jirkinet, *an outer jacket or jerkin worn by women.*
Jirt, *a jerk ; to squirt.*
Jo, *sweetheart, joy.*
Joctelegs, *clasp-knives.*
Joes, *lovers.*
Jorum, *the jug.*
Jouk, *to duck, to make obeisance.*
Jow, *to swing and ring.*
Jumpit, *jumped.*
Jundie, *to justle.*

Kaes, *daws.*
Kail, *broth.*
Kail-blade, *the leaf of the colewort.*
Kail-runt, *the stem of the colewort.*
Kain, *farm produce paid as rent.*
Kebars, *rafters.*
Kebbuck, *a cheese.*
Keckle, *to cackle, to laugh.*
Keekin'-glass, *a looking-glass.*
Keeks, *peeps.*
Keepit, *kept.*
Kelpies, *water-spirits.*
Ken, *know.*
Ken'les, *kindles.*
Kenn'd, *known.*
Kennin, *a little bit.*
Kent, *knew.*
Kep, *to catch anything when falling.*
Ket, *a fleece.*
Kiaugh, *anxiety, cark.*
Kilbagie, *the name of a certain kind of whisky.*
Kilt, *to tuck up.*
Kimmer, *a married woman, a gossip.*
Kin', *kind.*
King's-hood, *a part of the entrails of an ox.*
Kintra, *country.*
Kintra cooser, *a country stallion.*
Kirn, *a churn.*
Kirns, *harvest-homes.*
Kirsen, *to christen.*
Kist, *a chest.*
Kitchen, *anything that eats with bread to serve for a relish.*

Kitchens. *seasons, makes palatable.*
Kittle, *to tickle ; ticklish, difficult.*
Kittlin, *a kitten.*
Kiutlin, *fondling.*
Knaggie, *like knags, or points of rock.*
Knappin-hammers, *hammers for breaking stones.*
Knowe, *a knoll.*
Knurlin, *a dwarf, knotted, gnarled.*
Kye, *cows.*
Kytes, *bellies.*
Kythe, *discover, appear.*

Laddie, *a lad.*
Lade, *a load.*
Laggen, *the angle between the side and bottom of a wooden dish.*
Laigh, *low.*
Laik, *lack.*
Lair, *lore.*
Lairing, *sticking in mire or mud.*
Laith, *loth.*
Laithfu', *bashful.*
Lallan, *lowland.*
Lampit, *limpet.*
Lan', *land, estate.*
Lane, *alone.*
Lanely, *lonely.*
Lang, *long.*
Lap, *did leap.*
Lave, *the rest.*
Lav'rocks, *larks.*
Lawin, *shot, reckoning, bill.*
Lawlan', *lowland.*
Lea'e, *leave.*
Leal, *true, loyal.*
Lea-rig, *a grassy ridge.*
Lear, *lore, learning.*
Lee-lang, *live-long.*
Leesome, or lo'esome, *pleasant.*
Leeze me, *leif (or dear) is to me ; mine above everything else be.*
Leister, *a three-barbed instrument for sticking fish.*
Len', *lend.*
Leugh, *laughed.*
Leuk, *look, appearance.*
Libbet, *gelded.*
Licket, *beating.*
Licks, *a beating.*
Liein, *telling lies*
Lien, *lain.*

Lift, *heaven, a large quantity.*
Lightly, *to undervalue, to slight.*
Lilt, *sing.*
Limmer, *a woman of loose manners or morals.*
Limpit, *limped.*
Lin, *a waterfall.*
Linket, *tripped deftly.*
Linkin, *tripping.*
Linn, *a waterfall.*
Lint, *flax.*
Linties, *linnets.*
Lippened, *trusted.*
Loan, *lane.*
Lo'ed, *loved.*
Lon'on, *London.*
Loof, *palm of the hand.*
Loosome, *lovesome.*
Loot, *did let.*
Looves, *palms.*
Losh, *a petty oath.*
Lough, *a lake.*
Louns, *fellows, rascals.*
Loup, *to leap.*
Lowe, *flame.*
Lowan, *flaming.*
Lowin, *blazing.*
Lowpin, *leaping.*
Lowping, *leaping.*
Lowse, *to loosen.*
Luckie, *a designation applied to an elderly woman.*
Lug, *the ear.*
Lugget, *eared.*
Luggies, *small wooden dishes with straight handles.*
Luke, *look.*
Lum, *the chimney.*
Lunardie, *a bonnet called after Lunardi, the aëronaut.*
Lunt, *a column of smoke.*
Luntin, *smoking.*
Luve, *love.*
Luvers, *lovers.*
Lyart, *grey.*
Lynin, *lining.*

Maf, *more.*
Mair, *more.*
Maist, *almost.*
Mak, *make.*
Mailie, *Molly.*

Mailins, *farms.*
Mang, *among.*
Manteels, *mantles.*
Mashlum, *mixed corn.*
Maskin-pat, *a tea-pot.*
Maukin, *a hare.*
Maun, *must.*
Maunna, *must not.*
Maut, *malt.*
Mavis, *the thrush.*
Mawin, *mowing.*
Mawn, *a basket; mown.*
Meere, *a mare.*
Meikle, *as much.*
Melder, *corn sent to the mill to be ground.*
Mell, *to meddle.*
Melvie, *to soil with mud.*
Men', *mend.*
Mense, *good manners.*
Mess John, *the clergyman.*
Messin, *a dog of mixed breeds.*
Midden, *the dunghill.*
Midden-creels, *dunghill baskets.*
Midden-hole, *the dunghill.*
Mim, *prim.*
Mim-mou'd, *prim-mouthed.*
Min', *remembrance.*
Min', *mind.*
Minnie, *mother.*
Mirk, *night; murky.*
Misca'd, *abused.*
Misguidin', *misguiding.*
Mishanter, *misfortune, disaster.*
Mislear'd, *mischievous; ill-bred.*
Mist, *missed.*
Misteuk, *mistook.*
Mither, *mother.*
Mixtie-maxtie, *confusedly mixed.*
Moistify, *to make moist.*
Mony, *many.*
Mools, *the earth of graves.*
Moop, *to nibble, to keep company with.*
Moorlan', *moorland.*
Moss, *a morass.*
Mou', *mouth.*
Moudieworts, *moles.*
Muckle, *great, big, much.*
Muslin-kail, *thin broth*
Mutchkin, *an English pint.*
Mysel, *myself.*

Na', *not, no.*
Nae, *no.*
Naebody, *nobody.*
Naig, *a nag.*
Nane, *none.*
Nappy, *strong ale.*
Natch, *grip, hold.*
Neibors, *neighbours.*
Needna, *need not.*
Neist, *next.*
Neuk, *nook, corner.*
New-ca'd, *newly calved.*
Nick, *to break, to sever suddenly.*
Nickan, *cutting*
Nicket, *caught, cut off.*
Nick-nackets, *curiosities.*
Nicks, *notches.*
Niest, *next.*
Nieve-fu', *a fist-full.*
Nieves, *fists.*
Niffer, *exchange.*
Nits, *nuts.*
Nocht, *nothing.*
Norland, *Northland.*
Nowte, *cattle.*

O', *of.*
O'erlay, *an outside cravat, muffler.*
O'erword, *refrain.*
Ony, *any.*
Orra, *superfluous, extra.*
O't, *of it.*
Ought, *aught, anything.*
Oughtlins, *anything in the least.*
Ourie, *shivering, drooping.*
Oursel, *ourselves.*
Out-cast, *a quarrel.*
Outler, *un-housed, outlying.*
Owre, *over, too.*
Owsen, *oxen.*

Pack an' thick, *on intimate terms, closely familiar.*
Packs, *twelve stones.*
Paidle, *to paddle.*
Paidles, *wanders about without aim.*
Painch, *paunch, stomach.*
Paitricks, *partridges.*
Pangs, *crams.*
Parishen, *the parish.*
Parritch, *porridge.*
Parritch-pats, *porridge-pots.*

Pat, *put ; a pot.*
Pattle, *a plough-spade.*
Paughty, *haughty, petulant.*
Paukie, *cunning, sly.*
Pay't, *paid.*
Pechan, *the stomach.*
Pechin', *panting.*
Penny wheep, *small beer.*
Pettle, *a plough-spade.*
Phraisin, *flattering, coaxing.*
Pickle, *a small quantity.*
Pit, *put.*
Placads, *public proclamations.*
Plack, *an old Scotch coin, the third part of a Scotch penny, twelve of which make an English penny.*
Plaiden, *plaiding.*
Plenished, *stocked.*
Pleugh, *plough.*
Pliskie, *a mischievous trick.*
Pliver, *a plover.*
Plumpit, *plumped.*
Pocks, *wallets or bags.*
Poind, *to seize or distrain.*
Poortith, *poverty.*
Pou, *to pull ; to gather.*
Pouk, *to pluck.*
Poupit, *the pulpit.*
Pouse, *push or thrust.*
Poussie, *a hare.*
Pouts, *chicks.*
Pouther'd, *powdered.*
Pouthery, *powdery.*
Pow, *the head, the poll.*
Pownie, *a pony.*
Powther, *powder.*
Pree, *to taste.*
Preen, *a pin.*
Prent, *print.*
Prie'd, *tasted.*
Prief, *proof.*
Priggin', *haggling.*
Primsie, *demure, prim.*
Propone, *to propose.*
Proveses, *provosts.*
Pu', *to pull.*
Puddock-stools, *toadstools.*
Puir, *poor.*
Pund, *pounds.*
Pyet, *the magpie.*
Pyke, *to pick.*
Pyles, *grains.*

Quaick, *quack.*
Quat, *quit, quitted.*
Quaukin', *quaking.*
Quean, *a young woman.*
Quey, *a young cow.*
Quo', *quoth.*

Rab, Rob, *Robert.*
Rad, *afraid.*
Rade, *rode.*
Ragweed, *the plant ragwort.*
Raibles, *rattles nonsense.*
Rair, *to roar.*
Raise, *rose.*
Raize, *to madden, to inflame.*
Ramblin, *rambling.*
Ramfeezl'd, *fatigued.*
Ramgunshock, *rugged.*
Ram-stam, *forward, precipitate.*
Randie, *quarrelsome.*
Randy, *a vixen.*
Ranting, *noisy, full of animal spirits.*
Rants, *jollifications.*
Rape, *a rope.*
Raploch, *coarse cloth.*
Rask, *a rush.*
Rash-buss, *a bush of rushes.*
Rattan, *a rat.*
Rattons, *rats.*
Raucle, *rough, rash, sturdy.*
Raught, *reached.*
Raw, *a row.*
Rax, *to stretch.*
Ream, *cream.*
Rebute, *a rebut, a repulse, a rebuke.*
Rede, *counsel.*
Red-wud, *stark mad.*
Reekin, *smoking.*
Reekit, *smoked, smoky.*
Reeks, *smokes.*
Reestit, *smoke-dried ; stood restive.*
Reif randies, *roysterers.*
Remead, *remedy.*
Remuve, *remove.*
Rew, *to take pity.*
Rickles, *stocks of grain.*
Rig, *a ridge.*
Riggin, *rafters.*
Rigwoodie, *withered, sapless.*
Rin, *run.*
Rink, *the course of the stones in curling.*

Rinnin, *running.*
Ripp, *a handful of unthrashed corn.*
Ripple, *weakness in the back and reins.*
Ripplin-kame, *a flax-comb.*
Riskit, *made a noise like the tearing of roots.*
Rive, *to burst or tear.*
Rock, *a distaff.*
Rockin, *a social gathering, the women spinning on the rock or distaff.*
Roon, *round.*
Roose, *to praise.*
Roosty, *rusty.*
Roun', *round.*
Roupet, *hoarse as with a cold.*
Routhie, *well filled, abundant.*
Rowes, *rolls.*
Rowte, *to low, to bellow.*
Rowth, *abundance.*
Rowtin, *lowing.*
Rozet, *rosin.*
Ruefu', *rueful.*
Rung, *a cudgel.*
Runkl'd, *wrinkled.*
Runts, *the stems of cabbage.*
Ryke, *reach.*

Sabs, *sobs.*
Sae, *so.*
Saft, *soft.*
Sair, *sore ; to serve.*
Sairly, *sorely.*
Sair't, *served.*
Sang, *song.*
Sannock or Sawnie, *Alexander.*
Sark, *a shirt.*
Sarkit, *provided in shirts.*
Saugh, *the willow.*
Saul, *soul.*
Saunt, *saints.*
Saut, *salt.*
Saw, *to sow.*
Sawmont, *a salmon.*
Sax, *six.*
Scaith, *hurt.*
Scaur, *to scare.*
Scaur, *frightened.*
Scaud, *to scald.*
Scawl, *a scold.*
Scho, *she.*
Schoolin', *schooling, teaching.*

Scones, *barley cakes.*
Sconner, *to loathe ; disgust.*
Scraichin, *screeching.*
Screed, *a tear, a rent; to repeat glibly.*
Scriechin', *screeching.*
Scrievin', *gilding easily.*
Scrimpit, *scanty.*
Scrimply, *sparingly.*
Scroggie, *covered with stunted shrubs.*
Sculdudd'ry, *fornication.*
Seizins, *investitures.*
Sel, *self.*
Sell't, *sold.*
Sen', *send.*
Set, *lot.*
Sets, *becomes, set off, starts.*
Settlin', *settling.*
Shachl't, *loose and ill-shaped.*
Shaird, *a shred.*
Shangan, *a cleft stick.*
Shanna, *shall not.*
Shaul, *shallow.*
Shaver, *a wag.*
Shavie, *a trick.*
Shaw, *show.*
Shaw'd, *showed.*
Shaws, *wooded dells.*
Sheep-shank, Wha thinks himsel nae sheep-shank bane, *who thinks himself no unimportant person.*
Sheers, *shears.*
Sheugh, *a trench or ditch.*
Sheuk, *shook.*
Shiel, *a shieling, a hut.*
Shill, *shrill.*
Shog, *a shock.*
Shools, *shovels.*
Shoon, *shoes.*
Shor'd, *threatened, offered.*
Shore, *to threaten or offer.*
Shouldna, *should not.*
Shouther, *shoulder.*
Shure, *did shear* (corn).
Sic, *such.*
Siker, *secure.*
Siclike, *suchlike.*
Sidelins, *sidelong.*
Siller, *money, silver.*
Simmer, *summer.*
Sin', *since.*
Sindry, *sundry.*
Singet, *singed.*

Singin', *singing.*

Sinn, *the sun.*

Sinny, *sunny.*

Sinsyne, *since then.*

Skaith, *hurt.*

Skaithing, *injuring.*

Skeigh, *high-mettled, disdainful, skittish.*

Skellum, *a worthless fellow.*

Skelp, *a slap ; to run with a slapping vigorous sound of the feet on the ground.*

Skelpie-limmer, *a technical term in female scolding.*

Skinkin', *thin, liquid.*

Skinklin, *glittering,*

Skirl, *to shriek.*

Sklent, *to slope, to strike obliquely, to lie.*

Sklented, *slanted.*

Sklentin, *slanting.*

Skouth, *range, scope.*

Skreech, *to scream.*

Skriegh, *to scream.*

Skyrin, *parti-coloured.*

Skyte, *a glancing sliding stroke.*

Slade, *slid.*

Slae, *the sloe.*

Slaps, *gaps or breaches.*

Slaw, *slow.*

Slee, *sly, clever.*

Sleeest, *slyest.*

Sleekit, *sleek.*

Slidd'ry, *slippery.*

Sloken, *to quench, to allay thirst.*

Slypet, *slipped, fell over slowly.*

Sma', *small.*

Smeddum, *dust, mettle, sense.*

Smeek, *smoke.*

Smiddy, *a smithy.*

Smoor'd, *smothered.*

Smoutie, *smutty.*

Smytrie, *a number huddled together, a smatter.*

Snash, *abuse, impertinence.*

Snaw broo, *melted snow.*

Snawy, *snowy.*

Sned, *to lop, to cut off.*

Snell, *bitter, biting.*

Sneeshin-mill, *a snuff-box.*

Snick, *the latchet of a door.*

Snirtle, *to laugh slily.*

Snool, *to cringe, to sneak, to snub.*

Snoov'd, *went smoothly.*

Snowkit, *snuffed.*

Sodger, *a soldier.*

Soger, *a soldier.*

Sonsie, *jolly, comely, plump.*

Soom, *to swim.*

Soor, *sour.*

Sootie, *sooty.*

Sough, *a heavy sigh.*

Souk, *a suck.*

Soupe, *a spoonful, a small quantity of anything liquid.*

Souple, *supple.*

Souter, *a shoemaker.*

Sowps, *spoonfuls.*

Sowth, *to whistle over a tune.*

Sowther, *to solder, to make up.*

Spae, *to prophesy.*

Spails, *chips of wood.*

Spairges, *dashes or scatters about.*

Spairin, *sparing.*

Spak, *spake.*

Spate, *a flood.*

Spavie, *spavin (a disease).*

Spean, *to wean.*

Speel, *to climb.*

Speer, *to inquire.*

Spence, *the country parlour.*

Spier, *to ask, to inquire.*

Spleuchan, *a tobacco-pouch.*

Splore, *a frolic.*

Sprackled, *clambered.*

Sprattle, *to struggle.*

Spring, *a quick air in music, a Scottish reel.*

Spritty, *full of rushes or reed-grasses.*

Sprush, *spruce.*

Spunk, *fire, mettle.*

Spunkie, *full of spirit, mettlesome.*

Spunkies, *Wills-o'-the-wisp.*

Spurtle, *a stick with which porridge broth, &c. are stirred.*

Squattle, *to sprawl.*

Stacher'd, *staggered, walked un-steadily.*

Stack, *stuck.*

Staig, *a horse two years old.*

Stan', *stand.*

Stanes, *stones.*

Stang, *to sting.*

Stank, *a pool of stagnant water.*

Stap, *to stop.*
Stark, *strong, hardy.*
Starns, *stars.*
Staukin, *stalking.*
Staw, *to steal, to surfeit.*
Stechin, *cramming.*
Steek, *to close.*
Steeks, *stitches.*
Steer, *to molest, to stir up.*
Steeve, *firm.*
Stells, *stills—commonly illicit.*
Sten, *a leap or bound.*
Stents, *assessments, dues.*
Steyest, *steepest.*
Stibble, *stubble.*
Stibble-rig, *the reaper in harvest who takes the lead, a stubble-ridge.*
Stick-an-stowe, *totally, altogether.*
Stilt, *halt.*
Stimpart, *an eighth part of a Winchester bushel, half a peck.*
Stirk, *a cow or bullock a year or two old.*
Stockins, *stockings.*
Stockit, *stocked.*
Stocks, *plants of cabbage.*
Stoitered, *staggered.*
Stoor, *strong, harsh, deep.*
Stoppit, *stopped.*
Stot, *an ox.*
Stoure, *dust, dust blown on the wind, battle or confusion.*
Stown, *stolen.*
Stownlins, *by stealth.*
Stowrie, *dusty.*
Stoyte, *to stumble.*
Strade, *strode.*
Strae, *a fair strae-death, a natural death in bed.*
Straik, *to stroke.*
Straikit, *stroked.*
Strak, *struck.*
Strang, *strong.*
Strappin, *strapping.*
Straught, *straight.*
Streekit, *stretched.*
Striddle, *to straddle.*
Stringin, *stringing.*
Stroan't, *pissed.*
Studdie, *a stithy.*
Stumpie, dim. of *stump, a short quill.*

Strunt, *spirituous liquor of any kind; to strut.*
Stuff, *corn.*
Sturt, *trouble, stir, disturbance.*
Sturtin, *frighted.*
Styme, see a styme, *see in the least.*
Sucker, *sugar.*
Sud, *should.*
Sugh, *a rushing sound.*
Sumphs, *stupid fellows.*
Sune, *soon.*
Suthron, *Southern, English.*
Swaird, *sward.*
Swall'd, *swelled.*
Swank, *thin, agile, vigorous.*
Swankies, *strapping young fellows.*
Swap, *an exchange.*
Swarf, *to swoon.*
Swat, *did sweat.*
Swatch, *sample.*
Swats, *new ale.*
Swearin', *swearing.*
Sweatin, *sweating.*
Swinge, *to lash.*
Swirl, *a curve.*
Swith, *swift, suddenly.*
Swither, *hesitation.*
Swoor, *swore.*
Sybow, *a thick-necked onion.*
Syne, *since, then.*

Tack, *possession, lease.*
Tackets, *hob-nails.*
Tae, *toe.* Three-tae'd, *three-toed.*
Taed, *a toad.*
Taen, *taken.*
Tairge, *to task severely.*
Tak, *to take.*
Tald, *told.*
Tane, *the one.*
Tangs, *tongs.*
Tapetless, *heedless, foolish, pithless.*
Tapmost, *topmost.*
Tappit hen, *a quart measure.*
Taps, *tops.*
Tapsalteerie, *topsy-turvy.*
Tarrow, *to murmur.*
Tarry-breeks, *a sailor.*
Tassie, *a goblet or cup.*
Tauld, *told.*

Tawie, *that allows itself peaceably to be handled.*

Tawpies, *foolish young persons.*

Tawted, *matted.*

Teats, *small quantities.*

Teen, *sorrow.*

Tell'd, *told.*

Tellin', *telling.*

Temper-pin, *the wooden pin used for tempering or regulating the motion of a spinning-wheel.*

Tent, *to take heed, mark.*

Tentie, *heedful,*

Teughly, *toughly.*

Teuk, *took.*

Thack, *thatch.*

Thae, *these.*

Thairm, *fiddlestrings, intestines.*

Theekit, *thatched, covered up.*

Thegither, *together.*

Themsels, *themselves.*

Thieveless, *without an object, trifling, impotent.*

Thigger, *beggar.*

Thir, *these.*

Thirl'd, *thrilled, bound.*

Thole, *to suffer, to endure.*

Thou's, *thou art.*

Thowes, *thaws.*

Thowless, *slack, lazy.*

Thrang, *busy; a crowd.*

Thrapple, *the throat.*

Thrave, *twenty-four sheaves of corn, making two shocks.*

Thraw, *to sprain or twist, to cross or contradict.*

Thrawin', *twisting.*

Thrawn, *twisted.*

Thraws, *throes,*

Threap, *to assert.*

Thretteen, *thirteen.*

Thretty, *thirty.*

Thrissle, *the thistle.*

Throwther, *mixed, pell-mell.*

Thuds, *that makes a loud intermittent noise, resounding blows.*

Thummart, *the polecat.*

Thumpit, *thumped.*

Thysel', *thyself.*

Tidins, *tidings.*

Till, *to.*

Till't, *to it.*

Timmer, *timber.*

Timmer-propt, *timber-propped.*

Tine, *to lose or be lost.*

Tint, *lost.*

Tint as win, *lost as won.*

Tinkler, *a tinker.*

Tips, *rams.*

Tippence, *twopence.*

Tirl, *to strip or uncover.*

Tirl'd, *rasped (knocked).*

Tirlin, *unroofing.*

Tither, *the other.*

Tittlin, *whispering and laughing.*

Tocher, *marriage-portion.*

Todlin', *walking unsteadily or softly like an infant.*

Tods, *foxes.*

Toom, *empty.*

Toop, *a ram.*

Toun, *a hamlet, a farm-house.*

Tout, *the blast of a horn or trumpet.*

Touzie, *rough, shaggy.*

Touzle, *to rumple.*

Tow, *a rope.*

Towmond, *a twelvemonth.*

Toy, *a fashion of female head-dress.*

Toyte, *to totter.*

Transmugrify'd, *metamorphosed.*

Trashtrie, *trash.*

Treadin', *treading.*

Trews, *trousers.*

Trickie, *tricksy.*

Trig, *spruce, neat.*

Trinkling, *trickling.*

Troggin, *wares sold by wandering merchants or cadgers.*

Troke, *to exchange, to deal with.*

Trottin', *trotting.*

Trow't, *believed.*

Trowth! *in truth!*

Tulzie, *a quarrel.*

Tup, *a ram.*

Twa, *two.*

Twa-fauld, *twofold.*

Twa-three, *two or three.*

Twal, *twelve.*

Twalt, *the twelfth.*

Twang, *twinge.*

Twined, *reft, separated from.*

Twins, *bereaves, takes away from.*

Twistle, *a twist.*

Tyke, *a vagrant dog.*

Tyne, *to lose.*
Tysday 'teen, *Tuesday at evening.*

Unchancy, *dangerous.*
Unco, *very, great, extreme, strange.*
Uncos, *strange things, news of the country-side.*
Unkenn'd, *unknown.*
Unsicker, *unsecure.*
Unskaith'd, *unhurt.*
Upo', *upon.*
Upon't, *upon it.*

Vap'rin, *vapouring.*
Vauntie, *proud, in high spirits.*
Vera, *very.*
Viewin, *viewing.*
Virls, *rings.*
Vittel, *victual, grain.*
Vittle, *victual.*
Vogie, *proud, well-pleased.*
Vow, *an interjection of admiration or surprise.*

Wa', *a wall.*
Wa'-flower, *the wallflower.*
Wab, *a web.*
Wabster, *a weaver.*
Wad, *would; a wager; to wed.*
Wad a haen, *would have had.*
Wadna, *would not.*
Wadset, *a mortgage.*
Wae, *sorrowful.*
Wae days, *woful days.*
Waefu', *woful.*
Waes me, *woe's me.*
Waesucks ! *alas !*
Wae worth, *woe befall.*
Waft, *the cross thread that goes from the shuttle through the web.*
Waifs, *stray sheep.*
Wair't, *spend it.*
Wal'd, *chose.*
Wale, *choice.*
Walie, *ample, large.*
Wallop in a tow, *to hang one's self.*
Wame, *the belly.*
Wamefou, *bellyfull.*
Wan, *did win, earned.*
Wanchancie, *unlucky.*
Wanrestfu', *restless.*

War'd, *spent, bestowed.*
Ware, *to spend.*
Wark, *work.*
Wark-lume, *tool.*
Warks, *works.*
Warld, *world.*
Warlock, *a wizard.*
Warly, *worldly.*
Warran', *warrant.*
Warsle, *to wrestle.*
Warst, *worst.*
Warstl'd, *wrestled.*
Wasna, *was not.*
Wast, *west.*
Wastrie, *prodigality, riot.*
Wat, *wet; wot, know.*
Wat na, *wot not.*
Waterbrose, *meal and water.*
Wattle, *twisted wands.*
Wauble, *to wabble.*
Waught, *a big drink.*
Waukening, *awakening.*
Waukens, *wakens.*
Waukit, *thickened with toil.*
Waukrife, *wakeful.*
Wauks, *awakes.*
Waur, *to fight, to defeat; worse.*
Waur't, *worsted.*
Weans, *children.*
Weason, *the weasand.*
Wee, *little.*
    A wee, *a short period of time.*
    A wee a-back, *a small space behind.*
Weel, *well.*
Weel-gaun, *well-going.*
Weel-kent, *well-known.*
Weet, *wet.*
We'se, *we shall or will.*
Westlin, *western.*
Wha, *who.*
Wha e'er, *whoever.*
Whaizle, *to wheeze.*
Whalpit, *whelped.*
Wham, *whom.*
Whan, *when.*
Whang, *a large slice.*
Whar, *where.*
Whare, *where.*
Wha's, *whose.*
Whase, *whose.*
Whatfor no ? *for what reason not ?*

Whatt, *did whet or cut.*
Whaup, *a curlew.*
Whaur'll, *where will.*
Whiddin, *running as a hare.*
Whigmaleeries, *crochets.*
Whingin', *crying, complaining, fretting.*
Whins, *furze bushes.*
Whirlygigums, *useless ornaments.*
Whisht, *peace.*
Whiskit, *whisked.*
Whissle, *whistle.*
Whistle, *the throat.*
Whitter, *a hearty draught of liquor.*
Whun-stane, *whinstone, granite.*
Whup, *a whip.*
Whyles, *sometimes.*
Wi', *with.*
Wick, *a term in curling.*
Widdle, *a struggle or bustle.*
Wiel, *a small whirlpool.*
Wifie, *dim. of wife.*
Wight, *strong, powerful.*
Wil' cat, *the wild cat.*
Willow wicker, *the smaller species of willow.*
Willyart, *wild, strange.*
Wimplin, *flowing, meandering.*
Wimpl't, *wimpled.*
Win', *wind.*
Winkin, *winking.*
Winna, *will not.*
Winnock-bunker, *a seat in a window.*
Winnocks, *windows.*
Wins, *winds.*
Win't, *did wind.*
Wintle, *a staggering motion.*
Wintles, *struggles.*
Winze, *a curse.*
Wiss, *wish.*
Witha', *withal.*
Withoutten, *without.*

Wonner, *a wonder.*
Wons, *dwells.*
Woo', *wool.*
Woodie, *the gallows, a withe.*
Wooer-babs, *garters tied above the calf of the leg with two loops.*
Wordie, *dim. of word.*
Wordy, *worthy.*
Worl', *world.*
Worset, *worsted.*
Wow, *an exclamation of surprise or wonder.*
Wrang, *wrong.*
Wreeths, *wreaths.*
Wud, *mad.*
Wumble, *a wimble or auger.*
Wyle, *to beguile, to decoy.*
Wyliecoat, *a flannel vest.*
Wyling, *beguiling.*
Wyte, *to blame.*

Yard, *a garden.*
Yaud, *a worn-out horse.*
Yealings, *coevals.*
Yell, *barren, giving no milk.*
Yerd, *yard.*
Yerket, *jerked, lashed.*
Yerl, *an earl.*
Ye'se, *you shall or will.*
Yestreen, *yesternight.*
Yetts, *gates.*
Yeukin, *itching.*
Yeuks, *itches.*
Yill, *ale.*
Yill-caup, *ale-mug.*
Yird, *earth.*
Yirth, *the earth.*
Yokin, *yoking, a bout, a set to.*
Yont, *beyond.*
Yoursel, *yourselves, yourself.*
Yowes, *ewes.*
Yowie, *pet ewe.*
Yule, *Christmas.*

# INDEX OF FIRST LINES

# CHRONOLOGICAL LIST

(AS FAR AS KNOWN).

———•◦•———

### ROBERT BURNS,

Born January, 1759—Died July, 1796, aged 37½ years.

———•◦•———

1773.
Handsome Noll—'O, once I loved.'

1775.
? O Tibbie, I hae seen the day.
'I dreamed I lay.'

1776.
The sun he is sunk in the west.

1777.
Tragic Fragment—'All villain as
I am.'

1778.
The Tarbolton Lasses—'If ye gae
up.'
Jeremiad—'Ah, woe is me.'

1779.
Montgomerie's Peggy—'Altho' my
bed.'

1780.
As I was a wandering.

The Ronalds of the Bennals—'In
Tarbolton, ye ken.'
The Lass of Cessnock Banks.
Bonnie Peggy Alison—'Ilk care
an' fear.'
Mary Morison.
Here's to thy Health.

1781.
Winter—A Dirge : 'The wintry
wast.'
Prayer under the Pressure of
Anguish.
Paraphrase of the First Psalm.
Metrical Version of Part of Psalm
XC.
A Prayer in Prospect of Death.
Stanzas on the same Occasion
—'Why am I loth.'
Though Fickle Fortune.

1782.
O Raging Fortune's withering
Blast.
O why the Deuce.
My Father was a Farmer.
John Barleycorn.

The Death and Dying Words of Poor Mailie.
? Poor Mailie's Elegy.
? No Churchman am I.

### 1783.

The Rigs o' Barley—'It was upon a Lammas night.'
Now Westlin Winds.
My Nannie O—'Behind yon hills.'
Remorse—'Of all the numerous ills.'
Epitaph on Boghead.
Epitaph on Souter Hood.
Epitaph on William Muir of Tarbolton Mill.
Epitaph on his Father.

### 1784.

Wha is that at my Bower Door?
Green grows the Rashes O.
When Guildford good.
'I am a keeper of the law.'
Epistle to John Rankine—'O rough, rude.'
Welcome to his 'dear-bocht Bess'—'Thou's welcome, wean!'
O Leave Novels.
When First I came to Stewart Kyle.
Belles of Mauchline—'In Mauchline there dwells.'
Burns's 'Bletherin' Bitch'—'Below thir stanes.'
Epitaph on a Henpecked Husband.
Epigram on the same—'O Death, had'st thou.'
Another epigram—'One Queen Artemisia.'
On Tam the Chapman.
On John Rankine—'Ae day, as Death.'
'He who of Rankine sang.
Man was made to mourn.
The Twa Herds; or, the Holy Tulzie.

### 1785.

Holy Willie's Prayer.
Epitaph on Holy Willie.
? Epistle to Davie, a Brother Poet.

Death and Doctor Hornbook.
Epistle to John Lapraik—'While briers' (April 1).
Epistle to John Lapraik—'While new-ca'd kye' (April 21).
Epistle to William Simpson (May).
One Night as I did Wander.
Tho' Cruel Fate.
Rantin', Rovin' Robin.
Elegy on the Death of Robert Ruisseaux.
Epistle to John Goldie (August).
Epistle to John Lapraik—'Guid speed' (September).
Epistle to Rev. John M'Math (September 17).
Second Epistle to Davie—'I'm three times owre.'
'Young Peggy blooms.'
Farewell to Ballochmyle—'The Catrine woods.'
'Her flowing locks.'
Halloween (November).
To a Mouse (November).
Epitaph on John Dove, or Dow.
Adam Armour's Prayer.
The Jolly Beggars (November).
The Cotter's Saturday Night (November).
Address to the Deil.
Scotch Drink.

### 1786.

The Auld Farmer's New-Year Morning Salutation to his Auld Mare, Maggie.
The Twa Dogs.
The Author's Earnest Cry and Prayer.
The Ordination.
Epistle to James Smith—'Dear Smith.'
The Vision.
The Rantin' Dog, the Daddie o't.
'Here's his health in water.'
? Address to the Unco Guid.
The Inventory—'Sir, as your mandate' (Feb. 22).
To John Kennedy—'Now, Kennedy.'

Willie's Awa — 'Auld chuckie Reekie.'
At the Grave of Highland Mary— 'Strait is the spot.'
On the Death of Sir J. H. Blair.
To Miss Ferrier—' Nae heathen name.'
' Sad thy tale.'
On Carron Iron Works.
' Here Stuarts once.'
At Kenmore Inn.
Birks of Aberfeldy.
The Humble Petition of Bruar Water.
On the Fall of Fyers.
A Highland Welcome.
Strathallan's Lament.
Castle Gordon.
Lady Onlie, Honest Luckie.
Theniel Menzies' Bonnie Mary.
The Bonnie Lass of Albany.
On Scaring some Water-fowl.
Blythe and Merry was she.
A Rose-bud by my Early Walk.
Banks of Devon.
The Lofty Ochils.
My Peggy's Face.
Young Highland Rover.
On the Death of Robert Dundas.
Sylvander to Clarinda.
Ode for Dec. 31, 1787.

1788.

Clarinda, Mistress of my Soul.
Owre Young to Marry yet.
To the Weavers gin ye go.
Macpherson's Farewell.
Stay my Charmer.
? My Hoggie.
Raving Winds around her Blowing.
Up in the Morning.
How Lang and Dreary.
Hey, the Dusty Miller.
Duncan Davidson.
Her Daddie Forbad.
Musing on the Roaring Ocean.
The Blude-red Rose.
The Winter it is Past.
' Fair Empress of the Poet's soul.'
The Chevalier's Lament.

The Bonnie Lad that's Far Awa.
Epistle to Hugh Parker.
My Jean—'Of a' the airts.'
' I hae a wife o' my ain.'
Verses written in Friars-Carse Hermitage.'
' My god-like friend.'
' Anna, thy charms.'
The Fête Champêtre.
To Graham of Fintry—'When Nature.'
' The day returns.'
A Mother's Lament.
' O, were I on Parnassus Hill.'
The Lazy Mist.
' It is na, Jean, thy bonnie face.'
Go, fetch to me a Pint o' Wine.
Auld Lang Syne.
The First Kiss—'Humid seal.'
' Thee, Nature, partial Nature.'
Elegy on the Year 1788.
The Henpecked Husband.
Robin Shure in Hairst.
Ode, to the Memory of Mrs. Oswald.
' With Pegasus upon a day.'
' I burn, I burn.'
She's Fair an' Fause.
To Capt. Riddell—' Your news.'
Bonnie Ann.
To Miss Cruickshank—' Beauteous rose-bud.'
Ode on the Regency Bill.
Epistle on Glenconner—' Auld comrade.'
' O sing a new song.'
A Sketch—To the Hon. C. J. Fox.
The Wounded Hare.
On a Bank of Flowers.
Young Jockey.
Banks of Nith.
Jamie, come try me.
My Sandy O.
Sweet Tibbie Dunbar.
Mount and go.
John Anderson, my jo.
My Love, she's but a Lassie yet.
Tam Glen.
Carle, an the king come.
There's a Youth in this City.
Whistle o'er the Lave o't.

My Eppie Adair.
On Captain Grose's Peregrinations.
The Kirk's Alarm.
On Being appointed Exciseman.
On Receiving a Favour—' I call no Goddess' (*Aug.* 10).
Willie Brew'd a Peck o' Maut.
Ca' the Yowes.
Ee sae Bonnie Blue.
Highland Harry Back Again.
The Battle of Sherramuir—' O cam ye here.'
Killiecrankie Braes
Awa, Whigs.
Farewell to the Highlands.
The Whistle.
To Mary in Heaven.
Epistle to Dr. Blacklock (*Oct.* 21).
To the Toothache.
The Five Carlins.
Westerha—' The Laddies by the Banks o' Nith.'

1790.

Prologue—' No song nor dance' (*Jan.* 1.)
To Mrs. Dunlop—' This day Time winds' (*Jan.* 1)
Prologue—' What needs this din.'
On Receiving a Newspaper—' Kind Sir, I've read.'
Elegy on Willie Nicol's Mare ' Peg.'
' Yestreen I had a pint o' wine.'
' Gudewife, count the lawin.'
' I murder hate.'
Election Ballad—' Fintry, my stay.'
Elegy on Captain Matthew Henderson.
On Captain Grose—' Ken ye ought.'
Tam o' Shanter.
On the Birth of a Posthumous Child.
Elegy on the late Miss Burnet.

1791.

Lament of Mary, Queen of Scots.
' By yon castle wa'.'

' Out over the Forth.'
' Ye banks and braes o' bonnie Doon.'
Lament for the Earl of Glencairn.
Craigieburn Wood.
The Bonnie Wee Thing.
Lovely Davies.
' What can a Young Lassie do.'
The Posie.
On Glenriddel's Fox breaking his Chain
Caledonia—' There was once a day.'
? On Pastoral Poetry.
On the Destruction of Drumlanrig Woods.
The Gallant Weaver.
Welcome, Willie Stewart.
Lovely Polly Stewart.
Cock up your Beaver.
Eppie M'Nab.
My Tocher's the Jewel.
O for Ane an Twenty, Tam !
Fair Eliza—' Turn again.'
Bonnie Bell.
Sweet Afton.
To the Shade of Thomson.
Fareweel to a' our Scottish Fame.
Ye Jacobites.
Kenmure's on and awa.
To Maxwell of Terraughty.
Epistle to Graham of Fintry—' Late crippled.'
Song of Death on the Field of Battle.
Sensibility.
O May, thy Morn.
Ae Fond Kiss.
Behold the Hour.
Gloomy December.

1792.

? On Fergusson—' Ill-fated genius.'
The Weary Pund o' Tow.
Willie Wastle.
Lady Mary Ann.
Kellyburn Braes.
' It was in sweet Senegal.'

The De'il's awa wi' the Excise-
man.
Country Lassie—'In simmer
when the hay.'
Bessy and her Spinning-wheel.
Bonnie Lesley.
The Lea Rig—'When o'er the
hill.'
My Wife's a Winsome Wee Thing.
Highland Mary—'Ye banks and
braes.'
Spoken by Miss Fontenelle—
'While Europe's eye.'
Auld Rob Morris.
Duncan Gray.
Here's a Health.

### 1793.

Poortith Cauld—'O why should
Fate.'
Braw, braw Lads.
Sonnet—'Sing on, sweet thrush.'
Lord Gregory.
Wandering Willie.
'The wan Moon is setting.'
Young Jessie—'True-hearted was
he.'
Meg o' the Mill.
The Soldier's Return.
The Last Time I came o'er the
Moor.
Blythe hae I been.
Logan Braes.
O were my Love yon Lilac Fair.
Bonnie Jean.
Epigrams on the Earl of Gallo-
way, &c.
Had I a Cave.
Phillis the Fair.
By Allan Stream.
Whistle, and I'll come to you,
my Lad.
Adown Winding Nith.
Come, let me take thee.
Dainty Davie.
Scots wha hae.
Where are the Joys.
Deluded Swain.
Thine am I.
Spoken by Miss Fontenelle—
'Still anxious.'

### 1794.

Wilt thou be my Dearie?
A Vision—'As I stood by.'
Banks o' Cree.
Monody—'How cold is that
bosom.'
Epistle from Esopus to Maria.
Lovely Lass of Inverness.
Hee Balou.
'Bannocks o' bear meal.'
Highland Widow's Lament.
It was a' for our Rightfu' King.
On the Seas and Far Away.
'Sae flaxen were her ringlets.'
How Long and Dreary.
Let not woman e'er complain.
Sleep'st thou, or wak'st thou.
But lately seen.
Behold, my love, how green the
groves.
Lassie wi' the Lint-white Locks.
Willy and Philly—A duet.
Contented wi' Little.
Farewell thou Stream.
My Nannie's awa.'
For the Sake of Somebody.
A Man's a Man for a' that.

### 1795.

Let me in this ae night.
I'll aye ca' in by yon town.
Heron Election Ballads.
The Lass that made the Bed
to me.
'Does haughty Gaul invasion
threat.'
'O stay, sweet warbling.'
How Cruel are the Parents.
'Can I cease to care.'
Mark Yonder Pomp.
'Twas na her Bonnie Blue Ee.
Their Groves o' Sweet Myrtle.
'O wert thou, love, but near
me.'
Last May a Braw Wooer.
This is no' my ain Lassie.
O Bonnie was yon Rosy Brier.
Now Spring has clad.
'O, wat ye wha.'
To Chloris—''Tis Friendship's
pledge.'

News, Lasses, News.
' Mally's Meek, Mally's Sweet.
Jockey 's ta'en the Parting Kiss.
To Collector Mitchell—' Friend of
   the Poet.'

1796.

The Dean of Faculty.
Epistle to Col. de Peyster.

A Lass wi' a Tocher.
In Praise of Jessie Lewars.
' Here's a health to ane I lo'e
   dear.'
' O wert thou in the cauld blast.'
' Thine be the volumes, Jessy fair.'
   (*June* 26.)
' Fairest maid on Devon banks.'
   (*July* 12.)

Each eye it cheers when she appears,
  Like Phœbus in the morning,                          1C
When past the shower, and ev'ry flower
  The garden is adorning.
As the wretch looks o'er Siberia's shore,
  When winter-bound the wave is ;
Sae droops our heart when we maun part
  Frae charming lovely Davies.


Her smile's a gift frae 'boon the lift
  That maks us mair than princes ;
A scepter'd hand, a King's command,
  Is in her darting glances :                           20
The man in arms 'gainst female charms,
  Even he her willing slave is ;
He hugs his chain, and owns the reign
  Of conquering lovely Davies.


My Muse, to dream of such a theme,
  Thy feeble powers surrender !
The eagle's gaze alone surveys
  The sun's meridian splendour :
I wad in vain essay the strain,
  The deed too daring brave is ;                        30
I'll drap the lyre, and mute admire
  The charms o' lovely Davies.


## SAE FAR AWA.

O SAD and heavy should I part,
  But for her sake, sae far awa ;
Unknowing what my way may thwart,
  My native land sae far awa.
Thou that of a' things Maker art,
  That form'd this Fair sae far awa,
Gie body strength, then I'll ne'er start
  At this my way sae far awa.

To Mr. M'Adam—'Sir, o'er a gill.'

To a Louse.

'Thou flattering mark.'

The Holy Fair.

Menie's ee—'Again rejoicing nature.'

To a Mountain Daisy (*April*).

To Ruin—'All hail, inexorable lord.'

The Lament—'O thou pale orb.'

Despondency—'Oppressed with grief.'

To Gavin Hamilton—'I hold it, Sir' (*May* 3).

Reply to an Invitation—'Sir, yours this moment.'

'Will ye go to the Indies, my Mary?'

My Highland Lassie O.

Epistle to a Young Friend (*May*).

Address of Beelzebub to Lord Breadalbane (*June* 1).

A Dream (*June* 4).

A Dedication, to Gavin Hamilton.

Note to Dr. Mackenzie—'Friday first's the day.'

Farewell to St. James's Lodge —'Adieu.'

On a Scots Bard gone to the West Indies.

Farewell to Eliza.

A Bard's Epitaph.

Epitaphs—Robert Aiken, Gavin Hamilton, Wee Johnnie.

The Lass o' Ballochmyle.

Motto to the Kilmarnock Poems (*July*).

Lines to John Kennedy—'Farewell, dear friend.'

Lines to an Old Sweetheart— 'Once fondly loved.'

Lines on the Back of a Bank-note.

? On Naething.

The Farewell — 'Farewell, old Scotia's.'

The Calf (*September* 3).

Nature's Law—'Let other heroes.'

Willie Chalmers.

Reply to a Lousie Bitch of a Tailor.

The Brigs of Ayr.

'The night was still.'

Epigram on Bad Roads.

'O Thou dread Power.'

'The gloomy night.'

Lines on meeting Lord Daer (*October* 23).

Masonic Song—'Ye sons of old Killie' (*October* 26).

Tam Samson's Elegy.

Epistle to Major Logan—'Hail, thairm-inspiring' (*October* 30).

On Sensibility.

A Winter Night.

'Yon wild mossy mountains.'

Address to Edinburgh.

Address to a Haggis.

1787.

To Miss Logan—'Again the silent wheels' (*Jan.* 1).

'Crochallan came.'

Rattlin', Roarin' Willie.

'My blessings on ye.'

Extempore in the Court of Session.'

Inscription for Fergusson the Poet's gravestone.

Inscription under Fergusson the Poet's portrait.

Epistle to the Guidwife of Wauchope House (*March*).

Verses for a Noble Earl's Picture.

Prologue—'When by a generous' (*April* 16).

The Bonnie Moorhen.

'My lord a-hunting.'

Epigrams—At Roslin Inn, To an Artist, The Book-worms, On a Translation of Martial, To Miss Ainslie.

Epitaphs—Willie Michie, William Nicol.

'Here's a bottle.'

'Cease, ye prudes.'

'Hey, ca' throu.'

To William Tytler of Woodhouse-lee.